GERMAN NATIONAL CINEMA

German National Cinema is the first comprehensive history of German film from its origins to the present. In this new edition, Sabine Hake discusses film-making in economic, political, social, and cultural terms, and considers the contribution of Germany's most popular films to changing definitions of genre, authorship, and film form.

The book traces the central role of cinema in the nation's turbulent history from the Wilhelmine Empire to the Berlin Republic, with special attention paid to the competing demands of film as art, entertainment, and propaganda. Hake also explores the centrality of genre films and the star system to the development of a filmic imaginary.

Presenting the national as a highly unstable category, her discussions highlight the cross-cultural influences that situate German films within the European tradition and in ongoing dialogue with Hollywood.

Special issues discussed include:

- the preoccupation with German history and heritage
- the emphasis on questions of gender, class, race, and nation
- and the ongoing negotiation of regional, national, international, and transnational perspectives.

This fully revised and updated new edition will be required reading for everyone interested in German film and the history of modern Germany.

Sabine Hake is the Texas Chair of German Literature and Culture in the Department of Germanic Studies at the University of Texas at Austin. She is the author of several books on German cinema and Weimar culture, including *The Cinema's Third Machine: German Writings on Film 1907–1933* (1993) and *Popular Cinema of the Third Reich* (2001).

National Cinemas
Series Editor: Susan Hayward

GERMAN NATIONAL CINEMA

Second Edition

Sabine Hake

Routledge
Taylor & Francis Group

LONDON AND NEW YORK

First edition published 2002
by Routledge
2 Park Square, Milton Park, Abingdon, Oxon OX14 4RN

Simultaneously published in the USA and Canada
by Routledge
270 Madison Ave, New York, NY 10016

This edition published 2008

Transferred to Digital Printing 2008

Routledge is an imprint of the Taylor & Francis Group, an informa business

© 2002, 2008 Sabine Hake

Typeset in Galliard by
Keystroke, 28 High Street, Tettenhall, Wolverhampton

Printed and bound in Great Britain by
CPI Antony Rowe, Chippenham, Wiltshire

British Library Cataloguing in Publication Data
A catalogue record for this book is available from the British Library

Library of Congress Cataloging in Publication Data
Hake, Sabine, 1956–
German national cinema / Sabine Hake. — 2nd ed.
p. cm. – (National cinemas)
Includes index.
1. Motion pictures–Germany–History. 2. Motion picture
industry–Germany–History. I. Title.
PN1993.5.G3H28 2997
791.430943–dc22
2007019715

ISBN10: 0–415–42097–0 (hbk)
ISBN10: 0–415–42098–9 (pbk)

ISBN13: 978–0–415–42097–6 (hbk)
ISBN13: 978–0–415–42098–3 (pbk)

In memory of my father,
Günter Hake 1922–2000

CONTENTS

CONTENTS

ILLUSTRATIONS

Plates 15–21 appear on pages 186–189.

Plates 22–25 appear on pages 222–223.

ACKNOWLEDGEMENTS

Writing *German National Cinema* for the first time was an enormous, and at times overwhelming, project. By contrast, rewriting the book for this revised and expanded version has been not only a great privilege but, for the most part, a real pleasure. In taking on this task, I have been exceptionally fortunate to think about German cinema during a time of dramatic changes both in the academic disciplines of film studies and German studies and in the political, social, cultural, and intellectual landscapes called Germany. Colleagues gave me critical feedback on the first edition that proved extremely useful in the process of revision. I am grateful to Nathan Hill for editorial assistance and to Charlotte Wood and Maggie Lindsey-Jones for supporting the book's second edition and ushering it through. My special thanks go to Fred Nutt for his unwavering support for everything I am and do. This book would not have been possible without the important work done by the scholars and critics who established the study of German film during the last three decades and the younger generation of academics who continue to discover previously unexplored areas, challenge prevailing assessments, and introduce new critical perspectives. My work has also benefited immensely from the film archives, film museums, film festivals, and film book publishers that are so important to the continued existence of a vibrant film culture. I owe all of these individuals and institutions a great debt of gratitude.

INTRODUCTION

German National Cinema, which was published first in 2002 and which now appears in a revised and expanded edition, is the first comprehensive English-language history of German cinema from the beginning to the present. The book presents films in their social, political, and cultural context, approaches film-making as art, entertainment, and industry, and discusses the contribution of cinema to definitions of gender, class, and national identity. The most famous films and directors will be analysed next to the most popular genres and stars; questions of film form and style will be addressed as part of larger social and cultural developments; and the filmic organisation of meaning and fantasy will be examined in relation to politics and ideology.

This approach is predicated on the fact that feature films have played, and continue to play, a key role in the conception of national identity, in the definition of national culture, and in the making of the nation as an 'imagined community' (Benedict Anderson). At the same time, cinema from its inception has been part of aesthetic and political utopias about universal communication and international co-operation and always functioned as a hybrid phenomenon and transgressive force. In other words, it has also played a key role in the making of the transnational as an imagined community, whether in the name of internationalism, cosmo-politanism, or multiculturalism. Thus positioned between the national and transnational, and the local and the global, film must be seen as an integral part of social and cultural history, with the myriad stories, characters, places, images, and sounds amounting to an imaginary archive of hopes, desires, ambitions, joys, anxieties, resentments, and what Siegfried Kracauer calls the 'daydreams of society'. In the German context, this rich and diverse cultural memory includes domestic productions as well as foreign films, cross-cultural influences as well as nativist fantasies, integrative mechanisms as well as exclusionary strategies, dominant practices as well as countercultural sensibilities, and hybrid identities as well as nationalist ideologies.

The book's seven chapters are structured around the historical events, including two world wars and five regime changes, which mark German cinema as a site of crises, ruptures, and antagonisms, but also of unexpected influences, affinities, and continuities. Technological innovations, social practices, artistic movements, and

1

aesthetic sensibilities are an integral part of this history, as are prevailing attitudes toward high culture, popular culture, and national heritage and changing views about romance, love, and family life. The historical trajectory moves from the cinema of the Wilhelmine Empire (1895–1919), the Weimar Republic (1919–33), and the Third Reich (1933–45) to the complicated divisions characterising post-1945 Germany. From the divided, but still unified cinema of the postwar period (1945–61), the overview continues with two parallel chapters about the German Democratic Republic (1961–90) and the Federal Republic (1962–90), only to conclude with the cinema of the Berlin Republic (1990–2007). The chapter subheadings identify the competing perspectives of popular cinema and art cinema that, on the one hand, constitute German cinema as commercially viable and resisting easy integration into changing political systems and ideologies and that, on the other hand, confirm its powers as an artistically ambitious and socially conscious art cinema positioned uneasily between national interests and international effects.

The main goal of this historical overview is to present filmic practices in relation to larger social and political developments, to define the cinema's place within mass culture and modernity, and to analyse the creative exchanges with other art forms, mass media, and cultural practices. The remarkable ability of films to provide an archive of human fantasies and desires and to preserve the imaginary of the past within the present has influenced the overall conception of the book on several levels: the inclusion of brief discussions of film authorship, film genre, and the star system; repeated references to the impact of new scholarship on the historiography of German film; and the continuing influence of the classics on subsequent generations of directors and audiences. In contrast to the text-based approach found in *Geschichte des deutschen Films* (Jacobsen, Kaes, and Prinzler 2004), a multi-author work that privileges the art film and aesthetic readings, this historical overview presents films as part of larger social practices and insists on the centrality of popular traditions to German cinema. And in contrast to the cultural-studies-based *German Cinema Book* (Bergfelder, Carter, and Göktürk 2002), which is organised around case studies, this comprehensive account remains committed to the conceptual and didactic advantages of a master-narrative.

Within this framework, special emphasis will be placed on the changing function of the cinema as a mass medium, social space, public diversion, political weapon, and cultural institution. The role of film culture in negotiating local, regional, national, and international influences and the importance of genre films in constructing social, sexual, ethnic, and national identities will provide the organising principles in the presentation of individual films and directors. At the same time, the focus on German cinema will continuously be expanded toward its relationship to Hollywood and its place within European film-making, with the national understood as a category of inclusion as well as exclusion, homogeneity as well as diversity, and strength as well a crisis. Limitations of space make it necessary to restrict the material to mainstream cinema and feature film production. Throughout, special effort will be made to identify the various Others against which the narrative film defined its formal conventions and asserted its cultural hegemony, whether in

2

relation to the rich but little known traditions of experimental and documentary film-making (Zimmermann 2005), the strong ties with Austrian cinema as the other important German-speaking cinema (von Dassanowsky 2005), or the complicated dynamics of competition and collaboration with public and private television (Hickethier 1998).

Narrative films dominate not just filmic practices but also the history of film: reason enough to consider the complex ways in which they participate in the formation of private and public identities and contribute to the making of national history and collective memory. As historical documents, feature films offer unique insights into everyday life, uncover the social imaginary, and allow us to trace the formation of collective memory and national identity. As aesthetic products, they provide privileged access to the private fantasies that are a reflection of, and a reaction to, the social and political conditions at a particular historical juncture. Promising spectatorial pleasure and emotional catharsis, feature films since the beginnings of cinema have exerted a powerful influence over everything from sexual behaviour and consumer choices to aesthetic preferences and political attitudes. Film genres, stories, and characters have done as much to give expression to social aspirations and anxieties as they have served as catalysts for political controversies and new cultural trends. However, using narratives in the reconstruction of historical periods or, worse still, collective mentalities remains problematic, for such an undertaking is predicated on certain assumptions about the mimetic nature of the filmic medium, its relationship to alternative definitions of reality, and its psychological function both as an escape from, and a reflection of, everyday life. Yet which forces actually organise the relationship between fiction and society? What is the 'real' of filmic narrative, social reality or the reality of desires? Does the feature film reflect social experience or does it represent that which is absent, denied, and ignored? Can films influence social processes or do they simply condense, displace, and resolve existing conflicts and contradictions? Must we link their emotional appeal to a pervasive need for illusion and escape or are even the most superficial films part both of a continuous working through fundamental problems and of an authentic articulation of real lack? What is the relationship between narrative and sexual difference, and how are class, gender, and race configured differently in the prevailing narrative forms and modes of address developed within German cinema?

To continue this line of inquiry, how should we define a national cinema? Are its main features determined by economic, political, or aesthetic forces? What is the ultimate reference point: the nation state, the public sphere or some more elusive mixture of shared linguistic, cultural, and historical characteristics? Does the national refer to actual practices, whether of film-makers or film audiences, or is it a function of promotional strategies, public policies, market pressures, and the ideology of nationalism? Can we treat audiences as representative of the nation as a whole, or is it necessary to modify our conclusions based on the changing size and composition of the audience? Must we locate the meaning of national cinema in specific genres and styles, narrative themes and motifs, and more elusive definitions of social, sexual, and ethnic identity expressed through a highly codified national physiognomy and identified with particular actors and stars? Or is national cinema primarily an instrument of distinction and demarcation, evoked only in opposition to other national cinemas and then most often through various strategies of resisting, excluding, and competing with Hollywood? Finally, in what ways does film engage the nation differently, compared to other narrative traditions, such as folklore and literature, and other forms of public spectacle, such as opera and theatre?

Establishing its sphere of influence through texts and contexts, the cinema – this quintessential mixed medium – has succeeded like no other representational practice in incorporating diverse and often competing definitions of culture: high and low, national and regional, traditional and avant-garde, dominant and subversive, official and alternative. In offering a place of public assembly and in functioning as a public sphere, the cinema – this first truly democratic mass medium – has also facilitated important debates about culture, politics, and society, and it continues to serve as an instrument of innovation, provocation, and critical reflection. This function has been especially pronounced in the making of national culture and identity.

Where, then, can we locate the specific, if not unique, qualities of German cinema? In the conditions of film production defined through economic policies and legal frameworks and bounded through geographical and linguistic borders? Or in the marketing of German films as German on international markets but also, as a form of self-branding, to domestic audiences? In the efforts by innovative directors, ambitious studios, and cinephile critics to elevate cinema to the level of the other arts and infuse it with the kind of cultural relevance attributed to high literature and classical music as the main sites of German identity? Or in the repeated attempts by government agencies and political parties to control all aspects of fantasy production and to turn film into an instrument of political propaganda and ideological affirmation? In the efforts by the domestic film industry to gain support through public subsidies as well as through quotas and tariffs? Or in the complicated relationship of German audiences to their own filmic traditions and styles, whether in the aggressive terms of nationalist ideologies or in the banal versions of a nationalism of everyday life? In light of the predominance of Hollywood, can we even describe moviegoing and cinema culture in national terms? Given the non-identity of state and nation during the Third Reich and the Cold War, can we speak of a cinematic *Sonderweg* (special path) in the ways suggested for modern German history? Or must we emphasise the many similarities with other European cinemas, including Austria, France, Italy, and Great Britain, and highlight the presence of German films on international markets and in transnational contexts? The following comprehensive overview of German cinema does not attempt to answer all of these questions. However, the individual chapters present a number of interweaving and overlapping narratives that open up a space for new readings of national cinema.

Informed by all of these questions, *German National Cinema* moves beyond the usual catalogue of canonical films and famous *auteurs* to include the big blockbusters, popular stars, and favourite genres that have always defined German cinema, and often in marked opposition to the demands of film art and film propaganda. Similarly, the subcategories evoked to describe cinema as a public sphere – national cinema, art cinema, and popular cinema – will be developed not through normative definitions or theoretical models but through the complicated relationship between cinema and politics, on the one hand, and cinema and high culture, on the other. Concretely, this means that the notion of national cinema cannot be evoked without acknowledging the foreign influences, international developments, and global forces that are regularly described as a threat to national traditions but that in fact reveal the national as a production of internal coherence and a product of exclusion and demarcation; this point has been made repeatedly in the recent debates on national cinemas (Crofts 1993, Willemen 1994, Kaes 1995, Silberman 1996, Hjort and MacKenzie 2000).

As a critical category, the discourse of national cinema constructs an illusion of essential qualities, especially against Hollywood as the threatening and alluring other. Yet as a historically specific category, the nation serves very different functions at different times, preventing or promoting artistic innovation and cultivating or suppressing critical voices. Throughout, the function of national cinema remains inextricably linked to the role of the state and its changing cultural and economic policies. Consequently, no national cinema can be conceptualised without at least some reference to the mechanisms of integration, assimilation, and hybridisation that define and organise its relationship to other cinemas. Similarly, the close alliance between cinema and politics, including its ideological effects, can be understood only through its dialectical relationship to the practices of mass entertainment and the rituals of cultural consumption that are predicated on the suppression of the political. Last but not least, the innovative art films cannot be examined without considering their relationship to the popular genre films, whether in the competition over audiences or in the different approaches to the aesthetics and politics of representation.

Aware of the term's elusive and contested nature, this historical overview presents 'the national' both as a driving force behind, and as a desired effect of, mainstream filmic practices. Yet it also pays special attention to those sensibilities and imaginations that cannot be integrated as easily and often resist or subvert any attempts at appropriation and co-optation. Instead of subsuming everything under normative definitions of national culture and, even more problematically, national character, the following chapters thus draw attention to the tensions among national, regional, and local traditions; among national, international, and global perspectives; and among cultural, economic, and political definitions of nation. As noted, the status of national cinema as a contested category is especially evident in relation to foreign films, and the undisputed global dominance of Hollywood in particular. But it also comes into view through the large number of foreigners working in the German film industry; the many co-productions with other European countries; and the continuous waves of emigration and migration of German film-makers to Hollywood and elsewhere. Finally, to move on to aesthetic concerns, the inherent instability of the national as a function of cinema becomes most apparent in the intense debates about uniquely German topics and styles; about the relationship between film and the other arts; about the place of popular cinema in the division between high and low culture; and about the function of film censorship, economic protectionism, and public subsidies in aligning the cinema with national interests. All of these struggles and initiatives bring into sharp relief the precarious nature of a national cinema striving for the kind of internal coherence and unity that, in fact, can and will never be achieved.

Defining German cinema through such unstable constellations necessarily expands the scope of the historical project and raises many questions about the relationship among film, politics, and society and the power of narrative film as a form of social history and national imaginary. On a methodological level, these questions complicate even the most basic conceptual pairs such as film versus cinema, film as history versus history of film, and history in cinema versus cinema in history. At the same time, the emphasis on German cinema as a continuous compromise between art cinema and popular cinema opens up important new perspectives. The emphasis on cinema as a cultural practice shifts the focus from individual texts to the systems of production, distribution, and exhibition that make films part of other aspects of public life and cultural consumption. Locating the cinema at the centre of modern mass culture brings out its affinities with urbanism, consumerism, tourism, and distinctly modern sensibilities, and it underscores its changing alliances with working-class culture, white-collar culture, and youth culture. Likewise, the attention to film as an integral part of modern life expands the terms of historical analysis in productive ways: from the canonical works to popular successes; from the formal characteristics of texts to changing modes of perception; from the social function of stereotypes and clichés to the psychological effects of audio-visual pleasures and identifications. Last but not least, the predominance of feature film depends always on its creative exchanges with non-narrative forms such as documentary and experimental film-making; with established cultural practices such as literature, theatre, music, dance, and the visual arts; with the most advanced technologies of visuality and spatiality developed in architecture, photography, fashion, and design; and, finally, with the very different notions of reality and representation offered by other audio-visual media such as television, video, and the internet.

The notion of national cinema as a category of difference and contestation also complicates the understanding of film history as a linear narrative with distinct periods and movements, continuities and ruptures, and cycles of rise and decline. The relationship between film and history is usually established on a number of levels: through the formal means, artistic styles, and directorial visions that link one film to other films; through the presumed homologies among filmic narratives, cultural mentalities, and social experiences; and through the technological possibilities, financial resources, and organisational structures available at a given point in time. Yet what, for instance, is the function of the star phenomenon, the cult of authorship, the role of criticism and theory or, perhaps most difficult, the role of visual pleasure and the production of affect in the writing of film history? Which

6

of the available models is most suited for national histories? Can German cinema be approached from the perspective of social history, with everything from social and racial stereotypes to new cultural and political movements simultaneously reflected and prefigured in the films' recurring stories, characters, and themes? Or are the qualities of this particular cinema more accurately described through aesthetic categories that examine unique visual and narrative conventions and identify innovative directorial styles and artistic movements? Is it more important for an understanding of twentieth-century German history to pursue a diachronic model that establishes relationships of cause and effect and that explores long-range developments in social attitudes and behaviours? Or can the complicated dynamics of cinema and modern life be made more transparent through a synchronic model that explores relationships of mutual exchange and pays closer attention to contemporaneous phenomena as they are worked out in different mass media and representational forms?

The difficulties of writing film history and defining national cinema have only increased in light of the changed political landscape of Germany after unification and the uncertain future of cinema in the digital age. For instance, one might ask whether the renewed interest in film history is fuelled by nostalgia for a photographic medium increasingly marginalised by digital technologies. One might wonder to what degree the new research on national cinemas and, specifically, European cinemas marks the return of the national, whether on a sub-state or supra-state level, as a position of resistance to the levelling effect of a global entertainment culture ruled by Hollywood. And in the age of globalisation, one could speculate about the significance of the transnational as a category that emphasises movements, exchanges, and collaborations across borders. That feature films do play a crucial role in the making of national identities and the creation of national imaginaries is undeniable. On a less obvious level, the same holds true for film history. As the most important mass medium of the twentieth century, film not only continues to provide powerful stories and images but also uses its own historicity to convey a sense of cultural tradition and historical continuity. To what degree the transnational opens up entirely new ways of writing film history remains to be seen.

1

WILHELMINE CINEMA
1895–1919

Until recently, little was known about films from the Wilhelmine period, that is, the cinema before 1919. Some of the reasons for such neglect apply to other national cinemas as well: the large number of films lost or in danger of disintegrating; the inaccessibility of film copies, stills, and print sources from the period; and the limited resources available for preservation. But a renewed interest in early cinema, which peaked during the 1995 centennial of the invention of film, has finally brought more scholars to the archives and resulted in increased scholarly activity, published in journals such as *KINtop: Jahrbuch zur Erforschung des frühen Films*. Archival research has drawn attention to previously unknown films, directors, and producers and revealed the richness and complexity of early cinema as a technology, business, industry, art form, and popular diversion. But the study of early cinema has also allowed scholars to question basic assumptions of film historiography such as the privileging of the feature film and of a nation-based model of analysis and to reject any claims to a normative film aesthetic in favour of the historical manifestations of authorship, spectatorship, and media specificity. Cultural-studies-based approaches have shed new light on the embeddedness of the feature film within a wide range of representational modes and exhibition practices and clarified the relationship of early cinema to other media and communication technologies, including its contribution to the making of a post-bourgeois public sphere. Moreover, because of its precarious position between local influences, national initiatives, and international developments, early film-making has drawn attention to the constitutive tension within German cinema between a basic openness toward heterogeneous influences and cross-cultural exchanges, on the one hand, and its enlistment in the discourses of nationalism and the making of national identity, on the other.

In the process, the study of early cinema has raised more fundamental questions about the functioning of film as a powerful technology for expanding the boundaries of time and place, producing new identities and subjectivities, cultivating new modes of perception and experience, and redrawing the boundaries of fantasy and reality. Questions asked in this context include: Which technological, economic, social, and cultural forces contributed to the invention of cinematography? Did the technology of film create new forms of diversion or was cinema an expression of, and a response to, dramatic changes in modern mass society? What is the relationship of early cinema to other mass media (illustrated press, photography), technologies of space (railway, telegraph) and the discourses of the body (medicine, ethnography, criminology)? In what ways does early cinema engage with the concomitant processes of urbanisation, massification, mechanisation, and industrialisation (Segeberg 1996 and 1998)? Must we conceive of cinema as a radically new cultural practice or an eclectic mixture of popular traditions, established conventions, and modern diversions? How did the rise of film affect the formal registers and social significance of literature and the other arts, and how did it alter the relationship between high and low culture? Where must we place early cinema in relation to urban culture, bourgeois culture, working-class culture, regional culture, and folk culture? What is its contribution to the contemporaneous discourses of colonialism and nationalism and the aesthetic projects of turn-of-the-century decadence and life reform? Did early cinema provide an alternative public sphere in which marginalised and suppressed voices found expression, or did it prepare the ground for both the commodification of culture described by Adorno and Horkheimer in their notion of the culture industry and the aesthetics of simulation evoked by many post-structuralist critics? Finally, where can we locate the emergence of national cinema out of the internationalism of the early film business and the syncretism of early film forms and styles?

Addressing many of these questions, film historians have turned their attention to the beginnings of German cinema, both to fill considerable historical lacunae and to develop new methods of inquiry (Usai and Codelli 1990, Kessler et al. 1992, Elsaesser 1996a, Elsaesser and Wedel 2002, Garncarz 2007). They have challenged earlier characterisations of Wilhelmine cinema as technically inferior and formally undeveloped on the grounds that the conventions of the classical Hollywood style had inappropriately served as the standard for all critical evaluation. Correcting the almost exclusive emphasis on Berlin as the capital and the centre of film production, scholarship on early cinema culture in other cities (e.g., Munich, Düsseldorf, Frankfurt am Main) has shown regional influences working against the homogenising effect of the national in political debates and cultural practices. At the same time, studies on film exhibition in small towns and rural areas have documented how the cinema levelled the difference between city and country even where exhibition practices accommodated regional tastes and preferences (Warstat 1982). Feminist scholarship has shown the ability of early films to respond to the needs of women audiences, among other things through the heightened emotionality of the melodrama, and thus give rise to an alternative public sphere (Schlüpmann 1990). At the same time, detailed studies on local exhibition practices and early production companies have confirmed the socially integrative qualities of early cinema, especially during the transition from the short to the longer film, and thus put an end to persistent myths surrounding early cinema as a proletarian public sphere (Müller 1994).

Not surprisingly, there exists some disagreement on the meaning of new historical knowledge and its impact on periodisation and canonisation. Two basic models can be found: one based on continuous progression, and one defined through breaks and ruptures. Scholars either treat the cinema from 1895 to 1919 as a prehistory of the classical silent cinema or, conversely, see it as radically different in its approach to narrative continuity, psychological motivation, and visual spectacle. In the first case, the styles of the 1920s provide the normative standard for evaluating earlier film practices as deficient and flawed. Within a comparative framework, such evolutionary models are frequently evoked to explain alleged instances of retardation in the German cinema before 1919. Accordingly, some critics have described expressionist cinema as the result of yet insufficiently developed filmic techniques (Salt 1979). Taking a very different approach, other scholars have used early cinema and its presumed otherness to think about the formal shift from 'showing' to 'telling' as an abandonment of the subversive qualities derived from the greater emphasis on visual spectacle and the cult of attractions.

In most cases, film-making before 1919 has been examined as inseparable from the larger concerns of Wilhelmine culture and society and its constitutive tensions and contradictions: between an authoritarian state and its nationalist ideology and the democratising effects of civic involvement and social activism, between the modernising forces of industry and technology and the oppressive effects of a rigid class system, and between an official culture of pompous pretension and countless new initiatives for artistic innovation and cultural reform. The years between the founding of the Reich in 1871 and the collapse of the monarchy in 1918 brought dramatic changes in every area of public life, from belated industrialisation and urbanisation and the rise of a powerful working class to significant advances in social legislation and political representation. The Wilhelmine Empire under Emperor Wilhelm II was held together by the nationalist fervour and imperialist ambition that culminated in the cataclysm of the First World War, but it also saw the emergence of new industries and corporations and the kind of entrepreneurial spirit that, among other things, made possible the advent of cinema. Its earliest attractions appeared during a cultural period that thrived on conventionality, sentimentality, materialism, and kitsch. In the educated middle classes, moral double standards dominated social interactions, and public debates exuded pretentiousness and hypocrisy. The provocation of naturalism and, later, expression-ism, attested to the need for more fundamental changes in the existing power structures and the cultural institutions and practices that supported them. Around the turn of the century, new artistic movements began to challenge the sharp division between high and low culture, while progressive social movements worked to improve the living conditions of the lower classes. Committed to the idea of reform, these groups ranged from working-class cultural organisations to alternative lifestyle movements but also included activist groups fighting for better housing, sex reform, and women's rights. As an integral part of these developments, early cinema became a privileged symbol both of the destructive and constructive effects of modernisation and modernity.

Cinema: a new technology, industry, and mass medium

Playfully eclectic and unabashedly populist, early cinema exposed the shortcomings of high culture and, through its embeddedness in everyday life, brought into sharp relief the enormous power and appeal of modern mass culture. The strong resistance to the new medium among members of the educated middle class was based not only in their anxieties about the levelling effect on cultural life but also their fears of the modern masses for whom the cinema became a preferred form of entertainment. Strongly influenced by other public diversions such as the variety, the circus, the fairground, and the panorama, the first films had little need for, and even less interest in, the formal conventions of literature and bourgeois theatre. Cultivating decidedly modern sensibilities trained in the big cities and at the new places of work, the cinema quickly became an integral part of modern consumer culture and soon joined forces with other mass-produced forms of diversion such as illustrated magazines and trivial literature. But in contrast to the latter, cinema became a popular attraction through its double status as a technology in the narrow sense of machines and mechanisms and in the broader sense of producing and displaying illusions, a dynamic already apparent in the early phase of invention and experimentation.

The first cinematographers took full advantage of this unique convergence of perception and technology by exhibiting new optical devices (for example, Ottomar Anschütz's Tachyscope) and by presenting their 'magic tricks' as an integral part of the cinema of attractions. The move from scientific experimentation to public entertainment was completed when, from February to March 1895, Anschütz showed his 'living photographs' to a paying audience, thus also for the first time privileging collective over individual forms of reception (Rossell 2001). Max Skladanowsky, one of the many showmen and inventors from the period of early cinematography, usually gets credited with having organised the first public film screening as part of a variety show in the Wintergarten in Berlin on 1 November 1895. Emulating the variety format, the programme consisted of acrobatic acts, animal scenes, folk dances, and artistic presentations. A later series of Skladanowsky shorts from 1896 was more documentary-like and included street scenes from the neighbourhood around Alexanderplatz. Both programmes must be described as aesthetically and technically inferior to the actualities first screened by August and Louis Lumière in Paris on 28 December 1895. Because of its high-quality products, the Cinématographe Lumière soon achieved a dominant position on European markets, whereas the German competition remained small and underfinanced.

Most technological advances during the early years were connected with Oskar Messter and Guido Seeber. Messter was a talented cinematographer who not only improved the mechanics of cameras and projectors but also successfully marketed his products (Kessler et al. 1994a and 1994b, Rossell 1998). The Maltese cross for flicker-free projection is his invention as are the popular *Ton-Bilder* (sound images) that, through a gramophone, synchronised sound and image for short musical numbers. Messter made countless fictional shorts for Messter Film GmbH and, as

11

early as 1897, began producing regular newsreels following the popular success of a documentary short about the centennial of the birthday of Emperor Wilhelm I. After 1914, these newsreels appeared weekly as the famous *Messter-Woche*. Like Messter, Seeber combined business acumen and technological know-how with an almost intuitive grasp of the camera's artistic possibilities. Known for his innovative camerawork on *Der Totentanz* (The Dance of Death, 1912) and other films by Urban Gad, he specialised in trick photography and published the earliest manual on cinematography. Working for the Deutsche Bioscop, Seeber in 1912 also oversaw the construction of the Babelsberg studios, soon to become the famous Ufa-Stadt, the German Hollywood, on the south-western outskirts of Berlin.

In general, Wilhelmine cinema can be divided into three phases: the early years of emergence and experimentation (1895–1906), a phase of expansion and consolidation (1906–10), and the process of standardisation that gave rise to the longer feature film (1910–18). An often accelerating and sometimes retarding factor in this process was the alignment of cinema with national interests and its separation from international developments as a result of the First World War. During the period of travelling cinemas, which lasted until 1906 (and until 1915, in some rural areas), exhibitors either purchased or produced their own films and travelled from town to town to present their 'theatre of living photographs'. The programme usually included newsreels, nature scenes, humorous sketches, acrobatic acts, dramatic recitations, and documentary shorts about local events. Two filmic styles, respectively associated with the names of Lumière and Meliès, prevailed: a realist style, with the camera recording the visible world and favouring a mode of representation located in the pro-filmic event; and a fantastic style that took advantage of the camera's ability to create new imaginary worlds and overcome the limitations of everyday perception. Newsreels and documentaries increased the audience's interest in physical reality and confirmed to them the beauty of everyday life. By contrast, the *tableaux vivants* (staged group scenes) and the *féeries* (fairytales), as well as the popular shorts with musical numbers and acrobatic presentations, continued to adhere to the conventions of the proscenium stage, from the framing of the scenes to the frontal positioning of actors and performers. This celebration of an unabashedly sensationalist cinema modelled after the variety was most apparent in the fantastic effects achieved through trick animation, tinting or toning and had a lasting impact on the visual conventions of the early social drama and detective film.

Weekly changes in movie programmes and improvements in the design of exhibition spaces contributed to the cinema's growing popularity. Beginning in 1905, more and more storefronts, pubs, and coffee houses were converted into stationary cinemas, from then on alternatively referred to as *Kino, Kientopp* or *Kintop*. With the increase in numbers – in Berlin, from 165 cinemas in 1905 to 206 in 1913 – came greater attention to comfort and luxury, as evidenced by early spectacular movie palaces like Berlin's Marmorhaus. Usually located in the downtown areas, on the large thoroughfares, and near railway stations and shopping districts, these new cinemas catered to a diverse audience, from workers, employees, and middle-class women to adolescents, artisans, and the unemployed. In the big cities, screenings took place from eleven o'clock in the morning to ten at night, with patrons coming and going on a continuous basis. Programmes lasted approximately 15 minutes and almost always included piano or organ music accompaniment and, not infrequently, explanations by a commentator. Usually limited to the evenings, the more ambitious *Kinobühnenschauen* (cinema stage shows) offered an entertaining mixture of short films and live acts; these programmes remained popular until the late 1920s.

Movie audiences often came from the lower classes, but it would be misleading to characterise them as working-class or think of early cinema only in class-based terms. Sociological studies from the period, including Emilie Altenloh's *Zur Soziologie des Kino* (On the Sociology of the Cinema, 1914), described very heterogeneous groups, characterised above all by their precarious social positions and brought together by shared experiences of discrimination and marginalisation. Because of its provocative qualities, the new medium was regularly discussed in the antagonistic terms of class, with writers and critics frequently denouncing the movies as a threat to bourgeois culture and society. As such a potential source of social unrest, the cinema had to be controlled through various legal and administrative measures on the local, state, and federal levels. Initially the police had been responsible for making preventive censorship decisions, a practice which allowed for significant variation among municipalities. The introduction in 1906 of official pre-censorship, and the requirement of a censor's certificate after 1907, greatly simplified this process, with Prussia publicising its censorship decisions as a guideline for the other states. Additional new measures included admission monitoring for children and adolescents and the enforcement of city ordinances about safety standards and health codes. Eventually, municipalities found a workable compromise between controlling the cinema's presumably detrimental effect on public morality and profiting from its mass appeal through a local entertainment tax, from then on a major source of revenues (Kilchenstein 1997).

The cinema's rise from a small business to a national industry came about through the concentration of all resources, including financial capital, production facilities, and technological know-how, in the hands of fewer and larger companies. Additional factors included a more effective division of labour among film production, distribution, and exhibition; further specialisation in the film-related professions and industries; and technical and artistic standards and greater product differentiation. In 1913 alone, more than 350 new films were released nationwide. The founding of the Geyer printing lab in 1911 gave German companies some degree of independence from their French competitors. Known for its lively cultural scene, Berlin emerged as the centre of film-making, with the cafés and restaurants around Friedrichstrasse functioning as a kind of employment exchange, and with most of the studios located nearby in Tempelhof, Weissensee, and Babelsberg (Hanisch 1991). *Der Kinematograph* and *Die Lichtbild-Bühne*, the earliest trade papers, were founded in 1907 and 1908, respectively, to improve communication among the various branches of the industry and to offer advice on technical, financial, and legal questions. The first serious reviews in daily newspapers appeared around 1913 and were followed by extensive debates on the artistic merits of film in most mainstream publications.

Production companies from these early years include Jules Greenbaum's Deutsche Bioskop (1902) and Deutsche Vitascope (1909), as well as the first film producer who also functioned as a distributor, Alfred Duske's GmbH (1905). Exploring the possibilities of vertical integration, Paul Davidson first acquired a cinema chain in 1906, the ubiquitous Union-Theater, before creating the first German joint-stock film company, the Projektions-AG Union (PAGU), in 1909. Founded in 1915, Erich Pommer's Decla contributed to this process of economic concentration by operating on a national level from the very beginning. Like Paul Davidson of PAGU, Decla's Pommer belonged to a new generation of producers who believed in improving the technical and artistic quality of their products and in striving toward a broader social acceptance of the movies. In order to minimise financial risks, some companies experimented with restrictive practices such as the monopoly films, films available through only one distributor. The Asta Nielsen star vehicle *Der Abgrund / Afgrunden* (The Abyss, 1910), a Danish production, was distributed as a monopoly film. Practices such as blind booking and block booking had a similarly stabilising effect; so did advertising campaigns that made films part of other forms of cultural consumption. Commodity tie-ins appeared for the first time when the chocolate manufacturer Stollwerck & Co. in Cologne, distributor of the Cinématographe Lumière since 1896, installed vending machines in its cinemas (Loiperdinger 1999).

Responding to such developments, even conservative political groups and public institutions discovered film's untapped possibilities as a modern mass medium. The royal family turned to film as a promotional tool for the monarchy. Beginning with the grand opening of the Nord-Ostsee Canal in 1895, Wilhelm II repeatedly appeared in newsreels featuring military parades, victory celebrations, and manoeuvres of his beloved Royal Navy. For the celebrations surrounding the twenty-fifth anniversary of his rule, eight different production firms joined forces to produce *Der deutsche Kaiser im Film* (The German Emperor on Film, 1912). The enlistment of cinema in the scenarios of German nationalism, militarism, and monarchism, did not remain limited to the recording of public events. The *Deutsche Flottenverein*, an influential naval association, showed films extolling German military might and glory in order to mobilise civilian groups and increase patriotic sentiment. Colonial associations produced feature and non-feature films about South West Africa and German East Africa that took advantage of the widespread fascination with racial otherness to advance their racist and imperialist agendas. The underlying fascination with the primitive shared by ethnographers and anthropologists extended to the entertainment purposes served by colonial films and the popular *Völkerschauen* (ethnographic exhibitions) and continued in the search for an authentic experience thematised by early film theorists (Oksiloff 2001).

Turning film into a marketable and profitable commodity required not only the institutionalisation of cinema as a social practice but also a further standardisation of filmic means. Between 1911 and 1914, the longer narrative film emerged as the most popular cinematic form, a process that had a profound effect on prevailing forms and styles. The multi-reelers made popular by the so-called *Kinodrama* (film drama) introduced numerous new techniques related to camerawork, editing, and mise-en-scène. These included a greater variation in shot sizes, including close-ups, and a range of narrative devices such as superimposition, fade-in/fade-out, cross-cutting, and masking (for instance, through iris and keyhole masks). In aesthetic terms, the creation of a film-specific language allowed film-makers to overcome their dependence on the other arts and explore the unique qualities of the filmic medium. Yet in cultural terms, the emergence of the longer narrative film aligned the cinema also more closely with high-culture traditions in literature and theatre and made its stories beholden to bourgeois taste and morality (for example, in the insistence on social relevance and aesthetic value).

Above all, the longer film required a linear narrative within a clear time–space continuum, as well as consistent character development and psychological motivation. Despite these new rules and conventions, which laid the foundation for the classical narrative cinema, there was still sufficient opportunity for cultivating national styles and sensibilities. Rejecting action-driven plots for psychological conflicts, the early German film dramas continued to privilege relations of contiguity over continuity by treating the frame like a self-contained space. Some scholars have explained the close attention to mise-en-scène at the expense of other filmic techniques as a belated or only partial adaptation of the conventions of storytelling. Yet it might also have derived from the greater influence of well-established theatrical traditions or from a deliberate attempt at product differentiation, specifically by creating a German alternative to the plot-driven, action-oriented Hollywood films. In either case, older traditions of performance and visual spectacle remained an integral part of the cinematic apparatus and continued to assert their power against the increasingly conventional story lines and their underlying assumptions about gender, race, nation, and class.

Sometimes the provocation of early cinema found expression in humorous stories about the filmic medium itself. From *Der stellungslose Photograph* (The Unemployed Photographer, 1912) and *Wie sich das Kino rächt* (How the Cinema Takes Revenge, 1912) to *Die Filmprimadonna* (The Film Primadonna, 1913) and *Wo ist Coletti?* (Where Is Coletti?, 1913), films repeatedly thematised their conditions of production and thereby drew attention to the new popular diversion and its unique pleasures (Hake 1992b). Confronted with relentless attacks by cinema reformers and literary critics, directors used such self-referentiality to justify cinema's integration into mainstream culture and demonstrate film's artistic merits. Others responded to the demand for cultural respectability and the underlying fear of social disintegration by emphasising the educational values and political possibilities of the new medium.

Firmly established by the late 1910s, the longer narrative film gradually displaced other filmic modes such as documentary and animation, institutionalised the sharp distinction between narrative and non-narrative forms, and established fictionality and illusionism as the dominant representational paradigm. From then on, the exploration of physical reality ceded to the imaginary relations that constituted the cinema as a popular diversion with clearly defined social functions and affective structures. At the same time, the conventions of genre cinema provided an important framework for fusing public and private desires and for mediating between the legitimating fictions of identity, whether defined in terms of class or of nation, and the alternately transgressive and compensatory effects of sensation, suspense, romance, and fantasy. With the longer narrative film came more elaborate programmes and more refined programming practices. The inevitable reduction in daily screenings, in turn, required cinema owners to pay greater attention to the framework of presentation, which extended from cinema architecture and design to the rituals of attendance and cultural appreciation modelled on the theatre.

Local, regional, and national differences notwithstanding, film production and distribution during the prewar period took place in a decidedly European framework. The high degree of co-operation and collaboration and the relative lack of trade regulations kept European film markets open until the early 1910s. In fact, the majority of films shown in Germany before the First World War were of foreign origin, with domestic productions usually taking a market share of 10 to 20 per cent. While French films, and the Pathé newsreels in particular, dominated programmes before 1910, Italian films became very popular after 1910, largely because of the success of monumental epics such as *Cabiria* (1914). The many Danish directors working in Berlin, including Ole Olsen, Benjamin Christensen, Stellan Rye, and Urban Gad, contributed to the great popularity of Scandinavian cinema (Behn 1994). During a period when questions of authorship were still considered irrelevant from an artistic perspective, product differentiation was achieved primarily through the association of individual studios with specific genres. For instance, Nordisk was perceived as a company specialising in social-problem films, whereas Pathé and Gaumont became identified with ambitious literary projects. It was only in the course of the First World War that these differences were instrumentalised by the politics of nationalism and enlisted in the making of a national cinema.

In aesthetic matters as well, an initial disregard for clear boundaries and distinctions characterised the cinema's relationship to the other arts and made it the quintessential mixed medium. Film-makers creatively explored the possibilities of multi-medial cross-fertilisation, introducing elements from the serial novel, making references to the operetta, imitating the theatre, and alluding to painting and photography. They took advantage of the affinities among cinema, urbanism, tourism, and consumerism by, for instance, showing the dangers of urban living, exploring various social settings, and venturing on imaginary journeys to exotic places. Interestingly, this hybrid quality also made film particularly suited to the representation of difference and the validation of diversity. The large number of Jewish directors and producers such as Ernst Lubitsch, Max Mack and Joe May, as well as Jules Greenbaum and Paul Davidson not only attests to the absence of strong professional hierarchies and social prejudices in the early film industry but also confirms the relative openness of the new medium toward the exploration of diverse social, ethnic, and local milieux. Especially the representation of the Jewish milieu referenced in Lubitsch's early two- and three-reelers bears witness to the strong affinities between the hybrid aesthetics of early cinema and its heterogeneous social functions and contexts (Stratenwerth and Simon 2004).

Elements of a national cinema: stars, genres, directors

The emergence of the longer film and the development of a filmic language would not have been possible without the enterprising businessmen, inventors, technicians, designers, composers, actors, and performers who thrived in this volatile atmosphere of great economic risks and even greater opportunities. Aided by better cameras, lighting, and film stock, cinematographers like Messter, Seeber, and the famous Karl Freund developed new filmic techniques. Taking advantage of their background in theatre design, Rochus Gliese, Hermann Warm, and Paul Leni created beautiful mise-en-scènes through their alternately naturalistic, realistic, and illusionistic approaches to filmic space. Composers and musicians combined well-known repertory pieces and innovative original scores for so-called cue sheets, thus starting a tradition that resulted in the 1920 publication of Guiseppe Becce's famous *Kinothek*, a collection of mood music for movie accompanists.

Promoting their longer films as artistic works with distinct qualities, studios relied increasingly on the notion of authorship and its implicit claims about creativity and originality. Directors began to play a more significant role in the marketing of films and, like trademarks, became frequently identified with particular genres (Wedel 1996). Thus Ernst Lubitsch and Max Mack acquired a reputation for comedies, Joe May for detective films, and Franz Hofer for melodramas. Equally important were the narrative continuities established within genres through their stereotypical characters and formulaic story lines. Some studios designed their entire public image around one main character, as did the Stuart-Webbs Film Co. with its detective films. Others, like the Mia May films, relied on the drawing power of the company's leading female star. Serials and sequels turned out to be a most effective form for ensuring public interest and involvement; the short-lived *Preisrätselfilme* (quiz films) even required the audience's active participation.

Most importantly, the star system established a structure for harnessing the psychological process of identification and making its mechanisms of adoration, emulation, and imitation an integral part of film reception and spectatorship. Closely identified with established social and sexual stereotypes and often associated with 'typical' German physical traits, the film star blurred the boundaries between actor and role and created a much-needed sense of continuity among individual films and genres. The star phenomenon took advantage of the existing cult of personality but also opened up new possibilities for viewer identification through decidedly voyeuristic scenarios. What distinguished film acting in the silent era from other forms of performance was the strong sense of physical presence and, hence, of closeness and intimacy. Through their body types and facial expressions, film actors conveyed a unity of body and character not attainable on the stage. They gave new credence to older assumptions (for instance, taken from physiognomy) about outward appearance and inner self while at the same time promoting more fluid definitions of identity based on the modern concept of self-fashioning. At the same time, actors played a key role in the construction of national identity, evoking the other as a temptation as well as a threat and articulating normative concepts of Germanness in visual, narrative, and performative terms.

These contradictory qualities and effects were often articulated along gendered lines. Male stars such as Albert Bassermann and Paul Wegener projected an image of traditional masculinity indebted to dramatic conceptions of character. By contrast, female stars inspired effusive claims about a universal visual language, a superior form of communication located in the body. The first actresses to be perceived in this way were Asta Nielsen and Henny Porten. With her distinctive pageboy hairstyle and slender body, the Danish Nielsen brought an exceptional emotional intensity and erotic presence to the screen. She was idolised by an entire generation of intellectuals who saw her face as a symbol of the new poetics of film. Between 1910 and 1919, Nielsen made over 40 films for Nordisk, often under the direction of her husband Urban Gad. Her greatest successes were social dramas that placed her on the side of the underprivileged and the oppressed and offered compelling examples of female strength and autonomy. Nielsen's most famous films from the period were *Die arme Jenny* (Poor Jenny, 1912), *Das Mädchen ohne Vaterland* (The Girl Without Fatherland, 1912), *Die Sünden der Väter* (The Sins of the Fathers, 1913), *Engelein* (Little Angel, 1914), and *Vordertreppe – Hintertreppe* (Front Entrance – Back Entrance, 1915).

Whereas Nielsen was perceived as an almost disruptive force in silent cinema, Henny Porten became closely identified with the normative force of traditional gender roles (Belach 1986). With her long blonde hair, plain features, and buxom figure, Porten personified traditional Germanic womanhood even when she appeared in rustic comedies that showed off her considerable comic talents. This first genuine German film star had her greatest successes with melodramas in the literary tradition of middle-brow authors Eugenie Marlitt and Hedwig Courths-Mahler. Her identification with maternal qualities helped to placate widespread anxieties about women's emancipation and made her ideally suited for old-fashioned stories about female honour, duty, and sacrifice. None the less, Porten frequently used her talent and fame to draw attention to the most pressing issues of the time: working-class poverty in *Mütter, verzaget nicht!* (Mothers, Don't Despair!, 1911), labour unrest in *Tragödie eines Streiks* (Tragedy of a Strike, 1911), and unwed motherhood in *Abseits vom Glück* (Overlooked by Fortune, 1916). The career women, bluestockings, and single mothers in these films often resist male domination through moral rectitude and the renunciation of sexual pleasure. By incorporating such gestures of resistance into otherwise traditional female narratives, Porten emerged as the classical *femme forte* of early cinema who represented the problems of ordinary women more accurately than the cosmopolitan *femmes fatales* portrayed by Pola Negri and Mia May.

In the same way that the star system reflected dramatic changes in Wilhelmine society, including the emancipation of women and the rise of the working class,

18

the most successful film genres responded to new lifestyles and sensibilities, but again with a detour through established popular traditions. Drawing on fairytales, rustic comedies, trivial novels, and folk operettas, comedies and melodramas provided the most effective models for organising visual and narrative motifs and for linking them to specific problems in modern mass society: the conflicts between classes, sexes, and generations; the search for freedom and happiness; experiences of alienation and dislocation; the dangers of modern life; the fascination of the big city; and the changing face of labour and industry. At the same time, more action-oriented genres such as the detective film and the adventure film emulated the narrative formulas of the Hollywood cinema. The physical humour in early German comedies also took inspiration from American slapstick comedies. In all cases, American stories and characters were translated into German contexts or reinterpreted from a German perspective, with the resultant tensions between self and other an integral part of the appeal. Thus a short-lived series of westerns imitated the successful Tom Mix films while also taking cues from the ever-popular Karl May novels and their uniquely German romance with the Wild West.

The emerging genres of early cinema may have been formulaic but they also established a framework for the articulation of individual perspectives and sensibilities. Film directors, producers, and studios took full advantage of the inherent tension between tradition and innovation, often using the conventional genre structures in original and creative ways. Appropriating elements from the naturalist drama, the newspaper serial, and the trivial novel, the early melodramas often ended up containing social experiences within purely psychological categories, thereby depriving their protagonists of the possibility of real change. Yet these stories also focused on individual experiences of discrimination, exploitation, and oppression and, in so doing, acknowledged the reality of human suffering. Fantastic films appropriated established visual and narrative motifs from romantic painting and literature, as well as from the popular Gothic novels, but used their unsettling effects to give expression to a decidedly modern fear and dread of the other. The historical epics, sometimes also called costume dramas or period films, displaced political events into the material splendour of set and costume design and resolved questions of historical agency through the juxtaposition between active individuals and passive masses. Yet in their insistence on visual pleasure without regard for psychological motivation or historical accuracy, these elaborate costume dramas also preserved some of the anarchic qualities of early *Kientopp* in their material and performative excesses.

Meanwhile, detective films and suspense thrillers experimented with national stereotypes without necessarily promoting nationalistic sentiments. British crime fiction served as a model for Joe May's Stuart Webbs series with Ernst Reicher, as well as for the Joe Deebs series with Max Landa. The fascination with British rationality and pragmatism stood behind Richard Oswald's involvement with the Sherlock Holmes figure and inspired a surprising number of stories with smart women detectives such as Nobody and Ellen Grey. Started by Louis Feuillade in 1913, the French *Fantômas* series exerted a strong influence on mysteries like *Der*

19

Bär von Baskerville (The Bear of Baskerville, 1915) as well as on the Fritz Lang thrillers from the early 1920s. Last but not least, American action adventures left a noticeable mark in the work of actor-director Harry Piel, who became known for his penchant for big explosions, wild animals, and futuristic technologies and who, known in the 1920s as the 'German Douglas Fairbanks', continued to perform his own stunts till the 1950s.

The detective films, in particular, contributed to the emergence of a highly codified filmic language through their fast-paced stories and dramatic situations, their colourful characters from different backgrounds, and their unusual locations and exotic settings (Hesse 2003). Establishing narrative continuity across time and space and building suspense through framing and editing proved essential to such stock situations as the chase, the cliffhanger, and the last-minute rescue. All of these narrative conventions provided an opportunity for talented individual directors to develop a signature style. Thus Joseph Delmont's *Der geheimnisvolle Klub* (The Mysterious Club, 1913) stood out through the extensive use of real locations, whereas *Der Steckbrief* (The Wanted Poster, 1913) by Franz Hofer, a rediscovered early *auteur*, convinced through his poetic camerawork and atmospheric mise-en-scènes. Largely responsible for the strong female presence in the detective genre, Hofer favoured beautiful heroines who, as in *Die schwarze Natter* (The Black Snake, 1913) and *Die schwarze Kugel* (The Black Ball, 1913), solved all problems with intelligence and determination.

In the same way that the detective films used the filmic medium to complicate basic assumptions about knowledge, evidence, and truth, early film comedies enlisted the constitutive tension between affirmation and critique to engage with the most pressing social issues of the times: the disintegration of the traditional family, the battle between the sexes, the dangers of the big city, the provocation of youth, and conflicts in the workplace. Comedies from the Wilhelmine period covered the entire range from the humorous and the grotesque to the silly and the crude. What distinguished them from Weimar comedies were their close attention to local and ethnic milieux, an irreverent play with gender roles, and a marked penchant for sadistic pleasures and nihilistic sentiments. Laughter served two distinct functions: to provide release from the pressures of everyday life – for instance by showing its absurdities through a decidedly physical humour – and to affirm one's own identity, for instance by playing with gender, ethnic, racial, and national stereotypes. The tacit assumptions about shared values and beliefs made many of these comedies ill-suited for exportation but contributed to their success as simultaneous fantasies of transgression and acts of accommodation. To what degree these films contributed to the preservation of the status quo and in what ways they undermined hegemonic discourses of identity depended on a variety of factors, including the actor's or director's use of humour and irony as a critical tool. Taking a conciliatory approach, rustic comedies celebrated the country folk as the embodiment of old-fashioned gullibility and a more innocent past and usually played into a conservative worldview. By contrast, the many mistaken-identity plots in the sophisticated comedies made the individual problems caused by social mobility and the redrawing of class boundaries the source of an ultimately affirmative humour but did so in full recognition of the instability of identity.

In many cases, the involvement of individual actors determined a film's critical possibilities. Karl Valentin, the Munich comic, singer, and cabaret artist, uncovered the absurdities of everyday life in numerous grotesque comedies from *Karl Valentins Hochzeit* (Karl Valentin's Wedding, 1912) to *Mysterien eines Frisiersalons* (Mysteries of a Hair Dresser's Shop, 1922), a later collaboration with Bertolt Brecht and Erich Engel. Working in the tradition of the Bavarian folk play, Valentin deconstructed social conventions and regional traditions through an aggressive form of physical humour that produced almost surrealist effects. Introducing slapstick elements into ethnic milieux, Lubitsch focused on the Jewish clothing manufacture in *Der Stolz der Firma* (The Pride of the Firm, 1914) and *Schuhpalast Pinkus* (Shoe Salon Pinkus, 1916). His play with sexual stereotypes found expression in provocative stories of desire and deception, from the debunking of male chauvinism in *Don Juan heiratet* (Don Juan's Wedding, 1909) to the gender confusion caused by female cross-dressing in *Ich möchte kein Mann sein* (I Don't Want to Be a Man, 1918).

The early melodramas, and the social dramas even more critically, addressed the problem of female self-determination within a discernible social setting and with close attention to the performative aspects of femininity. Films such as *Mutterliebe* (Mother Love, 1909) and *Ich will keine Stiefmutter* (I Don't Want a Stepmother, 1911) offered sustained reflections on modern marriage and motherhood and addressed social problems without the usual moralising tone. Aesthetically, the melodramatic approaches remained indebted to social realist aesthetics and a firm belief in the visibility of social structures. By mapping the psychological dimensions of the bourgeois interior, the social dramas with Nielsen and Porten validated the emotionality of women and the importance of the private sphere. The translation of social relations into spatial terms created the highly symbolic mise-en-scènes that eventually gave rise to an artistically more ambitious sub-genre of melodrama, the *Kammerspielfilm* (chamber play film), which explored the claustrophobic interiors as part of a larger critique of bourgeois and petty-bourgeois family life. Only after the war and in the context of expressionism did the chamberplay films begin to privilege male over female perspectives and abandon the critique of gender and family relations for psychological introspection.

While the unjustly maligned melodrama staged the problem of femininity by taking advantage of popular traditions, the artistically more ambitious fantastic film addressed the crisis of masculinity through the literary and artistic traditions of the nineteenth century. Melodramatic forms were considered most suited for representation of the domestic sphere and female desire, whereas the fantastic with its precarious sense of reality proved ideal for articulating the problem of male subjectivity. The subversive effects of the uncanny found paradigmatic expression in the screen personas of Albert Bassermann, Olaf Fönss, Conrad Veidt, and Bernhard Goetzke, all of whom acted out traditional assumptions about masculinity within increasingly unstable configurations of identity, power, and desire. Filmic engagements with the fantastic restaged this modern uncanny as an experience of dissolving boundaries: between the animate and inanimate world, between awaking and dream, between the self and the other. This experience was often articulated in terms of visual perception, which explains the recurring motif of blindness and the frequent use of mirrors and doubles. The preoccupation with looking, and the underlying struggle for control, reflected a pervasive fear of losing oneself in the confrontation with women, workers, and foreigners – in short, with the vilified, demonised, and ostracised others of German modernity.

When emphasising film's closeness to the world of childhood, fantastic films frequently sought inspiration from the rich tradition of the fairytale and achieved the visualisation of the marvellous in elaborate dream sequences – like the ones from *Rübezahls Hochzeit* (Old Nip's Wedding, 1916). References to German romanticism appeared in Richard Oswald's *Hoffmanns Erzählungen* (Tales of Hoffmann, 1916), whereas a distinctly Gothic style prevailed in one of the earliest filmic reflections on the relationship between man and machine, *Homunculus* (1916) with Otto Rippert. More troublesome affinities between cinema and dream were first explored in Stellan Rye's *Der Student von Prag* (The Student of Prague, 1913), with Wegener in the title role. Written by Hanns Heinz Ewers, a prolific writer who specialised in mixing fantasy and myth, the film translates elements of the romantic imagination (the figure of the double, the pact with the devil) into filmic and, therefore, profoundly modern terms (Keiner 1987). *Der Golem* (The Golem, 1914), the first in a number of films about the eponymous mythological figure, uses the fascination with medieval life and cabalistic ritual both to rehearse familiar Jewish stereotypes and to reflect on the history of anti-Semitism (Ledig 1990). With their affinity for pre-industrial society, traditional folk culture, and small-town living, the fantastic films provided audiences with an imaginary space for expressing their ambivalence toward modern life. Onscreen, the allusions to myths and fairytales helped to displace the shock of technology into eternal times and archetypal situations. At the same time, the romantic figure of the double gave expression to an urgently contemporary sense of dissociation and alienation. Firm believers in the artistic possibilities of film, both Wegener and Ewers promoted the fantastic as an authentically German tradition that combined old thematic preferences with new technological possibilities. In so doing, they developed a model for reconciling modern and premodern elements and for eliminating the high/low-culture divide through the imaginary worlds created by film.

The controversies over silent cinema's allegedly negative impact on cultural life were most intense in relation to theatre and literature. Central to the formation of national identity since the late eighteenth century, the theatrical establishment felt threatened by the growing competition for audiences and feared loss of its historical role in the bourgeois public sphere. Writers speculated about the diminished role of literature in constituting Germany as a *Kulturnation*, that is, a nation defined more through its cultural traditions than through its social and political accomplishments. Much of early film theory must be seen in the context of these institutional rivalries and the underlying anxieties about the displacement of high culture by a mechanically produced mass culture. From Georg Lukács to Herbert

Tannenbaum, critics argued about the formal differences between cinema and theatre and formulated an aesthetic of cinema out of its inherent limitations, beginning with its 'muteness'. Some described the cinema's assault on the values represented by literature, including such cherished notions as the autonomy of art, as symptomatic of a deeper crisis of bourgeois individualism; others saw the cinema's visual language as the first step in the making of the new mass individual.

Whether vilified or glorified, the cinema offered many career opportunities for writers, actors, musicians, and artists. Because of the contribution of well-known writers, the so-called *Autorenfilm* (authors' film) earned the new medium middle-class respectability and cultural legitimacy. Inspired by the French *film d'art* and its acclaimed adaptations of canonical literary texts, the German *Autorenfilm* promoted a cinema of quality based on the great classics as well as contemporary literature. Under the motto 'Films of famous authors are the future of cinema!' production companies secured the film rights to the dramatic works of Gerhart Hauptmann, Hermann Sudermann, Max Halbe, and Arthur Schnitzler. While polemicists were still arguing whether or not film would ever be art, Kurt Pinthus already published *Das Kinobuch* (The Cinema Book, 1914), a collection of film scenarios that explored the medium's affinities with the fantastic, the supernatural, and the grotesque. After Bassermann's screen debut in the Max Mack adaptation of Paul Lindau's *Der Andere* (The Other, 1913), a variation on the Jekyll and Hyde motif, a growing number of stage actors began to appear regularly in films, attracted by the high pay and the promise of instant celebrity. Respected theatre producers such as Max Reinhardt and Leopold Jessner soon followed suit. Envisioning a new theatre for the masses, Reinhardt in the early 1910s adopted some of his stage productions to the screen and even directed two films that skilfully mixed fantastic and romantic motifs, *Die Insel der Seligen* (The Isle of the Blessed, 1913) and *Eine venezianische Nacht* (A Venetian Night, 1914).

Throughout, the cinema provided the educated middle class with an opportunity to affirm the place of literature in modern culture, to appropriate filmic techniques for the project of literary modernism and to reflect on the broader changes in culture and society; these debates have become known as the *Kino-Debatte* or cinema debate (Heller 1984, Hake 1992b). The literary and artistic avant-gardes either set out to rescue the project of high culture from the dangers of commodification or they tried to achieve the full integration of art into life. Writers as diverse as Alfred Döblin, Thomas Mann, and Else Lasker-Schüler engaged in a passionate debate for and against the cinema that lasted until the late 1920s and involved many literary forms and institutions (Kaes 1978, Güttinger 1984a and 1984b). Initial curiosity and disdain soon gave way to a more systematic involvement with a new art form simultaneously described as dramatic, epic, and poetic, and alternately compared to theatre, music, and pantomime. Throughout, the debater's preoccupation with new audiences and new modes of reception betrayed deep anxieties about the disappearance of the traditional bourgeois public sphere where intellectuals played a privileged role as the final arbiters of taste. In some cases, these controversies gave rise to utopian dreams of cinema as the only solution to a much diagnosed crisis of meaning. Through the cinema, many critics hoped, audiences could reclaim the unity of experience in the pure act of looking. Whereas literature and the other arts seemed weighted down by problems of mediation, the new medium conjured up an imaginary space of lifelike representations and immediate pleasures; hence Hugo von Hofmannsthal's and Ernst Bloch's enthusiastic comments on the close affinities between cinema and dream.

The debates about the corrupting influence of cinema took a decidedly political turn in the polemical writings by educators, politicians, public officials, and religious leaders (Degenhardt 2001). These cinema reformers fell into two groups: those primarily concerned with social reform and public health, and those interested in the cinema as a tool of German nationalism and cultural renewal. Thus, on the one hand, in numerous articles and books, the art historian Konrad Lange attacked the trashy film (*Schundfilm*) with moralistic arguments adopted from late nineteenth-century debates on trivial literature. On the other hand, the media activist Hermann Häfker and his associates from *Bild und Film* (Image and Film), a Catholic media organisation founded in 1912, emphasised film's pedagogical uses and actively promoted the so-called *Kulturfilm* (cultural film), a form of documentary committed to idealised representations of nature, culture, and science (Diederichs 1986). In their studies on the social relevance of cinema, the reformers developed the first psychological theories of film spectatorship and established the basic terms for an emerging sociology of film. They paid close attention to the mechanisms of mass manipulation and considered its potential uses for the promotion of public policies and education reforms. Above all, the cinema reformers spoke out passionately against the emotional excesses of a cinema that, in their view, were symptomatic of the problems of Wilhelmine society as a whole.

German cinema and the First World War

While the pre-war years saw the emergence of a popular cinema with strong international ties, the propagandistic uses of film during the First World War closely aligned the cinema with the goals of German nationalism. The war forged a powerful bond between the industry and the state and left an indelible mark on the cinema not only through new censorship practices and quota laws but also through the enlistment of film in political propaganda (Barkhausen 1982, Mühl-Benninghaus 1997 and 2004). Even more important, the declaration of war in 1914 by force created a national film market and, in so doing, completed the consolidation of the industry. Once French films were no longer in distribution, German companies encountered little other competition and expanded aggressively to meet the demands of an increasingly war-weary populace. Meanwhile, the increase in discretionary incomes and a growing need for escapist fare made moviegoing more attractive for larger segments of the population. Between 1914 and 1919, almost seven hundred new cinemas opened. The number of films produced in Berlin quadrupled, with countless smaller firms specialising in cheaply made sentimental dramas and comedies. Finally, German firms saw a chance to escape the French dominance and divide domestic markets among themselves. Hollywood films continued to be shown until 1916; Nordisk also remained a strong presence because of the close ties between German and Danish companies.

The cinema's contribution to the war effort and to the survival of the monarchy dramatically changed the economic and political status of the film industry. Granted, production companies lagged behind the British and the French in their use of propaganda as an ideological continuation of war. German films never achieved the kind of effects attributed to the British *The Beast of Berlin*, which portrayed the enemy as bloodthirsty Huns. However, concerted efforts to introduce national perspectives into the cinema, on both the institutional and the ideological level, resulted in a fundamental redefinition of popular culture and had far-reaching implications for the postwar years. The cinema's nationalistic awakening began with the organisation of patriotic film-days and screenings at the front. Military farces and sentimental dramas were produced to strengthen the bond between the soldiers and their families. Animated films (for example, those of Julius Pinschewer) relied on humour and wit to promote the sale of war bonds. In *Hurra! Einquartierung!* (Hurrah! Quartering!, 1913) and *Weihnachtsglocken* (Christmas Bells, 1914), Hofer used elements from rustic farce and social drama to offer assuring glimpses from the home front. Paul Leni's story of an army physician, *Das Tagebuch des Dr. Hart* (The Diary of Dr Hart, 1916), stood out through a surprising realism in its presentation of daily life in the military. Such exceptions notwithstanding, the majority of feature films produced between 1914 and 1918 avoided all references to the ongoing war and completely ignored the social problems that contributed to the fall of the monarchy.

None the less, the First World War must be described as the first truly modern media war. Through a clear division between aggressive propaganda and escapist entertainment, the cinema became part of a pervasive militarisation of culture. The heavy reliance on mass media in reports from the front and the enlistment of fantasy production in the war effort radically redefined the relationship between representation and reality. Newsreels aimed to disperse rumours about the horrors of trench warfare and maintain patriotic spirit and public morale. *Eiko-Woche* and *Messter-Woche* frequently abandoned the traditional tableaux format of battle panoramas for the shifting points-of-view normally found in feature films. Interested less in documentary accuracy than in emotional effects, these war newsreels adopted a distinctly narrative style (for instance, by including staged scenes from the trenches). Meanwhile the use of photography and cinematography in reconnaissance established aviation and cinema as compatible forms of visual control. Early ballistic studies, including the ones made possible by Anschütz's camera gun, had relied on similar technologies of vision and confirmed simulation as an integral part both of advanced warfare and of modern consciousness. Through these technologies of war, the filmic interventions into the real gave rise to a newly constituted unreal (for example, the disembodied enemy), a process predicated on the growing distance between human and machine and the absorption of cause and effect into more elusive notions of agency.

25

Two organisations closely identified with the military-industrial complex became instrumental in enlisting early cinema in the service of German nationalism and militarism. The Deutsche Lichtbild Gesellschaft (DLG, German Society for Visual Media) was formed in 1916 by Ludwig Klitzsch and Alfred Hugenberg as a promotional tool for German heavy industries pursuing expansionist plans in the Balkans and the Near East. Similar interests stood behind the Deutsche Kolonial-Filmgesellschaft (DEUKO, German Colonial Film Society), founded in 1917 to advance the colonial idea. The DLG, which after the war became the Deulig, produced countless documentaries and contributed significantly to the rise of the cultural film. In 1917, the German High Command under General Erich Ludendorff formed its own propaganda unit, the Bild-und Filmamt (Bufa, Office for Photography and Film); its goal was to co-ordinate all official media activities in one central agency and to support the war effort through all available photographic and filmic means. Ludendorff's plans for a large film company financed by the Reich extended these activities into an increasingly uncertain political future for the monarchy. With military victory no longer certain, government control over the production of images – and, by implication, the masses – seemed all the more important.

The Universum Film-AG (Ufa), the legendary film studio that still looms large in the German imagination, was the product of such political calculations. Founded on 18 December 1917 with a starting capital of 25 million Reichsmark (RM), of which the Reich contributed 7 million, the Ufa brought together the government, represented by the War Ministry under Ludendorff, with major industries and financial institutions, including the electrical giants AEG and Bosch, the Hamburg-America Line, and the Deutsche Bank, whose director Emil Georg von Stauß became chairman of the board. Alfred Hugenberg, director of the Krupp concern and a representative of the Rhine-Ruhr industrial complex, played an important role in co-ordinating corporate interests and right-wing politics over the next decade; so did Ludwig Klitzsch, who, as director of the Scherl publishing conglomerate, participated actively in the restructuring of Ufa during and after the war. Quickly establishing its influence in film production, distribution, and exhibition, Ufa bought the German sister companies of Nordisk, as well as the Messter and Union-studios in Berlin Tempelhof, and acquired large shares of PAGU. Following the collapse of the monarchy in 1918 and the adoption of a democratic constitution in 1919, the close ties between state and industry continued to haunt the German cinema for decades to come, with the presumed identity of Ufa and German cinema one of the most persistent after-effects of such political and economic alliances (Bock and Töteberg 1992, Borgelt 1993, Kreimeier 1996). Wielding almost monopolistic power, this powerful vertically integrated concern had a decisive influence on every aspect of cinema culture during the 1920s. Even when the Reich sold its shares to Deutsche Bank in 1921, Ludendorff's project of nationalistic propaganda through mass entertainment was far from finished; it simply continued in the alliance of economic power and right-wing politics that haunted all aspects of Weimar cinema.

2

WEIMAR CINEMA 1919–33

The years of the Weimar Republic have played a key role in the writing of German film history and contributed greatly to the recognition of film as an essential part of twentieth-century German culture. The signing of the constitution in 1919 ushered in a period of dramatic social, political, and cultural changes that, in the popular imagination, have become identified with the liberal, urban, and cosmopolitan atmosphere of the 'golden twenties'. The difficult conditions under which the various short-lived governments had to deal with civil war, putsches, strikes, inflation, mass poverty, unemployment, and political strife confirmed the persistence of prewar power structures and the lack of popular support for democratic processes and republican institutions. The new political, social, and cultural elites promised to move beyond the trauma of the First World War by placing the forces of modernisation, industrialisation, and urbanisation in the service of greater social mobility, economic opportunity, and individual freedom. After a brief period of stabilisation between 1924 and 1929, in which economic progress was palpable and cultural life flourished, the young republic confronted its most serious challenge in the worldwide economic depression and the rise of National Socialism. In 1933, the combined force of traditional conservative and right-wing parties and of a new political party held together by anti-communism and anti-Semitism brought an end to the first German republic.

As the product of non-synchronous developments and irreconcilable forces, Weimar culture must be defined less through distinct characteristics or clear tendencies than through its underlying conflicts and contradictions: emancipatory mass culture and provincial lifestyles; revolutionary mass movements and right-wing and pre-fascist tendencies; the culture of the big city and nostalgia for traditional communities; the fascination with all things American and campaigns against foreign influences and racial others; and female emancipation and sexual liberation and retreat to authoritarian models and all-male groups. The literary and artistic avant-gardes, from expressionism and Dadaism to New Objectivity promoted experimentation, innovation, and social change. Similarly, the alliance of urban culture, consumer culture, and new mass media gave rise to a progressive mass culture beyond the old divisions of high and low culture. Yet the adaptation of American notions of labour and leisure (for instance, in the embrace of Taylorism and Fordism) also created great anxieties that found expression in regressive fantasies, conservative attitudes, and reactionary politics. Articulating this dialectic of mass culture and modernity in its multifaceted stories and images, cinema represented an integral part of these heterogeneous discourses.

As in the case of Wilhelmine cinema, scholars distinguish three phases: the years from 1919 to 1924, which saw the rise of the expressionist film out of the trauma of the lost war, the failed revolution, and the hyperinflation; the years from 1924 to 1929, which brought greater economic stability and more realist approaches in the style of New Objectivity; and the years from 1929 to 1933, which began with the restructuring of the industry after the introduction of sound and ended with the politicisation of cinema before the Nazi takeover. Although only 10 per cent of the films have survived, the cinema of the Weimar Republic has inspired a wide range of socio-psychological, art historical, and cultural studies approaches. In Germany, the classics of the silent cinema have played a key role in the acceptance of film as an art form and the establishment of film studies as an academic discipline. Yet during the last decades, Weimar cinema has also provided a critical model for revisiting the complicated relationship between art and politics, popular cinema and dominant ideology; for exploring the larger configurations of cinema, modernism, and modernity; for studying cinema's relationship to other mass media and communication technologies; for tracing its connection to mass consumption, mass tourism, and Americanism; and for contemplating the affinities between cinema and the discourses of science, medicine, and the law. Not surprisingly, the most famous films from the period have frequently served as reference points in the revisions of German cinema from the 1950s to the 1990s and have allowed film-makers, whether through remakes, quotations or pastiches, to establish aesthetic and critical traditions across the cultural divide marked by the Third Reich.

Performing such paradigmatic functions, the study of Weimar cinema has raised many questions relevant for a better understanding not only of the period but also for all of German cinema and its continuing negotiation of art, politics, and entertainment. To begin with, was Weimar cinema an art cinema unloved by the masses or a popular cinema with artistic ambitions? Can the feature films made between 1919 and 1933 be read as a direct reflection of German society or are they more accurately described as an expression of society's dreams and fantasies? Are the films to be analysed through the categories of textual analysis or through the historical contexts that define their meaning and function? Is Weimar cinema to be conceptualised as part of a larger media history or history of audio-visual technologies? Or would it be more productive to focus on the cinema as a public sphere with changing alliances with high culture, mass culture, national culture, as well as the culture of subversion, alterity, and dissent? Can the historical trajectory of Weimar cinema be described in terms of artistic decline, with the expressionist film of the early 1920s as the high point, or as a series of incomplete projects that began with various initiatives for the quality film and that ended with the social realist films of the early 1930s? And is the end of Weimar cinema marked by the introduction of sound, an international phenomenon, or the return of nationalism with the advent of National Socialism?

Both written in the aftermath of the Third Reich, two famous studies by Siegfried Kracauer and Lotte Eisner have profoundly influenced the scholarly reception of the period. In *From Caligari to Hitler: A Psychological History of the German Film* (2004, first published in 1947), Kracauer examines the films for the prevailing psychological dispositions or tendencies within a nation at a particular historical juncture; in this case, Germany after the First World War. Focusing on recurring thematic preferences and narrative motifs, Kracauer sees the vacillation between anxiety and aggression, and revolt and submission, as a typical expression of German national character and its foundation in authoritarian social and political structures. According to his socio-psychological reading, Weimar films reveal hidden pre-fascist tendencies that make the rise of Hitler appear almost inevitable. Concentrating on the expressionist movement, Lotte Eisner uses stylistic categories to conclude that German cinema is a continuation of romanticism, a translation of its core themes and motifs into new technologies and techniques. The body of work thus constituted must be regarded as both profoundly anti-modernist in its cultural sensibilities and self-consciously German in its preoccupation with problems of identity and the metaphysics of space (Eisner 1977, first published in French in 1956).

Critics have responded to Kracauer's teleological construction of Weimar cinema as pre-fascist cinema through a number of historical studies that modify or challenge some of his claims: studies about the beginnings of a leftist film culture (Murray 1990); the economic and cultural predominance of Hollywood (Saunders 1994); the critical reception of films in the last years of the republic (Korte 1998); the corporate, legal, and institutional battles surrounding the new sound technology (Mühl-Benninghaus 1999); and the richness and complexity of late Weimar cinema as a realist cinema and modernist cinema (Koebner 2003). Kracauer's socio-psychological approach has been refined through closer attention to the modes of spectatorship that constitute modern subjectivity in relation to questions of gender, class, race, and national identity. Some studies have used the problematic of modern subjectivity to examine the visual and narrative strategies that constitute Weimar cinema as a decidedly modernist cinema (Elsaesser 1984 and 2000b), while other scholars have underscored its contribution to the emergence of a vernacular modernism. The unique aesthetic qualities of the silent films have been explored in recent studies both on the ongoing negotiation of modernist and anti-modernist influences (Calhoon 2001) and on the pivotal role of light and light metaphors in articulating the elusive mise-en-scènes of Weimar modernity (Guerin 2005).

Feminist approaches in particular have drawn attention to the importance of melodramatic forms in addressing women audiences and offering alternative models of female spectatorship (Petro 1989). The obsession with the crisis of masculinity and the traumas of the war have been traced in filmic conceptions of the modern (mechanised) body and in the subversive blurring of gender roles and sexual identities in the cult of the New Woman (McCormick 2002). The notion of shell shock as a collective experience and an allegory of modernity has been used to make sense of the preoccupation with vision and visuality and its underlying epistemological, perceptual, and affective crises (Kaes 2008). Under the influence of cultural studies, Weimar cinema continues to be read as an integral part of Weimar culture, with special attention paid to the profound impact of the lost war, failed revolution, and rampant inflation, the many overlaps with urbanism, consumerism, and Americanisation, and the strong affinities with new social movements, cultural mentalities, and lifestyle phenomena. Because of these changes in focus and methodology, it is no longer possible to describe Weimar cinema as pre-fascist cinema without also considering the many characteristics that define it as a postwar cinema.

Weimar cinema as art cinema

Robert Wiene's *Das Kabinett des Dr. Caligari* (The Cabinet of Dr Caligari, 1920) occupies a special place in many assessments of Weimar cinema, and the expressionist film in particular (Prawer 1980, Budd 1990, Jung and Schatzberg 1999). Often described as the quintessential expressionist film, *Caligari* has become famous for its painted backdrops, skewed angles, dark shadows, and claustrophobic interiors. The haunting story of the mysterious Caligari and his medium, the somnambulist Cesare, has been read as symptomatic of the unstable social and political situation after the First World War. Stylistically, the film combines elements from German romanticism and Gothic literature, including the device of the unreliable narrator, with the staging and acting conventions of expressionist theatre and early film melodrama. Yet historically, the film also re-enacts the transition between the so-called primitive early cinema and the classical silent film. And economically, *Caligari* must be described as a highly successful model for using style as a form of product differentiation on domestic and foreign markets.

The critical and popular success of *Caligari* paved the way for art films distinguished through their highly stylised sets, visual and spatial symbolisms, mysterious characters, and bizarre story lines. The subsequent emergence of a recognisable expressionist style was primarily the work of set designers such as Robert Herlth, Kurt Richter, Erich Kettelhut, and Hermann Warm who, often with no more than plaster, paper, and paint, created what some might call a mise-en-scène of the national unconscious. The screenwriter Carl Mayer, who often collaborated with Friedrich Wilhelm Murnau, translated these haunting stories of desire, death, and destruction into uniquely filmic effects. Known for his masterful use of atmosphere, or *Stimmung*, Mayer must be described as the unifying force behind the various manifestations of film expressionism (Omasta et al. 2003). While expressionist elements appear in a number of genres and oeuvres, only a few films aimed at a radical transformation of the physical world, a projection of psychological states into haunting, terrifying, fantastic or dreamlike mise-en-scènes. These films include Robert Wiene's *Genuine* (1920), *Raskolnikow* (1923), and *Orlacs Hände* (The Hands of Orlac, 1924); Karl Heinz Martin's *Von morgens bis mitternachts*

(From Morn to Midnight, 1920), based on the Georg Kaiser play, as well as Arthur Robison's *Schatten* (Warning Shadows, 1923), and Paul Leni's *Das Wachsfiguren-kabinett* (Waxworks, 1924), two early representatives of the horror genre. *Der Golem: Wie er in die Welt kam* (The Golem: How He Came into the World, 1920), by and with Paul Wegener, and Henrik Galeen's *Der Student von Prag* (The Student of Prague, 1926), a remake of the original featuring Conrad Veidt, are often included in the expressionist canon but actually stand closer to the traditions of the fantastic from the prewar years.

The expressionist film is notorious for the way it resists definitions, and comparisons to theatre and the visual arts have done as much to obscure as to clarify expressionism's stylistic debts (Barlow 1982, Kasten 1990). Similarly, the focus on the expressionist classics has distracted from the thematic concerns and filmic techniques shared with other popular genres and styles (Scheunemann 2003). Contributing to the eclectic nature of the expressionist film, important literary and artistic influences include romantic painting (Friedrich, Spitzweg) and literature (Hölderlin, Novalis, E. T. A. Hoffmann) as well as the rich tradition of the fantastic. Film-makers' partiality for the unreal and the interest in the uncanny reveal decidedly contemporary anxieties, beginning with the thematisation of new visual technologies in the intense preoccupation with looking. Expressionism in the cinema must therefore be approached on two levels: as a cluster of formal characteristics and narrative elements and as a particular atmosphere, a mood, that points to a profound crisis of identity in modern mass society. In the first sense, the expressionist film shares much with the expressionist drama, such as the emphasis on father–son conflicts and the provocation of female sexuality; the preference for identifiable stereotypes rather than psychologically developed characters; the interest in transgression, madness, and rebellion; and the fascination with ambiguity, difference, and otherness. These thematic explorations are not always free of racial stereotyping, as evidenced by the negative depiction of Jewish or Jewish-looking characters as the embodiment of otherness (e.g., in *Nosferatu* and the *Golem* films).

In the second sense, the expressionist film is primarily a visual phenomenon, a mise-en-scène of fear and desire. Internal conflicts and ambivalences are projected on to an external world that has become foreign and strange, a process that finds expression in the destabilisation of the subject at the centre of the narrative; hence the many overlaps with the horror genre (Coates 1991). Often created entirely in the studio, these films rely on a psychological conception of space which foregrounds the medium's affinity with transgressive states such as dream, intoxication, and insanity. Using modern techniques to escape into pre-industrial, premodern worlds allows the expressionist film to take full advantage of the cinema's precarious position between myth and modernity. Created through oblique angles, flat surfaces, skewed perspectives, sharp contrasts, and chiaroscuro lighting, the films' imaginary spaces undermine the spectator's belief in physical reality and the primacy of realism. This elusive metaphysics of space extends from landscapes and buildings to objects of everyday use and includes a similarly destabilising theatricalisation of performance through exaggerated gestures, dramatic costumes, and heavy makeup. Together set design, costume design, and acting styles provide the perfect mise-en-scène for the recurring plot structures and narrative motifs of the expressionist film: the dynamics of oppression and rebellion, domination and subordination; the burdens of the past and fear of the future; the spectacle of female sexuality and the violence of male desire; the threats posed by modern industry and technology; and the promises and dangers of the big city. Adding to these thematic patterns, the crisis moments in the expressionist film are often re-enacted through an almost obsessive concern with visual relations, modes of spectatorship, and problems of perception, which explains the privileging of frame composition over narrative continuity in the expressionist imaginary.

Many members of the film industry had welcomed the calls for a strong national cinema during the war years and made a concerted effort to advance film's usefulness as political propaganda. Yet after 1918, Ufa's corporate strategies were motivated primarily by economic concerns and focused almost exclusively on film as art and entertainment. Taking advantage of its privileged position, Ufa acquired the Messner and Union studios in Berlin, built more and better first-run cinemas, and began to publish film books and magazines – all with the goal of achieving dominance in the production, distribution, and exhibitions sectors. DECLA and Bioscop first merged in 1920 to become the second largest film studio and then joined forces with Ufa in 1921. In the same year, the Reich sold its Ufa shares to the Deutsche Bank and thereafter exerted its influence primarily through political and legal measures. By continuously expanding and diversifying, the Ufa studio pursued a double strategy: to protect its domestic interests against the growing influx of American films and to contribute to the development of a European alternative to the feared American cultural hegemony. This strategy included building the elaborate distribution and exhibition networks that, by the mid-1920s, made Ufa the only serious competitor for the Hollywood majors on European markets.

Classic silent cinema began as an inflation cinema that was able to realise its aesthetic ambitions because of the systemic power vacuum and legitimation crisis that defined the Weimar Republic as much as its authoritarian structures and conservative institutions. During the first years after the war, the devaluation of the currency and the low production costs, including the availability of cheap labour, contributed to an expansionist frenzy and hyper-activity. In the absence of foreign competitors, countless smaller firms flooded the market with mediocre productions made for quick consumption. Leading studios such as Ufa invested in big historical spectacles and ambitious art films that improved the reputation of the German film abroad and, in so doing, developed a business strategy for the entire next decade. The international success of *Caligari* confirmed that films with 'typical' German styles could be profitable and, moreover, that only the emphasis on the national would make German companies competitive internationally. Hailed as an artistic novelty after its 1921 New York premiere, *Caligari* was part of a brief export wave that started in 1920 with *Passion*, the American title of Lubitsch's *Madame*

Dubarry, and that also included *Carmen* (Gypsy Blood, 1918) and *Sumurun* (One Arabian Night, 1920). The positive reception of these films in the United States provoked fears of a 'German invasion' and prompted several studios to eliminate the unwanted competition by inviting some of the major players to Hollywood: Lubitsch and Negri as early as 1922, and Murnau in 1926.

The passing of the *Reichslichtspielgesetz* (Reich Film Law) in 1920 confirmed the continuing influence of prewar institutions and debates, including the early cinema reform initiatives against 'trash and smut'. Stricter censorship laws put an end to the wave of *Sittenfilme* or *Aufklärungsfilme* (sex education films) about brothel life, prostitution, venereal diseases, and back-alley abortions produced right after the war (Hagener 2000). These films responded to the changing attitudes toward sexuality and revealed growing insecurities about new gender roles. As in the sensationalist dramas about drug addiction such as *Opium* (1919) with the sexually ambiguous Conrad Veidt, taboo subject matter often provided little more than titillation and excitement. However, in rare cases, the new sense of tolerance also made possible the acknowledgement of alternative sexualities, including through the theory of the third sex advocated by Magnus Hirschfeld, the founder of the Institute for Sex Research, in Richard Oswald's controversial *Anders als die andern* (Different from the Others, 1919). As the first film about homosexuality, *Anders als die andern* not only opened up a space for the articulation of male–male desire but also took a clear political stance by speaking out against Clause 175, which criminalised homosexuality.

In response to these dramatic changes in public attitudes toward gender and sexuality but equally concerned with other, more fundamental threats to law and order, the new federal law unified and clarified censorship practices. After 1922, a film could be censored if it threatened the vital interests of the state or endangered public safety, if it damaged the image of Germany abroad or its relationships with other nations, and if it violated religious standards or had a brutalising effect on children. To preserve the freedom of speech, a clause was added to protect films with an artistic, religious, or philosophical message – a provision frequently ignored in actual censorship practices.

The tension between art and commodity found a productive compromise in the concept of quality film advocated by the most famous producer of the Weimar period, Erich Pommer (Jacobsen 1989, Hardt 1996). The founder of DECLA and head of DECLA-Bioscop since 1920, Pommer took over production at Ufa in 1923. He created a trademark style by promoting innovative set design and by demanding superior craftsmanship and technical expertise, one reason why his manufacture-based approach has been compared to the guild system of the medieval building associations. Beginning with *Caligari*, Pommer supervised the production of big-budget films that included such classics as *Der letzte Mann* (The Last Laugh, 1924), *Varieté* (Variety, 1925), *Ein Walzertraum* (A Waltz Dream, 1925), and *Metropolis* (1927). Bringing together a remarkable group of professionals, the Babelsberg studios in the mid-1920s became famous for maintaining the highest technical and artistic standards in Europe.

33

Technological innovations and technical skills were an essential part of the Ufa style. Contributing to the studio's good reputation, film architects Walter Röhrig, Otto Hunte, Erich Kettelhut, Robert Herlth, and Rochus Gliese lent their expertise to the monumentalism of period films, the naturalism of social dramas, and the modernism of urban comedies. Cinematographers Fritz Arno Wagner, Günter Anders, and Günther Rittau gave the filmic images brilliance and depth, while Carl Hoffmann created a highly symbolic, anti-naturalist look through his dynamic use of light and shadow (Esser 1994, Aurich and Jacobsen 1998). For his experiments with free camera movement in *Der letzte Mann*, Karl Freund built the famous 'unleashed camera', whereas Eugen Schüfftan used semi-permeable mirrors to introduce models into large-scale scenes for the futuristic city of *Metropolis*. Though not always commercially successful, Pommer's high-quality productions approached film-making as a collaborative effort and thus offered an important alternative to the privileging of individual creativity. More important yet, his definition of quality resided in an understanding of national culture still uncontaminated by nationalist politics and committed more to marking principles than political ideologies. Unfortunately, with *Metropolis* alone costing more than 6 million RM, Ufa experienced growing financial difficulties in the late 1920s and was eventually taken over by right-wing ideologues with enormous political ambitions and considerable financial means.

The structural problems in the film industry became apparent as early as 1924, when the introduction of a new currency, the Reichsmark (RM), stabilised the economy after years of galloping inflation. The Dawes plan channelled foreign capital back into Germany and opened up the market for new investors. Known as the stabilisation period, the years from 1924 to 1929 brought greater economic and political stability for society as a whole. In trying to control the influx of American investment capital and to limit the foreign competition, the government passed stricter protective laws. As in other European countries, import licences were given proportionally to distributors of American films. However, the Hollywood majors circumvented the new regulations by producing so-called quota quickies or contingency films – inexpensive films made solely to fulfil the quota of German productions necessary for keeping German and European markets open to US imports (Thompson 1996). Under the contingency system, the percentage of American films dropped from approximately 44 per cent in 1926 to 28 per cent in 1931. During the same period, the numbers of French films increased from 4 to 11 per cent, largely owing to the joint ventures and co-productions started under the heading of Film Europe. However, the fact that the market share of domestic productions increased from 39 to 58 per cent did not improve revenue streams for the studios, for such an increase had little to do with actual box office receipts. In fact, Ufa was almost brought to the brink of financial ruin by its expensive high-quality films. Thus, in exchange for a ten-year loan of $4 million, the studio in 1925 was forced to enter into a mutually profitable agreement over distribution rights with Metro-Goldwyn-Mayer and Paramount, known as the Parufamet agreement, which gave the Hollywood majors access to Ufa's prestigious first-run cinemas. Other film companies signed similar contracts, including, for instance, Terra-Film with Universal and Phoebus with MGM. Meanwhile, Universal Pictures under Carl Laemmle used its sister company Deutsche Universal to produce films in Germany, often by using emigrant or remigrant directors such as Wilhelm Dieterle, Kurt Bernhardt, and Hermann Kosterlitz (Wottrich 2002).

After 1924, an average of four to five hundred domestic and foreign films were released annually. For the German studios, rising expenditures – the average cost per film grew from 12,000 RM in 1920 to 175,000 RM in 1928 – rarely translated into higher profits. Increasingly, film distribution was used to offset financial losses in production, and the largest production companies soon controlled the distribution networks. The exhibition sector, for the most part, remained decentralised, and that despite the fact that several major studios began to acquire national movie theatre chains, with the Ufa cinemas and UT cinemas a ubiquitous presence in most big cities. The studios' growing dependence on international investment capital was another matter, as were the new alliances between right-wing parties and big industries. The considerable power of banks and corporations over film production became glaringly obvious when the publishing house and media concern Ullstein sold the Terra studio to IG Farben, the chemical giant. In 1928, Emelka bought Phoebus-Film, which had secretly received government financing – a fact that, when it was made public, caused a political scandal, but also seemed symptomatic of the increasing politicisation of cinema.

Such difficult political and economic conditions gave rise to the innovative art cinema closely identified with the names of Ernst Lubitsch, Fritz Lang, Friedrich Wilhelm Murnau and, to a lesser extent, Georg Wilhelm Pabst. These famous directors moved beyond the conventions of genre to impose their unmistakable styles on established forms. As a result, their films can be described less through a fixed set of themes or motifs than through the articulation of a particular problematic across narrative and visual conventions. To begin with the most prolific member in this distinguished group, Lubitsch continued to cultivate the mixture of enlightened eroticism and irreverent materialism known from his early one- and two-reelers. Yet increasingly, the humorous effects were achieved through uniquely filmic devices such as point-of-view shots, shot/counter shots, and parallel editing. Through his calculated use of doors, windows, and mirrors, the director confirmed the centrality of vision to the conception of the world and revealed the social and psychological obstacles to the fulfilment of individual ambition and desire. The rustic comedy *Kohlhiesels Töchter* (Kohlhiesel's Daughters, 1920), with Henny Porten in the double role as the pretty and ugly sister, still relies on the frontal staging and acting conventions known from the theatre. Romantic comedies such as *Die Austernprinzessin* (The Oyster Princess, 1919), *Die Puppe* (The Doll, 1919), and *Die Bergkatze* (The Wildcat, 1921) present the trials and tribulations of female desire through a highly filmic mixture of fairytale elements, slapstick humour, and filmic irony. The tension between the excesses of power and the fickleness of love results in more fatal consequences in *Madame Dubarry* (Passion, 1919) and *Anna Boleyn* (Deception, 1920), two period films set during the French Revolution and the reign of Henry VIII respectively. What made Lubitsch so important for Ufa marketing strategies and what brought attractive offers from Hollywood was his uncanny ability to combine artistic quality with popular appeal and to make films that were innovative and provocative, but also conventional in the best sense of the word.

Equally competent in urban comedies and historical spectacles, Lubitsch was the first director to use the camera as an instrument of ironic commentary. He has remained an important model for many later romantic comedies and sophisticated comedies (Prinzler and Patalas 1984, Hake 1992a). Always maintaining a critical distance from the narrative, this early *auteur* combined a fundamental scepticism about human nature with a deep understanding for individual flaws and weaknesses. While making Jannings and Negri major stars, Lubitsch never really became an actor's director and cared little about psychological nuances and complexities. Instead, he relied primarily on objects in conveying the inner reality of the characters. His acute awareness of the difference between public and private behaviour laid the foundation for what later became known as the 'Lubitsch touch'. Whether in historical, contemporary, or fantastic settings, with melodramatic or comic overtones, Lubitsch always returned to this constitutive tension between appearance and truth in order to confirm the power of the gaze, and of surface phenomena, in sustained reflections both on the nature of human desire and on the cinema's visual attractions. Though reaching the high point of his German career during the transition toward narrative integration, he remained under the sway of early cinema and its nihilistic irreverence. He mocked moral rectitude and high-mindedness and debunked cherished notions such as love, honesty, responsibility, and integrity; hence the frequent characterisation of his period films as 'history from the keyhole perspective'. Yet his scorn for grand ideas and romantic ideals also betrayed a deeply cynical view of gender relations, social structures, and political processes; in that sense, Lubitsch remained a profoundly conservative director.

Fritz Lang appropriated popular, classical, and modernist traditions for a highly original auteurist vision that covered a wide range of themes and motifs and that found foremost expression, after 1934, in his contribution to *film noir*. Some critics have interpreted his interest in power relations as a premonition of pre-fascist tendencies and read his heavy reliance on set design as a symptom of social paralysis. Eclectic in the use of literary, mythological, philosophical, religious, and contemporary references but consistent in the emphasis on stylisation and symbolism, Lang worked primarily in two genres, the monumental epic and the urban thriller. Both are structured around a limited number of dramatic constellations: the helplessness of the individual in the face of evil; the will to power and the need for reconciliation; the fascination with death and destruction; and, most importantly, the inescapable forces of fate and destiny. Whether in the oriental episodes of *Der müde Tod* (Destiny, 1921), the epic settings of the two-part *Die Nibelungen* (The Nibelungs, 1922–24) or the social dystopia of *Metropolis* (1927), Lang relied on architectural elements and styles to stage the movements of individuals and masses and to achieve the reconciliation of life and death, history and myth, and labour and capital, in the figure of a mediator. His mass choreographies reflected a profoundly pessimistic worldview ameliorated only by the sentimental touch and metaphysical speculation provided by his wife and collaborator, Thea von Harbou. Her screenplays combined the trivial and the profound with an acute awareness of their sensationalist potential. Moreover, Harbou introduced the kind of political ambiguities in his work that continue to divide scholars in their assessment of its ideological effects (Keiner 1991, Schönemann 1992, Bruns 1995). All of these heterogeneous influences and contradictory tendencies came together in *Metropolis* which, together with *Caligari*, has assumed almost mythical stature in film histories as a metaphor of German modernity and Weimar society (Gehler and Kasten 1990b, Minden and Bachmann 2000, Elsaesser 2000a).

Lang's thrillers and detective films examine the consequences of power and fate in more contemporary settings and with a distinctly modernist sensibility. All of his filmic reflections on urban life, modern technology, and the fascination of crime and violence are structured around the centrality of vision and spectacle and the underlying struggle for narrative and, by extension, discursive authority. The anti-humanism that in the monumental films gives rise to a populist mythology with not unproblematic political resonances becomes in the thrillers an instrument of critical analysis and aesthetic intervention. Thus the Weimar thrillers re-enact the alienation of modern man, his struggle with anonymous power structures, and his fear and paranoia through distinctly filmic ciphers, with the pervasive crisis of masculinity an integral part of the story lines. Significantly, the scenarios of perpetual crisis and imminent catastrophe are always mediated or inflected by other modes of representation such as photographs, recordings, writings, and mirror reflections. Applying these self-reflexive strategies to explicitly political material, the two-part *Dr. Mabuse, der Spieler* (Dr Mabuse, the Gambler, 1922) and its sequel, *Das Testament des Dr. Mabuse* (The Testament of Dr Mabuse, 1933), evoke the pathologies of Weimar society with sensationalist flair and uncanny foresight. Not surprisingly, the second film was banned by Goebbels. Through the confrontation between the representatives of law and order and the criminal organisation of its mad mastermind, the popular *Mabuse* films reveal the interdependencies between legality and illegality, rationality and irrationality, and draw attention to the power of new technologies of communication and surveillance. Similarly, the diagnosis of a breakdown in the available models of cognition and interpretation stands behind the financial intrigues and market manipulations depicted in *Spione* (Spies, 1928) and gives emotional urgency to the story of the child murderer in *M* (1931), Lang's first sound film and a brilliant continuation of his filmic inquiries in the acoustic and auditory realm (Kaes 2000).

While the work of Lubitsch and Lang is usually examined in the context of larger social changes and developments, the films of Friedrich Wilhelm Murnau tend to invite close readings that emphasise the formal qualities of mise-en-scène, lighting, framing, and editing (Eisner 1973, Prinzler 2003). His explorations into the poetics and metaphysics of filmic space place Murnau both at the centre and on the margins

37

of Weimar art cinema. The director often adapted canonical literary texts and developed his visual strategies around established iconographies, above all those of nineteenth-century romantic painting. This influence is most apparent in two fantastic films, *Nosferatu* (1922), based on the Bram Stoker novel *Dracula*, and *Phantom* (1922), an adaptation of the Gerhart Hauptmann novella. Combining naturalistic landscapes and stylised studio interiors, the Murnau films systematically resist conventional definitions of filmic realism. Instead they produce, or rather reproduce, dreamlike images that emerge from the unconscious and the imagination. Even the contemporary settings are constructed around imaginary thresholds that dissolve the boundaries between past and present, nature and culture, and, most importantly, fantasy and reality. The most famous example for the latter is *Der letzte Mann* (The Last Laugh, 1924), his most socially conscious film and a brilliant example of a dynamisation of narrative space achieved entirely through filmic effects.

Murnau's poetic realism thrives on powerful dichotomies between interiority and exteriority, temporality and spatiality, and subjectivity and objectivity that resist all efforts at integration and mediation. These polarisations find expression in his continual fascination with extreme states (blindness, madness, dream) and liminal places (deserted castles, remote estates). Even his subtle exploration of homoerotic attractions cannot be separated from the desired, or feared, overcoming of boundaries in the act of looking. He directed highly stylised rural melodramas such as *Der brennende Acker* (Burning Soil, 1922), thus expanding the imaginary topographies of the chamber play drama, but also contributed literary adaptations like *Tartüff* (Tartuffe, 1925), a modern interpretation of the Molière figure, and *Faust* (1926), Ufa's big-budget adaptation of Goethe's most famous drama. In Murnau's filmic oeuvre, the idylls of small-town Biedermeier culture and the horrors of modern urban life alternate with deceptively beautiful landscapes that, each in their own way, conjure up an uncanny atmosphere, and awareness of the sublime, that has been called quintessentially German (Gehler and Kasten 1990a). Yet, despite his strong influence on other film-makers, Murnau's filmic sensibility ultimately remained the exception in an art cinema struggling to strike a workable compromise between convention and innovation. While Lubitsch and Lang enjoyed long and distinguished American careers, the one with sophisticated comedies, the other with crime thrillers, Murnau completed only two projects in Hollywood – *Sunrise* (1927) and *Taboo* (1931) – before his premature death.

Directing most of his films during the stabilisation period, Georg Wilhelm Pabst is often associated with New Objectivity and its realist aesthetics. While usually identified with an attitude of sobriety or matter-of-factness, the fascination with the physical world that distinguishes his approach to camerawork and mise-en-scène sometimes also invites decidedly voyeuristic and fetishistic scenarios. The absence of a core set of themes and his association with the mentality of the stabilisation period have contributed to the conflicting judgements about Pabst's status as an auteur (Rentschler 1990). His films deal with such diverse problems as war, inflation, prostitution, labour struggles, marital problems, and revolutionary politics. Significantly, the same principle of detached enchantment guides the visual representation of women, interiors, and the objects of everyday life. Celebrating the beauty of appearances and the surface character of things, Pabst conjured up a fictional world that was both provocatively materialist and profoundly consumerist in orientation and marked a fundamental break with the metaphysics of the image in the expressionist film. From the social criticism of the inflation drama *Die freudlose Gasse* (Joyless Street, 1925) and the psychological subtleties of *Geheimnisse einer Seele* (Secrets of a Soul, 1926), the first film to explore the relationship between psychoanalysis and cinema, to the engaged humanism of the anti-war film *Westfront 1918* (Comrades of 1918, 1930), Pabst registers the individual gestures of resistance, surrender, and compliance with the same formal brilliance and technical perfection. His films with Louise Brooks, *Tagebuch einer Verlorenen* (Diary of a Lost Girl, 1929), the account of a young girl's descent into prostitution, and *Die Büchse der Pandora* (Pandora's Box, 1929) based on Frank Wedekind's famous *Lulu* plays, move beyond the objectification of the female body to create a pure eroticism of the filmic image. Finally, the German–French encounter in the mining drama *Kameradschaft* (Comradeship, 1931) allowed Pabst to demonstrate his mastery of the new sound technology through a veritable cacophony of languages, voices, and sounds.

The creation of a distinct filmic style beyond the literary ambitions of the early *Autorenfilm* also involved other well-known directors whose names are frequently, and sometimes incorrectly, connected to specific genres. Known for his early sex education films, Richard Oswald later became a specialist in costume films and melodramas. He showed his dramatic skills in an adaptation of the successful Vicki Baum novel *Feme* (Assassination, 1927), one of the few films from the period that dealt with the problem of right-wing terrorism (Belach and Jacobsen 1990). Ewald André Dupont, who was repeatedly drawn to circus settings after the international success of *Variety*, applied his talent for characterisation and his power of observation to other social and ethnic milieux, including traditional Yiddish life in *Das alte Gesetz* (The Ancient Law, 1923) (Bretschneider 1992). Henrik Galeen, who is usually identified with the Gothic sensibilities of *Der Golem* and *Alraune* (Mandrake, 1928), had much more commercial success with sophisticated comedies set among the upper class. And Gerhard Lamprecht, who was well known for social dramas with a critical agenda, demonstrated his contemporary sensibilities in several successful literary adaptations, including the charming *Emil und die Detektive* (Emil and the Detectives, 1931), based on Erich Kästner's famous children's book.

The high-quality work of these directors contributed to the productive exchanges between film and the other arts that transformed cinema into a middle-class diversion and gradually dissolved the hierarchies between high and low culture. Moving more freely between stage and screen, actors developed a greater range of styles, from the heightened theatricality of Kraus and Jannings to the nuanced psychological performances of Veidt and Kortner. After the commercial success of *Hamlet* (1921), which featured Asta Nielsen in the title role, studios scoured nineteenth-century and twentieth-century literature for suitable stories and

39

characters. Confronted with the decline of the literary public sphere, Béla Balázs, Rudolf Leonhardt, and countless other writers turned to film criticism and scenario writing as a source of income. The large oeuvre of Gerhart Hauptmann, whose account of a transatlantic voyage in *Atlantis* was brought to the screen as early as 1913, inspired numerous adaptations, including of his famous naturalist dramas *Rose Bernd* (1919) and *Die Weber* (The Weavers, 1927). Critically acclaimed films such as *Die Hose* (The Pants, 1927), based on the play by Carl Sternheim, and *Heimkehr* (Homecoming, 1928), based on the Leonhard Frank novella, proved that literary sources did not necessarily preclude an adequate filmic treatment. Depending increasingly on such inter-textual, multi-media effects, conglomerates such as Ullstein and Scherl began to novelise famous films through elaborately designed 'books to the film'. They used illustrated magazines to promote rising stars and published newspaper serials to advertise films in production, a practice repeatedly chosen in the marketing of Ullstein success author Vicki Baum.

The close ties between film and literature changed not only the conditions of cultural production and consumption; the resultant cross-fertilisation also brought into relief the formative influence of the cinema on other art forms. There was an unmistakable trend toward narrative continuity, psychological motivation, and realist or naturalist styles. The thus defined ideal of a seamless narrative was modelled on the formal conventions of the nineteenth-century realist novel, including its more trivial forms, and the thematic concerns of the so-called *Zeitroman* (topical novel); the latter often included filmic metaphors or references to moviegoing (Rutz 2000). Meanwhile, innovative literary authors and theatre producers incorporated filmic elements – the approach to montage and mise-en-scène, the affinity for the quotidian and the ephemeral – into literary texts and stage productions. In fact, the conventional screen adaptation of Alfred Döblin's famous novel, Piel Jutzi's *Berlin Alexanderplatz* (1931), showed that literary modernism could be more radical than its celluloid counterpart in exploring modern sensibilities, including through montage techniques inspired by film. Sometimes literary adaptations caused legal problems that unintentionally drew attention to the competing definitions of authorship in film and literature. Bertolt Brecht, in a polemical treatise about his law suit against Nero-Film, the company that had produced the screen version of *Die Dreigroschenoper* (The Threepenny Opera, 1931), analysed the contradictions between the conservatism of the film industry and the revolutionary potential of the filmic medium in order to unmask the conditions of film-making under capitalism (Gersch 1975, Silberman 2000).

Marginalised by the overwhelming trend toward verisimilitude, formal experimentation continued to thrive in avant-garde practices but also left a strong impact on cultural films and advertising films (Wilmesmeier 1994, Agde 1998). Unlike the documentary, which used non-narrative forms for clearly defined purposes, the abstract or absolute film focused on the free play with movement, rhythm, light, contrast, and form and maintained strong links to modern painting and photography. Lotte Reiniger remained one of the few film artists to combine the possibilities of animation and storytelling in beautiful silhouette films such as *Die*

Abenteuer des Prinzen Achmed (The Adventures of Prince Achmed, 1926). For the most part, encounters between film and art remained limited to non-representational works that rejected narrative forms on principle. Viking Eggeling in *Diagonal-Symphonie* (Diagonal Symphony, 1923) worked with painted scrolls, while Oskar Fischinger developed elaborate graphic systems to explore the synaesthetic relationship between music and image, an interest that continued in his reflections on colour and form in the later *Komposition in Blau* (Composition in Blue, 1934). By contrast, Hans Richter moved from formalist studies in the style of *Rhythmus* (Rhythm, 1921–25) to the social commentary offered in experimental shorts such as *Inflation* (1928). His belief in formal experimentation as the foundation of progressive politics inspired an early avant-garde pamphlet, *Filmfeinde von gestern – Filmfreunde von morgen* (Enemies of Film Yesterday – Friends of Film Tomorrow, 1929), and stood behind later calls for a socially responsible film in *Der Kampf um den Film* (The Struggle for the Film, 1939), his most important contribution to film theory.

During the 1920s, abstract film-makers often found employment, and a showcase for their ideas, in advertising films, which used the most advanced animation techniques to sell sweets, drinks, and cigarettes. Film-makers with a background in photography and painting resorted to similar strategies when making cultural films and industrial films. All of these films were strongly influenced by the cult of objectivity and factuality associated with New Objectivity painting and photography. Blurring the boundaries between narrative and non-narrative forms, directors and cinematographers treated the camera as a powerful instrument for representing, or reinventing, the visible world and enlisted the documentary aesthetic in the creation of fictional worlds; the resultant tension between creative expression and realistic representation must be considered a constitutive trait of Weimar cinema after expressionism (Keitz and Hoffmann 2001). In the work of Walter Ruttmann, the synergies among painting, photography, and film can be traced from the abstract quality of the *Opus*-films (1918–23) to the celebration of urban life in *Berlin, die Symphonie der Grosstadt* (Berlin, Symphony of the Big City, 1927), the famous Berlin film that served as inspiration for many later city films (Goergen 1989). Whereas Ruttmann relied on the principle of cross-section, Alexis Granowsky in *Das Lied vom Leben* (Song of Life, 1931) used montage and its affinities to machine aesthetics to celebrate the technological spirit as the foundation of modern life. Toward the end of the New Objectivity period, film-makers also combined narrative, documentary, and avant-garde techniques to foreground the epistemological status of filmic reality as a construction. Examples include Ernö Metzner's haunting scenes of big-city life in *Polizeibericht Überfall* (Accident, 1928) and a filmic collaboration by Robert Siodmak, Edgar Ulmer, and Billy Wilder on *Menschen am Sonntag* (People on Sunday, 1930), which shows young Berliners during their weekend activities. Combining narrative and non-narrative elements and enlisting documentary styles for social observations, many of these films offered an important model for leftist film-makers trying to develop a self-consciously proletarian cinema during the early 1930s.

Weimar cinema as popular cinema

Weimar cinema is frequently portrayed as an innovative art cinema that eschewed generic traditions and resisted the formal conventions of an emerging classical cinema. However, a closer look at the entire production, especially from the period between 1924 and 1929, points to the dominance of popular genres developed during the Wilhelmine period. As a system for organising meanings, genre proved especially effective in responding to contemporary social and political problems and in giving expression to individual experiences of uncertainty, instability, and change. The established modalities of humour, drama, action, and adventure could at once articulate and contain the underlying conflicts and contradictions of modern mass society. Contemporary social types such as the war profiteer, the society lady, the small-time con artist, the class-conscious worker, the proletarian mother, the aspiring actress or the pretty salesgirl offered spectators multiple positions for identifying with the countless stories about the big city and the small town and for experimenting with alternately optimistic, sentimental, pragmatic, and cynical attitudes toward modern life. Dreams of social advancement and financial gain, the rivalries between old money and new money, the lure of the criminal underworld, conflicts among the generations, romance in the workplace, marital crises and infidelities, high-spirited sparring between the sexes – these are only some of the themes that sustained the effective mixture of social commentary and escapist fantasy in most comedies and dramas with a contemporary setting.

The stereotypes, formulas, and clichés of genre cinema provided directors both famous and unknown with a structural framework for engaging with social fantasies and, even more than in the Wilhelmine period, for introducing new critical perspectives. Directors working almost exclusively in this fashion included Ludwig Berger, who cultivated a fondness for romantic fairytale motifs, Wilhelm Thiele, who was known for his light comic touch, and Richard Eichberg, whose name became synonymous with action-driven, effect-filled plots. Formal innovation, social commentary, and popular appeal came together in an almost programmatic fashion in two genres often considered part of expressionist cinema: the *Kammer-spielfilm* (chamber play film), whose origins lay in the early 1910s, and its more contemporary manifestation in the *Strassenfilm* (street film). These sub-genres of the melodrama projected psychological conflicts on to spatial configurations and presented their troubled protagonists within highly codified spaces: in the first case, the interior with its protective as well as confining qualities and, in the second, the street as the ultimate symbol of the city's dangers and attractions. Like the social dramas from the prewar period, the chamber play film and the street film used a limited number of characters and locations, preferred slow editing and constructed mise-en-scènes, and paid close attention to psychological details and nuances. Whereas the early expressionist films relied on fantastic and mythological elements, the later chamber play films and street films preferred contemporary settings to restage the process of modernisation and make visible the German middle class's deepening sense of alienation and disorientation.

The chamber play film expressed conservative attitudes especially in its opposition to big city life and its affirmation of traditional family values. In *Scherben* (Shattered, 1921) and *Sylvester* (New Year's Eve, 1924), the petty-bourgeois interior provided Lupu Pick with an opportunity for testing naturalist milieu theories and applying them to the psychodramas of petty-bourgeois life. These cautionary tales about the contested spaces of modern subjectivity usually articulate the protagonists' experiences of oppression, transgression, and final resignation through the aesthetic registers of the modern uncanny. Social conflicts are projected into sexual relations and suppressed desires translated into the unstable terms of visual perception. Taking inspiration from the Oedipal family drama, many stories feature stock characters such as the rebellious son, the weak father, the maternal wife, and the seductive *femme fatale*. Typically the male characters respond to the comforts of the bourgeois home with claustrophobia. Any brief sojourns into the world of freedom and adventure promised by the street invariably end with their remorseful return to the safety of family life. Both the private and the public sphere are presented as places dominated by women, and the male characters fight this perceived loss of authority through a mixture of resentment, dread, and self-pity that often culminates in the symbolic punishment of the sexually threatening woman.

Following in the tradition of the social drama, the street film concentrates more directly on the conflict between the upper and lower classes and takes on typical urban problems such as bad housing, poverty, unemployment, violence, crime, and discrimination. Yet in Karl Grune's *Die Strasse* (The Street, 1923), the street also facilitates new experiences and allows the protagonists to reflect critically on their living conditions, a tradition that continues in the social realist films of the late 1920s and early 1930s. When these stories are told from the female perspective – Leopold Jessner's *Hintertreppe* (Backstairs, 1921) with Henny Porten is a good example – a frequent solution to personal problems seems to be the flight into madness. *Dirnentragödie* (Tragedy of the Street, 1927), with Nielsen, confirms the identification of a liberated female sexuality with criminality, for instance in the figure of the shrewd prostitute. Despite the neutralisation of such disruptive energies, these women characters are often portrayed with surprising psychological complexity, which explains the genre's considerable appeal to female audiences who identified with the emotional excesses of the melodramatic form (Wager 1999). Popular throughout the 1920s, the genre of the street film covered the entire range from conventional melodramas with strong doses of Wilhelmine morality to sleek city symphonies with a more pragmatic, if not also more cynical attitude toward love and sexuality. Joe May's *Asphalt* (1929) brought together both sides, the sentimentality of modern love and the fascination with surface phenomena, in what would be a final demonstration of the genre's filmic possibilities before the introduction of sound.

Although postwar German cinema built its artistic reputation on the contribution of expressionism, its greatest commercial successes came with big-budget period films, sometimes also referred to as historical dramas or costume films. These productions changed the public perception of cinema as a cheap diversion and contributed notably to product differentiation at Ufa and other leading studios. The staging of a alternately more heroic and idyllic past and the focus on human nature and universal messages provided an important vehicle for working through contemporary problems, from the deprivations of the war years and the 'shameful peace of Versailles' to the many challenges faced by the young republic under siege. The popularity of historical spectacles peaked around 1919, indicating a widespread desire both for escapist fantasy and material excess and for adequate representations of the modern masses, if only as extras in historical costumes. The work of Griffith and DeMille proved very influential in the development of the genre, as did the eclectic styles of late nineteenth-century painting and architecture and Max Reinhardt's spectacular theatre productions with their dynamic mass choreography. The period films presented their tragic love stories on the grand scales of history and with a fatalist attitude toward progress and change. At the same time, the monumental sets, spectacular costumes, and numerous extras were counterbalanced by a highly personalised view of history that affirmed the individual at the centre of the narrative.

Two directors were largely responsible for the commercial success of the period film. After *Veritas vincit* (1919), an episodic film reminiscent of *Intolerance* (1916), Joe May perfected the sensationalist formula in *Die Herrin der Welt* (Mistress of the World, 1919–20), an eight-part epic starring his wife Mia May. He also directed *Das indische Grabmal* (The Indian Tomb, 1921), the first of many screen adaptations of von Harbous's famous oriental fantasy of love, death, and tyranny (Bock and Lenssen 1992). May appealed through the enormous scale and sheer volume of his productions and cultivated an unmitigated penchant for exotic settings and characters, whereas Lubitsch infused his dynamic mass choreographies with more suspicious glances at the relationship between public power and private desire. Whether in the revolutionary Paris of *Madame Dubarry* or the Tudor London of *Anna Boleyn*, the historical settings provided Lubitsch with a convenient backdrop for reflecting on the libidinal forces behind political power struggles. Both modes of representing distant times and places, May's monumental spectacles and Lubitsch's intimate vignettes, had a lasting influence on the costume drama in the form of orientalist sensibilities and mythologising elements and, more generally, through the celebration of the other as a category of fascination and resentment. Whether associated with exotic and distant locations or identified with strangers and foreigners, the notion of otherness subsequently emerged as a key category for organising meanings and channelling desires in the Weimar cinema, including in the expressionist film (Kabatek 2003).

After the First World War, historical subject matter became highly charged with contemporary meanings, including mourning for missed political opportunities and yearning for the days of national strength and glory. Several films about the French Revolution, from Buchowetzki's expressionistic *Danton* (1921) to the Kortner vehicle *Danton* (1931), concentrated on the figure of the revolutionary hero, an obvious allusion to the failed German revolution of 1919. Meanwhile, the Prussian films promised nostalgic views of Prussia under Frederick the Great and, again with obvious compensatory functions, depicted this period of aggressive expansionism as a rare moment of greatness for the German nation. Adding to Prussian history's appeal for dreams of nation and empire, the actor Otto Gebühr became closely identified with the figure of the king after the influential four-part *Fridericus Rex* series produced by Arzen von Cserépy between 1922 and 1923. Most films about Frederick the Great celebrated the authoritarian, paternalistic relationship between leader and nation and confirmed the camaraderie of all-male groups as the true foundation of society. Later films also explored other, more problematic aspects of the Prussian myth, including the renunciation of personal happiness for the good of the state and the role of the military as an ideal model for private and public life.

Another popular genre, the *Bergfilm* (mountain film), is often linked to the cult of heroic masculinity. However, given its modernist qualities, the mountain film occupies a much more precarious position between the celebration of archetypal landscapes and their enlistment in nationalist ideologies. In terms of aesthetic sensibilities, the genre's leading practitioners stand closer to the realist aesthetics of New Objectivity, the documentary ethos of New Photography, and, of course, the non-narrative form of the cultural film. All of these influences came together in the remarkable technical tricks and physical stunts performed by the genre's leading cinematographer, Hans Schneeberger. The enthusiastic embrace of cinema as a technology of conquest and discovery and the preference for a camera aesthetic modelled on the pro-filmic event distinguish many mountain films as modernist works. At the same time, the glorification of primordial nature, the metaphysics of place and belonging, and the idealisation of pre-industrial communities reveal the genre's debts to right-wing rhetoric and negative utopianism. Resisting any simplistic equation with (pre)fascism or reactionary modernism, the mountain films must be described as a privileged expression of the dialectics of myth and modernity. With these ambiguous qualities, these films contributed greatly to the proliferation of various irrationalisms and nationalisms toward the end of the Weimar Republic (Rentschler 1990, Rapp 1997).

Arnold Fanck, the best-known representative of the genre during the 1920s, showed in *Der heilige Berg* (The Sacred Mountain, 1926) and *Die weisse Hölle vom Piz Palü* (The White Hell of Pitz Palu, 1929) how to combine melodramatic and documentary elements to great effect; both films feature Leni Riefenstahl in the female lead. By reflecting on the overdetermined place of mountains in the national imagination, the director achieved a precarious balance among the apotheosis of man, the cult of technology, and the poetics of cinema. In contrast to Fanck, whose contemporary sensibilities included extensive references to mass tourism and modern technology, other directors exploited this uniquely German genre for more essentialising positions on nature and culture that combined anti-capitalist arguments with folk mythology and ethnic stereotyping. Contributing to this trend, Riefenstahl in her first directorial effort, *Das blaue Licht* (The Blue Light, 1932), turned the mountains into a highly symbolic mise-en-scène for the exceptional individual; in this case: a young mountain girl played by the director herself.

Riefenstahl worked again for Fanck in *S.O.S. Eisberg* (S.O.S. Iceberg, 1933), the account of an Arctic rescue expedition that took them to the eternal landscapes of ice and water – just when momentous events were taking place in Germany.

The more problematic elements of the mountain film came together in the career of the Tyrolian alpinist, actor, cameraman, and director Luis Trenker, whose name, beginning with *Der Rebell* (The Rebel, 1932), has come to personify the genre's inherent tension between rebellion and authoritarianism and its changing political alliances during the 1920s and 1930s. To what degree the mountains of Weimar cinema offered both a model and a counter-model of modernity can be seen in the famous dissolve from the Dolomites to the Manhattan skyline from *Der verlorene Sohn* (The Prodigal Son, 1934), the film that continued the genre's metaphysics of form within decidedly nationalist ideologies. Not surprisingly, the apotheosis of physical beauty and courageous strength culminated in the figure of the solitary hero as a prefiguration of the mixture of cold idealism and sentimental megalomania that also characterises much of official Nazi art.

Weimar cinema's close identification with the early expressionist film and the focus on a few innovative directors has distracted attention from a popular genre that embodied the period's productive compromise between art and entertainment: the critical *Zeitfilm* (topical film). These films stood apart from the mass of escapist fare – the countless military farces, ethnic comedies, rural melodramas, and sentimental *Heimatfilme* (literally: homeland films) – by actually engaging with contemporary problems, even if in a conciliatory fashion. Exhibiting the typical limitations of the genre, the so-called Zille films offered sympathetic accounts of working-class life but rarely moved beyond a naturalist depiction of milieu such as the one presented in Lamprecht's *Die Verrufenen* (The Slums of Berlin, 1925), about the social rehabilitation of an unjustly incarcerated engineer, or *Die Unehelichen* (Children of No Importance, 1926), about the plight of illegitimate children in an abusive foster home. In both films, sympathetic identification with the victims of misfortune and prejudice is achieved through the moral oppositions (rich versus poor, good versus evil) leading up to the inevitable reward of virtue in the end. *Die Brüder Schellenberg* (The Brothers Schellenberg, 1926) demonstrated the power of the individual faced with economic hardship by casting Conrad Veidt in the double role of optimistic and pessimistic brother. Similarly, *Kreuzzug des Weibes* (The Woman's Crusade, 1926) juxtaposed the story of a rich and a poor pregnant woman to highlight the social injustices of the abortion clause. Profiting from years of sex education and reform, *Geschlecht in Fesseln* (Sex in Chains, 1928) drew attention to the sexual problems of male prison inmates, a subject that made the film open to accusations of sensationalism but also underscored the need for prison reform. The youth movement, reform pedagogy, and the cult of youth in the mass media produced numerous dramas of youthful rebellion that, such as *Primanerliebe* (High School Love, 1927), either emulated the intensely emotional constellations of the expressionist drama, or, such as *Revolte im Erziehungshaus* (Revolt in the Reformatory, 1930), aimed at a more detached critique of society's authoritarian structures and institutions.

Through their association with specific roles and performance styles, Weimar's leading stars played a key role in the making of a popular cinema defined as much by international trends in screen-acting as by the development of a national physiognomy and gestural code (Hickethier 1986). Refining the traditions of typecasting established in the 1910s, actors and actresses were cast in a way that allowed for the equation of specific body types with specific character traits. From Nielsen and Porten to Wegener and Goetzke, many stars reached the height of their fame during the 1920s by abandoning the histrionics of the prewar years and by cultivating a more economical, though not necessarily more subdued, acting style. Unrivalled in her minimalist and subtle style, Nielsen used literary adaptations of classics such as *Der Reigen* (The Merry-Go-Round, 1920), based on Arthur Schnitzler, and *Erdgeist* (Earth Spirit, 1923), based on Frank Wedekind, to introduce a seldom seen eroticism to the silent screen. Other well-known actresses covered the entire range of female stereotypes from the classical *grandes dames*, *demimondaines*, and *ingénues* of the stage to the emancipated New Woman who, whether as a working girl or a society wife, stood out through her fashionable looks and her enlightened attitude toward love, romance, and sexuality. Brunettes such as Mia May and Lil Dagover were usually cast as seductive *femmes fatales* in melodramas and sophisticated comedies. As portrayed by Lilian Harvey, Dolly Haas, and Käthe von Nagy, the contemporary type of the *Girl* became identified with a refreshingly pragmatic approach to the complications of love and work. By contrast, Brigitte Helm and, later, Marlene Dietrich acquired a reputation for infusing a sense of danger and cruelty into the battle of the sexes. As the perfect embodiment of modern androgyny and female neurasthenia, the celebrated theatre and film actress Elisabeth Bergner was adored by an entire generation of moviegoers.

Compared to actresses, whose screen personas remained closely linked to the problem of gender and sexuality, male actors covered a much broader range of dramatic conflicts and constellations. Character actors from the classical stage were often enlisted to give credence to the cinema's artistic ambitions. These actors brought with them the acting conventions that equated heterosexual masculinity with specific physical types, facial expressions, and gestural codes. Consequently, the portrayal of male authority remained the prerogative of older, larger-than-life character actors who, quite literally, filled the screen with their enormous bodies. The dynamics of domination and submission found a privileged expression in the brutal vitality projected by massive types such as Albert Bassermann, Fritz Kortner, and Werner Krauss. By contrast, the crises of masculinity were explored through the slightly neurotic styles developed by the ascetic Conrad Veidt and the gaunt Rudolf Klein-Rogge. Emil Jannings perfected the unsettling combination of strength and weakness that, from the role of Henry VIII in *Anna Boleyn* to Professor Unrat in *Der blaue Engel*, made him equally convincing as the most 'German' actor at home and abroad. For the most part, the celebration of modern masculinity remained limited to younger actors without pronounced star appeal and, for that reason, with limited international success. Combining old-fashioned charm and bonhomie with the new body consciousness, Harry Liedtke, Willy

Fritsch, and Gustav Fröhlich appeared as the young lovers, best friends, and average guys in countless romantic comedies and social dramas. Often performing together, the massive Kurt Gerron and the scrawny Siegfried Arno developed further the physiognomic qualities of slapstick acting, but with clear awareness of the precarious relationship between physical body and social identity and the kind of ethnic stereotypes that limited most Jewish actors to comic registers.

The development of genre cinema and the rise of film stars cannot be separated from the popular reception of other national cinemas. Foreign films returned to Germany with the lifting of the import ban in 1921, initially in the form of re-releases. By the mid-1920s, after the currency reform, more than half of all new releases were imports, evidence of a growing crisis in the industry after years of economic growth. The diatribes by many intellectuals against German films contributed to the impression that audiences preferred the offerings from Hollywood, a claim that actual box office receipts fail to confirm (Garncarz in Jung and Schatzberg 1992). Foreign films dominated the market in numbers, but domestic productions generated most of the revenues. Moreover, German actors regularly won in the annual popularity contests. In 1924, to mention only one year, the winners were Lya de Putti and Harry Piel. The top ten films from 1925 to 1932, according to audience polls, included only a few critical successes such as *Die Drei von der Tankstelle* (Three from the Gas Station, 1930) and *Der Kongress tanzt* (The Congress Dances, 1931). The American films in these lists often featured European actors such as Greta Garbo (in *Anna Karenina*) and Emil Jannings (in *His Last Command*) or dealt with German subject matter, as did the Lewis Milestone adaptation of Remarque's anti-war novel *All Quiet on the Western Front* (1930). Among the classics, only *Metropolis, Heimkehr, Asphalt, Die weisse Hölle vom Piz Palü, Westfront 1918*, and *Der blaue Engel* reached larger audiences who otherwise preferred big-budget films with conventional stories and famous stars.

The influence of American culture on modern mass culture permeated all areas of everyday life, from beauty ideals and fashion styles to consumption patterns and recreational activities; but the allure of these new designs for living was most noticeable in the cinema. In the *feuilleton*, Americanism was used as a cipher for the attitude of confidence and optimism – or, in negative terms, of brashness and superficiality – characterising the new generation of white-collar workers and young city-dwellers. Critics' polemical attacks on, and the equally passionate defence of, the American way of life represented an important way of addressing the Americanisation of German culture and society. In the filmic imagination, America provided an amalgam of sensibilities, mentalities, and attitudes that seemed at once worth emulating and opposing. Some critics saw Americanisation as a precondition for the democratisation of high culture, others as a sign of its inevitable corruption and decline (Horak 1993, Saunders 1994).

Largely indifferent to these debates, mass audiences valued Hollywood films for their pronounced physical humour and strong emphasis on action and suspense. Box office hits from the time included works by Griffith, von Stroheim, and von Sternberg as well as almost every film with Jackie Coogan, Buster Keaton, Douglas

Fairbanks, and Rin Tin Tin, the famous German shepherd. The ambivalent attitudes toward America culminated in Charlie Chaplin, whose *The Gold Rush* (1925), *The Circus* (1928), and *City Lights* (1931) were critical and commercial successes and made him an instant celebrity in Germany during the late 1920s. But where leftist intellectuals welcomed the figure of the little tramp as the embodiment of a truly democratic mass culture, conservatives saw Chaplin's particular brand of slapstick humour as a poignant expression of modern alienation that could be overcome only through a return to German values and traditions.

The popular successes of the so-called *Russenfilme* (Russian films) followed the alliances built by the international communist movement and developed further through the avant-garde sensibilities of constructivism and productivism. Throughout the 1920s, many German films were exported to the Soviet Union but their critical reception never came close to the German infatuation with the revolutionary Soviet cinema (Bulgakowa 1995, Schöning 1995, Saunders 1997). From the first showing of Sergei Eisenstein's *Bronenosets Potyomkin* (Battleship Potemkin, 1925) to a succession of films by Vsevolod Pudovkin, including *Mat* (Mother, 1926), *Konets Sankt-Petersburga* (The End of St Petersburg, 1928), and *Potomok Chingis-Khana* (Storm over Asia, 1929), Russian films repeatedly experienced censorship problems and became the subject of ongoing political debates and legal battles that usually involved their German distributor, Prometheus Film. Founded in 1925 with the goal of promoting Russian films in Germany, Prometheus operated as part of various communist media initiatives that included Willi Münzenberg's influential publishing empire and the activist IAH (International Workers Relief Fund). Initially conceived as a distribution company for the Moscow-based Meschrabpom-Rus, Prometheus ended up producing Slatan Dudow's and Bertolt Brecht's *Kuhle Wampe* (To Whom Does the World Belong?, 1932), the politically most radical and formally most innovative film of the period. For many left-liberal intellectuals, Eisenstein, Pudovkin, Vertov, and Dovzhenko personified the future of cinema under communism, and, even though some dogmatic Marxist thinkers took issue with their formalist tendencies, references to the *Russenfilme* were ubiquitous in public debates on film and politics and played a central role in the left-wing conceptualisation of a revolutionary film art. By presenting the masses as the new subject of history, the Russian films provided audiences with a strategy for revolutionary action. Likewise, by privileging conceptual approaches to montage that uncovered the ideological investments behind bourgeois culture, these films offered a compelling alternative to classical narrative cinema.

Benefiting from the close ties between Germany and the Soviet Union, many Russians came to work in Berlin, including directors Dimitri Buchowetzki, Alexis Granowsky, and Fjodor Ozep. Directed by Ozep, the German–Soviet co-production *Der lebende Leichnam / Zhivoy trup* (The Living Corpse, 1929) combined a German approach to social milieu with Soviet-style editing. In the Dostoevsky adaptation *Der Mörder Dimitri Karamasoff* (The Brothers Karamasov, 1931), the director used Kortner's expressive physiognomy to confirm the primacy of the image over the sound track. Taking advantage of the German infatuation with all things Russian, some Russian directors specialised in historical epics that celebrated the simple peasant life and explored the depths of the 'Russian soul', among other things through the tragic endings known as 'Russian endings'. Meanwhile Austrian and Hungarian directors developed a reputation for sensuality and sentimentality by adapting turn-of-the-century settings to contemporary tastes. Through the many arrivals from Vienna – Lang, Oswald, May, and Pabst, not to mention a seemingly unending stream of stage actors – Central European traditions left an indelible mark on the romantic comedy and the musical comedy and added a much-needed touch of lightness, sophistication, and self-irony to Weimar art cinema.

The large number of foreigners working in the German film industry was also a product of the growing number of co-productions and cross-cultural exchanges in what, during the 1920s, became known as Film Europe (Thompson 1996). Spurred on by their dreams of film as an international language, European directors, designers, producers, and actors worked across national boundaries – only to become specialists in the genres associated with their particular ethnic or national background. These developments added further to the reputation of the Babelsberg studios as the centre of European film production and made Berlin particularly attractive for Scandinavian film professionals. Danish actors and directors continued to work in Berlin – especially Urban Gad, Benjamin Christensen, and, of course, Carl Theodor Dreyer, who directed the equally sombre *Michael / Mikael* (Chained, 1924) and *Vampyr, der Traum des Allan Grey* (The Vampire, 1932). But their contribution to the vision of Film Europe should not be described in terms of production alone. Indicative of a parallel internationalisation in the patterns of cultural consumption and mass tourism, German–Swedish relations received new impulses by the popularity of cultural films about Nordic landscapes and the travel preferences of the educated middle classes (Vonderau 2007).

It was precisely this model of European co-operation and collaboration that, in combination with early protectionist measures, offered a valid alternative to the feared Americanisation and seemed to guarantee some degree of artistic autonomy for a self-consciously European cinema. Young directors such as Alfred Hitchcock went to Berlin to study the acclaimed Ufa style, and the Ufa studios were frequently rented out to French and British companies. In fact, Ufa signed formal agreements with the French Etablissements Aubert in 1924, and with Gaumont-British in 1927; a German–Russian production and distribution company, the Derussa, was formed in 1926. That same year, the International Committee on Intellectual Co-operation of the League of Nations in Paris passed a resolution urging film artists to avoid racist and nationalist stereotypes and, in so doing, to advance the international spirit of film. Only a few years later, the situation in Europe looked quite different, with the world economic crisis and the resurgence of nationalism as a political force severely curtailing both the spirit and the reality of cultural exchange within Europe. The emerging sound technology made co-productions increasingly unprofitable, but it was above the new politics of cultural isolationism and national expansionism that, after 1933, put an end to the ethos of inter-nationalism and the aesthetics of multiculturalism.

The struggle for economic survival after the currency reform in 1924 manifested itself in an intense competition over film audiences that affected everything from advertising, journalism, and fandom to programming practices, admission policies, and theatre architecture and design. Two simultaneous developments informed the transformation of cinema as a public sphere: the unification of audiences under the guiding idea of a homogeneous middle-class society and the diversification of markets according to differences in class, gender, age, and geographical region. The cinema gained cultural respectability by emphasising quality, originality, and novelty; by imitating exhibition practices from the theatre and the variety; and by integrating its attractions into other urban and contemporary lifestyles. To a large degree, popular tastes and preferences reflected the attitudes of white-collar workers, the fastest-growing social group of the 1920s and the main consumers of popular entertainment. Their needs and desires found privileged expression in cinema and its cult of surfaces, its celebration of movement and change, its unabashed sensationalism and sentimentality, and its emphatic promotion of social mobility, material culture, and vernacular modernism.

These contradictory impulses were nowhere more evident than in the changing conditions of moviegoing. The number of cinemas increased from approximately 2,300 in 1918 to 3,700 in 1920. By 1930, there were more than five thousand movie theatres in Germany. In terms of architectural styles, Berlin's theatres covered the entire range, from the eclectic historicism of the Capitol and the Ufa Palast am Zoo to the functionalist style of the Universum built in 1928 by Erich Mendelsohn. Opening nights became elaborate productions that included introductory lectures, short variety acts, and live music performed by large orchestras. Part of regular programming since the early 1920s, the Ufa newsreels, which appeared in a sound version as *Ufa-Tonwoche* after 1930, typically offered a mixture of political events, sports competitions, cultural news, and scientific travelogues. Special attention was paid to the so-called pre-films, which included animated shorts, comic sketches, and cultural films about flora and fauna, distant continents and foreign customs, and the beauty of German landscapes and peoples. Even visual pleasure found its proper place in the introductory programme through the celebration of the beautiful nude body in cultural films such as the feature-length *Wege zu Kraft und Schönheit* (Ways to Strength and Beauty, 1925).

The transformation of cinema into a middle-class diversion radically changed the ways critics thought about individual films. From the beginning, film criticism had played a central role in educating audiences, especially in a culture with a long tradition of addressing questions of national identity through literature and literary criticism. Daily newspapers, illustrated magazines, and cultural journals took part in extensive debates on the relationship between film and society and the future of film as an art form. Trade journals such as *Lichtbild-Bühne* and *Der Kinematograph* continued to represent the interests of the film industry and its various branches. Founded in 1919 as the first journal to be published on a daily basis, *Film-Kurier* made a concerted effort to include artistic perspectives. In its pages, the lively exchanges among Willy Haas, Hans Siemsen, and Rudolf Kurtz about the responsibilities of movie reviewers set high standards for journalistic writing but also pointed to the difficulties of independent film criticism.

Critics often turned to the cinema to address other problems, from the future of literature and the experience of modernity to the relationship between art and technology. Leading theatre critics Herbert Ihering, Alfred Kerr, and Alfred Polgar used the provocation of film to consider new approaches to acting and staging and to redefine the task of modern theatre with regard to changing audience needs. In countless reviews and articles for the liberal *Frankfurter Zeitung*, Siegfried Kracauer scrutinised the surface manifestations of modern mass culture – movie theatre design, modern dance styles, and star personas – to uncover underlying social and economic processes. Informed by his sociological studies on white-collar workers, his early essays on cinema aimed at a critical rereading of key concepts like entertainment and *Zerstreuung* (distraction) that acknowledged the products of mass culture as necessary, legitimate, and inherently progressive. Confronted with the escapist fare and reactionary tone of the early 1930s, Kracauer developed a more critical approach that anticipated Theodor W. Adorno's and Max Horkheimer's notion of the culture industry. Meanwhile Béla Balázs extolled film as the first democratic mass medium and introduced the notion of modern film folklore to measure its revolutionary potential. His study on *Der sichtbare Mensch* (The Visible Man, 1924) focused on the relationship between the camera and the face and analysed the importance of filmic devices like the close-up in revealing the universal language of the body. His later *Der Geist des Films* (The Spirit of Film, 1930) revised some of these findings under the influence of the early sound film. Finally, Rudolf Arnheim in *Film als Kunst* (Film as Art, 1932) identified the formal qualities that distinguished film from the other arts and evaluated the new medium's approach to movement, time, space, and perspective through the inherent laws of visual perception. Influenced by Gestalt psychology, Arnheim paid close attention to the difference between normal perception and filmic perception and, for that reason, rejected the new sound technology as a betrayal of film's original possibilities (Arnheim 1974 and 1977).

Film, politics, and the coming of sound

The discourse of art cinema established through the expressionist film and the conventions of genre cinema perfected during the 1920s developed as part of an ongoing negotiation between indigenous traditions and national exigencies, on the one hand, and international developments and economic pressures, especially those identified with Hollywood, on the other. Whether through their literary references or stylistic choices, many art films and prestige productions used Germanness as both an aspect of the commodity (i.e., a form of self-branding) and a strategy of resistance to the commodification of art associated with Hollywood. To foreign audiences, German films confirmed national stereotypes – especially prevalent after the First World War – and remained closely identified with difficult subject matter, an unsentimental view of love, and a tragic conception of life. For domestic audiences, German film evoked either high culture and humanistic education or nationalist sentiments and ideologies. These references to shared cultural traditions allowed for specific forms of viewer identification that validated the cinema's role in sustaining national history and culture and that confirmed the leadership role of the educated middle class in sustaining the alliance of cinema and nation.

Because of the public debates on Americanism, consumerism, urbanism, and modernism, it is often assumed that Weimar cinema existed within a predominantly metropolitan culture characterised by cosmopolitan tastes, liberal views, and progressive politics. However, the majority of films from the period point to a much more heterogeneous film culture. Regional differences, folk traditions, provincial mentalities, and rural lifestyles continued to exert a powerful influence over the filmic imagination, fuelling the fascination with myths and legends but also guaranteeing the continued popularity of rustic comedies and farces. Fairytale elements could be found in literary adaptations, comedies and fantastic films, as well as legends and sagas, adding a decidedly folkloristic element to the filmic imagination (Jörg 1994). Nostalgia for the empire inspired countless sentimental stories of Heidelberg student life and of honour and glory in the officer corps. But the wistful glances toward the prewar years and the romantic images of primordial landscapes also responded to more contemporary investments in the idea of nation that, especially in the late 1920s, took increasingly conservative and reactionary forms.

Three originally unrelated events contributed to the problems of the film industry in the last years of the republic: the introduction of sound, the world economic crisis, and the rise of National Socialism. The enormous costs involved in the transition to sound and the legal battles over sound patents forced the industry to streamline its operations. Ufa, Terra, and Emelka, the largest studios at the time, consolidated their holdings and looked for much-needed infusions of investment capital. Under these difficult conditions, closer contact with the state as the self-declared protector of German culture and industry seemed a valid alternative to domination by the Hollywood majors. The resultant economic restructuring coincided with Alfred Hugenberg's aggressive expansion of his vast media empire, and the growing influence of right-wing groups on media politics. A prominent member of the DNVP (German National People's Party) and an influential supporter of Hitler in the Harzburg Front of 1931, Hugenberg bought out the American interests in Ufa in 1927 in order to use film more effectively for his ultra-nationalist agenda. Under the directorship of Ludwig Klitzsch, Ufa's increasing conservatism in artistic matters resulted in a growing preference for formulaic story lines and escapist fare, including spectacular musical comedies and sentimental patriotic dramas. The growing anti-Semitism in the industry became glaringly obvious with the dismissal of Pommer who, like many other producers and directors, was Jewish. Ernst Hugo Correll, who remained head of production until 1939, replaced him.

Outside the centre of German film-making, the situation was equally grim. The Munich-based Emelka, which had been founded in 1919 by Peter Ostermayr, continued to provide a counterweight to Berlin by specialising in regional fare such as the popular Ludwig Ganghofer adaptations. During the 1920s, Geiselgasteig emerged as the second-largest production centre after Babelsberg. However, repeated attempts to develop a more international profile through monumental historical epics such as *Waterloo* (1928) and orientalist fantasies such as the Indian production *Die Leuchte Asiens / Prem Sanyas* (The Light of Asia, 1925) could not prevent the studio from eventually declaring bankruptcy in 1932 (Putz 1996). Faced with the world economic crisis and the giant Ufa concern, most of the smaller films studios and production units suffered a similar fate during the last years of the Republic.

Because of the cinema's central importance to Weimar culture, nationalistic groups during the early 1930s often used controversial films to bolster their arguments about the failure of modern democracies and the double threat of Bolshevism and Americanism. Nazi groups organised boycotts of *All Quiet on the Western Front*. Like its American counterpart, the Pabst anti-war film *Westfront 1918* experienced repeated censorship problems. Openly political films such as the German–Soviet co-production *Salamander / Salamadra* (Forgers, 1928), which exposed the right-wing assault on academic freedom from a leftist position, and *Cyankali* (Cyanide, 1930), which was based on the Friedrich Wolf play against the anti-abortion Clause 218, experienced similar opposition. The difficulties encountered by *Kuhle Wampe oder Wem gehört die Welt?* in 1931 and the banning of *Das Testament des Dr. Mabuse* in 1933 represented the endpoint of a politicisation of film culture that culminated in the Nazi takeover of the industry. These famous censorship cases as well as the more hidden pressures on writers, directors, and producers revealed the deep crisis in the democratic institutions of the Weimar Republic and attested to the shifting balance of power in culture and society as a whole (Plummer et al. 1982).

Confronted with aggressive right-wing campaigns, left-liberal activists began to speak out forcefully against the politicisation of cinema and organised campaigns against nationalistic Prussian films such as *Das Flötenkonzert von Sanssouci* (The Flute Concert of Sans-Souci, 1930). The Volksverband für Filmkunst (People's Association for Film Art) was founded in 1928 by, among others, Erwin Piscator, G. W. Pabst, and Heinrich Mann to support progressive causes. Members organised political and cultural events and published *Film und Volk* which, in 1930, merged with a theatre journal to become *Arbeiterbühne und Film*. It was only after long debates about the educational value of film that the political parties on the left, too, discovered the new medium as an important weapon in the revolutionary struggle (Lüdeke 1973, Kühn et al. 1975, Berger et al. 1977, Kinter 1985). The Social Democrats abandoned their traditional views of working-class culture as a version of bourgeois culture for more media-based initiatives in political education and financed Werner Hochbaum's *Brüder* (Brothers, 1929), about the 1896 dockworkers' strike in Hamburg. Insisting on the primacy of the economic base even in cultural matters, the communists continued to promote the revolutionary Russian films and focused on attacking mainstream German films for their reactionary content. Their belief that all art under capitalism reflected bourgeois ideology and that only socialism could give rise to a truly new cinema severely limited their film activities, as did their lack of financial resources.

In leftist film-making, classical realist styles, including the cathartic effects advocated by Lukács, coexisted productively with the avant-garde techniques promoted by the Russian *Proletkult* and developed further in Brecht's theory of epic theatre, with its emphasis on active audience participation and forms of critical detachment achieved through the so-called alienation effect (Mueller 1989, Silberman 2000). The man most closely associated with leftist film-making was Piel (or Phil) Jutzi, whose work combined social critique with melodramatic effects. His *Hunger in Waldenburg* (Hunger in Waldenburg, 1929) documents the mass poverty caused by the textile industries of Upper Silesia. In *Mutter Krausens Fahrt ins Glück* (Mother Krause's Journey to Happiness, 1929), Jutzi ventures into the tenements of Berlin to show both the destitution of working-class life and the importance of class solidarity. Using similar locations, *Kuhle Wampe*, the Dudow–Brecht collaboration with music by Hanns Eisler, conveyed its political message through a combination of documentary sequences and epic devices such as extended montage sequences and non-psychological acting. The participants also used discussions and songs, including the famous Solidarity Song, to uncover the connection in capitalist societies between economic exploitation and political oppression. Enormously successful with Berlin audiences, *Kuhle Wampe* was banned several times and released only in a truncated version.

Initially, film companies showed little interest in the artistic possibilities and commercial applications of sound. It took the worldwide success of *The Jazz Singer* (1927) with Al Jolson – his *The Singing Fool* was the first sound film shown in Germany – to convince studio heads of the inevitability of technological change. Hans Vogt, Joseph Engl, and Joseph Massolle had first tested their Tri-Ergon sound system in the short *Das Mädchen mit den Schwefelhölzern* (The Matchbox Girl, 1925). Because the results were so disastrous, Ufa sold the Tri-Ergon patent to a Swiss concern in 1926, fully convinced, as were many critics, that the art of film had already reached its ideal form in the silents. Only two years later, pending patents wars and competing sound systems prompted several companies to join forces under the name of Tobis (Sound Image Syndicate). The 'Paris Sound Film Peace' of 1929 established compatibility between American and European systems and divided international markets into their respective zones of influence. In 1929, Tobis and the Klangfilm GmbH, financed by AEG and Siemens-Halske, entered into another agreement under the name Tobis-Klangfilm that, from then on, controlled European markets; among the studio's specialities were multi-language versions (Diestelmeyer 2003).

On 12 March 1929, Ruttmann's compilation film *Melodie der Welt* (Melody of the World) was released as the first long German sound film. Soon after, in December, came the first feature-length Ufa sound film, *Melodie des Herzens*

(Melody of the Heart), which was shot in a silent version and four different language versions. The new technology eventually prevailed, but only after considerable improvements in sound recording and closer attention to the creative possibilities of music and dialogue. The addition of the so-called *Tonkreuz*, a cross-shaped building equipped for sound recording, made the Ufa studios in Babelsberg the technically most advanced studio facility in Europe. During this transitional period, countless smaller companies went bankrupt or were bought out by others. Contributing to the process of economic concentration, the large studios received much-needed capital through new alliances with electrical concerns and media conglomerates. Because of the high costs, the process of equipping cinemas with sound projection facilities was not completed until 1935. In 1928, of a total 183 German feature films, eight were sound films; by 1931, only two of a total of 157 new releases did not have a sound track. As production costs increased, the total number of films declined from 224 in 1928 to 132 in 1932; German exports to other countries also decreased dramatically. Film attendance fell from 328 million tickets sold in 1929 to 238 million in 1932, an indication also of the worsening economic situation. The representatives of the film industry responded to these troubling developments with the SPIO plan of 1932, which called for more state intervention and spoke out in favour of a centralised German film industry.

Despite the rise of nationalism, xenophobia, and anti-Semitism, the spirit of collaboration within Film Europe continued to influence film-making until the mid-1930s. The arrival of the sound film coincided with a second wave of emigration, during which Marlene Dietrich, Wilhelm Dieterle, Vicki Baum, and Karl Freund left for Hollywood; but the new technology also brought fresh talent from the former Austro-Hungarian Empire to Berlin. Because of the high level of technical expertise among its studio personnel, the Ufa studios were often rented out, especially for German–French co-productions featuring actors and producers who worked successfully in both national cinemas. Some companies tried to overcome the new language barriers by casting French and British stars in foreign versions of the same film. During a transitional period that lasted until 1935, almost one-third of all sound films were made with these multi-language versions. For instance, Dupont's *Atlantic* (1929), promoted as 'the first 100 per cent sound film', was shot in three versions in the British Elstree studios. Carl Froelich's *Die Nacht gehört uns / La nuit est à nous* (The Night Belongs to Us, 1929) became the first French–German sound production and the first sound film to use the new technology in more creative ways (for instance, by experimenting with offscreen sound). After 1933, the practice of multi-language versions was eventually abandoned because of the exorbitant production costs and the changing political landscape (Schöning 2005).

International in their mode of production, multi-language versions contributed to the identification of famous stars with national characteristics and played into the growing preoccupation with language and voice as a locus of national identity. Stylistically, the addition of dialogue put an end to the more expressive acting styles from the silent period and introduced many conventions from the stage, including idiosyncratic pronunciations like the guttural 'r'. Whereas actors became closely identified with the question of national character, actresses continued to work in an international framework. For example, Lilian Harvey appeared in the German version of *Der Kongress tanzt* with her usual partner Willy Fritsch but was cast vis-à-vis Henri Garat in the French version. By contrast, the futuristic adventure film *F.P. 1 antwortet nicht* (F.P.1 Doesn't Answer, 1932) featured Hans Albers, Conrad Veidt, and Charles Boyer as the male leads in the respective German, English, and French versions. Partly because of such casting problems, the practice of multi-language versions was soon abandoned in favour of dubbed versions. After that, dubbing, which often had well-known German actors lend their distinct voices to famous Hollywood stars, became the industry standard for popular films, with subtitled versions usually reserved for art films.

Tobis was not the only company that emerged in the late 1920s as part of the transnational project of Film Europe. The stabilisation period and the introduction of film sound brought a second flourishing of film-making, but this time with a decidedly European bend and with extensive contributions by Jewish film professionals. Many of the new companies were headed by strong producer personalities, some of them Austrians or Hungarians, who, after 1933, continued their film activities first in other European countries and, later, in the United States. Nero-Film, founded in 1925 by Seymour Nebenzahl, produced many of the Pabst films, including the scandal-ridden *Threepenny Opera*, as well as the last two German Lang films, before relocating after 1933, first to Paris and then to Hollywood (Wottrich 2002). From 1928 to 1935 the Deutsche Universal, a subsidiary of the famous Hollywood studio founded by the German émigré Carl Laemmle, produced numerous German-language films, including all of the Fanck films (Wottrich 2001). Under these conditions of relative openness, a new generation of actors, screenwriters, composers, and directors moved freely within Europe and pursued their work in an expanding media landscape that also included broadcasting and the recording industry. Organised around numerous smaller studios and independent producer units, the film industry also became more flexible in accommodating enterprising actors-producers such as Porten, Nielsen, and Piel and in giving relative freedom to directors who, like Fanck or Siodmak, worked in narrative as well as non-narrative formats.

The early sound film found its greatest inspiration in the musical traditions that had been central to definitions of Germanness since the nineteenth century. It forced film-makers to rethink major assumptions about film art and reconsider definitions of filmic realism in light of new aesthetic paradigms and new media alliances (Müller 2003). On the one hand, the early sound film advanced the trend toward verisimilitude, principally by expanding the terms of fictionality into audio-visual terms. On the other hand, it further standardised the terms of film spectatorship and fantasy production and aligned them more closely with normative categories of identity and subjectivity and the underlying discourses of gender, ethnicity, class, and race. Just as the added possibilities of dialogue reconnected the early sound film with the legacies of the bourgeois theatre as a 'moral institution', music aligned the project of nationalism with the alternately contemplative and heroic tones of Germany's rich musical culture. At the same time, the new alliances among film, music, and dance allowed for the translation of contemporary American sounds and rhythms into the elevated mood and frenetic pace of late Weimar entertainment culture. Two forms predominated: the Viennese operetta with its obligatory waltzes and old-fashioned arias, and the musical comedy with its optimistic hit songs and exuberant dance numbers (Uhlenbrok 1998, Hagener and Hans 1999). Evoking an imaginary nineteenth-century Vienna populated by charming noblemen, sweet girls, and dashing officers, *Liebeswalzer* (Love Waltz, 1930) and *Walzerkrieg* (Waltz Wars, 1933) played into the widespread yearning for the 'good old days' of the Austro-Hungarian Empire. Known for his extravagant stage revues, Eric Charell made *Der Kongress tanzt* the most expensive German film made until that point when he brought together the dream couple of the German film, Harvey and Fritsch, and used the most spectacular sets, beautiful costumes, and intricate camera movements for a charming anecdote from the Congress of Vienna.

Whereas the past allowed for brief episodes of merriment and sentimentality, contemporary settings usually required the kind of healthy pragmatism and can-do attitude that distinguished depression comedies such as the smash hits *Die Drei von der Tankstelle* and *Ein blonder Traum* (A Blonde's Dream, 1932) and the charmingly self-reflexive *Ich bei Tag und du bei Nacht* (I by Day, You by Night, 1932). These films typically featured young actresses such as Hertha Thiele, Dolly Haas, or Renate Müller, who combined aspects of the classical *ingénue* and the modern city girl. In his contribution to early sound comedy, the actor-turned-director Reinhold Schünzel used ironic commentaries and sexual innuendoes in ways reminiscent of the early Lubitsch, but with a new edginess that betrayed the compensatory function of these early sound comedies as fantasies of individual survival. Many white-collar comedies from the 1930s used the workplace as a backdrop for inspiring stories of individual endurance and resourcefulness. In *Die Privatsekretärin* (Private Secretary, 1931), a typical example of the genre, all problems, from unemployment and sexual harassment, are overcome through witty dialogues and cheerful tunes. The frequent concern with appearances, especially in difficult personal or professional situations, is most apparent in the many stories that involve cross-dressing, from *Ein steinreicher Mann* (A Tremendously Rich Man, 1932) with Curt Bois to *Der Page vom Dalmasse Hotel* (The Page from the Dalmasse Hotel, 1933) with Dolly Haas. The protagonist's unusual choices in these comedies often hide an existential struggle for economic survival that cannot be separated from the underlying dynamics of money and power and the mechanisms of sexual and racial discrimination.

The flourishing of film comedy during the early sound period also brought a return to the traditions of Jewish humour that had been an integral part of German cinema from the beginning and that, whether through comic actors such as Arno, Gerron, and Bois or successful directors such as Schünzel, added a sophisticated, ironic, and urbane attitude to the early sound film comedy. However, the validation of Jewish life worlds and the celebration of German-Jewish culture cannot be separated from the anti-Semitic stereotyping that accompanied the genre's ongoing transformations, as evidenced by the repeated adaptation of *Robert und Bertram*, based on the nineteenth-century farce by Gustav Raeder, in 1915, 1928, 1939, and 1961 (Prawer 2005, Diestelmeyer 2006).

In exploring the mise-en-scènes of sound, the early sound film opened up new opportunities for provocative subject matter. Based on the famous Heinrich Mann novel, Josef von Sternberg's *Der blaue Engel* (The Blue Angel, 1930) brilliantly staged the seduction and humiliation of a middle-aged German school teacher by a beautiful variety singer and, in so doing, laid the foundation for Dietrich's international career. Melodramatic forms relied heavily on the possibilities of sound to explore the emotional range of the auditory realm. Bergner continued her collaboration with Paul Czinner with *Ariane* (1931) and *Der träumende Mund* (Dreaming Lips, 1932), two melancholy reflections on the soundscapes of loss. Similarly, Max Ophüls in the Schnitzler adaptation *Liebelei* (La Ronde, 1932/33) explored the connections among desire, renunciation, and auditory pleasure to conjure up a distinctly masochistic aesthetic. Combining subtle psychological portraits with a sharp critique of Prussian authoritarianism, the all-female cast of Leontine Sagan's *Mädchen in Uniform* (Girls in Uniform, 1931) gave rise to the first sympathetic depiction of lesbianism on the screen. The continuities and ruptures that defined Weimar film-making in artistic and political terms became especially evident in the remarkable diversity of the 1933 lineup, which included Schünzel's light-hearted cross-dressing comedy *Viktor und Viktoria* (Viktor and Viktoria), Ophüls's charming take on the Smetana opera *Die verkaufte Braut* (The Bartered Bride, 1932), and Froelich's celebration of Prussian military history in *Der Choral von Leuthen* (The Choral of Leuthen).

When viewed retrospectively, the cinema of the Weimar Republic may be described best through its productive tensions: between the discourses of popular entertainment and film art, the call for a homogeneous mass culture and a class-conscious cinema, the emphasis on artistic and technical quality and the excesses of escapism and triviality, the industry's demands for autonomy and its calls for protectionism, the advancement of German traditions and the emulation of American styles, and, last but not least, the promotion of nationalist policies and the belief in European co-operations. Perhaps it was this lack of full integration that gave cohesion to Weimar cinema in the form of overlapping and competing practices. Perhaps it was the fragmentation of movie audiences, artistic movements, and political debates that allowed for the coexistence of mass cultural as well as elitist, populist, and modernist elements and that distinguished the cinema as a public sphere where the disintegration of society could at once be exposed and magically overcome. From the postwar manifestations of trauma and the brief period of confidence to the growing political and economic problems, the cinema of the Weimar Republic continued to hold on to the utopian dream of film as a progressive, democratic mass medium and, in so doing, inspired not only contemporaries but many later generations of film-makers and critics as well.

1 Conradt Veidt and Lil Dagover in *Das Kabinett des Dr. Caligari*. Courtesy BFI Stills, Posters and Designs.

2 Gustav von Wangenheim and Henny Porten in *Kohlhiesels Töchter*. Courtesy BFI Stills, Posters and Designs.

3 Aud Egede Nissen and Eugen Klöpfer in *Die Strasse*. Courtesy BFI Stills, Posters and Designs.

4 Alfred Abel and Rudolf Klein-Rogge in *Metropolis*. Courtesy BFI Stills, Posters and Designs.

5 Marlene Dietrich and Emil Jannings in *Der blaue Engel*. Courtesy BFI Stills, Posters and Designs.

6 Ernst Busch and Hertha Thiele in *Kuhle Wampe*. Courtesy BFI Stills, Posters and Designs.

7 Adolf Wohlbrück, Hilde Hildebrand, Renate Müller, and Hermann Thimig in *Viktor
und Viktoria*. Courtesy BFI Stills, Posters and Designs.

3

THIRD REICH CINEMA 1933–45

From 1933 to 1945, the German film industry produced more than one thousand feature-length films and an even larger number of short films, newsreels, and documentaries. These numbers suggest three things: that the industry under the Nazis was a formidable economic force, that films provided powerful narratives of identity and community, and that the cinema functioned as an integral part of everyday life, promoting National Socialist ideas and promising distraction along the lines defined by the regime. Yet in analysing this complicated relationship between entertainment and politics, one needs to approach filmic practices in a way that does not reduplicate the period's own obsession with boundaries. Labels such as 'Nazi cinema' or 'Nazi film' suggest a complete convergence of popular cinema, cultural politics, and Nazi ideology that was never achieved, given the repeated clashes between industry representatives, special interest groups, and the Propaganda Ministry; the continuing popularity of foreign films and the dominance of Hollywood as a model of industrially produced mass entertainment; the politicisation of cinema and the aestheticisation of politics before and during the Second World War; the elusive nature of film spectatorship and the ambiguities of fantasy production; and the overall difficulties of controlling the conditions of moviegoing in the Reich and its occupied countries.

In coming to power in 1933, Adolf Hitler and the National Socialist German Workers Party (NSDAP) promised a spiritual renewal and a national awakening in all areas of German culture and society; in reality, they established a dictatorship and murderous regime. National Socialism combined conservative, nationalist, racist, anti-communist, and, above all, anti-Semitic attitudes within an extremist *völkisch* ideology that culminated in the glorification of the Aryan race, the celebration of *Volksgemeinschaft* (national community), the myth of *Blut und Boden* (blood and soil), and the rejection of liberal democracy for the hierarchical, authoritarian structures embodied by the leadership principle. Art and culture in the Third Reich were characterised by traditionalism, classicism, anti-intellectualism, and the denunciation of modernism as alien and degenerate. However, the Nazi culture industry also relied on the most advanced media technologies and marketing techniques to achieve the integration of regional, folkloric, and popular traditions and to reconcile official Nazi art and literature with the legacies of high culture and the demands of modern mass culture. Despite the essentialist rhetoric about German spirit and German soul, culture in the Third Reich was held together less through any innate qualities or stylistic traits than through its repression of progressive, democratic, and critical voices and its exclusion of international and cosmopolitan influences.

While the basic structure of cinema under National Socialism was firmly in place by 1934, the years until 1945 still saw considerable changes in the organisation of film production and distribution, the approach to exhibition practices and market-ing, and the definition of entertainment and propaganda. Three main phases can be distinguished: first, 1933–37: institutional restructuring and consolidation; second, 1937–42: further economic concentration and expansion as part of the war effort; and third, 1942–45: monopolisation and mobilisation of all filmic resources for the so-called final victory. On the institutional level, the alignment of every aspect of cinema culture with the interests of the state began with the purging of the professions in 1933 and culminated in the nationalisation of the industry after 1938. None the less, as a popular mass medium, the cinema continued to function through the double myth of being both within and outside ideology.

This raises a number of important questions of relevance not only to the period in question: Were all films made during the Third Reich Nazi films? Can we distinguish between propaganda films and so-called apolitical entertainment films? Are there moments of aesthetic resistance in particular genres or in the work of individual directors? Is it productive to describe most of the films as escapist in nature, and political only through their socio-psychological function, or must we see the influence of Nazi ideology as all-pervasive and all-powerful? Can the effectiveness of film as a form of mass manipulation be identified on the level of textual characteristics, or are the ideological effects only realised in the larger social and political context and under specific conditions of reception? Do the films exhibit aspects of what has been called fascist aesthetics, or do the continuities with Weimar cinema and Hollywood cinema predominate?

Two approaches have defined the scholarship on this period: historical studies on propaganda, which take a thematic approach and usually include narrative and non-narrative forms, and more theoretically informed studies on the relationship between cinema and ideology that focus on genres, narratives, and fantasy effects. In the beginning, most film historians limited their inquiries to the propaganda films while ignoring the vast number of genre films (Hull 1973, Leiser 1974, Welch 1985 and 1993). In mapping this *terra incognita* of individual pleasures and private desires, some historians used quantitative analyses and thematic overviews to differentiate between the popular and the political (Albrecht 1969, Drewniak 1987). Other scholars focused on the strategies of economic concentration and cultural hegemony and examined the complicated relationship between narrative and ideology (Becker 1973, Petley 1979, Lowry 1991). More recently, a number of critical studies have been published that show how popular genres offered fictional solutions to unresolved conflicts and contradictions in society, and how modern mass media radically redefined the relationship between art and politics in terms of fantasy production and public spectacle (Witte 1995, Rentschler 1996,

Schulte-Sasse 1996, Reimer 2000, Hake 2002). This revisionist process has drawn attention to the stylistic and thematic continuities of German cinema, including its complicated relationship to Hollywood as an economic and aesthetic model; the similarities between Third Reich cinema and other 1930s state-controlled cinemas in Italy and the Soviet Union; and the role of classical narrative in the textual articulation of ideologies of difference, including sexism, racism, and nationalism. This kind of historical contextualisation, coupled with theoretically informed definitions of popular cinema, has moved the debates beyond the conceptual binaries of cinema versus politics, propaganda versus entertainment, and art versus ideology that, until recently, dominated critical assessments in not always productive terms.

The restructuring of the film industry

The Nazi takeover of the film industry began on 13 March 1933 with the creation of the Reichsministerium für Volksaufklärung und Propaganda (Reich Ministry for People's Enlightenment and Propaganda). As the minister in charge, Joseph Goebbels assumed control over all aspects of cultural life, from film, radio, broadcasting, and the press to literature and visual and performing arts, and set out to co-ordinate all areas of cultural production and consumption with the political goals of the new regime. The so-called *Gleichschaltung* (forced integration) of the industry in 1933 and 1934 completed the process of economic concentration that had started in the late 1920s with the internal struggles at Ufa. Benefiting from the accompanying shift to the right, Ufa, Tobis, Bavaria, and Terra quickly consolidated their positions as the largest film studios of the 1930s. Together they produced more than 80 per cent of all feature films and maintained high levels of production up to the establishment of a state monopoly during the war years.

After 1933, all writers, artists, actors, musicians, directors, and so forth had to be organised in the Reich Culture Chamber, whose corporatist guild model established the institutional structure for cultural production in a one-party state. The Reichsfilmkammer (Reich Film Chamber) was the first chamber to be created, an indication of the great importance given to film-making by the new regime. Only Germans, as defined by the new citizenship and racial laws, were eligible for membership in the Reich Film Chamber. This rule allowed the Propaganda Ministry to exclude so-called non-Aryans and politically unreliable persons from working in the industry and, in so doing, to purge German cinema of all 'alien' influences. In 1935, the provisional revoking of screening licences for all films made before 1933 effectively rewrote film history from a National Socialist perspective. The names of Jewish directors were removed from the credits of older films, and political rallies organised against films that featured Jewish actors.

The forced integration of the film industry had a devastating effect on individual lives; but it also destroyed a lively cinema culture that had emerged in the 1920s with significant contributions by Jewish actors, directors, and producers. Confronted with discriminatory laws and exclusionary practices, most Jews working in the industry left Germany in 1933 and 1934 for other European countries, often with hopes of a speedy return. Like the European border crossings during the 1920s, the exile experience after 1933 must be considered an integral part of German cinema, whether in the context of exile film or through the import of German – or, to be more precise, Central European – traditions into other national and cultural contexts, especially the Hollywood film of the 1930s and 1940s (Hilchenbach 1982, Belach and Prinzler 1983, Horak 1984 and 1996). Conceptualising the relationship between Babelsberg and Hollywood in dialogic terms, some scholars have denounced Nazi film-makers for their strategies of aesthetic and ideological compliance while identifying exile film-makers with a position of subversive otherness within Hollywood (Koepnick 2002a). Undoubtedly, the émigrés added new filmic sensibilities, most famously through their contribution to the pessimistic and cynical worldview of *film noir*. But like Hollywood, even Babelsberg after 1933 was dependent on the spectacle of difference and the fascination of otherness, primarily through the association of famous stars with particular national stereotypes and ethnic identities.

Pommer and Wilder were among the lucky few to leave for Hollywood as early as 1934, with studio contracts in hand. The largest number of exiles came to Hollywood in the late 1930s under less favourable conditions; many were aided by the agency of Paul Kohner. The difficulties of exile were greatest for actors, whom language problems often limited to bit parts and 'accent parts'. Apart from Marlene Dietrich, only Peter Lorre and Conrad Veidt had significant American careers. Known for their professionalism and technical expertise, cameramen Rudolf Maté and Eugen Schüfftan quickly found artistic recognition, as did composers Friedrich Hollaender and Erich Wolfgang Korngold. Directors Fritz Lang, Billy Wilder, Curtis (Kurt) Bernhardt, Robert Siodmak, and Douglas Sirk (Detlef Sierck) gained critical acclaim for infusing classical Hollywood genres with European sensibilities and for offering critical perspectives on the United States coloured by the experience of exile. In Britain, the contribution of German-speaking émigrés was most noticeable in cinematography and set design (Bergfelder and Gargnelli 2007). By contrast, the few film-makers who, like Gustav von Wangenheim, went to the Soviet Union put their artistic skills in the service of popular-front politics and the anti-fascist struggle (May and Jackson 2001).

The purging of the professional organisations and the subsequent exile waves were only the beginning of more fundamental changes that gave the state greater control over the legal, financial, and creative aspects of film-making. The Reich Film Law of 1934 clearly spelled out the new principles of film censorship. Any film considered critical of National Socialism, whether through moral judgements or aesthetic styles, could be prohibited, banned, and confiscated (Maiwald 1983). A far-reaching system of pre-censorship based on submitted film scripts replaced the standard post-production censorship; now a Reich Film Dramaturge was in charge of the approval process. The close involvement of the Ministry in the pre-production phase limited the economic risks for the studios while extending ministerial control to all stages of production. Not surprisingly, the total number of censored films was small, with the majority of cases occurring during the early 1940s. Most of the 27 known films were censored because the director or main lead had become *persona non grata* (Wetzel and Hagemann 1982). Suggesting internal disagreements over the role of artistic quality in film propaganda, a few films were banned despite, or even because, of their National Socialist fervour. In other cases, the censors considered certain representations – for instance, of bombed cityscapes – too demoralising for wartime audiences.

An elaborate system of direct and indirect financing offered new incentives for struggling film companies and proved just as effective as more punitive mechanisms of control. Financial support was available through the Film Credit Bank that, as early as 1935, provided financing to almost 70 per cent of all films in production; many loans were never repaid. Almost one-third of feature films received distinctions, or ratings, of some sort, with the rating system quickly emerging as one of Goebbels's favourite tools for promoting specific genres and subjects. This system of distinctions, which included 'educational' and 'artistically (especially) valuable', came with certificates of tax reduction or, in the highest category, with tax exemption. To the existing distinctions, the Film Office added 'politically (especially) valuable' and the honorary designation 'film of the nation', which was awarded only five times: to *Ohm Krüger* (1941), *Heimkehr* (Homecoming, 1941), *Der grosse König* (The Great King, 1942), *Die Entlassung* (The Dismissal, 1942), and *Kolberg* (1945). All five films were so-called *Staatsauftragsfilme* (state-commissioned films), big-budget productions commissioned by the Propaganda Ministry to promote key concepts of Nazi ideology through the lens of German history. Their melodramatic stories typically focus on the heroic deeds of great Germans, the triumphs and defeats of the German nation, and the struggles of ethnic Germans abroad. Many contributions confirmed race as the foundation of German character and transformed the past into a preview of German manifest destiny. Because of their overdetermined conditions of production and reception, the state-commissioned films must be considered a genre in its own right, defined less through particular formal characteristics than through the propagandistic intentions that established clear parallels between the events on the screen and concurrent political developments and that made fantasy production an integral part of the mobilisation of emotions in the broader propaganda effort (Kanzog 1994, von der Osten 1998).

Goebbels, who supervised the implementation of all new film policies, never provided a clear definition for the National Socialist film. In speeches to industry representatives, he early on announced that films should have a political tendency but that tendency could not be separated from artistic quality. Repeated calls for more *Gesinnung* (political attitude) and *Volkstümlichkeit* (popular taste) in the cinema remained empty political rhetoric, with day-to-day decisions guided primarily by economic and political considerations. Sometimes complicating matters, Goebbels had a strong personal interest in film and, like Hitler, socialised extensively with film actresses. Indeed, the film community – and, in other contexts, the literary and musical establishment – played an important role in giving cultural legitimacy to the new regime. Courted by the power elite, many actors and directors lived in a world of luxury and privilege. For the most part, their dealings with representatives of the Ministry took place in a collaborative spirit, with both sides profiting equally from the undiminished popularity of German films with German audiences. Aware of the importance of skill and talent, Goebbels repeatedly gave special permission to individuals deemed too valuable to be lost to the new membership laws. These exceptions included several Jewish actors and directors and banned authors such as Erich Kästner who, under the pseudonym Berthold Bürger, wrote the screenplay for *Münchhausen* (1943). However, the brute force with which insubordination could be punished at any point became glaringly obvious in two tragic incidents: the 1942 suicide of actor Joachim Gottschalk, who had refused to divorce his Jewish wife, and the 1943 death of director Herbert Selpin in a Gestapo prison after quarrels during the making of *Titanic*.

Supported by the new political elites, the cinema after 1933 quickly emerged as the most important mass medium for forging a national community beyond class boundaries and for rearticulating the problem of identity within the public–private divide. Central to the cinema's overdetermined function within the Nazi culture industry was its uncanny ability to enforce conformity and consensus while allowing for moments of difference and dissent. The new contingency system sharply reduced the numbers of imported films and limited the participation of non-Germans in domestic productions. But even concerted efforts to imitate Hollywood styles and incorporate American mentalities did not diminish the appeal of foreign films, which remained a strong presence until the war and compensated for the dearth of quality films with artistic ambition and social relevance. In 1933, almost half of all films shown were made in the United States. After the first year of the regime, their market share declined to 20 per cent. None the less, more than six hundred foreign feature films were still shown during the Third Reich, with the majority released between 1933 and 1939 in subtitled or dubbed versions. Confirming the undiminished influence of American popular culture in all areas of everyday life, audience favourites included the Nelson Eddy and Jeanette MacDonald operetta films, the musicals with Fred Astaire and Ginger Rogers, and, of course, anything involving Tarzan or Mickey Mouse. Clark Gable, Shirley Temple, Greta Garbo, Joan Crawford, and Gary Cooper all had a large following among German movie fans. In 1936, Dietrich could still appear in the Lubitsch production *Desire*, despite official polemics against émigrés appearing in foreign films. It was only in 1939, after the release of Anatole Litvak's *Confessions of a Nazi Spy* (1939) that American films were taken out of distribution (Spieker 1999).

The Propaganda Ministry's close attention to the conditions of film exhibition and the psychology of mass reception reflected persistent anxieties about the possibility of subversive meanings and resistant readings. Feature-length films always ran as part of a mandatory programme that consisted of newsreels and short cultural films. Because audiences often skipped these pre-films, cinema owners were advised during the war years to close their doors to latecomers once the newsreel had started. None the less, the unpredictability of audience tastes and reactions remained a source of deep concern, only partly allayed by the regular reports from the movies by the Security Service. In an effort to reach larger segments of the population, the Propaganda Ministry instituted the Film People's Day, on which audiences could attend special screenings for a nominal fee. Meanwhile the Youth Film Hours, organised by the Hitler Youth since 1934, showed documentaries and short feature films aimed specifically at children and adolescents. In the 1942/43 season, more than eleven million young people attended these popular events (Kleinhans 2003).

While firmly ensconced on domestic markets, leading film companies still had to deal with a dramatic decline of their export business and, more generally, the negative effects of cultural isolationism on a visual medium that had always thrived on international connections and cosmopolitan tastes. There was little competition for German films in neighbouring countries such as Austria and Switzerland, but film exports, especially to the United States, declined by almost 80 per cent. Remarkably, as late as 1939, 85 of the 272 foreign films shown in the United States were still produced by German (or Austrian) companies. Usually shown in the German original, these films found a receptive audience in states and cities with a large German-speaking immigrant population, including New York and Chicago. After 1939, the activities of various anti-Nazi groups complicated such patterns of reception and increased public awareness of the dangerous situation in Europe. The anti-Nazi films made in Hollywood with the involvement of exile actors and directors played an important role in this process.

The lack of creative talent after the purging of the industry in 1933 remained a serious obstacle to the studios' competitiveness in foreign markets and resulted in the conventional style and mediocre quality of most new films in production. Co-productions remained limited to Austria, Hungary, Czechoslovakia, and, after 1939, to Italy and Japan. The Venice Film Festival was reduced to a showcase for expensive but undistinguished productions by the Axis powers. Contributing to the systematic suppression of creative and critical impulses, film criticism after 1936 was redefined to comprise only factual information and appreciative commentary. *Lichtbild-Bühne* and *Film-Kurier*, the major trade journals, were turned into mere mouthpieces for the Propaganda Ministry. Under such conditions, the founding of the Deutsche Akademie für Filmkunst (German Academy for Film Art) in 1938 came much too late to reverse the negative effects of artistic conformity and intellectual opportunism.

The years 1937 to 1942 saw the elimination of all remaining independent companies through a series of calculated economic and political interventions. Film attendance increased steadily and significantly; during the record year 1938, for instance, almost 440 million tickets were sold. However, shrinking export revenues and growing production costs forced even Tobis to accept secret loans from the Ministry. The average costs of making a feature film more than doubled from 250,000 RM in 1933 to 537,000 RM in 1937. In 1937, when the losses at Ufa approached 15 million RM, the Reich secretly bought more than 70 per cent of the Ufa stock through a middleman, Max Winkler of the Cautio Trust; a similar takeover of Terra took place soon thereafter. Now effectively under state ownership, Tobis, Terra, and Bavaria kept their names but began to play a more active role in the mutual instrumentalisation of cinema and politics. The occupation of most neighbouring countries opened up new export markets, set new attendance records, and eventually turned the film industry into the country's fourth-largest industry and the only serious competitor of the Hollywood majors in Europe. At the same time, after the invasion of Sudentenland in 1938 and the attack on Poland in 1939, the increasing militarisation of everyday life resulted in a sharper distinction between entertainment and propaganda, with expensive prestige productions openly fuelling anti-Semitic and anti-Slavic sentiments and with conventional genre films offering brief escapes from the problems of the home front.

The annexation of Austria in 1938 destroyed a German-speaking cinema that had thrived on shared cultural traditions and facilitated extensive artistic exchanges (Fritz 1988 and 1991). In the larger context of national fictions and iconographies, Austrian cinema had always projected an alternative image of Germanness, more Central European than Prussian, and with a heavy dose of self-irony. With its decadent charm, ironic sentimentality, and old-fashioned *Gemütlichkeit*, the myth of Vienna provided more light-hearted but also more ambiguous interpretations of generic formulas. Film studios concentrated on sound comedies with the inexhaustible Hans Moser, melancholy love stories with Willi Forst, and countless musical comedies and operetta films inspired by the close identification of Vienna with classical music. The new Wien-Film, a state-controlled company established in 1938 under Karl Hartl, continued to specialise in fictional constructions of Austrianness, producing musical biographies such as the Mozart films *Eine kleine Nachtmusik* (A Little Night Music, 1940) and *Wen die Götter lieben* (Whom the Gods Love, 1942), as well as Forst's famous Vienna trilogy, *Operette* (Operetta, 1940), *Wiener Blut* (Viennese Blood, 1942), and *Wiener Mädeln* (Viennese Maidens, 1945/1949).

The situation in France after the German invasion in 1939 was very different. Since the invention of cinematography, France and Germany had enjoyed a close relationship, from the sharing of technologies and the exchange of actors to the many co-productions that continued throughout the 1930s (Hurst and Gassen 1991, Sturm and Wohlgemuth 1996). Yet in 1940 the Nazis took over film production in occupied France through a sister company of Ufa, Continental-Films, which, among others, made Henri-Georges Clouzot's critically acclaimed *Le corbeau* (The Raven, 1943). Goebbels's overall goal in France was to produce films that retained their French qualities and could be advertised as domestic productions. Maintaining an appearance of openness and diversity was all the more important as Hollywood imports had an increasingly difficult time reaching European markets. None the less, these strategies failed to extinguish the spirit of resistance that found expression, among other things, in the organised boycotting of German films in the Balkans and the Netherlands.

Inside the Third Reich, the transformation of the movie audience into a model of the national community involved the most mundane aspects of cinema culture, beginning with programming practices and rules of admission. After 1938, Jews were no longer admitted to cinemas; similar prohibitions applied to foreign labourers and POWs. These practices implicated audiences directly in the staging of the body politic and made them an integral part of the fantasies subsumed under the concept of *Volksgemeinschaft*. The mobilisation of cinema as a place of collective experiences and an instrument of ideological positioning was further aided by obligatory screenings of war newsreels, organised group viewings of propaganda films, and free admission to highly politicised film events. There aesthetic pleasures, social rituals, and media effects all came together to transform the motion-picture theatre into a public sphere where an illusory sense of national identity could be achieved, if only in the realm of fantasy.

The year 1942 brought the full nationalisation of the film industry, with Cautio acting as a trust company and with the newly formed Ufa-Film GmbH, sometimes also referred to as UFI, operating as a holding company with several subsidiaries. Ufa-Film was headed by Fritz Hippler as the newly appointed Reich Film Administrator responsible for co-ordinating film production and distribution with official policies. Eleven firms were now united in one huge state-owned trust, including the Ufa-Filmkunst, Terra-Filmkunst, Tobis-Filmkunst, Bavaria-Filmkunst, Wien-Film, Prag-Film, and Continental-Film. This monopoly structure made possible a more effective division of labour between the competing demands of propaganda and entertainment. After an initial phase of politicisation, the Ministry returned to the double strategy of producing a few big-budget propaganda films and a large number of conventional genre films with strong entertainment value. Expanding the market for German films and setting new attendance records, the war proved highly profitable to the industry, with the number of tickets sold increasing from 624 million in 1939 to more than 1,117 billion in 1943. By the early 1940s, only the United States had more exhibition venues than the Third Reich with its approximately 8,600 cinemas throughout Europe. Revelling in these successes, Ufa celebrated its 25-year anniversary in 1943 with the blockbuster production of *Münchhausen*, an all-star historical action adventure, shot in colour, which cost the studio an unprecedented 6.5 million RM.

During the last years of the war, frivolous subject matter and escapist fare returned to the cinema with a vengeance, as did more defeatist attitudes and melancholy styles. Avoiding direct references to the worsening situation on the home front and the strong possibility of military defeat, most film stories were set in a distant past or indiscernible present. Within such an illusionist structure, the eruptions of the real, whether in the form of particular sentences or images, proved a constant source of concern for the Propaganda Ministry. The inclusion of documentary material in war films such as *U-Boote westwärts!* (Submarines Westward!, 1941) or *Stukas* (1941) validated the myth of individual heroism, but also drew attention to the difference between actual war experience and filmic representation. Likewise, in 1940, the commercial failure of the anti-Semitic historical drama *Die Rothschilds* (The Rothschilds), as well as some audiences' uneasiness about the hateful tone of *Der ewige Jude* (The Eternal Jew) brought into sharp relief the danger of relying on simplistic assumptions about intended filmic effects and actual audience responses. Despite such problems, the Propaganda Ministry continued to supply war-wary audiences with a steady stream of escapist fare, including many re-releases. The Barrandov studios in Prague became the preferred destination for film professionals fleeing the capital. Because of the massive destruction caused by allied bombing of cities, venerable state theatres were turned into cinemas to provide the population with shelter, literally and figuratively speaking. Until the very end, even Goebbels remained convinced of a German victory – if not on the battlefield of war, then in some imaginary cinema of the future.

Third Reich cinema as political cinema

The image of Goebbels as an all-powerful director of mass-produced fantasies and the characterisation of audiences as highly susceptible and manipulable continue to inform popular perceptions of Nazi cinema as a cinema of propaganda. In fact, propaganda films, which included the state-commissioned films, made up only 10 per cent of the entire production and remained limited to historical dramas, war films, genius films, and a few home front films. Most genre films avoided direct references to the regime – only to serve it by promoting the sexist, nationalist, and racist ideologies essential to its continued existence and by sustaining the illusory division between an official culture of political spectacle and the seemingly apolitical sphere of private pleasures, individual choices, and modern diversions. Ministerial directives about everything from the appropriate length of films to the adequate portrayal of different nationalities indicate to what degree the regime tried to control the circulation of meanings. Tensions between various branches of the state bureaucracy and the film industry and personal rivalries among studio managers, party leaders, and government officials simultaneously undermined and strengthened the integrative power of a cinema described alternatively as escapist, populist, and propagandistic. In the same way that Nazi ideology was based on an eclectic and largely derivative mixture of theories and philosophies, the cinema of the Third Reich was held together less through a monolithic aesthetic vision or ideological project than through the effective management of scenarios of difference and instances of resistance.

The competing definitions of film propaganda can be traced back to the different positions taken by Hitler and Goebbels in the early 1930s. Hitler had very clear ideas about propaganda and its relevance to the Nazi movement. Film and other modern media, he argued, could be instrumental in winning political followers and propagating National Socialist ideas; hence the importance of direct emotional appeal. For Hitler, propaganda meant the reduction of complicated issues to a few simple slogans and their further intensification through repetition, exaggeration, and visual symbolism. Goebbels favoured a more indirect approach to propaganda that concealed its intentions and placed greater emphasis on the mode of presentation. For him, the politics of representation was more important than the representation of politics. Their differences first became apparent in the heated

73

controversies over three early feature films about the beginnings of the Nazi movement. These movement films shared a number of characteristics: the celebration of youthful idealism and martyrdom; the validation of community, discipline, and solidarity; and the close attention to public ritual and the symbolic power of flags and uniforms. Time and again, National Socialism was presented as the result of an ongoing process of self-discovery rather than a set of distinct political beliefs. By equating political commitment with emotional experiences, the three films in question established a not unproblematic model of identification for many later propaganda films. *Hitlerjunge Quex* (Hitler Youth Quex, 1933) showed the conversion of a communist working-class youth in a style reminiscent of Weimar social realism. By contrast, *SA-Mann Brand* (SA-Man Brand, 1933) presented the early years of the movement so crudely that it was shunned by critics and audiences. And *Hans Westmar* (1933), inspired by the story of Horst Wessel, was initially withdrawn from distribution because the Nazis feared the commercialisation of their symbols and rituals.

To what degree the aestheticisation of politics gave rise to a distinctly fascist aesthetic has been the central question behind the critical reception of the most famous film of the period, Leni Riefenstahl's *Triumph des Willens* (Triumph of the Will, 1935). Shot during the 1934 Party Congress in Nuremberg, the film stages the encounter between the *Führer* and the *Volk* in tightly choreographed sequences that mythologise social and political processes (Barsam 1975). This convergence of modernity and myth takes place through visual symbols such as flags, clouds, and fire and filmic devices such as repetition, symmetry, and counterpoint. The underlying ideological process is predicated on the transformation both of the historical city into a stage set and of the party event into a cinematic spectacle. Riefenstahl's apotheosis of the national community finds expression in the human ornaments that become an integral part of the monumental architecture and the cult of the beautiful that motivates the many close-ups of ecstatic faces and steely bodies. This aesthetics of racial perfection, including the apotheosis of physical strength, also permeates Riefenstahl's documentary about the 1936 Olympic Games, *Olympia* (1938), with its two parts *Fest der Völker* (Festival of Nations) and *Fest der Schönheit* (Festival of Beauty) infused with metaphysical significance through the rich Wagnerian score by Herbert Windt (Hinton 1991). Since then, Riefenstahl's work has been debated by defenders who praise its technical brilliance and remarkable formal qualities and detractors for whom the obsession with beauty functions as an essential part of 'fascinating fascism' (Susan Sontag). Riefenstahl's appearance in the much discussed documentary by Ray Müller, *Die Macht der Bilder* (The Wonderful, Horrible Life of Leni Riefenstahl, 1993), and her death in 2003 have brought renewed interest in a director who continues to personify Nazi cinema and fascist aesthetics, including the highly problematic cult of the body (Downing 1992, Riefenstahl 1993, Filmmuseum Potsdam 1999, Rother 2000, Pages et al. 2007).

Confirming the inherent problems in using film for political purposes, professional associations and party organisations continued to argue over their adequate representation in the grand narratives of *Volk* and nation and make bold pronouncements about the appropriate portrayal of Germany's political enemies. To give only one example: when generals complained about the cursory treatment of the army in *Triumph des Willens*, Riefenstahl made a short documentary, *Tag der Freiheit* (Day of Freedom, 1935), to appease them. During the war years, propagandistic intentions could not always keep up with changing military objectives. While Bolshevism had always invited negative stereotyping, especially in the conflation of Bolsheviks with Jews, the Non-Aggression Pact in 1939 inspired a brief wave of sentimental films about Old Russia, including the Pushkin adaptation *Der Postmeister* (The Postmaster, 1940). The anti-Russian film *Friesennot* (Frisian Plight, 1935) was first banned in 1939 but, after the German attack on the Soviet Union, reissued in 1941 as *Dorf im roten Sturm* (Village in the Red Storm).

Triumph des Willens illustrates well the workings of the fascist aesthetic, but its exceptional status also confirms the fact that the Third Reich never gave rise to an ideologically coherent body of work or a consistent set of artistic practices, even where official pronouncements suggest otherwise. The fundamental problem of controlling images and their meanings can be seen in the Ministry's close attention to non-narrative forms with a greater investment in, or proximity to, the material world and documentary praxis. Whether as party convention films, weekly newsreels or cultural films, these non-narrative forms played as key a role in the obscuration of political reality and its realignment with fantasy and illusion. Considered the most effective tool of political propaganda, newsreels after 1933 became increasingly sophisticated in their use of nationalist rhetoric and a visual style that relied heavily on rapid editing and trick photography. Newsreels changed even more under the conditions of total media warfare and the complete militarisation of public life. Already the invasion of the Rhineland in 1936 had taken place in front of camera teams. After 1939, all independent newsreels were consolidated in the *Ufa-Tonwoche* which, in 1940, was given the more patriotic name of *Deutsche Wochenschau* (German Newsreel). Film footage from the front was provided by special military units, the so-called propaganda companies. Lasting up to one hour, war newsreels relied heavily on incendiary commentary and dramatic music in order to create an aestheticised view of warfare that had no place for death and suffering. Documentary footage and staged scenes were combined to create a filmic reality ruled less by the ethical standards of news reporting than by the regime's need to enlist the powers of the imagination in the desperate pursuit of a final victory. Especially in *Feldzug in Polen* (The Polish Campaign, 1940) and *Sieg im Westen* (Victory in the West, 1941), the cinematographer Svend Noldan relied heavily on maps, graphics, and trick animation to make visible the strength of the German army.

National Socialist ideology found privileged expression in the countless cultural films that were an essential part of the supporting programme but differed from the newsreel in their educational goals and artistic ambitions. Since the 1920s, screenings had typically included pre-films on topics ranging from geography and biology to ethnography and art history. After 1933, these themes, while always closely linked to the question of Germanness, were presented in more nationalistic tones. Compilation films such as *Blut und Boden* (Blood and Soil, 1933) and *Der ewige Wald* (The Eternal Forest, 1936) enlisted the familiar iconography of German landscape, nature, and *Heimat* in anti-urban and anti-modern diatribes. Countless shorts celebrated the Reich's technological, architectural, and organisational accomplishments, from the projects of the Reich Labour Service and the cultural programmes of the Strength through Joy organisation to Albert Speer's grandiose plans for Berlin as the future Germania. Sometimes these non-narrative forms offered a rare opportunity for formal experimentation. Resisting the romantic accounts of technical innovation and skill found in *Wunder des Fliegens* (The Wonders of Flying, 1935), with famous aviator Ernst Udet, a few film-makers continued to present modern industries and technologies in the cool, detached New Objectivist style. Willy Zielke's *Das Stahltier* (The Steel Animal, 1935), commissioned for the centennial of the first German railway line, as well as Ruttmann's *Deutsche Waffenschmieden* (German Armaments Factories, 1939) and *Deutsche Panzer* (German Tanks, 1940), relied extensively on modernist techniques such as associative montage, rapid editing, unusual perspectives, and extreme close-ups to celebrate the convergence of fascism and modernism in the machine aesthetic. The influence of the Weimar cross-section film can also be seen in Leo de Laforgue's *Symphonie einer Weltstadt* (Symphony of a World City), completed in 1942 and shown for the first time in 1950 as the last filmic record of Berlin before the mass bombings.

The division of labour among film, radio, and television played a crucial role in maintaining ideological coherence on the level of institutional structures and representational practices. Public broadcasting, which operated under total state control, offered unlimited opportunities for mass manipulation by bringing the voice of Hitler into almost every household. Fully aware of radio's untapped possibilities, the Nazis produced an inexpensive model, known as the *Volks-empfänger* (people's receiver), that allowed them to address an instant community of eight million listeners. The underlying sense of simultaneity, omnipresence, and connectedness was cleverly exploited in the famous Christmas broadcasts from the front. At the same time, the conditions of listening in the private home further fragmented the public sphere and limited participation in political events to the auditory realm. Programming practices offered various surrogate forms of participation, from live broadcasts of classical concerts and variety shows to the popular request concert series depicted in *Wunschkonzert*.

Even in its early experimental stage, television promised to expand further the possibilities of mass manipulation (Reiss 1979, Uricchio 1990, Zeutschner 1995). Telefunken first presented the new technology at the Fifth German Radio Exhibition in 1928, and public television was experimentally introduced as early as 1935, though only on a limited basis. With the cost of a television set too high for most consumers, screenings took place in public television lounges. The daily television broadcasts included newsreels, narrative shorts, cultural films, variety shows, popular music, and comic sketches; older films were sometimes shown in abbreviated form. Even after 1939, when viewers in the Berlin area could already receive regular programmes, television remained a technological and aesthetically unsatisfactory experience.

The state-commissioned films presented their political messages as part of such larger media networks and public events, and they realised their ideological effects through the convergence of mass media and high culture in new patterns of cultural consumption. Highly contextualised film propaganda involved the translation of racist and nationalist ideologies into dramatic constellations and fictitious scenarios. Their affective charge extended beyond the simple mechanisms of mass manipulation to give rise to an aesthetic conception of the national community. From the casting of stars to the conception of characters, the narratives were held together by highly normative and exclusionary definitions of race, nation, and *Volk* that combined utopian dreams of plenitude and belonging with more aggressive visions of greatness and domination. With national identity conceptualised along these lines, the propaganda films of the late 1930s and early 1940s aimed at a radical redefinition of the political from the perspective of individual fantasy and desire. The resultant fictionalisation of politics made the cinema the model of an illusory public sphere held together through media technologies and media productions. The underlying narratives of identity formation produced an imaginary space where private desires could be acknowledged and fulfilled through their inscription into new political scenarios, including the exclusionary mechanisms of nation and race. Narrative denouement, the deliverance from alienation, could finally be achieved, if not on the screen, then in the reality of war and genocide. All filmic elements contributed to the dissolution of psychological and social conflicts into this unifying vision of national community and the mapping of identity across the body of the racialised other. The reintroduction of these fiction effects into the spaces of everyday life completed the cycle of projections and displacements sustained by the discourses of history, biography, mythology, and folklore. Without such mediations, the propaganda film betrayed its political intentions all too clearly and, despite its heavy reliance on racial and national stereotyping, failed to mobilise the power of imagination.

The main contribution of the propaganda films to the re-emergence of German nationalism lay in the displacement of present concerns into past events and the rewriting of collective history as individual melodrama and tragedy. Most propaganda films – and all state-commissioned films – were historical films, with the meaning of history significantly changed in the process of adaptation and actualisation. Especially the films about the trauma of the First World War and the failure of the Weimar Republic relied on simplistic assumptions about cause and effect to give rise to lurid fantasies of humiliation and revenge. With the Third Reich firmly installed as the *telos* of German history, the emotional purpose of these narratives was one not of historicity but of urgent contemporaneity. To the degree that the prevailing modes of address achieved the full identity of protagonists and spectators, the latter were confirmed as the executors of history's unfulfilled promises. The revenge for past suffering was a narrative construction that legitimised new racial policies and military actions. Moreover, through the notion of *Volk*, the historical films created a collective identity beyond the problems of the present and provided a sense of manifest destiny that offered advance justification for future aggressive acts.

Accordingly, *Flüchtlinge* (Refugees, 1933) focuses on the fate of Volga Germans persecuted by the Bolsheviks after the First World War. *Menschen ohne Vaterland* (People Without Fatherland, 1937) has German civilians fighting in the Baltics, whereas *Patrioten* (Patriots, 1937) stages the drama of national identity through the fate of a German pilot captured by the French. *Pour le mérite* (1938) reaches narrative denouement with the rearmament of Germany after a long period of self-denial, whereas Rabenalt's famous . . . *reitet für Deutschland* (Riding for Germany, 1941) has an injured war veteran regain his physical strength once he commits himself to the project of nationalism. Responding to ongoing military conflicts, *Menschen im Sturm* (People in the Storm, 1941) uses the suffering of Germans under the Serbs to justify the attack on Yugoslavia. And one of the most infamous contributions to the genre, *Heimkehr* (Homecoming, 1941), dramatises the discrimination of ethnic Germans in Volhynia in a way that retroactively 'makes sense' of the invasion of Poland in 1939.

Under the special conditions of production and reception reserved for the state-commissioned film, historical subject matter quickly emerged as the preferred vehicle for the dissemination of racist and nationalist ideologies (Happel 1984, Schulte-Sasse 1996). The conflation of history and narrative blurred the distinctions between public and private, individual and collective, and fiction and reality. Everybody could become part of the nation's struggle for survival and, through identification with the historical leader, find a place in the interstices of the imaginary and the real. Perhaps most importantly, historical films provided the critical categories for dissolving the contingencies of history into the eternal categories of nation and race. In so doing, the historical imagination allowed for a temporary return to the pre-industrial world of peasantry and agriculture; a validation of the community of *Volk* and the rootedness of *Heimat*; and an idealised view of the German nation based on its beautiful landscapes, indigenous peoples, and ancient traditions.

Historical re-enactments of wars and revolutions, and of political crises and colonial ambitions, provided the material for the founding myths of a new Germany, with the Third Reich a ubiquitous reference point as the culmination of German history. Accordingly, *Bismarck* (1940) retells the early years of the Wilhelmine Empire from the perspective of the strong leader figure, whereas *Die Entlassung* (The Dismissal, 1942) links the leadership crisis after Bismarck's dismissal to the rise of liberal parliamentarianism. *Carl Peters* (1941) explains the fight for German colonies in Africa through the continuous threat of British imperialism, while *Ohm Krüger* (1941) uses the Boer Wars to justify the Reich's military actions against Great Britain. Parallels between past and present also coloured the approach to other national histories. Thus *Der Fuchs von Glenarvon* (The Fox of Glenarvon, 1940) and *Mein Leben für Irland* (My Life for Ireland,

1941), two anti-British films about the Irish uprising of 1921, served as historical models for the struggle of the Nazi movement during the 1920s.

A sub-genre of the historical film, the Prussian film stood out through its unabashed glorification of the absolutist state and its autocratic ruler. Associated with authoritarianism, the myth of Prussia gave expression to National Socialist fantasies about a complete militarisation of public life. In the figure of the Aryan, Prussian virtues such as discipline, order, duty, and obedience returned triumphant. Prussian history showed the conditions under which war, to paraphrase Clausewitz, became a continuation of politics through other means. The Prussian films focused on two historical periods: the period of Frederick II the Great, which culminated in the Seven Years War (1756–63) and the rise of Prussia as a major European power, and the War of Liberation (1812–14), through which Prussia freed itself from Napoleonic rule and laid the ground for the emergence of German nationalism. The Fridericus films, whose popularity during the 1920s and 1930s took full advantage of the uncanny resemblance of Otto Gebühr to the Prussian king, articulated key ideological positions: the need for a political system based on absolute power; the importance of internal unity as a defence against foreign influences; the celebration of all-male groups in the building of a fully militarised society; and the acceptance of patriarchy as a model for the family and the state. Often structured around the equation of love and death, the genre reconciled the underlying tension between discipline and punishment, on the one hand, and suppressed desire and deferred satisfaction, on the other, in the almost godlike portrayal of Frederick the Great. Showing the transformation from the rebellious son into the lonely soldier king, *Der Choral von Leuthen*, *Der alte und der junge König* (The Old and the Young King, 1935), and *Der grosse König* outlined an ideal-typical trajectory for the making of the soldierly male and national comrade. However, with *Kolberg*, Veit Harlan pushed the emotional investments of the Prussian film to its perverse conclusion when he worked with more extras than soldiers in the actual siege in 1807 and requisitioned scarce resources from the soldiers on the front. The film premiered in the beleaguered Atlantic fortress of La Rochelle and a bombed-out Berlin: a telling indication of the ways in which the relationship between fantasy and reality had finally been reversed.

The representation of the leader figure as rebel and tyrant played a key role in the Nazis' uses and abuses of history. Whether focusing on political figures, great scientists or famous artists, the so-called genius films emphatically confirmed male subjectivity as the foundation of German identity. In accordance with National Socialist myths about its revolutionary origins, these 'great men' frequently expressed their opposition to tradition and convention through patriotic feelings and nationalist ideas. The genre exhibited a marked preference for innovators – the physician *Robert Koch* (1939), the inventor [Rudolf] *Diesel* (1942), and the fifteenth-century Swiss scientist *Paracelsus* (1943) – whose quest for knowledge and truth invariably put them in conflict with the prejudices of their times. The apotheosis of the creative genius and his quintessential Germanness found further confirmation in the idealism of *Friedrich Schiller* (1940), whose call for a national theatre contributed to the reclamation of the young playwright as a precursor of National Socialism; the stubbornness of 'Prussian Michelangelo' *Andreas Schlüter* (1942), whose dreams of a national architecture prefigured the contributions of Albert Speer; and the personal struggles portrayed in *Friedemann Bach* (1941), whose artistic and political rebellion against a dominant father resonated deeply with the Oedipal self-representation of the Nazis as a movement of the sons.

The necessity of articulating nation and race within fully developed narratives proved of particular relevance to the few anti-Semitic films made between 1939 and 1942. Using anti-Semitic stereotypes to provide justification for the 'final solution of the Jewish question', these films contributed greatly to the reconfiguration of fantasy and ideology at the beginning of the Second World War. The centrality of anti-Semitism to Nazi ideology and the scarcity of anti-Semitic representations in Nazi cinema suggest a carefully maintained and continuously adjusted division of labour between the fascist mass spectacle and an entertainment culture presumably free of politics. Ideological positions were expressed not just through the dynamics of manifest and latent meanings. In fact, the discourses of discrimination and persecution relied much more heavily on the structuring absences and suggestive silences that, until 1939, prohibited film reviewers from mentioning the existence of Jewish characters on the screen. Accordingly, anti-Semitic stereotypes functioned as part of a larger system of defining others in ethnic or national terms. Because of the potentially disruptive effects of negative stereotyping, questions of racial difference were often displaced on to the problem of sexual difference, with the (sexualised) body of the woman standing in for the provocation of race that needed to be contained. As a result, anti-Semitic attitudes can also be found in the unflattering portrayal of intellectuals and small-business men, in the casting of presumably Jewish-looking actors as unsympathetic characters, and in the ridiculing or demonising of modernist tastes and cosmopolitan lifestyles. Without these mediations, anti-Semitic representations ended up uncovering the hidden workings of ideology, an unintended effect that made the conflation of Jew, Russian, and Bolshevik in *GPU* (The Red Terror, 1942) a perfect case study for the ultimate failure of film propaganda.

Harlan's infamous *Jud Süss* (Jew Suess, 1940) proved so effective because its anti-Semitic images are presented within the structures of classical bourgeois tragedy. Based on the story of Joseph Süss-Oppenheimer at the eighteenth-century court of the Duke of Württemberg, the film offers justification for the persecution of Jews by juxtaposing the corrupt system of autocratic rule financed by the Jewish banker and the emerging nation state based on traditional family values and sustained through 'typical' German traits such as duty, honour, and modesty. By adding the rape and subsequent suicide of a young German woman, the director exploited widespread beliefs about Jewish sexuality to articulate the question of race along gendered lines and to link the imagined threat of racial impurity and miscegenation to the crisis of national community. In so doing, Harlan's film combined two key aspects of anti-Semitism, namely, the projection on to the Jews of those qualities that were considered threatening to society and the identification of the Jews with exceptional abilities that were bound to incite envy and resentment (Hollstein 1983).

The most rabidly anti-Semitic film of the period, *Der ewige Jude*, combined documentary images of ceremonial prayer and ritual slaughtering with brief excerpts from Weimar feature films betraying 'Semitic tendencies'. Made under the supervision of Reich Film Administrator Hippler and obligatory viewing on the eastern front, this vicious compilation film about the 'world Jewish conspiracy' claimed to reveal the truth through an incendiary mixture of allusions, insinuations, and comparisons, including the metaphor of swarming rats. The centrality of filmic images to the organisation of an industrialised genocide became glaringly evident in a later pseudo-documentary about Theresienstadt, made expressly to deceive a concerned international community about the nature of concentration camps. Directed by one of the inmates, the Jewish actor Kurt Gerron, *Der Führer schenkt den Juden eine Stadt* (The Führer Gives a City to the Jews, 1945) presents the camp as a model community, a place of healthy work and wholesome play – a more than troubling comment on the role of modern mass media in international relations.

Third Reich cinema as popular cinema

While the propaganda films shed an important light on the mutual instrumentalisation of ideology and fantasy and allow us to better understand the aestheticisation of politics during the Nazi period, they reveal very little about popular tastes, private fantasies, and mainstream diversions. In fact, cinema during the Third Reich was overwhelmingly a popular cinema defined through famous stars and familiar genres. Its primarily goal was entertainment, not indoctrination, with the artificial distinction between both terms an integral part of cinema's emotional appeal and political function. Confirming the success of this approach, the list of greatest hits was led by *Die goldene Stadt* (The Golden City, 1942) with 12.5 million tickets sold, followed by *Der weisse Traum* (The White Dream, 1943) and *Immensee* (1943), each with 10.1 million, *Die grosse Liebe* (The Great Love, 1942) and *Wiener Blut* (Viennese Blood, 1942), each with 9.2 million, and *Wunschkonzert* (Request Concert, 1940) with 8.8 million tickets. A number of factors contributed to these phenomenal successes: their reliance on genre as the most efficient way of addressing diverse audiences; their cultivation of the star system as a convenient structure for spectator identification; their incorporation of other popular diversions such as music, radio, literature, and sports; and, most importantly, their reliance on the conventions and styles identified with the classical Hollywood film.

Nazi cinema was from the beginning a cinema organised around male and, above all, female stars. Famous stars established patterns of identification, imitation, and admiration beyond the individual films. The collapsing of actor and role in the persona of the star created compelling figures of identification in a society obsessed with sexual and racial difference and the negotiation of public and private identities. In contrast to character actors such as Gustav Gründgens, Heinrich George, and

Werner Krauss, who conveyed a sense of artistic significance and cultural respectability, and unlike supporting actors such as Grete Weiser and Theo Lingen, who added local wit and regional humour, the leading stars of Goebbels's dream factory were constituted through, and sustained by, the filmic construction of national identity, character, and physiognomy. Distinguished through their beauty, charm, and sex appeal, actresses in particular were considered central to the highly gendered narratives of nation and community and the equally important visions of an alluring sexuality and eroticism marked as fundamentally other. In projecting an image of elegance, style, and worldliness, actresses embodied cinema's international ambitions and compensatory effects. Yet the transformation of the female body into a site of authenticity and essence also introduced more problematic ideas about race and gender that, even outside conventional definitions of Aryan womanhood, proved essential to the socio-psychological function of mass entertainment during the Third Reich (Beyer 1991, Romani 1992, Ascheid 2003, Carter 2004).

Adored by their fans, photographed in the illustrated press, and written up in gossip columns, film actors and actresses evoked a fully modern society far removed from the reactionary strains within Nazi ideology and fully committed to adventure, leisure, pleasure, and merriment. The Propaganda Ministry recognised the stars' vital public function by accommodating personal requests and paying exorbitant salaries. In 1937, for instance, Albers earned as much as 562,000 RM. By contrast, a skilled worker earned only 2,500 RM a year. Secret lists circulated with the names of those actors to be employed at all times and those to be avoided as 'box-office poison'. Many famous actresses modelled themselves on Hollywood stars, with sultry Zarah Leander promoted as a German Garbo, gamine Lilian Harvey resembling Miriam Hopkins, and perky Marika Rökk frequently compared to Eleanor Powell and Ginger Rogers. With the exception of blond *ingénue* Kristina Söderbaum, the majority of actresses appealed through physical features and character traits that bore little resemblance to the ideal of womanhood celebrated in Nazi painting. Through their exotic looks, refined tastes, and sophisticated styles, these actresses evoked the world of glamour and eroticism that had been largely eliminated from official culture. The fascination with otherness was especially pronounced in actresses whose careers had started after 1933. Many such as Söderbaum, Leander, and Rökk were foreigners or made foreignness part of their screen persona. Especially Leander, the statuesque Swedish-born singer and actress, inspired a cult-like admiration that suggests more unsettling identifications and sexual ambiguities. This acute awareness of femininity as masquerade continues in her present-day status as a gay icon.

For the most part, female stars were closely identified with specific genres. Romantic comedies continued to promote the slender, androgynous types embodied by Käthe von Nagy and Brigitte Helm. Olga Tschechowa excelled in playing the worldly older woman. Combining simplicity and inner strength, Austrian Paula Wessely brought emotional complexity to the woman's film. After Renate Müller's premature death in 1938, the young Ilse Werner became audiences' favourite 'girl next door'. Often cast as a dangerous *femme fatale*, Brigitte Horney appeared regularly in melodramas but, like Tschechowa and

Wessely, also lent her quiet intensity to several propaganda vehicles. Sibylle Schmitz, whose suicide later inspired Fassbinder's *Die Sehnsucht der Veronika Voss* (Veronika Voss, 1982), found a perfect showcase for her dark exotic beauty in highly stylised melodramatic settings.

With her classical features and theatrical training, Marianne Hoppe covered the widest range as an actress, playing in light-hearted sophisticated comedies in the style of *Capriolen* (Capers, 1937) and melancholy marital dramas such as *Romanze in Moll* (Romance in a Minor Key, 1943), but also adding her dramatic skill and emotional depth to home front films such as *Auf Wiedersehn, Franziska!* (Goodbye, Franziska!, 1941). While possessing some of the pragmatic, androgynous charm that linked *ingénues* such as Harvey, Müller, and Nagy to their Weimar precursors, Hoppe remained defined by the difficulties of modern women in reconciling the conflicting demands of career, marriage, and motherhood. Her screen persona combined strong character traits such as independence, ambition, and confidence with a knowing recognition and resigned acceptance of the expectations placed upon women in bourgeois society. The casting of Hoppe as Effi Briest in the Fontane adaptation *Der Schritt vom Wege* (The Step off the Path, 1939) took full advantage of this tension and offered a subtle commentary on the emotional dynamics of unfulfilled yearning and quiet subordination.

In contrast to the close identification of female stars with the problem of modern femininity, male actors were more directly implicated in the politics of national identity, including its foundation on normative heterosexuality and patriarchal family structures. Romantic leads Willy Fritsch and Gustav Fröhlich personified the confidence, optimism, and energy of the younger generation, whereas the more mature, heavy-set character actors from the theatre projected the kind of male authority usually associated with the past. Heinrich George brought his intense physicality to many historical personalities. Werner Krauss and Emil Jannings specialised in rulers, industrialists, and inventors. All three regularly took leading roles in propaganda vehicles. With the exception of the brash Hans Albers and the suave Willy Birgel, whose ambiguous screen personas included elements of weakness and cruelty, most actors appeared either in romantic or dramatic parts. The prevailing stereotypes included urbane charmers such as Hans Söhnker, quiet masculine types such as Paul Hartmann, and, in more heroic roles, Carl Raddatz and Paul Klinger.

The enormous popular appeal of Heinz Rühmann derived from his uncanny ability as a comic actor to articulate the petty-bourgeois desire for social acceptance and private contentment with all of its humorous and pathetic consequences. As the personification of the little man – oppressed, repressed, but always in a good mood – Rühmann comically re-enacted the crises of modern masculinity in numerous comedies about the difficulties of everyday life. Especially his most famous films, *Quax der Bruchpilot* (Quax the Crash Pilot, 1941) and *Die Feuerzangenbowle* (The Red Wine Punch, 1944), took full advantage of the underlying tension between male aggression and regression that sustained Rühmann's phenomenal career as the Reich's most popular comedian.

83

While there was no shortage of good actors, the lack of innovative directors after the introduction of the Aryan clause remained a serious problem throughout the decade. Most directors were little more than seasoned professionals who had started making films before 1933 and would continue working after 1945. The prolific Carl Boese directed almost 50 films for Goebbel's Ministry, including many comedies set in the petty-bourgeois milieu. The credits of screenwriter and director Robert A. Stemmle are equally extensive. Carl Froelich worked with Henny Porten in the early 1920s, directed and produced throughout the 1930s, and, as an active member of the Nazi party, was appointed president of the Reich Film Chamber in 1939. Froelich's best known films include *Heimat* (Homeland, 1938), a melodrama featuring George and Leander as estranged father and daughter, and *Die vier Gesellen* (The Four Companions, 1938), a romantic comedy about female friendship with a very young Ingrid Bergman. Appointed head of production at Ufa in 1942, Wolfgang Liebeneiner used his background in the theatre and his adaptable filmic sensibility to work with some of the greatest actors from the German stage. He made a name for himself with light comedies, only to take on more problematic subject matter with the infamous euthanasia film, *Ich klage an* (I Accuse, 1941) and two biographical films about the 'Iron Chancellor', *Bismarck* (1940) and the aforementioned *Die Entlassung*; both offering historical justification for the leadership principle.

Many directors established close working relationships with certain actors, screenwriters, and cameramen, or they specialised in popular genres that allowed them to capitalise on their cultural or ethnic background. Often in collaboration with composer Robert Stolz, the Hungarian Géza von Bolvary made film operettas that nostalgically evoked Old Vienna in the style of *Wiener G'schichten* (Viennese Tales, 1940). Known for his subtle use of stylisation, the Ukrainian Viktor Tourjansky made a name for himself with marital melodramas such as *Der Blaufuchs* (The Blue Fox, 1938) and murky political parables in the style of *Der Gouverneur* (The Governor, 1939). Beginning with *Liebespremiere* (Love Premiere, 1943), Austrian Arthur Maria Rabenalt directed several films set in the world of show business, whereas Herbert Selpin – not surprising given his penchant for physical challenges – specialised in adventure dramas such as *Sergeant Berry* (1938) and *Titanic* (1943).

Film-makers with strong political convictions exhibited a pronounced preference for the biographical or historical film. Hans Steinhoff, who emerged as a leading director after *Hitlerjunge Quex*, became a master at portraying great men, whether in the field of medicine (*Robert Koch* (1939)), colonial politics (*Ohm Krüger*) or high art (*Rembrandt* (1942)). From *Flüchtlinge* (Refugees, 1933) to *Heimkehr*, Gustav Ucicky mined historical experiences of displacement and discrimination for nationalist fantasies, not least by extolling the virtues of male friendship and personal sacrifice. The problems with using feature films for political messages repeatedly threatened the career of Karl Ritter, an ardent German nationalist and anti-communist whose propagandistic zeal in *Verräter* (Traitors, 1936), *Patrioten* (Patriots, 1937), and *Pour le mérite* (1938) was not always appreciated by the

Propaganda Ministry. Although labelled 'politically valuable', his high-profile films found outspoken critics even among polemicists such as Alfred Rosenberg who regarded their nationalist, rather than National Socialist, rhetoric as an obstacle to a quality-based definition of political film-making.

In a national cinema built primarily around popular genres and famous stars, was there any room for individual styles and critical perspectives? Experiments were certainly not encouraged, but it would be simplistic to explain the lack of innovative film-making solely with the oppressive conditions of production. Similarly, it would be misguided to read all signs of creativity as a manifestation of aesthetic opposition. The early sound film brought back many dramatic techniques and staging conventions from the theatre and contributed greatly to the growing preference for seamless narratives without authorial interventions. Film-makers' emphatic rejection of modernist techniques such as associative montage and unreliable narration was also driven by their opposition to the two filmic styles that had distinguished German art cinema until that point: social realism and expressionism. However, a number of traditions from the 1920s survived in modified form. Using musical comedies as a conduit to the irreverent atmosphere of the so-called 'golden twenties', Reinhold Schünzel continued to cultivate his visual and verbal witticisms in *Amphitryon* (1935), a daring political parody set among the gods of Antiquity. Similarly, Willi Forst conjured up an almost forgotten atmosphere of charm, sophistication, and irreverence in the amusing comedy-of-errors *Allotria* (Hokum, 1936).

During the same time period, the rediscovery of melodramatic forms allowed newcomers such as Detlef Sierck to explore stylisation as a means of distanciation in *Schlussakkord* (Final Chord, 1936), before perfecting his compelling mixture of formal and emotional excess in two critically acclaimed films with Leander, *Zu neuen Ufern* (To New Shores, 1937) and *La Habanera* (1937). These rare moments of stylistic innovation were part of larger developments within 1930s cinema internationally (for instance, in the woman's film), whereas later examples of film authorship must be explained through the gradual erosion of institutional controls during the final years of the war. In this light, Helmut Käutner's melancholy study of the Hamburg harbour milieu in *Grosse Freiheit Nr. 7* (Great Freedom Street No. 7, 1944) and his poetic realist portrayal of Berlin's canals and bridges in *Unter den Brücken* (Under the Bridges, 1946) can alternatively be read as moral defeatism, individual resignation, or passive resistance – qualities that made Käutner well suited for a career in postwar West German cinema.

Only one other director besides Leni Riefenstahl was able to develop a unique filmic style in full accordance with Nazi ideology: Veit Harlan (Noack 2000). The visual and narrative elements that distinguished his most infamous films, *Jud Süss* and *Kolberg*, can also be found in his melodramas, but without the exploitative mixture of racist ideology, family melodrama, and stylistic excess. Harlan usually worked with the same actors, including his wife Kristina Söderbaum, and often relied on realist and naturalist authors in staging his deterministic views on identity and fate. Thus Hermann Sudermann inspired *Die Reise nach Tilsit* (The Journey to Tilsit, 1939), Theodor Storm *Immensee* (1943), and Rudolf Binding *Opfergang* (Sacrifice, 1944). Stylistically, Harlan aimed at a level of intensification and exaggeration that, from the use of ethereal music to the heavy colour symbolism, surrounded even idyllic rural settings with an unsettling atmosphere of artificiality, decadence and, ironically, degeneracy. His insistence on the sublimation of sexual desires and his morbid fascination with death found expression in the compulsive scenarios of fate, desire, and renunciation that made him the most recognisable *auteur* of the Third Reich. During the period of de-Nazification in West Germany, the director of *Jud Süss* was singled to stand trial for crimes against humanity. The first trial in 1949/50 resulted in a not-guilty verdict; even subsequent lawsuits failed to stop Harlan from continuing his prolific career throughout the 1950s.

With few exceptions, the denigration of authorship and the validation of genre in the most affirmative sense meant the suppression of all artistic ambitions and critical intentions. Recycling familiar story lines and relying on well-known stereotypes and clichés, genre films after 1933 operated within clearly defined rules and structures. The introduction of variations on a theme created aesthetic pleasure and provided emotional release, while at the same time confirming the power of dominant ideology. In general, one of the functions of genre is to produce emotions such as joy, fear, anger or sadness and to inscribe them into predetermined narrative forms. During the Third Reich, the prohibition on addressing more serious issues put severe constraints on the underlying negotiation of affirmation and critique. Film producers were told to avoid detective films, courtroom dramas, and suspense thrillers that might draw attention to taboo subjects such as the existence of crime and violence. Meanwhile the popularity of literary adaptations and the high status of literature in the public sphere allowed some directors to infuse canonical texts with potentially subversive subtexts. The proliferation of musical forms confirmed the centrality of music to constructions of national identity but also attested to the incalculable power of emotions. Last but not least, the performative registers of the comical and the grotesque allowed for some expression of resistance to the conventions ruling private and public life, but they did so primarily through the socially stabilising effects of laughter.

Inherently conservative as a form, genre cinema during the Third Reich contributed to the normative discourse on identity shared by popular culture, official culture, and high culture. The narrativising of identity gave coherence to an eclectic system of beliefs, ideas, and attitudes about gender, sexuality, love, marriage, family, community, and society and played a key role in organising the divisions between public and private life that guaranteed the functioning of Nazi ideology. At the same time, the almost compulsive preoccupation with issues of identity opened up an imaginary space both for visualising a feared other defined in racial, national, and political terms and for reaffirming one's sense of self through the projection of all negative qualities into a thus constituted system of differences and exclusions.

Precisely because of this inherent tension between conventional form and specific application, genre films were able to accommodate the different social imaginaries and reconcile the conflicting perspectives that presumably had been absorbed into the unifying discourses of nation and race. While the openly political films defined the viewing subject in collective terms and addressed the audience as a unified body, the genre films participated more indirectly in the ongoing negotiation of difference: between social and individual norms, between public and private behaviour, and between social classes, ethnic groups, and different nationalities. This institutionalised division between the collective experiences promised by the propaganda films and the individual desires satisfied by the entertainment films acknowledged the irruptions of class and gender as continuing sources of individual frustration but refused to translate this diagnosis of crisis into explicitly political terms.

Genre films addressed audiences through a process of identification – often associated with the ideology of populism or, to use the Nazi term, *Volkstümlichkeit* – that allowed them to participate, though only symbolically, in the creation of a unified, imaginary subject constituted through socially specific conflicts but articulated through allegedly universal human traits. That this subject position can often be described as petty-bourgeois must be explained through the petty-bourgeois origins of the Nazi movement and its exploitation both of economic fears in the impoverished middle class and of fantasies of social ascent among members of the working class and lower middle class. The terms of spectatorship completed the necessary shift from a political ideology that recognised social tensions, though only in order to deny them, to the filmic fictions that used national and racial difference as the organising principle behind the all-encompassing discourse of *Volk*. A thus conceived notion of Germanness allowed audiences to participate in fantasies of national greatness while at the same time confronting their own failures and inadequacies. In validating the perspective of the 'little man', which itself is marked by ambivalence, films were able to reconcile contradictory impulses in the overarching principle of common sense and to celebrate the virtues of compliance through the pleasures of being or acting average. These stabilising effects informed the filmic articulation of petty-bourgeois consciousness and sustained the attraction of genre cinema throughout the 1930s, namely as a cinema in which popular, populist, petty-bourgeois, and *völkisch* positions had finally been united through the integrative category of national community.

Almost half of the feature-length films produced during the Third Reich were comedies: romantic comedies, sophisticated comedies, family comedies, rustic comedies, and, above all, musical comedies. Many carried on in the nineteenth-century tradition of the drawing-room comedy, with infidelity, boredom, temptation, intrigue, and deception as the driving forces behind heated exchanges, compromising situations, and inevitable happy endings. Comedies inspired by regional peculiarities and urban milieux specialised in formulaic stories about personal rivalries, family feuds, and neighbourhood scandals. Only the white-collar comedies, which continued in the tradition of the early 1930s, retained some awareness of social and economic problems through their focus on competent young women and, increasingly, insecure and resentful petty-bourgeois men.

The continuing influence of Hollywood found paradigmatic expression in the irreverent spirit and quick pacing of sophisticated comedies in the style of *Glückskinder* (Children of Fortune, 1936), the successful Fritsch–Harvey vehicle modelled on Frank Capra's 1934 *It Happened One Night*. However, these adaptations did not just imitate the American originals or translate American stories and characters into recognisably German contexts. Film-makers also created their own versions of a Germanised America by incorporating German traditions and peculiarities. Likewise they modified Weimar cinema's modernist interpretation of Americanism by drawing more heavily on the traditional Central European tastes and sensibilities that had informed comic registers during the 1920s and early 1930s. Whereas the spirited banter between the sexes in the New Deal comedies was based on the recognition of social and economic inequities, the men and women in the comparable German versions expressed their resentments primarily in personal terms. Highly normative assumptions about love, romance, and sexuality guided the characters' short-lived revolts against bigotry and hypocrisy. Without the kind of visual commentaries developed to perfection by Lubitsch, the humour remained language-based and exhausted itself in the confirmation of social prejudices and sexual stereotypes. The anxieties over questions of gender and class found an emotional outlet only in brief moments of transgression. Especially the possibilities of social mimicry, false identity, and cross-dressing provided a welcome release from typical 'German' qualities such as discipline, modesty, and reliability. Yet by acknowledging the constructed nature of identity, the comedies demonstrated the importance of compliance and conformity; therein lay their conservative socio-psychological function.

The equally popular musical genres enlisted the symbolic function of music in defining national identity while also promising an escape from the pressures of everyday life through a greater emphasis on pleasure, illusion, and fantasy. Film operettas, opera films, musical comedies, revue films, and films about great composers and musicians all took advantage of the studios' close ties to public broadcasting and the recording industry. Musical styles ranged from the operetta scores of Eduard Künneke and Robert Stolz to the more contemporary sound of Michael Jary and the hit songs by Peter Kreuder. Many films featured international recording stars such as Jan Kiepura and Marta Eggerth. The strong Austro-Hungarian influence was evident in countless productions barely held together by the sentimental melodies and nostalgic feelings associated with Old Vienna. Only *Wir machen Musik* (We Make Music, 1942) and a few other musical comedies from the early 1940s experimented with more contemporary styles, including the kind of modified jazz tunes officially denounced as 'degenerate music'. Through the enlistment of various acoustic media, musical styles, and auditory pleasures, film music and film sound functioned as an integral part of the soundscapes of nationalism that connected the 1920s to the 1930s and that linked newer definitions of community to established practices of sonic envelopment reaching back to Richard Wagner and his notion of *Gesamtkunstwerk* (Vogelsang 1990, Currid 2005).

A generic hybrid, the revue film offered an attractive alternative to the Hollywood musical through elaborate song-and-dance numbers that celebrated the creative individual (Belach 1979). In accordance with the prohibition on erotic imagery, even La Jana's semi-nude dances in *Es leuchten die Sterne* (The Stars Are Shining, 1938) and *Stern von Rio* (Star of Rio, 1940) inspired primarily comparisons to classical sculpture and racial health. Hollywood influences were most pronounced in revue films that, like *Wir tanzen um die Welt* (We Dance around the World, 1939), used a professional dancing troupe to create ornamental choreographies suggestive of Busby Berkeley but also eerily reminiscent of the fascist mass ornament, given the clear preference for military costumes and formations. Famous for her Hungarian Puszta charm, the inexhaustible Marika Rökk personified the revue film's peculiar mixture of optimism and aggression. Working under the direction of her husband, Georg Jacoby, Rökk appeared in *Hallo Janine!* (Hello Janine!, 1939), *Kora Terry* (1940), and *Die Frau meiner Träume* (The Woman of My Dreams, 1944). The Rökk character frequently had to choose between the freedom of artistic lifestyles and the security of love and marriage – a typical female dilemma that only underscored the symptomatic function of the modern career woman as the object of aggressive and transgressive fantasies.

With renunciation firmly established as a central motif in the romantic comedy and the revue film, only the melodrama was able to explore more ambiguous perspectives on gender and sexuality. During the early 1930s, melodramatic modes became part of the elusive mixture of sentimentality, melancholy, and irony cultivated by Forst in critically acclaimed Vienna films such as *Maskerade* (Masquerade, 1934). Taking on more tragic tones in the late 1930s, the genre's heightened emotionality and formal stylisation found perfect expression in the collaboration of Detlef Sierck and Zarah Leander and took a decidedly propagandistic turn with Leander's appearance in the wartime love story of *Die grosse Liebe*. The narrative constellations are always the same: guilt and redemption, love and renunciation, transgression and punishment. The visual representation of female desire and its constant companion, female suffering, relies extensively on close-ups, dramatic lighting, claustrophobic settings, and theatrical costumes. The increased production of melodramas during the last years confirms their primary psychological function of translating human suffering into aesthetic terms and of making pleasurable the delay of personal gratification. Yet even as the late melodramas contributed to the preservation of the status quo by presenting women as victims, they at least recognised the strengths borne of victimisation and turned them into an instrument of spectatorial identification and masochistic pleasure.

As the ostensible guardians of morality and protectors of life, women played a key role in the enforcement of normative gender roles and the production of idealised images of nation and community. However, instead of promoting official policies directly, the filmic representation of women functioned primarily in a complementary and supplementary fashion. Maternal melodramas such as *Mutterliebe* (Mother Love, 1939), with Käthe Dorsch as the woman who sacrifices everything for her children, remained the exception in a popular cinema that, despite the official cult of motherhood, treated women above all as objects of male desire. Modern femininity remained identified with an alluring but also threatening sexuality that had to be either punished or contained, with the clichéd opposition between virgin and whore an integral part of the filmic articulation of that ambivalence. The definition of appropriate female characteristics, attitudes, and behaviours were constantly adjusted to the changing demands of the times, especially during the war years. Throughout the 1930s, working women of the kind depicted in the misogynistic *Frau am Steuer* (Woman at the Wheel, 1939) usually inspired mockery and ridicule. Labour shortages in the war economy and the difficulties of the home front introduced more positive portrayals of working women like the competent female math teacher in *Unser Fräulein Doktor* (Our Miss PhD, 1940). Concerns about low birth rates stood behind the idealisation of family life in romantic comedies such as *Paradies der Junggesellen* (Paradise of Bachelors, 1939) and allowed even for sympathetic portrayals of unwed mothers. At the same time, the deprivations of war gave rise to exaggerated images of female sensuality, elegance, and self-possession that, in combination with an excessive attention to costumes and set design, can be interpreted only as compensatory fantasies addressed to an all-female audience. Associated with alternately fetishistic, voyeuristic, and narcissistic scenarios, the provocation on modern femininity could never be resolved, not even through the melodrama's imbalance between strong women and weak men or the rustic comedy's precarious compromise between male indolence and female competence (Bechdolf 1992, Traudisch 1993, Fox 2000, O'Brien 2003).

In sharp contrast to the psychological interiors explored in the female-dominated comedies and melodramas, the male-dominated action adventures thrived on movement, speed, tension, suspense, and individual initiative. Their cult of heroic masculinity often revolved around technological innovations, scientific discoveries, and territorial conquests. Remarkable athletic stunts and action scenes verging on slapstick distinguished the countless Harry Piel films in the style of *Der unmögliche Herr Pitt* (The Impossible Mr Pitt, 1938). More dramatic films featured Hans Albers who, with his blond hair, blue eyes, sharp profile, and tall muscular frame, came to personify the Aryan ideal of masculinity. Albers played modern adventurers in the futuristic thriller *Gold* (1934) and the seafaring drama *Unter heissem Himmel* (Under Hot Skies, 1936) and conquered new lands in the Canadian Western *Wasser für Canitoga* (Water for Canitoga, 1939). The genre's foreign locations and exotic settings provided an imaginary landscape for the articulation of nationalist and colonialist fantasies. Yet these narratives also opened up another space, unmarked by social conventions and political objectives, that facilitated temporary escapes from the ordinary and the familiar.

Closely connected to Nazi fantasies about *Volk* and *Heimat*, the *Heimatfilm* has often been described as the most appropriate genre for promoting a romanticised, but completely depoliticised view of country and nation. Quintessential German landscapes such as the Bavarian Alps, the Rhine valley, and the Baltic coast provided idyllic images of rural life where simple peasants lived in complete harmony with nature; but these settings also allowed for a return of the repressed in the form of mythological figures and archaic traditions. The genre's strong regionalist orientation, especially in the folk dramas and rustic comedies made in Bavaria, sometimes prevented co-optation by the categories of racial theory and the ideology of 'blood and soil'. Featuring well-known folk actors, these comedies stubbornly insisted on their own brand of provincialism and xenophobia. The validation of traditional Bavarian culture, including as a counter-design to the Prussian dominance, found expression in numerous Ganghofer adaptations, rustic farces with Karl Valentin and Liesl Karlstadt, and humorous vignettes of traditional village life by the prolific actor/director Joe Stöckel. More dramatic treatments gave rise to rare instances of local resistance and anti-capitalist struggle in the style of *Der ewige Quell* (The Eternal Spring, 1940) and *Der ewige Klang* (The Eternal Sound, 1943). By contrast, the association of *Heimat* with female strength and independence inspired yet another screen adaptation of *Die Geierwally* (The Vulture Wally, 1940), this time with Heidemarie Hatheyer. Throughout the period, the genre's emphasis on regional culture offered a welcome alternative to the highly politicised idea of nation that, in the historical films, culminated in the equation of Prussia with the Reich and that, in the state-commissioned films, reduced the abstract idea of *Volk* to that of race, rather than of ethnicity. Because of these elusive connections, the genre frequently associated with the Nazi cult of blood and soil also became the one with the most problematic relationship to political definitions of national community, a fact that contributed to the ascendancy of the *Heimatfilm* as the most popular genre during the Adenauer era.

Ultimately, the cinema of the Third Reich remained a work of compromise, serving the contradictory functions of entertainment and propaganda, satisfying different interests and tastes, and accommodating both the populist arguments and politicised attitudes considered essential to its functioning within the Nazi culture industry. No matter whether genres continued in the tradition of Weimar cinema and imitated Hollywood formulas or whether styles specifically marked as German fed into the National Socialist propaganda machine, ideology remained an integral part of representational practices, from the way subjectivities were positioned within social and political structures to the way they partook in the remaking of national identity through filmic images and narratives. While the Propaganda Ministry determined the conditions of production and consumption until 1945, the enduring popularity of these films, as evidenced by their regular appearance on television, has made them an integral part of German cinema. Starting such ongoing patterns of adaptation and reception, the so-called *Überläuferfilme* (literally, deserter films), film projects started before 1945 but only completed after 1945, first brought into relief the continuities and ruptures that constituted the cinema of the Third Reich and that, to this day, make it a perfect historical case study for general reflections on cinema, nation, and ideology.

4

POSTWAR CINEMA 1945–61

Until recently, most writings on postwar cinema – which almost always means West German cinema – followed the logic of those on Third Reich cinema by insisting on an interrelation between ideological contamination and aesthetic deprivation. Behind the seemingly harmless, trivial subject matter, went the argument, most of the films made after 1945 promoted conservative social values and political beliefs, while perpetuating the view of cinema as a popular diversion without artistic ambition or critical potential. Audiences were characterised as addicted to trivial entertainment, uninterested in art or politics, and above all determined to forget the traumas of the past and ignore the problems of the present. Described in these negative terms, postwar cinema seemed to consist of little more than the displaced fears, desires, and resentments that gave rise to the culture of amnesia after the Second World War, that sustained the project of economic and social reconstruction during the Adenauer era, and that ultimately prevented a truly new beginning for German cinema after 1945 (Schnurre 1950, Schmieding 1961, Hembus 1981).

These alleged failures of postwar cinema allowed the directors of the Young German Cinema to announce cinema's own *Stunde Null* (Zero Hour) in the 1962 Oberhausen Manifesto and to embark on a decade of experimentation, innovation, and provocation. In an Oedipal gesture that reveals as much about the dire state of cinema internationally as about the depth of generational conflict in postwar Europe, the Oberhausen signatories polemically declared 'Papa's cinema is dead'. In film histories, their blanket dismissal of an entire period of film-making has produced many blind spots, resulted in misinterpretations, and obscured the continuities of German cinema. Influenced by the aesthetic vision of the New Waves and a literature-inspired notion of authorship, West German scholars have either dismissed popular cinema between 1945 and 1962 as unworthy of critical attention or limited themselves to socio-psychological readings in the larger context of postwar history and society. West and East German accounts of early DEFA cinema have tended to focus on a few prestige productions while ignoring most efforts at creating a socialist popular cinema. Under the influence of the Cold War, the many movements across German–German borders and the strong stylistic and thematic similarities in what still can be described as one German cinema have been ignored in favour of two separate accounts of the cinema of the Federal Republic of Germany (FRG) and the German Democratic Republic (GDR).

Since unification, several comparative studies have opened up new perspectives on the intensively reciprocal relationship between East and West German cinema. Scholars have drawn attention to the dialogic structures and strange mirroring effects that informed much political reporting in documentary film and television and that characterised the antagonistic relationship between the two German states during the Cold War (Steinle 2003, *Film History* 18.1 (2006)). Other studies have focused on the similarities and differences between East and West German representations of the Third Reich and the Holocaust (Schmitt-Sasse 1993, Kannapin 2005). Such comparative approaches have also highlighted the profound differences in the treatment of important social issues such as women's rights and workers' rights (Strauß 1996, Moldenhauer and Zimmermann 2000). Last but not least, the ongoing reassessment of German cinema as part of a decidedly European popular cinema has brought into sharper relief the many connections between West and East postwar cinema and other European cinemas, beginning with the special case of Austrian cinema (Fritz 1984, Dassanowsky 2005).

The prevailing tendencies in West German and Anglo-American scholarship have produced two critical paradigms in the assessment of postwar cinema. Several popular accounts have placed the films made after 1945 within the formal and thematic traditions of Ufa and tried to explain the remarkable continuities through apologetic, nostalgic, and even ironic rereadings (Seidl 1987, Jary 1993, Bertram 1998). Scholarly approaches committed to ideology critique have analysed the close connection between conventional genre cinema and the reconstruction of the film industry under the conditions of late capitalism (Kreimeier 1973). Others have used feature films to gain access to the psychological mechanisms and unconscious processes identified with *Vergangenheitsbewältigung*, the difficult process of coming to terms with the Nazi past (Becker and Schöll 1995, Greffrath 1995).

Already the restorative tendencies of the 1980s brought greater awareness of the institutional struggles and ideological contradictions that informed the period of economic and cultural reconstruction and enlisted cinema in the remapping of national identity across the divided landscapes of the Cold War (Berger et al. 1989, Westermann 1990). Yet above all, it was German reunification that, since the 1990s, has drawn attention to the continuities of popular cinema before and after 1945 and forced scholars to look more closely at the correspondences between filmic practices in East and West Germany from the 1950s to the 1980s. Less obvious connections beyond the politicised East–West divide have finally come into view: between the few prestige productions and the mass of undistinguished adaptations, serials, and remakes; between an unabashedly popular cinema of petty-bourgeois tastes and sensibilities and a highly politicised film culture of bans, boycotts, and controversies; and between an intense interest in international film movements and an equally strong commitment to high culture traditions, including music and literature. On the basis of such an expanded definition of film culture, scholars have also begun to discuss postwar cinema's contribution to the process of economic and political reconstruction and to map more long-term changes in the cultural landscape after 1945 brought about by the Americanisation of postwar Europe and frequently identified with the making of the postwar generation (Fehrenbach 1995, Fisher 2007, Davidson and Hake 2007, Kapczynski 2008).

The reconstruction of the film industry

Like the forced co-ordination in 1933, the reconstruction of the film industry after 1945 must be described in terms of historical ruptures and continuities. The first and foremost goal of the Allies after German capitulation was the dismantling of the hierarchically organised, monopolistic structure of production facilities, distribution companies, and motion-picture theatres overseen by the Propaganda Ministry. In the beginning, the Allies fought over Ufa studio's technological equipment and film archives as valuable war booty but soon more urgent political considerations and long-term objectives prevailed. The Information Control Division (ICD) of the US Army approached the rebuilding of cinema as a project of political re-education. Mandatory screenings of *Die Todesmühlen* (Death Mills, 1945), about the Nazi death camps, confronted Germans with the truth about the Holocaust. American newsreels such as 'Welt im Film' reported extensively on Nazi atrocities and, later, the Nuremberg war tribunals, but did so with less and less emphasis on German collective guilt; similar tendencies can be found in the Soviet-made newsreel 'Der Augenzeuge'. Initially, the military governments tried to reach a workable compromise among the demands of political re-education, economic recovery, and cultural renewal. Moving away from an openly political approach to mass manipulation, the Allies soon recognised that they could promote their political and economic interests far more effectively through the film imports, including the many re-releases, that soon established competing spheres of influence: old Hollywood films in the Western sectors and the classics of Stalinist cinema in the Eastern sector. Under these conditions, the difficult assignment taken on by the Ufa Liquidation Committee (ULC) after the passing of the Lex Ufi in 1949 would not be completed until 1953. And because of persistent legal problems, Bavaria studio was turned over to private ownership only in 1956.

Immediately after the war, all new releases and projects required licensing in their respective zones, and film professionals had to undergo a process of de-Nazification (for example, through questionnaires). The difficulties during this early phase of re-education were acknowledged in *Die goldene Pest* (The Golden Plague, 1954), a realistic depiction of the pervasiveness of German moral and spiritual corruption. The Allied Commission reviewed all German films produced between 1933 and 1945 and established a list of films banned from public exhibition – primarily state-commissioned films – that remains binding to this day (Kelson 1996). At the same time, the Allies agreed on the importance of feature films in stabilising the political situation after 1945; hence their willingness to re-release many presumably harmless entertainment films from the Nazi period. Soon, however, disagreements erupted between the Soviets and the Western Allies over the future of the German film industry and the role of cinema in the project of ideological reconstruction. The Western Allies treated films as an integral part of modern mass culture and the institutionalised division, associated with film, radio, television, and the press, between profit and art, entertainment and information, and fantasy and reality. Accordingly, the reorganisation of public broadcasting followed the model of the BBC in the greater commitment to local, regional, and national culture and the insistence on radio as an important forum of public debate in a liberal democracy. Yet in the rebuilding of the film industry, the Hollywood model prevailed, resulting both in the adoption of many industry practices, including the practice of block booking and blind booking, and in the eventual domination of the distribution section by US companies.

In the Eastern zone, the Soviets quickly instituted their model of centralised production and state control. Founded on 17 May 1946, the Deutsche Film AG (DEFA) became the first German film studio to resume production in the old Ufa studios in Berlin-Babelsberg after receiving a licence from the Soviets for its first project, *Die Mörder sind unter uns* (Murderers Are among Us, 1946), featuring the young Hildegard Knef. The director Wolfgang Staudte belonged to the Filmaktiv, a group of exiled writers and directors – most of them communists – that included Friedrich Wolf, Kurt Maetzig, and Gerhard Lamprecht. In their efforts to rebuild German cinema in the spirit of democratic anti-fascism, they were actively supported by Sergei Tulpanov, the cultural officer of the Soviet Military Administration in Germany (SMAD). The foremost goal of DEFA was, on the one hand, to move beyond the filmic traditions of Ufa and the political legacies of the Third Reich and, on the other, to enlist Germany's 'positive cultural legacy' in the making of a socialist society. Committed to humanistic principles, the DEFA founders set out to make films that, through their new stories and different characters, countered the forces of nationalism and militarism and promoted the principles of international co-operation (Mückenberger and Jordan 1994).

The beginning of the Cold War complicated the rebuilding of the German film industry in the West and highlighted the different interests of the Information Control Division (ICD) as the propaganda branch of the US Army, the Motion Picture Export Association (MPEA), which represented the Hollywood majors, and the struggling new German-owned production and distribution companies (Hauser 1989). The initial spirit of peaceful co-operation among the four Allies gave way to the ideological divisions that emerged with the Berlin Blockade in 1948 and the founding in 1949 of the two German states, the Federal Republic of Germany and the German Democratic Republic. These developments had a significant impact on the rebuilding of the industry according to market principles in the West, especially after the currency reform in 1948. But they also contributed to DEFA's transformation into a state-owned company with close ties to the Socialist Unity Party (SED) and direct involvement in the political 'freezes' and 'thaws' of the 1950s. None the less, in the transitional period between the first and second phase of the German division (i.e., between 1949 and 1962), the daily business of film production and the mundane rituals of moviegoing especially in the divided city of Berlin still allowed for many border crossings in the literal and figurative sense.

While East German cinema got an early start through the establishment of a centralised production and distribution system, the rebuilding of the film industry in West Germany required very different organisational structures. This process began in 1949 with the founding of the SPIO, the main professional organisation of the West German film industry. The SPIO instituted the Freiwillige Selbstkontrolle (FSK, Voluntary Self Control) as an agency of self-censorship modelled after the MPPDA and its catalogue of taboo subjects – nudity, vulgarity, blasphemy, and so forth. After 1951, the Filmbewertungsstelle (FBS, Film Evaluation Board) established a system of economic support – and not infrequently political censorship – based on many of the same quality distinctions (for example, 'artistically valuable') used already during the Third Reich. The Federal government created specific agencies for controlling the production and exhibition of films in accordance with two overarching principles: the country's integration into the Western alliance and the enlistment of all mass media in the fight against communism. While guaranteeing the freedom of speech, the Federal Film Law allowed for the banning of all films that promoted nationalist, racist, or communist ideas or that posed a serious threat to national security. Working under the auspices of the Ministry of Finance, the new Interministerial Film Commission oversaw the import of all films from Eastern Bloc countries. Of the more than a thousand films examined during the 1950s, 90 were banned because of allegedly communist tendencies.

As the first to be licensed by the Western Allies in the late 1940s, distribution companies supplemented the small offerings of German productions by showing old Hollywood films, including many B pictures, as well as a large number of Ufa films reclassified as harmless entertainment. With the resources and networks to finance new films and bring these films into the theatres, distributors became the true power brokers of the postwar industry. Ilse Kubaschewski's Gloria-Verleih, known as the main purveyor of *Schnulzen* (weepies), played a key role in providing postwar audiences with the desired mixture of melodrama, romance, and fantasy. Surpassing smaller companies such as Herzog- und Schorcht-Verleih, Constantin under Wandfried Bartels in the late 1950s established itself as the second-largest distributor, and eventually also an important producer, by specialising in inexpensive but commercially successful film serials.

In the early years, film companies confronted a number of seemingly insurmountable problems: bombed-out and plundered production facilities; lack of basic materials and resources; and technical and creative personnel unaccustomed to working under makeshift conditions. In the American zone, production soon resumed in the Bavaria studios in Munich-Geiselgasteig, and it was in Munich that Harald Braun started the Neue Deutsche Filmgesellschaft (NDF). Contributing to the trend toward decentralisation, the short-lived Junge Film-Union built its production facilities in Lower Saxony (Stettner 1992). Also in the British zone, Rolf Thiele and Hans Abich established a small centre of film-making in Göttingen with Filmaufbau AG, a studio known for exploring controversial subject matter.

Led by Gyula Trebitsch and Walter Koppel, two strong producer personalities, the Hamburg-based Real-Film emerged as one of the most successful studios of the 1950s. Known for colourful revue films as well as gritty realist dramas, Real-Film built a reputation for quality films by working with skilled professionals such as the cameraman Heinz Pehlke and set designer Herbert Kirchhoff (Winkler and von Rauch 2001).

In the western sectors of Berlin, a number of smaller companies took advantage of the high concentration of talent in the former capital. They included Kurt Ulrich's Berolina-Film, which launched the successful *Heimatfilm* wave of the 1950s, and Horst Wendlandt's Rialto-Film, which started the popular Edgar Wallace and Karl May series in the early 1960s. The most important Berlin-based company was Artur Brauner's Central Cinema Company (CCC), whose mixture of literary adaptations, social dramas, and lifestyle comedies embodied the postwar compromise between cultural ambition and economic growth (Dillmann-Kühn 1990). The head of CCC played a key role in bringing back the exiled directors Lang and Siodmak and in producing several 'Jewish films' about the Holocaust. Balancing the demands of art and commerce, Brauner experimented repeatedly with European co-productions featuring international stars such as Maria Schell, Lilli Palmer, and Curd Jürgens. Other companies also tried to build up their European presence but, with the exception of the German–French co-production *Lola Montez* (1955), directed by Max Ophüls, few achieved critical recognition or established longer-lasting connections.

With the financial help of the American Marshall Plan and under the conservative government of Chancellor Konrad Adenauer, the Federal Republic in the 1950s embarked on the ambitious project that has become known as the *Wirtschafts-wunder* (Economic Miracle). These years of economic and political normalisation were characterised by an almost desperate focus on improving basic living conditions, a compulsive insistence on conformity in social and cultural matters, and a pronounced unwillingness on the part of the political and cultural institutions to deal with the Third Reich and the Holocaust. The ethos of the Economic Miracle gave rise to an affluent middle-class society in which an American-style materialism coexisted with the conservative Christian values advanced by the leading political party, the Christian Democrats (CDU). In the same way that the narrow-mindedness of this emerging *Wohlstandsgesellschaft* (affluent society) functioned as a protection against past trauma, the insistence on social conventions helped to ward off uncomfortable questions about collective guilt and responsibility. Growing prosperity brought a return to the conservative family values shared by the educated bourgeoisie and the nouveau riche, whereas the anxieties caused by increased social mobility and widespread dislocation found compensation in the promises of self-realisation through consumerism.

The first films made after 1945 still acknowledged the forces of history through the images of destroyed cities, occupying armies, displaced populations, and other postwar phenomena such as the black-market economy. Eventually, these realities disappeared from filmic representation and public consciousness. They were replaced by a depoliticised genre cinema that depended on the complete absorption of politics into the apolitical discourses of humanism but that also made possible the inevitable return of ideology in the form of a fanatical anti-communism. This process began with the so-called *Trümmerfilme* (rubble films), which used locations in the rubble of the cities, and stories of the victims of war and mass bombings, to come to terms with the nation's political defeat and wartime destruction; these films were among the first to give expression to German guilt and suffering (Shandley 2001). Enlisting expressionist styles and melodramatic effects in the rebirth of a defeated nation, *Die Mörder sind unter uns* not only introduced the main elements of the rubble genre but also outlined the position of depoliticised humanism that, often with an existentialist bent, characterised subsequent representations of the Third Reich and its postwar legacies. The film's ending captures the new public morality in its famous closing lines: 'We don't have the right to judge but we have the duty to bring charges and demand atonement in the name of those millions murdered innocently.'

Unlike foreign rubble films such as Roberto Rossellini's neo-realist *Germania anno zero* (Germany Zero Hour, 1947) and Billy Wilder's *A Foreign Affair* (1949), German productions rarely took full advantage of the destroyed cityscapes and their extraordinary spatial and visual effects. Only Lamprecht's *Irgendwo in Berlin* (Somewhere in Berlin, 1946), another DEFA production, relied on extensive documentary footage and on-location shooting to imagine a future committed to socialist humanism. The majority of rubble films took a more metaphorical approach to mise-en-scène and enlisted the rubble in the creation of psychological landscapes. Typically, in these films, a man returns home from the war and, confronted with the ubiquitous signs of destruction, is forced to make sense of his personal tragedy and, by extension, that of the German people. The ruins attest to the desired erasure of the past and the promise of a new beginning captured in the myth of Zero Hour. But in providing the appropriate setting for feelings of shame, guilt, doubt, hope, and renewal, the ruins also visualise the crisis of postwar masculinity and set the stage for the prescribed return to traditional family values.

In accordance with these restorative strategies, the rubble films offered individual solutions that extricated their protagonists from the burdens of history. Accordingly, *Zwischen gestern und morgen* (Between Yesterday and Tomorrow, 1947) and . . . *und über uns der Himmel* (And the Sky Above Us, 1947) rely on family problems and generational conflicts to work through the traumas of nation. Through the choice of a car as the narrator, *In jenen Tagen* (In Those Days, 1947) avoids the question of agency altogether and presents its seven owners as innocent victims of circumstance. Offering a welcome break from such approaches, R. A. Stemmle's *Berliner Ballade* (Berlin Ballad, 1948) enlists the proverbial 'Otto Normalverbraucher' (i.e., the average German) in a satirical commentary on the compromises of everyday life during the years of housing crises and food shortages. To what degree satire and farce served to justify a position of non-involvement can be seen in Käutner's post-lapsarian fantasy in *Der Apfel ist ab* (The Original Sin, 1948) and its promotion of Christian values as a protection against the threat of totalitarianism. On the other hand, the over-ambitious attempt to portray the existential crisis of the lost war generation through a combination of expressionist, surrealist, and realist styles contributed to the critical failure of Liebeneiner's Borchert adaptation, *Liebe 47* (Love '47, 1949).

All rubble films partook in the difficult process of working through and coming to terms with the past, a process that included professions of self-hatred as well as attempts at self-exculpation. Despite the bitter pronouncements on the inhumanity of the world, the essential goodness of humankind was always reaffirmed in the end. By shifting the focus from collective to individual experiences, these stories served psychological functions not dissimilar to the process of secondary revision; hence the frequent use of flashbacks and voice-over narration. The scenarios of victimisation protected postwar audiences against feelings of guilt; yet the cathartic effects also gave them hope and confidence for the future. Through the emphasis on human suffering, the main protagonists could be portrayed as innocent, and history be explained through the forces of fate. The bracketing of politics made possible the vindication of ordinary Germans as victims of anonymous forces, while distracting attention from the real victims and perpetrators, the Jews and the Nazis. Alternately melancholy, cynical, resigned, or defiantly optimistic in tone, the rubble films remained haunted by the experience of war and defeat and the loss of nation and homeland. That explains why this unwelcome intrusion of reality in the form of new themes and styles was short-lived; the rubble film disappeared from the screen as early as 1948. Soon film-makers in the West returned to the generic formulas perfected during the Third Reich and adapted its conciliatory narratives and affirmative effects to the very different demands of postwar audiences.

The product of such continuities, the career of Helmut Käutner, as well as of several other well-known directors, can be described as symptomatic of the difficult relationship between film and politics in postwar cinema as a whole (Jacobsen and Prinzler 1992). Having been associated with 'inner emigration' (i.e. those who remained in Germany after 1933 but expressed their opposition quietly or obliquely), Käutner after 1945 continued to translate political conflicts into the heightened terms of (unfulfilled) romantic love, first in *Die letzte Brücke* (The Last Bridge, 1954), about Bosnian partisans during the Second World War, and then in *Himmel ohne Sterne* (Sky Without Stars, 1955), one of the earliest films to acknowledge the existence of the zonal border. The director's neutral stance on the German division earned him sharp criticism from conservatives, but also guaranteed him regular screenings by the anti-communist 'Committee for an Inseparable Germany'. During the 1950s, Käutner developed a reputation for commercially viable and technically accomplished films; some critics attacked his work for being conciliatory and defeatist. His famous adaptation of Carl Zuckmayer's *Des Teufels General* (The Devil's General, 1955) offered West German audiences a positive self-image based on the cult of heroic masculinity. By contrast, the much more innovative *Ludwig II., Glanz und Elend eines Königs* (Ludwig II, 1955) explored the decadent cult of beauty and madness around the master builder of Neuschwanstein through filmic sensibilities that otherwise had no place in the conformist atmosphere of the 1950s.

In the same way that Käutner's oeuvre draws attention to the problematic legacies of the 1940s, Wolfgang Staudte's career after 1945 bears witness to the many movements between East and West in a society polarised by the Cold War (Orbanz 1977). Staudte frequently experienced censorship problems, first in his work for DEFA, and later with several films made in the Federal Republic. Already during the making of *Die Mörder sind unter uns*, the Soviets demanded that the director should change the original ending because it allegedly advocated violence as a means of political justice; after all, the film's original title had been 'The Man I Am Going to Kill'. His next film about working-class life in the Berlin of the 1930s and 1940s, *Rotation* (1949), focused on an apolitical 'little man' torn between the desire for personal happiness and the necessity of political action. Here, too, Staudte had to change several scenes because their pacifist message was deemed inappropriate in light of the beginning remilitarisation of the GDR. His most famous film from the period, *Der Untertan* (The Subject, 1951), based on the eponymous Heinrich Mann novel, traces the prehistory of National Socialism back to the authoritarian structures of Wilhelmine Germany; this film was banned in the Federal Republic. Working on both sides of the Cold War divide, Staudte was repeatedly attacked for formalist tendencies in the East and denounced as a communist in the West. Although the director refused to sign a statement of political loyalty for a West German producer, he ended up spending the latter part of the decade as an 'apolitical moralist' in the affirmative culture of the Adenauer era. Even after the critical success of *Rosen für den Staatsanwalt* (Roses for the Prosecutor, 1959), a political satire about the postwar career of a high-ranking Nazi officer, this last 'all-German' film director found himself increasingly marginalised among a new generation of apolitical directors led by the prolific and versatile Kurt Hoffmann.

Responsible for more than 20 films during the period under discussion, Hoffmann provided good middle-brow entertainment for the entire family (Tornow 1990). He found his ideal actress in the young Liselotte Pulver, whose perky, energetic personality carried such audience favourites as the Hungarian summer romance *Ich denke oft an Piroschka* (I Often Think of Piroschka, 1955). In most Hoffmann films, the world of make-believe offers a convenient way of playing with different identities, of testing new behaviours and attitudes, but always within the confines of private desires and with a clear view toward a harmonious integration of differences. When not indulging his preference for bygone eras, rural settings, or vacation stories, Hoffmann occasionally took on more ambitious literary projects. Yet in the same way that sentimentality diffused the humour in his comedies, it softened the ironic or satirical elements in his adaptations of Thomas Mann's *Bekenntnisse des Hochstaplers Felix Krull* (Confessions of Felix Krull, 1957) and Friedrich Dürrenmatt's *Die Ehe des Herrn Mississippi* (The Marriage of Mr Mississippi, 1961). The most political of his films, *Wir Wunderkinder* (Aren't We Wonderful?, 1958), reconstructs the German past through the different biographies

100

of two school friends, a decent 'little man' and an opportunistic social climber. But even here, Hoffmann's insistence on the modesty of desires and the virtue of contentment ends up validating the petty-bourgeois mentality that fuelled the Economic Miracle in the West. Not surprisingly, this film became a welcome target for cabaret artist Wolfgang Neuss when he made *Wir Kellerkinder* (We Cellar Children, 1960), a bitter parody of the entire discourse of *Vergangenheitsbewältigung*.

In terms of aesthetic and ideological commitments, no director could be more removed from Hoffmann than Slatan Dudow. His films for the DEFA studio continued in the Weimar tradition of social realist film-making, with the early Russian films and Brecht's theory of epic theatre as the main reference points. Known for his precise typologies of class, the Bulgarian director asserted his modernist sensibilities through montage and music as effective means of defamiliarisation and critical analysis; he repeatedly worked with Hanns Eisler. His name is often linked to the so-called *Aufbaufilme* (reconstruction films) and their highly didactic stories about the difficulties of building a socialist society. In *Unser täglich Brot* (Our Daily Bread, 1949), for instance, Dudow shows how a group of workers take ownership of a bombed-out factory in East Berlin. In the process, they overcome their petty-bourgeois attitudes and learn the socialist virtues of responsibility, solidarity, and commitment to the collective. *Frauenschicksale* (Women's Fates, 1952) introduces several women searching for love and marriage in a divided Berlin to demonstrate the superiority of socialism even in personal matters. Again the happy ending confirms the collective as the true agent of history and fiction. Dudow applied his critical method to the recent past when he made *Stärker als die Nacht* (Stronger than the Night, 1954), one of the few DEFA films about the communist resistance during the Third Reich and an important contribution to the filmic history of the German working-class movement.

The DEFA director Kurt Maetzig is regarded as one of the leading proponents of the so-called *Chronikfilm* (chronicle film) of the 1950s. As a kind of socialist epic, the chronicle films with their multi-generational narratives and didactic histories played an important role in the formation of early GDR identity. The director's first film, *Ehe im Schatten* (Marriage in the Shadows, 1947), still used melodramatic elements to make the all-important connection between political oppression and human suffering; its tragic story of a German-Jewish couple during the Third Reich was inspired by the fate of the actor Joachim Gottschalk. Focusing on one working-class family, *Die Buntkarierten* (Chequered Sheets, 1949) followed three generations of women from the 1920s to the 1940s to chronicle their gradual political awakening after difficult personal experiences. Similar elements can be found in *Roman einer jungen Ehe* (Story of a Young Couple, 1952) where the marital problems of two actors serve to illustrate the ideological struggles in a divided postwar Berlin. In accordance with the early rhetoric of anti-fascism, Maetzig holds his apolitical or opportunistic protagonists partly responsible for the rise of fascism and, by extension, anti-communism. The same sense of moral judgement and personal accountability informs *Der Rat der Götter* (Council of the

Gods, 1950), which reconstructs the history of IG Farben during the Third Reich – the company provided Zyklon B for the gas chambers – through the conflicting perspectives of workers, scientists, managers, and industrialists.

In the late 1950s, Maetzig abandoned such nuanced reflections on individual and collective guilt for more straightforward propagandistic messages. Shot in the obligatory socialist realist style, his grand socialist epics often concentrated on the revolutionary working class and its heroic achievements. Set in the largely rural Mecklenburg province, the two-part chronicle *Schlösser und Katen* (Palaces and Huts, 1957), introduced a large cast of characters to document the nationalisation and collectivisation of agriculture in what might be called the DEFA version of the *Heimatfilm*. The state-commissioned, two-part *Ernst Thälmann – Sohn seiner Klasse* (Ernst Thälmann, Son of His Class, 1954) and *Führer seiner Klasse* (Ernst Thälmann, Leader of His Class, 1955), with Günther Simon in the title role, used an idealised biography of the famous communist party leader to legitimise the existence of the German Democratic Republic; the formal debts to the genius films from the Third Reich are undeniable. An incredible success, the Thälmann films were seen by millions of spectators, often as part of official party events.

The only other DEFA director whose work was closely linked to the building of the socialist state is Konrad Wolf; he spent the Nazi years in the Soviet Union. A formal innovator, political artist, and influential public figure, Wolf is generally regarded as the most important DEFA director (Georgi and Hoff 1990, Jacobsen and Aurich 2005). His divided identities as a communist and a German Jew made him particularly susceptible to the contradictions within postwar German society. Especially his films from the 1950s to the 1970s played a key role in the revisions of German history and identity and offered complex filmic reflections on the project of socialism both in its utopian and its 'real-existent' forms (Silberman 1990). In his contribution to the chronicle film, Wolf often chose a female protagonist to present the GDR as part of the continuities and discontinuities of German history. Thus *Lissy* (1957) revisits the rise of National Socialism through a young woman from Berlin's working class forced to confront the consequences of her political apathy. The formally remarkable *Sonnensucher* (Sun Seekers, 1958/1972), about life and work in a uranium mine in Wismut, portrays a motley group of hard-working miners, ruthless adventurers, free-spirited women, and idealistic party cadres with a surprising sensitivity toward individual differences; the indirect references to the Soviet nuclear programme were one of the reasons of that film's censorship problems.

Wolf's tendency toward stylisation is most apparent in two films that directly address German anti-Semitism and the Holocaust. At the end of a decade closely and problematically associated with the universalist rhetoric of (socialist) humanism, the director affirmed his commitment to anti-fascism precisely by insisting on the specificity of the Jewish experience. In the first German film about the Holocaust, the German–Bulgarian co-production *Sterne* (Stars, 1959), Wolf tells of the encounter between a Jewish woman on her way to Auschwitz and a German officer who, in an ending removed from the West German version, ends up joining the

Bulgarian partisans. Then, adapting a play by his father Friedrich Wolf, *Professor Mamlock* (1961), the director uses the figure of a respected physician from Weimar Berlin's upper middle class to uncover the shortcomings of traditional bourgeois notions of class in understanding the historical roots of anti-Semitism.

Rewriting history, forging new identities

Käutner, Staudte, Dudow, Hoffmann, and Wolf participated in the corresponding processes of nation-building that, in the FRG and the GDR, hinged on a critical assessment of the Third Reich and the Holocaust. This representational project involved two equally important steps: the construction of a historical trajectory that gave political legitimacy to the new regimes in East and West Germany; and the interpretation of these opposing political and economic systems as radical departures from National Socialism and its problematic legacies. Bourgeois individualism, economic liberalism, and social conservatism made up the new identity of the Federal Republic; the primacy of the collective and the necessity of struggle and sacrifice that of the German Democratic Republic. The West subsumed the Holocaust under the category of crimes against humanity, whereas the East incorporated the Jewish question into the grand narratives of anti-fascism. In both cases, the creation of a postwar identity involved a complicated process of inclusion and exclusion, acceptance and denial.

The broader implications can be seen in the filmic reflections on the history of anti-Semitism. In the DEFA film *Affäre Blum* (The Affair Blum, 1948), Erich Engel reconstructed a famous murder trial against a Magdeburg Jewish businessman to show the rise of anti-Semitism in the Weimar Republic. *Morituri* (1948), Artur Brauner and Eugen York's rarely seen film about the inmates in a concentration camp in Poland, drew on personal experiences by the CCC producer. Beyond the depiction of real historical figures and events, a lingering sense of trauma could also be found in various registers of the uncanny that spoke to specifically German sensibilities. The underlying mechanisms of displacement and denial and the inevitable return of the repressed inspired two highly allegorical films about haunted ships and passengers lost at sea, the mystery drama *Epilog: Das Geheimis der 'Orplid'* (Epilogue, 1950) and the Traven adaptation *Das Totenschiff* (Ship of the Dead, 1959).

The few exiles and émigrés who returned to Germany after the war addressed the legacies of anti-Semitism in direct and indirect ways. In *Der Ruf* (The Last Illusion, 1949), Fritz Kortner played an exiled university professor who resumed teaching only to face anti-Semitic sentiments among his students and colleagues. When addressing the traumas of the past, rémigré directors frequently turned to the psychological motif of doubling to explore the relationship between victim and perpetrator or to uncover the defensive mechanisms behind hypocrisy, indifference, and cowardice. Thus in the highly allegorical *Der Verlorene* (The Lost One, 1951), Peter Lorre uses the familiar Dr Jekyll and Mr Hyde motif to conjure up the emotional reality of a nation ravaged by guilt. In the noirish thriller *Nachts wenn der Teufel kam* (The Devil Strikes at Night, 1957) and the political satire *Mein Schulfreund* (My School Chum, 1960), Robert Siodmak focuses on the representatives of law and order who, before and after 1945, protected their interests through all means necessary. Indicative of the broad resonances of the German dilemma within postwar Europe, even Rossellini returned to make *Angst / Paura* (Fear, 1954), an expressionist melodrama about a happy marriage almost destroyed by a dark secret from the past.

The early West German films about the Third Reich were an integral part of the project of political stabilisation and economic recovery. Not surprisingly, film-makers frequently used the recent past to give legitimacy to the Adenauer government in the antagonistic terms of the Cold War. Thus the category of the 'purely human' gave rise to a number of fictional oppositions introduced to distinguish the Federal Republic from the Third Reich and the East German regime. The purported rejection of ideology was achieved through the insistence on individual rather than public morality and a preference for ethical rather than political categories of historical explanation. With the Nazis depicted either as classic villains with a neurotic lust for power or as mere executioners of anonymous power structures, melodramatic forms proved most effective in demonising the Third Reich as an aberration of German history. Only a sharp distinction between the regime and the nation, between the political leadership and ordinary people, could exculpate the Germans as the victims of history: reason enough for many film-makers to abandon earlier notions of collective guilt for the celebration of individual heroism.

These ideological realignments stood behind the enormous commercial success of two films that focused on resistance among the military leadership, *Des Teufels General*, about the famous aviator Ernst Udet, and *Canaris* (Canaris Master Spy, 1954), about the well-known admiral and head of counter intelligence. Both films identified the opposition to the Nazi regime with two military men whose actions in the films are guided by an old-fashioned sense of duty and honour. Perhaps even more important, the directors relied heavily on the famous Ufa style in their chamber play approach to mise-en-scène and their treatment of Curd Jürgens and O. E. Hasse, respectively, as icons of German masculinity. Two other films about the failed assassination attempt on Hitler by the resistance group around Count Stauffenberg, Pabst's *Es geschah am 20. Juli* (It Happened on July 20th, 1955), and Falk Harnack's *Der 20. Juli* (The Plot to Assassinate Hitler, 1955), took a more restrained approach by combining pseudo-documentary scenes with theatrical dialogues and interiors; both films failed at the box office.

In the beginning, West German audiences had to turn to war films made in Hollywood, including Henry Hathaway's *The Desert Fox* (1951) and Anatole Litvak's *Decision before Dawn* (1951), to satisfy their desire for images of male heroism unburdened by political ideologies. With the creation of the Federal Armed Forces and the country's entry into NATO in 1955, the Second World War emerged as an important subject matter in genres ranging from historical dramas to military comedies – and that in sharp contrast to DEFA cinema where the war remained an absent referent, absorbed into the discourse of anti-fascism (Heimann

2000). Paul May's trilogy *08/15* (1954–55), based on the best-seller by Hans Hellmut Kirst, set the tone by romanticising military life in the barracks and at the front, all the while paying lip service to pacifist themes. In *Hunde, wollt ihr ewig leben?* (Dogs, Do You Want to Live Forever?, 1959), about the historical battle in the encircled city of Stalingrad, Frank Wisbar (or Wysbar) affirmed the military code of honour and the value of discipline; references to National Socialism remained conspicuously absent. Similarly, *Nacht fiel über Gotenhafen* (Night Fell over Gotenhafen, 1959), about the sinking of the *Wilhelm Gustloff* during the last days of the war, presented the war only as a human tragedy. In light of such revisionist tendencies, the submarine warfare depicted in *U47 – Kapitänleutnant Prien* (U47 – Lieutenant Commander Prien, 1958) proved ideally suited to separate the sheer excitement of battle from the political motives behind German territorial aggression. In *Der Arzt von Stalingrad* (The Doctor of Stalingrad, 1958), the brutal treatment of German soldiers in a Soviet POW camp offered an opportunity even for some anti-Russian stereotypes and anti-Soviet remarks. In such an atmosphere of remilitarisation, *Kinder, Mütter und ein General* (Children, Mothers, and a General, 1955), a well-intended anti-war parable told from the female perspective, failed to find a receptive audience – in sharp contrast to the sympathetic group of young boys depicted in Bernhard Wicki's internationally acclaimed anti-war drama *Die Brücke* (The Bridge, 1959).

The Cold War resonated in postwar film-making on all levels: in the visual and narrative representation of German history, including of the early years of reconstruction; in the official positions on the German–German division and their impact on institutional practices; and in the highly politicised circumstances under which some films were made, shown, and reviewed. In the Federal Republic, the emphatic rejection of all political ideologies in the name of humanist liberalism established anti-communism as the unifying doctrine that at once legitimated the retreat from politics in cultural life and made possible its return in the form of a Manichean worldview. The institutional structures established by the Allies – initially as part of the de-Nazification process – proved very useful in campaigns against alleged communists that either took the form of secret investigations against producers Koppel and Trebitsch or resulted in the denial of federal subsidies to directors working on both sides of the Iron Curtain. The Federal government's policy on DEFA films changed from a general ban in the early 1950s to a more selective approach that remained in place throughout the 1960s. Despite the political polemics about the threat of communism, few West German films ever addressed the profound impact of the Cold War on public and private life. With the exception of the sentimental love story of *Himmel ohne Sterne* and Will Tremper's sensationalist adaptation of a story from *Stern* magazine, *Flucht nach Berlin* (Escape to Berlin, 1961), West German film-makers avoided direct references to the border with East Germany. By contrast, the DEFA studio provided ready-made arguments for the German division in a series of cheaply made espionage films that depicted the decadent, corrupt capitalist West as a serious threat to the new socialist state and world peace.

Aside from the few films that thematised the German division, the continuities and discontinuities of German cinema in East and West found privileged expression in the enduring preference for literary adaptations. The dramas of Gerhart Hauptmann inspired two Maria Schell vehicles, Siodmak's *Die Ratten* (The Rats, 1955) and Staudte's *Rose Bernd* (The Sins of Rose Bernd, 1957), which applied the naturalist notion of milieu to the difficult situation of refugees from the East. At DEFA, the critical engagement with the legacies of nineteenth-century realism prompted Artur Pohl to rewrite the *nouveau-riche* narrative of Fontane's *Frau Jenny Treibel* in the class-conscious terms of *Corinna Schmidt* (1951). With its adaptation of *Der Untertan*, the DEFA studio in 1951 claimed Heinrich Mann for a Lukácsian tradition of critical realism. Meanwhile Thomas Mann inspired West German director Harald Braun to use the happy marriage between German culture and American money depicted in *Königliche Hoheit* (His Royal Highness, 1953) as a thinly veiled comment on postwar Americanisation. Competing claims on the illustrious Mann family also stood behind the first failed attempt at a German–German co-production; that project was later completed in the West as a conventional two-part star vehicle, *Buddenbrooks* (The Buddenbrooks, 1959).

The classics of German literature allowed DEFA directors both to claim the traditions of humanism for socialism and, on some occasions, to express marginalised sensibilities through new interpretations of well-known texts. Thus *Wozzeck* (1947), based on the Georg Büchner play, allowed its director to visualise experiences of individual oppression through starkly expressionist styles. The adaptation of *Das Fräulein von Scuderi* (Mademoiselle de Scuderi, 1955), a story by E. T. A. Hoffmann, explored the attractions of the uncanny with little regard for the ongoing debates about the problematic legacies of German romanticism. Taking a more conventional approach, later adaptations of Schiller's *Kabale und Liebe* (Intrigue and Love, 1959) and Lessing's *Minna von Barnhelm* (1962) complied fully with the cultural ambitions of the regime by appropriating the values of bourgeois emancipation for the new socialist ethics and morality. Similar intentions stood behind big-budget DEFA opera films such as *Die lustigen Weiber von Windsor* (The Merry Wives of Windsor, 1950) and *Zar und Zimmermann* (The Tsar and the Carpenter, 1956) that sought to reconcile petty-bourgeois tastes and high-culture pretensions by adding some populist flourishes.

The politicisation of cinema in the East

Bringing together young and old communist elites, DEFA was founded in the spirit of democratic anti-fascism: to aid in the project of reconstruction, to disseminate the ideals of humanism, and to fight the dangers of nationalism and militarism. Thematically, most prestige productions from the 1940s and 1950s responded to two interrelated sets of concerns, the role of film in the building of a socialist society and the meaning of anti-fascism in defining past and present. Both agendas gave rise to rarely told stories from the working class that showed the conditions of industrial labour and the history of labour struggles, a tradition developed further

106

in numerous later documentaries (Moldenhauer and Zimmermann 2000). New approaches to characterisation and audience identification (for example, through collective agency) conveyed the studio's obligation to the existing socialist state and showed its commitment to Marxist ideology, including the notion of class struggle. Central to the self-understanding of early DEFA, the meaning of anti-fascism as a foundational myth and its relevance to GDR identity underwent significant changes during the 1950s before deteriorating to an obligatory gesture in the official narratives of historical legitimacy (Kannapin 1997).

Even though the self-declared 'all-German' studio defined film production in political rather than economic terms, it still had to deal with disappointing attendance figures; often DEFA films were simply not as popular as foreign films. Throughout the 1950s, the studio suffered from low annual productivity rates, with individual projects slowed down by long pre-production meetings, repeated script revisions, and last-minute re-shooting of scenes. In several cases, the studio withdrew films from distribution before or right after their public release. Adding to these problems, the Babelsberg studio had to respond to the conflicting requests by party officials and cultural bureaucrats and accommodate their changing views of film-making under socialism. Official positions on culture and entertainment wavered between half-hearted attempts at liberalisation and demonstrations of hard-line dogmatism (Schittly 2002). Initially, communications between the DEFA and the SED were facilitated by the Central Cultural Commission. It ceded power to the DEFA Commission in 1950 and the State Committee for Film Questions in 1952. After 1954, all DEFA-related questions were handled by the Ministry of Culture. The infamous Hauptverwaltung Film (HV Film), which consisted of studio representatives, party members, and cultural functionaries, was respon-sible for the approval of all new film projects. During this period of ideological realignment, DEFA in 1953 became a state-owned company that united the various branches of the industry in one hierarchical structure. Separate units were created for feature film production, newsreels, documentaries, scientific films and children's films, as well as for animation and dubbing. Film distribution from then on was handled through Progress Film-Verleih and, in export matters, through the DEFA-Aussenhandel (Export Office).

The first phase in the subsequent freezes and thaws lasted approximately until 1953. It began with the 1947 First German Film Authors Conference, which called for a national cinema united beyond zonal boundaries. While eager to take on contemporary subject matter, DEFA film-makers initially showed little interest in developing a new filmic language and instead relied heavily on the familiar Ufa aesthetic. As a result, the early reconstruction films utilised established generic conventions to address the most pressing problems in the GDR such as the collectivisation in agriculture in *Freies Land* (Free Land, 1946) or the restructuring of the mining industry in *Grube Morgenrot* (The 'Dawn' Mine, 1948). Even the first film about the early working-class movement, Pohl's *Die Unbesiegbaren* (The Invincible, 1953), took an individual, psychological approach to the representation of proletarian subjectivity and collective agency. Soon after the founding of the

107

GDR, functionaries began to demand a more active contribution from the DEFA studio to the first five-year plan and, more generally, the building of socialist society. There was growing pressure on film-makers to support the fight against US cultural imperialism and to resist the influence of cosmopolitanism and what was now denounced as bourgeois psychologism. With these arguments, the infamous formalism debate of the early 1950s put an end to the kind of aesthetic experiments still found in the rubble films. Until the 1960s, modernist elements survived only in the form of expressionist or neorealist styles and the almost noirish sensibility in some of the later espionage films.

The official debates about realism, history, and class consciousness were based on the doctrine of socialist realism, which combined Georg Lukács's formal requirements for the realist novel with the ideological fervour of the Stalinist epics from the 1930s. With realism in the cinema no longer defined as a mere reflection of what exists but a representation of what should be, narrative films were called upon to support social change through typical stories and average characters, effective mechanisms of identification and idealisation, and through what later critics denounced as overly schematic dramatic conflicts and glaringly obvious didactic intentions. Yet more often than not, the anticipatory power of the aesthetic and the utopian potential of art were instrumentalised in the name of politics and ideology. The doctrine of socialist realism gave rise to a national cinema presumably sustained by, and accountable to, the socialist collective; responsive to the questions and debates most relevant to GDR society; and committed to the fight against monopoly capitalism and imperialist aggression. As the first casualty of the new dogmatism, Harnack's *Das Beil von Wandsbek* (The Axe of Wandsbek, 1951) was withdrawn from cinemas because of its complex treatment of Nazi supporters and fellow travellers.

Soon thereafter, the so-called New Course in 1953 ushered in a brief period of intellectual and artistic freedom. The death of Stalin, public mistrust of the party leadership, and dissatisfaction among workers contributed to the deep crisis of legitimisation that culminated in the uprising of 17 June. Reversing earlier pronouncements on the socialist realist style that produced the famous Thälmann epics, the Central Committee now called for more films about everyday problems such as love, marriage, and family life. This tentative opening toward the question of subjectivity and the social construction of identity, experience, and history brought greater possibilities for experimenting with modernist aesthetic sensibilities, recognising different filmic traditions, and even articulating dissenting political views. The new films from Poland, including Andrzej Wajda's *Kanal* (1957) and *Popiol i diament* (Ashes and Diamonds, 1958), inspired younger DEFA directors such as Kurt Jung-Alsen in *Betrogen bis zum jüngsten Tag* (Duped till Doomsday, 1957) to question the heroic anti-fascist narrative and emphasise the disillusionment of the war generation. In rewriting the Third Reich from an individual perspective, film-makers also learned to validate the contribution of children and women as the subjects of a very different history and historiography. Heiner Carow's *Sie nannten ihn Amigo* (They Called Him Amigo, 1959), about

108

a working-class boy sent to a concentration camp, and Frank Beyer's first DEFA film, *Zwei Mütter* (Two Mothers, 1957), about a French child caught between two mothers, were part of this larger project of rewriting history from below.

Meanwhile, the growing attention to the problem of rebellious youth – and its implicit challenge to traditional notions of class struggle – posed a serious challenge to the official emphasis on unity and harmony. Maetzig's *Vergesst mir meine Traudel nicht* (Don't Forget My Traudel, 1957), with Eva-Maria Hagen in the title role, still used the experiences of a rebellious young woman to promote the new ethos of social responsibility. Yet already the Berlin films by Gerhard Klein and Wolfgang Kohlhaase, *Alarm im Zirkus* (Alarm at the Circus, 1954), *Eine Berliner Romanze* (A Berlin Romance, 1956), and *Berlin – Ecke Schönhauser* (Berlin – Schönhauser Corner, 1957), initiated a more direct engagement with American youth culture and its symbolic function in the countercultural rituals shared by urban youths in East and West Berlin. Engaging with the quotidian on a thematic and aesthetic level, these three films proved as provocative in their contemporary subject matter as in their documentary, neo-realist style. Not surprisingly, both *Eine Berliner Romanze* and *Berlin – Ecke Schönhauser* encountered difficulties prior to their official release.

As part of the paradoxical logic behind the freezes and thaws of the Cold War and in response to persistent economic difficulties and social problems in the transition to a fully socialist society, the partial relaxing and tentative opening of official positions after 1953 eventually made necessary a re-ideologisation of culture in the late 1950s. After the Hungarian uprising and Khrushchev's denunciation of Stalin in 1956, dissatisfaction and dissent spread throughout the Eastern bloc countries. These developments prompted the SED leadership to re-examine their cultural policies and to look more closely at the new DEFA films in production. Determined to return to the dogma of socialist realism, the 1958 Film Conference organised by the Ministry of Culture evoked the spectre of revisionism to justify their punitive campaigns against those film-makers still committed to the project of a critical realism. Even highly respected directors such as Wolf and Maetzig had to go through humiliating exercises of self-criticism because they had acknowledged the continued existence of alienation in a non-capitalist society. Opposed to any exploration of estrangement or disaffection through innovative narrative and visual techniques, the party leadership insisted on filmic approaches that showed the ideal conditions in the workers' and peasants' state. They also demanded more heroic accounts of the historical struggles of the working class in the style of *Thomas Müntzer* (1956), about the religious leader of the Reformation, and *Tilman Riemenschneider* (1958), about the great medieval wood sculptor: two films that applied the hard lessons of the past to the present times.

DEFA's low productivity rate, inefficient use of resources, and lack of skilled personnel left studio heads no choice but to rely heavily on employees commuting from West Berlin. At times, they constituted 70 per cent of all full-time employees. Those with a considerable Ufa past included the veteran director Arthur Maria Rabenalt and prolific screenwriter Georg C. Klaren, the first chief dramaturge at

DEFA. Even silent star Henny Porten appeared in two historical dramas made in Babelsberg, including *Das Fräulein von Scuderi*. Among the better-known actors with screen credits in East and West were Werner Peters, since his appearance in *Der Untertan* the quintessential authoritarian subject, and Wolfgang Kieling who, like Peters, specialised in evil Germans, including in Hitchcock's 1966 Cold War thriller *Torn Curtain*. In response to the party's increasingly isolationist stance, DEFA made a concerted effort to dismiss employees who still commuted from the West. Yet the hope that the absence of such 'alien' elements would give the studio a more coherent artistic profile remained unfulfilled.

Since DEFA failed to produce enough feature films for the domestic market, motion-picture theatres depended heavily on imports, especially from the Federal Republic. Almost 70 such films were released in the GDR during the 1950s. Audiences in East and West often enjoyed the same hit films but significant differences in taste could also be noted. Musical comedies and romantic comedies proved extremely popular in the East – but not the sentimental *Heimatfilme*. In many ways, the West German imports fulfilled an entertainment function comparable to that of Hollywood films in Western Europe; the growing interest in art films was satisfied by French and Italian productions. Foreign films critical of the Federal Republic or, like *Salt of the Earth* (1954), of the United States often failed at the box office despite aggressive marketing campaigns. New releases from other East European countries, including innovative Polish and Czech films and Soviet prestige productions such as *Letyat zhuravli* (The Cranes Are Flying, 1957), could always be seen in the capital. In the smaller cities, film audiences preferred the conventional genre films produced by Bavaria, Rialto, and CCC. Especially the inexpensive border cinemas in West Berlin attracted scores of East Berlin youth with their sensationalist fare. By the late 1950s, these uncontrollable movements within the former German capital and citizen's exposure to Western television in many border regions were considered a serious problem by the party leadership. To counteract such outside influences, DEFA made a concerted effort to promote the so-called *Auftragsfilme* (commissioned films), short documentaries about social and political topics, and to make feature and non-feature films an integral part of party seminars, national anniversaries, and public events. However, these measures still did not prevent audiences from flocking to the melodramas of Harlan, Rabenalt, and others.

Searching for a popular or populist socialist cinema, DEFA studio officials already experimented with their own version of genre cinema in the midst of the heated debates about socialist realism and critical realism. As early as the late 1940s, filmmakers appropriated familiar formulas to address everyday problems and contemporary sensibilities. Known as *Gegenwartsfilme* (contemporary dramas), these films placed a strong emphasis on the private sphere but maintained their socialist perspective by showing the present as part of a historical continuum and depicting the individual as part of a larger collective. In the more successful contributions, narrative and visual pleasures absorbed the underlying political rhetoric. Conceived in that vein, *Razzia* (Raid, 1947) used the black market setting for a cautionary

110

tale about crime and money, and the melodramatic *Strassenbekanntschaft* (Street Acquaintances, 1948) by the unjustly forgotten Peter Pewas introduced a sexually liberated woman to educate audiences about sexually transmitted diseases. Predictable story lines and simple modes of identification prevailed in countless stories of everyday life under socialism, especially those set in the modern workplace. Thus *Modell Bianka* (Model Bianca, 1951) extolled the socialist work ethic in the collectivised clothing manufacture through the lens of romantic comedy, whereas *Sommerliebe* (Summer Love, 1955) relied on the same narrative devices to show young workers in love at their favourite vacation resorts on the Baltic coast.

In the pursuit of socialist entertainment, the DEFA studio experimented with a wide range of genres and styles, from expressionistic melodramas such as *Leuchtfeuer* (The Beacon, 1954) and realistic milieu studies such as *Alter Kahn und junge Liebe* (Old Barge and Young Love, 1957) to colourful revue films in the manner of *Silvesterpunsch* (New Year's Eve Punch, 1960). As in the West, film-makers referenced the classical Ufa style not only in the approach to camerawork, lighting, and mise-en-scène but also in the filmic production of emotions, pleasures, and identity effects. To give only two examples, the postwar preference for melo-dramas produced *Genesung* (Recovery, 1956) about a young man who practises medicine without a licence, a dilemma known from similar West German medical dramas. Reminiscent of the society dramas made before 1945, *Ehesache Lorenz* (Lorenz vs. Lorenz, 1959) approached the problems of a dual-career couple by presenting the neglected husband in the throes of an adulterous affair. Meanwhile, extreme forms of socialist kitsch could be found in the cheaply produced dramas and comedies that idealised workers' heroic efforts to reach their annual quotas in the nationalised industries and romanticised farmers' struggles to deal with petty jealousies on the collectivised farms.

The DEFA studio achieved its greatest successes with fairytale films that were critically acclaimed and enthusiastically received throughout Eastern Europe (König et al. 1996). The production of children's films increased the studio's export business and led to fruitful collaborations with other East European studios during the 1960s and with GDR television throughout the 1970s. In the same way that the West German adaptations of Kästner's famous children's book *Das doppelte Lottchen* (Two Times Lotte, 1950) and *Emil und die Detektive* (Emil and the Detectives, 1954) served the affirmation of traditional family values and con-servative social policies, the East German children's films enlisted German folk traditions in pressing political agendas. The various genres subsumed under the category extended from adaptations of popular folk tales and literary fairytales, including Brothers Grimm fairytales such as Rumpelstiltskin, the Golden Goose, Snow White, and Mother Hulda, to contemporary stories with youthful pro-tagonists and child-specific subject matter. The creative contribution of set designers and effects specialists such as Ernst Kunstmann proved essential to the genre's exploration of different realities and its experimentation with magical effects. Especially the fairytale films provided a utopian space for examining the social and economic conditions that prevented the fulfilment of true human needs and desires.

Accordingly, *Das kalte Herz* (The Cold Heart, 1950), the first DEFA colour film, offered an alternative to the capitalist money economy in the ethos of Protestantism and, by extension, socialism. *Die Geschichte vom kleinen Muck* (The Story of Little Mook, 1953), another Wilhelm Hauff adaptation, similarly pitted the superficial rewards of money and power against the real wealth found in friendship. And in *Das singende klingende Bäumchen* (The Singing Ringing Tree, 1957), the re-education of a beautiful but spoiled princess played by youth idol Christel Bodenstein allowed young audiences to appreciate the importance of work as a humanising force.

The depoliticisation of cinema in the West

A number of oppositions or, rather, triangulations defined postwar cinema on both sides of the border: German high culture, American mass culture, and socialist working-class culture; conventional entertainment films, cultural prestige productions, and political propaganda films; and, to move to aesthetic categories, the inherent tension among generic traditions, realist tendencies, and modernist elements. Political considerations permeated every aspect of cinema culture in the GDR, from the debates about socialist realism to the calls for more films about everyday life. By contrast, an ostensible absence of political perspectives characterised the self-representation of cinema in the FRG, from the promotion of new genres and stars to the official decisions about film imports and public subsidies. For that reason, the filmic fantasies produced in the West have most frequently been examined as a reflection of, and reaction to, the new ethos of hard work and social mobility; the return to conservative family values and a repressive sexual morality; and society's enthusiastic embrace of modern mass media and consumer goods. None the less, this highly circumscribed fantasy world still provided a framework for the articulation both of difficult questions related to gender, class, and national identity and of suppressed feelings of guilt, shame, and mourning.

In the Western zones, the cinema after 1945 supported and often mirrored the aggressive self-transformation of postwar culture and society. Catering to a growing audience, the number of cinemas increased from one thousand in 1945 to three thousand by the end of the decade. In 1956, an attendance record was reached with the average West German going to the movies 15.6 times a year. After that, numbers declined steadily from 817 million tickets sold in 1956 to 443 million tickets sold in 1962. Popular tastes during these years tended toward conventional fare; the four-sector city of Berlin, with its more cosmopolitan tastes, remained an exception. After the box-office failure of the rubble films and the anti-war films, film producers found their stories in either the distant past or the immediate present. Especially popular were so-called *Zeitfilme* or *Problemfilme* (contemporary dramas) that presented social problems in accordance with established narrative conventions and filmic styles. Questionnaires from the period suggest that audiences wanted to see familiar stories, characters, and settings; aesthetic experimentation was generally frowned upon. Producers accommodated their demands by emphasising the continuities with pre-1945 genre cinema. In 1950 even a mediocre Leander melodrama like *Gabriela* was more successful than the innovative British noir classic *The Third Man*. Dispelling widespread fears about postwar Americanisation and Coca-Colonisation, audiences also continued to prefer domestic productions, with the typical ratio of two-thirds German films to one-third foreign films changing only gradually until Hollywood provided half of all imports by the end of the decade. Foreign films gained wider acceptance with the improvement of dubbing technologies at specialised dubbing studios in Berlin and Munich. This form of *eindeutschen* (literally, Germanising) not only made the foreign more familiar, and hence more palatable, but also allowed for subtle forms of censorship, as evidenced by the changed dialogue lines in *Casablanca*, *Notorious*, and other foreign films with presumably anti-German subject matter.

The star phenomenon played a key role in organising audience preferences and channelling patterns of identification. The old Ufa stars satisfied widespread nostalgia for a period instantly rewritten as the 'good old times' and provided the familiar emotional registers: obnoxious cheerfulness in the case of supporting actors such as Grete Weiser, Hans Moser, and Theo Lingen and more subdued, melancholy tones in the case of former mega-stars such as Albers, Birgel, and Leander. Old Ufa directors Viktor Tourjansky and Veit Harlan continued to indulge their penchant for melodramatic excess, thus belying the critical diagnosis of postwar culture as a culture of emotional sterility. In less noticeable ways, the famous Ufa style continued to set artistic and technical standards through the expert work of the cinematographers Friedl Behn-Grund and Konstantin Irmen-Tschet, set designers Otto Hunte and Hermann Warm, screenwriters Bobby E. Lüthge and Herbert Reinecker, and composers Werner Richard Heymann and Herbert Windt. From the use of light and space to framing and editing, from the conception of characters to the nuances of dialogue and film sound, these consummate professionals established the conditions that, more than any new or daring topics, suggested an unbroken tradition in terms of aesthetic preferences, cultural mentalities, and social dispositions.

The political implications of such continuities were most apparent in genres that, like the genius film, had been enlisted in the discourses of nationalism during the Third Reich. Satisfying the audience's regressive yearning for patriarchal figures, new biographical films in the style of *Sauerbruch – das war mein Leben* (Sauerbruch – This Was My Life, 1954) presented the famous surgeon Ferdinand Sauerbruch as a quintessential German, that is, as someone capable of saving, rather than destroying lives – a not insignificant achievement in the aftermath of the Holocaust. Similarly, *Made in Germany* (1957) used the first director of the Zeiss optical company Ernst von Abbe to enlist the historical marriage of science and technology in the founding myths of German industries after the Second World War. In interweaving past and present, these biographical films provided a model of individual accomplishment that found its real-life versions in entrepreneurial figures such as Max Grundig, Rudolf August Oetker, and Josef Neckermann, the true heroes of the Economic Miracle. Extending these authoritarian fantasies into the political realm, the conservative thrust of the genre found its most telling expression in *Stresemann* (1957), a biographical film about the liberal Weimar politician that revisited the problems of the first German republic from the perspective of Adenauer's politics of stability and compromise.

The historical subject matter satisfied the nostalgia for strong leader figures and for visions of nation and empire unburdened by questions of guilt; some of the more escapist productions even provided harmless fantasies of individual resistance and antiauthoritarian struggle. The Biedermeier period emerged as the preferred setting for folkloric tales about noble robbers and rebels in the style of *Das Wirtshaus im Spessart* (The Spessart Inn, 1958) and *Der Schinderhannes* (Schinderhannes, 1958). The Wilhelmine era inspired the kind of inconsequential critiques of German militarism and authoritarianism offered by Heinz Rühmann in star vehicles such as *Der Hauptmann von Köpenick* (The Captain of Köpenick, 1956), *Der eiserne Gustav* (Iron Gustav, 1958), and, in a different context, *Der brave Soldat Schweijk* (The Good Soldier Schweijk, 1960). The Austro-Hungarian Empire provided a colourful backdrop for many classic film operettas, whereas Prussian history inspired more solemn lessons on duty, honour, and sacrifice. Aided by elaborate costumes and spectacular settings, the romantic identification of dynastic power with female beauty and youth gave rise to unabashedly positive images of empire. From Ruth Leuwerik as *Königin Luise* (Queen Luise, 1957), beloved for her dignified behaviour during the Napoleonic Wars, to Elisabeth of Bavaria who, in the incarnation of young Romy Schneider, gained cult-like status after the phenomenal success of the Austrian-made *Sissi* trilogy (1955–57), the simultaneously erotic, sentimental, and allegorical figures of female power made possible the rediscovery of nation as a category of positive emotional investments. Whereas Leuwerik performed that function through her wifely qualities, the over-identification of star and role in the case of *Sissi*, one of the few postwar films still regularly shown on German television, was achieved through the archetype of the good daughter who alone could restore the reputation of Germans at home and abroad; the clever marketing of commodity tie-ins like Romy fashion dolls also contributed greatly to the *Sissi* phenomenon.

The fantasy of the fairytale princess projected by Schneider, just like the independent young women portrayed by Knef, remained the exception during a decade in which most actresses were loved and admired for their maternal, wifely, or sisterly qualities. The cinema of the Economic Miracle is best known for the kind of hard-working wives and mothers portrayed by Luise Ulrich in *Vergiss die Liebe nicht* (Don't Forget Love, 1953) and *Eine Frau von heute* (A Woman of Today, 1954) and the attractive married career women depicted by Heidemarie Hatheyer as a physician in *Liebe ohne Illusion* (Love Without Illusion, 1955). One of the most popular actresses of the 1950s, Ruth Leuwerik repeatedly played highly capable, but non-threatening modern women, whether as the mayor of a small town in *Die ideale Frau* (The Ideal Woman, 1959) or as the Ufa star Renate Müller in *Liebling der Götter* (Sweetheart of the Gods, 1960). Her pragmatic approach to marital problems and family crises, combined with traditional female qualities such as modesty and charm, made Leuwerik a favourite among women audiences. By contrast, Maria Schell's penchant for melodrama allowed her fans to identify with a rarely expressed female masochism and submissive eroticism; like Knef, she enjoyed a brief international career.

Leuwerik and Schell were frequently cast vis-à-vis Dieter Borsche and O. W. Fischer, the two leading male stars of the decade. These famous screen couples paired strong or overpowering women with weak and indecisive men, thus responding to growing concerns about the crisis of postwar masculinity. Whereas the rigid Borsche personified an old-fashioned masculinity unsettled by new demands for flexibility, the charming Fischer displayed a narcissistic nervousness suggestive of more contemporary sensibilities. Borsche appeared in several *Arztfilme* (medical dramas) that used the ethos of the medical profession to offer a counter-image to the pervasive materialism of postwar society. The wave started with the Christian symbolism of death, faith, and the power of healing that gave credence to the critically acclaimed *Nachtwache* (Keepers of the Night, 1949). However, religion soon gave way to a highly gendered aesthetic of sacrifice and guilt. Thus the drama of life and death in two later Borsche films, *Dr. Holl* (Affairs of Dr Holl, 1951) and *Die grosse Versuchung* (The Great Temptation, 1952), ended up confirming not Christian values, as the Catholic and Protestant Churches had hoped, but the necessity of male authority in the public and the private sphere (Reuter 1997).

The return to traditional gender roles and sexual stereotypes during the 1950s began with the *Heimatfilm* and the successful pairing of a young Sonja Ziemann with the much older Rudolf Prack. It continued in the stereotypical casting of Curd Jürgens as the brooding hero, Nadja Tiller as the seductress, Liselotte Pulver as the *ingénue*, Lilli Palmer as the lady, and Paul Hubschmid as the ladies' man. Offscreen, film magazines such as *Film-Revue*, *Film und Frau*, and *Star-Revue* catered to a growing interest in luxury, gossip, and the cult of celebrity. Stars and starlets provided an interested readership with the inevitable scandals caused by affairs, divorces, and suicides, but the annual society galas and charity events organised by a struggling film industry failed to reproduce the glamour of the prewar years. It was left to a younger generation of actors and actresses to reintroduce 1950s audiences to the explosive mixture of liberated sexuality and social rebellion last seen in the films of the 1920s. Appearing in the new youth films, sultry blonde Karin Baal in *Die junge Sünderin* (The Young Sinner, 1960) and sunny boy Hardy Krüger in *Zwei unter Millionen* (Two among Millions, 1961) personified a more contemporary and decidedly American version of stardom. With their petty-bourgeois or working-class origins, their characters openly acknowledged and took advantage of the relationship between sex, money, and power. Their rebellious spirit sometimes led these new screen idols into the world of petty crime depicted for the first time in *Die Halbstarken* (The Hooligans, 1956), the cult film that established Horst Buchholz as the German James Dean. Yet whereas the young men were usually strengthened by such experiences, the androgynous child women made fashionable by Sabine Sinjen in the cautionary tale of *Die Frühreifen* (Precocious

Youth, 1957) invariably sought refuge in the safety of the family or an early marriage. The depiction of female delinquents in the starkly realist *Mädchen hinter Gittern* (Girls behind Bars, 1949) remained an exception.

Searching for more authentic forms of self-expression, the critical youth films derived their subversive qualities from the polemical opposition between German high culture and American popular culture and the radical break with the burdens of German history. Their stories, characters, and settings introduced a rebellious young generation distinguished through specific consumer objects such as blue jeans, leather jackets, and motor scooters and brought together by particular idioms, tastes, attitudes, and recreational activities. After *Die Halbstarken*, the team of Georg Tressler and Will Tremper extended their inquiries into contemporary sexual mores and social rituals to the young workers from *Endstation Liebe* (Last Stop Love, 1958). The preference for black-and-white cinematography and on-location shooting in these early youth films betrayed the strong influence of Hollywood classics such as *On the Waterfront* (1954) and *Rebel without a Cause* (1955). Yet what the films with James Dean or Marlon Brando celebrated as a desire for new experiences, for intensity as a value in itself, the highly didactic German versions presented as a dangerous threat to bourgeois moral values and conventions. Consequently, the disruptive potential of youth had to be contained, and its vital energies controlled through the social contract between the generations. Whereas the youth films from the East aimed at the characters' reintegration into the socialist collective, those from the West resolved their dramatic conflicts through the return to traditional gender roles and normative heterosexuality.

Many films about contemporary problems were surprisingly open about the crisis of patriarchy, the threat of female sexuality, and the corrosive effect of youth rebellion. Beginning with the rubble films, contemporary dramas repeatedly used the attractions of the big city to translate the tensions within postwar society into the heightened registers of emerging or alternative sexualities. From the criminal activities depicted in the noirish *Nachts auf den Strassen* (Nights on the Road, 1952) to the illicit world of drug addiction, prostitution, and homosexuality conjured up in Harlan's exploitative *Liebe kann wie Gift sein* (Love Can Be like Poison, 1958) and *Anders als du und ich* (Different from You and Me, 1957), the narrative strategies and emotional effects always are the same. On the surface, these films diagnose the crisis of postwar society by focusing on the dysfunctional middle-class family and its neglected young sons and daughters. However, the voyeuristic fixation on individual transgressions precludes any real insights into the complicated dynamics of the personal and the political. Whereas the rubble films and the chronicle films still articulated the contradictions of German history and society through archetypal family conflicts, the contemporary dramas reduced everything to the libidinal force of lust, greed, anger, and resentment. Central to all conflicts was the aggressive pursuit of individual pleasure and self-interest; but behind the sensationalism and the flirtation with decadence always lurked a fundamental unwillingness to confront the obsessively diagnosed loss of value and meaning and what it stood for: the unresolved legacies of the Third Reich and the Holocaust.

Three film scandals from the decade confirm the centrality of gender and sexuality to the unstable power relations that propelled the melodramatic imagination but also coloured the public perception of rebellious youth. Forst's *Die Sünderin* (The Story of a Sinner, 1951) with Hildegard Knef was the first case. Because the film dealt with female nudity and extramarital sex, Catholic bishops called for a nationwide boycott. Tapping into more fundamental fears about the disappearance of all distinctions between the respectable middle-class woman and the emancipated woman with her own needs and desires, *Das Mädchen Rosemarie* (The Girl Rosemarie, 1958), with Nadja Tiller in the title role, used the unresolved murder case of the prostitute Rosemarie Nitribitt to show the close link between woman's economic independence and sexual liberation. The hostile reactions to the film drew attention to the system of double standards unifying the simultaneously prudish and lascivious society of the Economic Miracle. In such an atmosphere, the nude female body provided a projection screen also for the new/old phantasmagoria of race that stood behind the surprise success of *Liane, das Mädchen aus dem Urwald* (Liane, Jungle Goddess, 1956), a German version of the Tarzan story with blonde newcomer Marion Michael.

The power of social convention and the need for individual conformity found foremost expression in the *Gesellschaftsfilm* (society drama) that, like the Weimar chamber play film, used intimate settings and internal conflicts to show the difficulty of reconciling private and public identities; this genre appealed primarily to older audiences. Confirming the diagnosis of an amnesiac postwar culture, these melodramatic stories frequently revolved around double or false identities and concerned dangerous secrets or resentments from the past. The individual rituals of self-denial and self-repression and the ongoing adjustments to new social and economic pressures usually took place in an upper-middle-class milieu reminiscent of the nineteenth-century literary salon. Entertained by the obligatory token artists and intellectuals, the old and new social elites came together in these luxurious settings to reaffirm the rituals of postwar public life, including its subtle regimes of exclusion. Unable to move beyond these increasingly self-contained and artificial worlds, convoluted society dramas such as *Ein Herz spielt falsch* (A Heart's Foul Play, 1953), *Teufel in Seide* (Devil in Silk, 1956), and *Herz ohne Gnade* (Heart Without Mercy, 1958) eventually disappeared from the screen – only to be revived in the context of television, the preferred new form of entertainment during the 1960s and 1970s for lower-class families, housewives, and senior citizens.

Consequently, it was left to the *Heimatfilm* and its spatial scenarios to provide the kind of cross-cultural and cross-generational encounters necessary for rejuvenating genre cinema and for envisioning a postwar identity for the Federal Republic. The apolitical notion of homeland promised an alternative both to the compromised history of German nationalism and to the contested status of the two Germanys during the Cold War. Beginning with Hans Deppe's *Schwarzwaldmädel* (Black Forest Girl, 1950) and *Grün ist die Heide* (The Heather Is Green,

1951), two famous Ziemann–Prack vehicles, the *Heimatfilme* emerged as the commercially most successful product of postwar cinema and regularly attracted more than five million spectators. Many scholars have explained the genre's enormous popular appeal through its essentially conservative nature: the validation of the patriarchal family, the return to normative morality, and the retreat to the pre-industrial communities found in typical landscapes such as the Bavarian Alps, the Black Forest, and the Lüneburg Heath. Yet the discourse of *Heimat* was also inextricably linked to the historical experience of war, expulsion, and relocation and the ongoing negotiation of tradition and modernity (Höfig 1973, von Moltke 2005).

As the quintessential genre of the Adenauer era, the *Heimatfilm* and its many variants showed an acute awareness of contemporary problems in their preoccupation with incomplete, dysfunctional, or unconventional families; their emphasis on the trauma of displacement and the experience of loss; and their attention to the difficult question of heritage, whether in the form of a sudden inheritance or a particular way of life. Through the conflicts between the generations and through the stereotypical figure of the stranger, the *Heimatfilm* established a spatial imaginary for coming to terms with the loss of nation and for turning the Federal Republic into a new homeland. Significantly, many of the strangers arriving in the genre's idyllic villages and beautiful landscapes were refugees from East Prussia and Pomerania or rémigrés from the United States. The efforts to reunite displaced families or create new ones found paradigmatic expression in *Suchkind 312* (Looking for Child 312, 1955), about a family separated during the war. Yet these efforts also extended to the unusual circumstances depicted in *Toxi* (1952) where an Afro-German child appears on the doorstep of an average middle-class family. The driving impulse behind these restoration narratives was the desire for a harmonious reconciliation of traditional social structures with contemporary economic and political realities; often that process hinged on the confrontation with difference and its successful assimilation and incorporation. In light of these contradictory tendencies, the *Heimatfilm* conjured up a simultaneously regressive and progressive fantasy of belonging that enlisted the well-known iconography of *Heimat* in the creation of a new collective identity based less on the old opposition of city versus country than on the shared belief in modernity as a precondition of social peace and economic prosperity for all West Germans.

The necessary symbolic acts of reconciliation in the *Heimatfilm* often took place during folk festivals, religious holidays, and communal celebrations and involved musical forms ranging from the folk songs in *Am Brunnen vor dem Tore* (At the Well outside the Gate, 1952) to the operatic arias in *Wenn der weisse Flieder wieder blüht* (When the White Lilac Blooms Again, 1953). *Rosen blühen auf dem Heidegrab* (Roses Bloom on the Grave in the Meadow, 1952), with its mixture of folklore, superstition, and mysticism, still acknowledged the dangerous sides of rural life, including (sexual) violence. Contributing to the genre's own repetition compulsion, remakes such as *Der Meineidbauer* (The Perjured Farmer, 1956) and

Das Mädchen vom Moorhof (The Girl of the Moors, 1958) still articulated melodramatic conflicts in the gendered terms that invariably end up penalising the independent woman. Yet the contemporary setting of *Die Landärztin* (Lady Country Doctor, 1958) already allowed for the integration of a modern career woman into the traditional village community. The Austrian mega-hit *Der Förster vom Silberwald* (The Forester of the Silver Forest, 1954) seemed to imply that the homeland existed outside all national boundaries and historical determinants, while *Die Fischerin vom Bodensee* (The Fisher Woman from Lake Constance, 1956) confirmed the importance of nation in preserving regional cultures. Liebeneiner's two-part homage to Austria's most famous singing family, *Die Trapp-Familie* (The Trapp Family, 1956) and *Die Trapp-Familie in Amerika* (The Trapp Family in America, 1958), showed how to reconcile traditions with the demands of the marketplace. The close association of the *Heimatfilm* with mass tourism was key to this process; but so was its contribution to the ongoing negotiation of gender and sexuality which accounted for the popularity of the sentimental *Heimatfilm* in West German and Austrian cinema during the 1950s and its later variant in the sexually explicit *Frau Wirtin* (Sexy Susan) cycle as part of 1960s German–Austrian co-productions.

Frequently, the *Heimatfilm* overlapped with another profoundly spatial genre of the 1950s, the travel or vacation film. Basically an extension of the tourist industry, the travel film served as a promotional vehicle for new recreational activities and consumerist attitudes. While the Americans in these films returned to the Old Country to experience their own *Heidelberger Romanze* (Heidelberg Romance, 1951), the Germans ventured forth once again to conquer Europe, but this time as paying tourists. With programmatic titles like *Ferien vom Ich* (Vacation from the Self, 1952), the travel films showed their overworked audiences how to take a break from the pressures of economic growth and prosperity. Viewers revisited favourite destinations such as Italy, France, and Hungary and discovered new ones such as the idyllic Schleswig-Hollstein depicted in the popular *Die Mädels vom Immenhof* series (The Immenhof Girls, 1955). While some travel narratives still referenced the romantic search for the authentic self and the exoticised other, film-makers increasingly relied on the rituals of mass consumption to achieve the desired recuperative effects. More importantly, these imaginary journeys to foreign locations also prepared West German audiences for dealing with different cultures and nationalities, including the growing numbers of Italian, Spanish, and Greek *Gastarbeiter* (guest workers) arriving in the country of the Economic Miracle.

Meanwhile old-fashioned film operettas in the tradition of *Die Czardasfürstin* (The Czardas Princess, 1951) and *Im Weissen Rössl* (The White Horse Inn, 1952) and spectacular revue films in the style of *Nachts im grünen Kakadu* (At Green Cockatoo at Night, 1957) and *La Paloma* (1959) showed a remarkable resilience in adapting to contemporary tastes and sensibilities. Especially in the international music and dance numbers, postwar society encountered a spectacular reflection of its own culture of material excess and bourgeois solidity, a point underscored by the films' colourful set designs and elaborate stage numbers (Winkler and Rauch

119

2001). From nightclubs and variety shows to resort hotels and country inns, the social milieu depicted in the revue films (and, to a lesser degree, the travel films as well) appeared deceptively open toward other cultures. Under such conditions, the ever-popular combination of film, song, and dance even helped to assuage widespread concerns about Americanisation, as illustrated by the fraternisation comedy *Hallo, Fräulein!* (Hello Fraulein!, 1949) and its happy compromise between American big band music and German folk song. Hybrid forms such as the *Schlagerfilm* (hit song film) achieved similar effects through the revitalisation of indigenous popular traditions under the influence of contemporary jazz and rock 'n' roll. Taking advantage of the industry's ties to the recording industry, films such as *Liebe, Tanz und 1000 Schlager* (Love, Dance, and 1000 Songs, 1955) featured such popular singers as Caterina Valente and Peter Alexander, or launched new talents such as Cornelia Froboess and Peter Kraus, the youthful stars of the popular success *Wenn die Conny mit dem Peter* (When Conny and Peter Do It Together, 1958). Modelled on the Elvis Presley films but also inspired by the bohemian culture of coffee houses and jazz clubs, these *Schlagerfilme* addressed a younger audience not interested in melodramatic society dramas or sentimental *Heimatfilme* (Hobsch 1999).

The problems of mass consumption, mass transportation, and mass tourism found a most telling expression in the petty-bourgeois comedies with Heinz Erhardt. Beginning with *Drillinge an Bord* (Triplets on Board, 1959), this popular comedian was repeatedly cast as a middle-aged, overweight bachelor or single parent who responds to the challenges of everyday life in the Economic Miracle with a mixture of gullibility, slyness, and old-fashioned eccentricity. From his driving lessons in *Natürlich die Autofahrer* (Of Course, the Motorists, 1959) to his vacation choices in *Der letzte Fussgänger* (The Last Pedestrian, 1960), Erhardt experimented with various survival strategies that, since the nostalgic rediscovery of the 1950s in 1980s, have made him a favourite icon of conformist non-conformity.

From the very beginning, cinema in the Federal Republic had to deal with two sets of problems: the institutional and ideological legacies of the Third Reich and the Allied Occupation, on the one side, and the continuing lack of interest in new aesthetic and critical perspectives among film-makers and their audiences, on the other. While successful with moviegoers on both sides of the zonal border, West German productions proved more or less unsuited for the export business, with the exception of Austria and Switzerland. Lacking the financial and technical resources of Hollywood, but also missing the artistic ambitions of their Italian and French colleagues, most directors resigned themselves to working exclusively for the domestic market. Because of the ageing of the cinema's core audience and the growing competition from television and other mass diversions, this market was shrinking rapidly by the late 1950s. To slow down this process, the federal government early on had introduced a number of subsidy programmes for the ailing film industry. These were financed in part by the so-called *Filmgroschen*, a levy on every box-office ticket sold.

Between 1950 and 1955, the Bundesbürgschaften (Federally Guaranteed Bonds) subsidised almost half of the annual production by absorbing the financial losses suffered by production companies. Favouring big-budget productions and discouraging difficult subject matter, these government bonds did little to promote innovative art films. On the contrary, the all-powerful distributors often used federal guarantees to finance an entire line-up of mediocre films. Later subsidy programmes created additional tax loopholes especially attractive to individual investors who supported unprofitable projects as a way of reducing their tax liabilities. Even the introduction of the federally funded Deutsche Filmpreis (German Film Prize), which came with a generous monetary award, did not improve the artistic quality of films. Few German films were ever shown at international festivals, and the films chosen for export were generally regarded as low-brow entertainment by more discerning audiences in Austria, Switzerland, Italy, and France.

First changes in the public awareness of film as an art form came with the film club movement, which was organised in the Verband der deutschen Filmclubs (Association of German Film Clubs). Modelled after similar organisations in France and Britain, local clubs studied the classics of world cinema – Weimar silents included – and learned about new film movements. Committed to an apolitical notion of film art, discussions in these clubs remained for the most part limited to aesthetic questions. Greater awareness of the relationship between cinema and society prevailed among the media organisations of the Catholic and Protestant Churches. Both denominations paid close attention to films in order better to understand modern mass culture and to develop strategies for restoring Christian values to contemporary life. Despite their occasional diatribes against immoral films, publications such as the Catholic *Film-Dienst* and the *Evangelischer Filmbeobachter* functioned as invaluable sources of information for the growing number of movie buffs and cinephiles.

The revival of film criticism and scholarship after the war occurred much more slowly. Gunter Groll remained one of the few journalists to practice an informed film criticism; Walter Hagemann and his Institut für Publizistik (Institute for Journalism) proved instrumental in reclaiming a place for film studies within communication studies. The new art theatres joined forces in the Gilde deutscher Filmkunsttheater (Guild of German Film Art Theatres) to promote aesthetically innovative films and raise awareness of the artistic possibilities of the medium. In 1957, Enno Patalas and Wilfried Berghahn started the journal *Filmkritik* as an alternative to the impressionistic style of the daily *feuilleton*. Committed to ideology critique, these young critics set out to practice film criticism as social criticism: that is to say, as a form of intervening into the oppressive conditions of postwar society. The writing in *Filmkritik* betrayed the strong influence of Kracauer, including his history of Weimar cinema and his theory of filmic realism. Supported by these discursive networks, a lively film culture emerged gradually at small film festivals such as the one in Mannheim, which was limited to cultural films, and the famous Oberhausen Short Film Festival, which provided a forum for experimental films. All these initiatives were started in sharp opposition to the Berlin Film Festival, also known as Berlinale, which was conceived in 1951 with the explicit goal of turning the divided city into a symbol of the Cold War and a showcase of Western consumerism.

The arrival of television increased the intense competition over audiences and further accelerated the decline of cinema culture during the late 1950s. Public television became part of the institutional structures initially developed in 1948 for NWDR, a precursor of the North and West German radio stations and the model for the organisation of broadcasting as a public service. The ARD (Arbeitsgemeinschaft der öffentlich-rechtlichen Rundfunkanstalten der Bundesrepublik Deutschlands), an association of regional broadcasting channels, started the First Channel in 1954; a Second Channel, the ZDF (Zweites Deutsches Fernsehen), began to transmit in 1963. Initially, film and television officials emphasised the differences between both visual media, with television regarded as a live medium committed, like radio, to providing information. The arrival of the *Fernsehspiel* (television play), including that of such big productions as the six-part war epic *Soweit die Füsse tragen* (As Far as My Feet Will Carry Me, 1959), complicated this convenient division of labour. Film companies began to rent out their facilities to television productions or functioned as co-producers of television plays. With the televising of old Ufa classics, the new medium became a serious competitor in the production and distribution of mass-produced fantasies. Public television deprived the motion-picture theatres of their most faithful audience, the older Germans raised on conventional genre films. Meanwhile young people embraced American mass culture with a vengeance and, under the sway of new musical styles and recreational activities, gradually lost interest in German-made films. As a result, postwar culture segmented more and more into high culture, folk culture, mass culture, and various artistic and intellectual subcultures. In such an atmosphere, going to the movies was increasingly perceived as irrelevant and outdated, and that despite the new slogan of the SPIO 'Enjoy a few relaxing hours. Go to the movies!'

The often cited 'death of the movies' came when the market share of German films fell to less than 30 per cent in the early 1960s, down from 40 per cent in the mid-1950s. A series of bankruptcies accompanied this seemingly inevitable decline, including that of the Allianz distribution company in 1956 and of the distribution branch of the dismantled Ufa concern in 1961. Some production companies responded to the crisis by shooting films in Cinemascope and Technicolor and by taking on more sensationalist subject matter. Other producers promoted European co-productions as a cure-all, hoping that big-name international stars would guarantee at least some commercial success. And yet other companies took advantage of mass media synergies by making films based on best-sellers by Johannes Mario Simmel or by adapting serial novels published in the television guide *Hör Zu* or the daily tabloid *Bild-Zeitung*. However, even the most innovative or most thought out marketing strategies could not disguise the fact that the formulas of genre cinema had reached a serious impasse. In a highly symbolic gesture that acknowledged the profound crisis of German cinema, the Berlin Film Festival in 1961 refused to hand out any Federal Film Prizes to the new releases from that fateful year.

8 Lilian Harvey and Willi Fritsch in *Glückskinder*. Courtesy BFI Stills, Posters and Designs.

9 Paul Hörbiger and Zarah Leander in *Die grosse Liebe*. Courtesy BFI Stills, Posters and Designs.

10 Carl Raddatz and Kristina Söderbaum in *Immensee*. Courtesy BFI Stills, Posters and Designs.

11 Hans Albers and Hilde Hildebrandt in *Grosse Freiheit Nr. 7*. Courtesy BFI Stills, Posters and Designs.

12 Hildegard Knef and Ernst Wilhelm Borchardt in *Die Mörder sind unter uns*. Courtesy BFI Stills, Posters and Designs.

13 Dieter Borsche and Renate Mannhardt in *Die grosse Versuchung*. Courtesy BFI Stills, Posters and Designs.

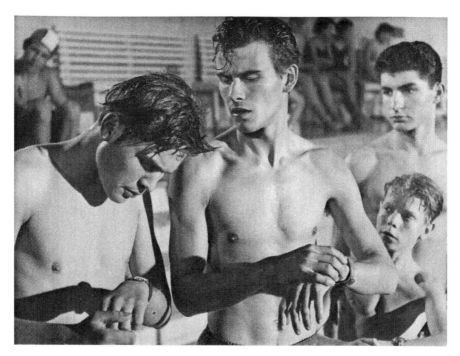

14 Horst Buchholz in *Die Halbstarken*. Courtesy BFI Stills, Posters and Designs.

5

EAST GERMAN CINEMA 1961–90

The asymmetrical relationship between East and West in postwar cinema ended with two equally significant events: the building of the Berlin Wall on 13 August 1961 and the signing of the Oberhausen Manifesto on 28 February 1962 (to be discussed in Chapter 6). The Wall enabled the German Democratic Republic to stabilise its political, economic, and cultural identity in relation to the Federal Republic and the threat of Western capitalism. According to official rhetoric, the 'construction of socialism' (*Aufbau des Sozialismus*) had been completed; the new phase was devoted to the 'consolidation of socialism' (*Ankunft im Sozialismus*). Insisting on a specific GDR identity subsequently allowed the SED regime to appropriate traditional notions of Germanness while resisting the reform initiatives started in other East European countries. Introduced in 1963 under Walter Ulbricht, the New Economic System promised to decentralise production, improve managerial and technical competence, and make the state-owned companies more compatible (and competitive) with other market economies. The liberalisation of the criminal justice system and greater attention to the nation's youth during a decade of international protest movements brought some improvements in the organisation of social relations. Under such conditions, some DEFA film-makers hoped – in vain – that the real and imaginary boundaries drawn by the Wall would also create more favourable conditions for artistic expression and critical exchange.

The years between the building and the fall of the Wall gave rise to a distinct GDR culture that, even in the sphere of popular culture, remained indebted to German high culture and the ideas of the Enlightenment, and that, even as part of an emerging socialist culture, continued to validate bourgeois notions of individual agency and public morality. The resultant mixture of cultural ambition and political compliance, social critique and aesthetic convention, defined DEFA cinema from the 1960s to the 1980s and made it an essential part of socialism, German style. The building of the Wall completed the bifurcation of postwar cinema into two national cinemas, with the one a private enterprise organised according to free market principles, the other a state-owned company involved in the building of a socialist society. The shared generic traditions and filmic styles and the competing ideological systems that had characterised postwar cinema as both unified and divided were overshadowed by the growing political divisions reflected in the FRG's hollow rhetoric of unification and the GDR's official doctrine of 'two Germanys'. None the less both cinemas continued to respond to the same political and social developments and engage with the same cultural trends and sensibilities, and that despite the lack of a sustained critical engagement with each other's films.

DEFA, like Ufa, has since become part of film history. More than seven hundred feature films were produced during its existence, and a large number are now considered classics of German cinema. Since reunification, many of the studio's leading actors and directors have begun new careers in film and television. The retrospectives, publications, and public debates of the 1990s reveal lingering bitterness about the sacrifices, battles, and lost opportunities in the search for a socialist film culture; they also raise many questions about DEFA's place in the national film heritage (Byg 1990, Hochmuth 1993, Poss 1997, Finke 2001). Studies on film reception in the GDR have challenged simplistic notions of mass manipulation, while others have provided a more detailed account of the intricate system of censorship and control (Blunk and Jungnickel 1990, Spielhagen 1993, Glaß 1999). Since the sixtieth anniversary of DEFA in 2006, there has also been cautious appreciation, occasional nostalgia, and a surprising return to symptomatic readings that use the films to diagnose the fundamental failure of the GDR and the socialist system (Poss and Warnecke 2006, Gersch 2006).

Like Third Reich cinema, GDR cinema raises fundamental questions about the relationship between film and politics in a state-controlled industry; the contribution of cinema to the construction of national identity; and the interchanges between the cinema and other art forms and popular diversions. And, like their West German counterparts, East German films from the 1960s and 1970s draw attention to the continuities of national cinema, including the various attempts to contribute to a tradition of art cinema and establish connections to international film movements (Meurer 2000). Since 1989, German and Anglo-American scholars have begun to address some of these issues through comprehensive overviews of DEFA's feature film and documentary production, case studies of individual genres and directors, and critical reflections on the historiography of GDR cinema (Schenk 1994, Jordan and Schenk 1996, Allan and Sanford 1999, Finke 2001, Byg and Moore 2002). There has also been growing attention to the contribution of cinema to the experience of everyday life, the role of film in cultivating a modernist aesthetic beyond national boundaries, and the emergence of a socialist film culture within Eastern Europe (Glaß 1999, Berghahn 2005, Trumpener forthcoming).

The New Waves and the Eleventh Plenary

The DEFA films made after 1962 can be understood only in the larger context of GDR culture and the cinema's privileged position in debates over socialist art and national identity. Largely absent from international markets, DEFA films addressed their audience specifically as a GDR audience who shared core beliefs about the individual and the collective and who, especially during the 1970s and 1980s, relied on similar strategies of disengaging from the official rhetoric and retreating into private life. As a result, the process of building a national cinema remained fraught with difficulties and contradictions. Films functioned at once as a stabilising force in the management of political dissent and public disaffection and as a corroding influence on sexual morality and social harmony. Meanwhile, the self-representation of the socialist state remained closely tied to high culture, especially literature and the legacy of the classics, with film enlisted repeatedly to reaffirm the bond between masses and party leadership and to realign public and private fantasies in the interest of the state.

As an integral part of the socialist public sphere, film occupied a special place in this difficult balancing act between affirmation and subversion, containment and release. The more the party leadership relied on intellectual and artistic elites in maintaining the status quo, the more cultural practices functioned as an extension of, and substitute for, political debates. Produced within greater constraints than literature but under fewer pressures than television, films had to answer to the competing demands of art, education, information, and entertainment. As a cultural and, by extension, political institution and as an integral part of socialist society, the DEFA studio was subjected to considerable political pressures from the Hauptverwaltung Film (HV Film) within the Ministry of Culture. At the same time, film-makers enjoyed optimal working conditions that included the luxury of time and money, vast studio resources and professional support, and, perhaps most problematically, the great relevance accorded to their work by the party leadership. In its best moments, the DEFA studio thrived on the spirit of artistic collaboration and critical debate. Yet more often than not, film-making took place in a stifling atmosphere of consensus building, forceful persuasion, and brutal silencing. The so-called Künstlerische Arbeitsgruppen (KAGs), which formed under names such as 'Johannisthal', 'Babelsberg,', Berlin', and 'Roter Kreis', developed alternatives to the bourgeois cult of individual creativity by approaching film-making as a collaborative process and collective experience. Enjoying some autonomy especially during the 1960s, these production groups typically formed around the integrative figure of a dramaturge – one of the many reasons why DEFA films resist conventional notions of film authorship and frequently lack a distinct artistic signature.

The shared belief in consensus building and social relevance makes it also difficult to speak of film-making either as a typical struggle between artistic freedom and political pressure or as yet another historical example of opportunist, conformist, or subversive artists working under an oppressive regime. The close relationship between the studio and the SED as well as that between the studio's director and its most respected writers, actors, and directors was sustained by an ongoing dialogue that recognised their work's contribution to the larger project of socialism. Under these conditions, censorship took place both through official bans and punitive measures and the more pernicious kind of self-censorship carried out in the name of socialism and allegiance to the party. Not surprisingly, the most controversial film-makers were also the ones most fiercely committed to Marxist ideas; and it was precisely their elevated position in GDR society that required repeated acts of self-criticism from Wolf, Maetzig, and others.

However, the question of ideological and artistic conformity cannot be reduced to the conditions of film-making in a state-controlled industry. Exceptional events such as the Eleventh Plenary and the waves of emigration during the 1970s and 1980s have focused too much attention on individual films and film-makers, and distracted attention from popular cinema as a social phenomenon beyond local sensibilities and national boundaries (Glaß 1999). Moreover, cinema in the GDR also included the reception of foreign films, especially the popular Hollywood films and the innovative films from Eastern Europe; the role of film criticism in establishing evaluative categories; the public discussions about specific films by working collectives, party associations, and other more informal communities; and the rituals of fandom inspired by a few cult films and popular stars.

Adding to these diverse influences, the emergence of the New Waves in East and West was not just part of a politicisation of cinema attributable to the work of innovative directors and their radicalised audiences. In fact, these movements responded also to the decline of classical genre cinema and the diminished appeal of film as the dominant form of popular entertainment. The convergence of politics and aesthetics in the various avant-garde movements of the 1960s must therefore be considered a product of the intensified competition among modern mass media, including television, and the resultant fragmentation of audiences. This diversi-fication – and, in the case of cinema, incipient marginalisation – made possible a greater emphasis on the creative and critical possibilities of film. By the end of the decade, the formal challenges to established patterns of perception would only increase the separation between a younger movie audience and educated art house regulars and make domestic productions at once more powerful and less influential – a contradiction that contributed to the subsequent crises of film-making during the 1970s and was acknowledged in many DEFA films' self-depreciating references to their own lack of popular appeal.

During the 1960s, East German cinema occupied an unusual position between the New Waves in France, Italy, Great Britain, and the Federal Republic, on the one hand, and the New Waves in Poland, Hungary, Czechoslovakia, and the Soviet Union, on the other. Like their Western colleagues, film-makers studied the neo-realist films by Roberto Rossellini, Vittorio de Sica, and later, Michelangelo Antonioni and Pier Paolo Pasolini, and they were familiar with the main repre-sentatives of the Nouvelle Vague, above all Alain Resnais and François Truffaut. They also took note of the British Free Cinema's renewed commitment to the documentary tradition and its interest in social activism. The influence of these movements can be seen in the growing awareness of film as a construction of, and an intervention into, social reality. Frequently, this critical sensibility took the form of a cool modernist style distinguished by stark black-and-white cinematography, fragmented narrative structures, and an analytical, self-reflective approach to the filmic medium. For instance, *Der geteilte Himmel* (The Divided Heaven, 1964), Konrad Wolf's adaptation of the famous novel by Christa Wolf, was strongly influenced by the West European literary and filmic avant-gardes, including Resnais's *Hiroshima mon amour* (1959). A strong presence in the GDR, Soviet film-makers after the XX Party Congress in 1956 had begun to explore alternatives to artistic and political dogmas; here the work of Mikhail Romm, Mikhail Kalatozov, and Andrei Tarkovsky proved especially influential. To mention only one example, Kalatozov's *The Cranes Are Flying* served as an important inspiration for the expressionist imagery in Frank Beyer's *Fünf Patronenhülsen* (Five Cartridges, 1960). Perhaps even more relevant to the double articulation of aesthetic and political modernism as a critique of conventional genre cinema and official cultural politics were the films by a younger generation of Polish and Czech film-makers, including Andrzej Wajda and Milos Forman, whose decentred perspectives on socialism Soviet-style gave DEFA film-makers new ides for their own work.

Throughout the decade, the leading directors of the 1960s received crucial impulses from contemporary literature. Literature had always played a central role in defining GDR culture, beginning with the First Bitterfeld Conference in 1959, which had insisted that the critique of productivism should come with closer attention to the problems of everyday life. Instrumental in challenging the dominant realist paradigm, writers moved tentatively toward literary modernism at the Second Bitterfeld Conference in 1964. Sharing a strong commitment to literature with both the political leadership and the cultural establishment, DEFA encouraged close working relationships between screenwriters and directors, thereby fostering Wolfgang Kohlhaase's work with Gerhard Klein and, later, Konrad Wolf; Helga Schütz's collaboration with Egon Günther; and Ulrich Plenzdorf's screenplays for Herrmann Zschoche, Frank Beyer, and Heiner Carow. Some of the most provocative contributions came from younger writers such as Christa Wolf and Günter Kunert, who experimented with avant-garde elements in order to revive an increasingly ossified socialist culture. In so doing, these writers also resorted to a well-established tradition, associated with the historical avant-gardes, of enlisting formal strategies in social and political critique.

Profiting from the new alliances between aesthetic and political modernism, film-makers once again turned their attention to what, to this day, remains DEFA's most significant contribution to German cinema: the anti-fascist film. In one of the most provocative reflections on the aesthetics of fascism, Gerhard Klein in *Der Fall Gleiwitz* (The Gleiwitz Case, 1961) reconstructed the attack on a radio station on the German–Polish border, which was staged by the SS to justify the German invasion of Poland. Shot in a highly experimental documentary style, this film faced accusations of objectivism because of its cool detachment from the physiognomy of power and the rituals of violence. Even more remarkable, the two-part *Die gefrorenen Blitze* (Frozen Flashes, 1967) by János Veiczi presented the Third Reich's secret military experiments with rocket technology through a daring combination of narrative and pseudo-documentary elements, including archival footage and still photography. Analytical in tone, Veiczi's depiction of the German war effort avoided the usual fireworks of drama and suspense. The same formal qualities had already distinguished his earlier political thriller, *For Eyes Only* (1962), whose story about a GDR agent working under cover at the CIA profited from the myths surrounding Markus Wolf, then the head of East German counter-intelligence.

The spirit of formal experimentation and critical re-examination extended even to the founding principles of GDR identity from the reconstruction in the late 1940s through the freezes and thaws of the 1950s. Some of the more influential films, including Günther Rücker's *Die besten Jahre* (The Best Years, 1965), still showed the personal sacrifices of the GDR's founding generation through the lens of collective agency and historical necessity, but did not shy away from acknowledging the growing sense of disappointment and disillusionment. In *Der Frühling braucht Zeit* (Spring Needs Time, 1965), Günter Stahnke presented the disagreements between an apolitical engineer and an ambitious manager over technical problems at a power plant through strategies of defamiliarisation that shed a critical light on the New Economic System and its fixation on production quotas. The critical potential of modernist strategies also extended to the filmic representation of love and marriage and the oppressive effect of social conventions on personal relations. Here Günther's *Lots Weib* (Lot's Wife, 1965), about a woman who forces her status-conscious husband to grant her a divorce by committing petty theft, made a compelling argument for a woman's right to personal happiness, and it did so through an almost clinical tone of detachment.

During the same time, the DEFA studio was repeatedly enlisted in the ideological confrontations that required clear statements of loyalty and commitment. The implications were particularly pronounced in the filmic representation of the German division. *Und deine Liebe auch* (And Your Love, Too, 1962) and the critically acclaimed *Der geteilte Himmel* in 1964 had been the first films to explore the profound impact of the Wall on personal relationships, one through a love triangle set in the divided capital, the other through a couple's growing personal and political disagreements. Such subtle psychological treatments soon gave way to the hyperbole of espionage thrillers like *Reserviert für den Tod* (Reserved for Death, 1963) and the propagandistic zeal of *Geschichten jener Nacht* (Stories of that Night, 1967), an omnibus film with several episodes about exemplary citizens who had made the right choice on the night of 12/13 August 1961. Many of these films articulated the power imbalance between East and West Germany in gendered terms, with the ambitious young men leaving for better professional opportunities in the West and with the idealistic young women affirming their commitment to the socialist collective.

The Central Committee of the SED convened the Eleventh Plenary in December 1965 at a high point of innovative film-making. Planned as a forum on economic policies, the Plenary ended up banning an entire year's production of 12 films. The studio director Jochen Mückenberger was dismissed, and many careers interrupted or destroyed. In discussions, the Plenary focused on *Denk bloss nicht, ich heule* (Just Don't Think that I Am Crying) and *Das Kaninchen bin ich* (I Am the Rabbit); hence the frequent reference in the scholarship to the so-called *Kaninchenfilme* (rabbit films). The main charges against these films can be summarised as 'scepticism', 'nihilism', 'relativism', and 'subjectivism'. The directors' failure or unwillingness to develop a dialectical conception of reality, the argument went, had produced characters and stories that were irrelevant, if not detrimental, to the self-understanding of GDR society. Some scholars have ascribed far more complex reasons for the banning of films – among them, the party's desire to distract from the failures of the New Economic System and to put an end to the process of liberalisation that would soon erupt in the Prague Spring of 1968. Accordingly, the events surrounding the Plenary must be seen less as a demonstration of power than a manifestation of crisis in the political leadership. For film-makers, the Eleventh Plenary destroyed any remaining illusions about the beneficial effects of the Wall and prompted many to retreat to uncontroversial topics and styles (Mückenberger 1990, Dalichow in Hoff and Wiedemann 1992).

The famous *Regalfilme* (shelved films), as the *Kaninchenfilme* are also called, included a rather diverse group defined less by some political agenda than by their shared historical fate. In Maetzig's *Das Kaninchen bin ich*, the love story between a young woman and the married judge who earlier convicted her dissident brother occasions a sharp critique of the political justice system and the opportunism of the party elites. *Karla* by Zschoche uses a young idealistic female teacher to question authoritarian teaching methods. That film's diagnosis of a growing rift between the first and second generation of GDR citizens and its impassioned plea for open dialogue still assumes some basic agreement about the utopian project of socialism. Similar assumptions can be found in three other *Regalfilme* that focus on younger protagonists: a high-school student who rails against the hypocrisy of adult society in Frank Vogel's *Denk bloss nicht, ich heule*; a young boy with a magical flashlight capable of identifying liars in Günther's *Wenn du gross bist, lieber Adam* (When You Are Grown up, Dear Adam); and the rebellious adolescents in *Berlin um die Ecke* (Berlin around the Corner), another Berlin film by the well-known team of Klein and Kohlhaase. In a marked departure from their earlier Berlin films, the central conflict could no longer be reduced to the seduction of urban youth by American mass culture. Instead, the film-makers focused on the growing sense of alienation between those who had lived through reconstruction and those who, born after 1945, no longer shared all of their unquestioned values and beliefs. Also experimenting with the conventions of the city film, the formally most radical film among the *Regalfilme*, Jürgen Böttcher's *Jahrgang 45* (Born in '45), focused on the problems of a young couple from Berlin's Prenzlauer Berg neighbourhood to diagnose the lacking sense of critical dialogue for social reform.

The Eleventh Plenary had a devastating impact on GDR film culture as a whole. The bans diminished the role of cinema as a repository of the grand narratives of socialism and curtailed its possibilities in offering alternative stories and inter-pretations. It became clear after 1965 that even the most basic assumptions about GDR history, society, and culture and, more specifically, the relationship between social reality and filmic representation, could become subject to critical inquiry and, by extension, political controversy. Under such conditions, some officials wondered whether DEFA films still allowed for any positive engagement with Marxist theory and practice. Were film-makers responding to the existing condi-tions or expressing their desire for more radical changes? Were the modernist forms a result of, or a reaction against, the loss of social consensus and cohesion? Such questions not only revealed the deep ideological schism between film-makers and party leadership. The recurring diagnosis of a crisis in production also responded to the further segmentation of film audiences into a large and predominantly young audience interested in conventional entertainment; a smaller middle-class audience still committed to the original project of cinema under socialism; and an even smaller group of artists, intellectuals, and cinephiles supportive of the international New Waves. As a consequence, the conformist political elites and the nonconformist artistic groups continued to clash repeatedly over the appropriate contribution of the DEFA studio to definitions of national identity and socialist mass culture. Meanwhile, movie audiences satisfied their entertainment needs through Hollywood films, and, increasingly, through East and West German television.

The events surrounding the Eleventh Plenary profoundly affected the career of the only new director to emerge during the 1960s, Frank Beyer. Working with the conventions of classical narrative cinema and taking advantage of its emotional powers, Beyer repeatedly pushed the limits of verisimilitude to create new filmic realities through dream sequences, fairytale elements, visual symbolism, and so forth (Schenk 1995a). Anti-fascism remained a central concern in his work, but less as a historical master-narrative than as a critical reflection on the relevance of the past to the present. Accordingly, the setting of the Spanish Civil War in *Fünf Patronenhülsen* allowed him to ponder the possibility of resistance and the importance of solidarity. In *Königskinder* (Royal Children, 1962), Beyer introduced the romantic motif of unrequited love to examine the different personal and political choices of three Berlin working-class children from the 1920s to the 1940s. In *Karbid und Sauerampfer* (Carbide and Sorrel, 1963), he relied on picaresque elements to uncover the ideological divisions of the Cold War through the adventures of a Don Quixote-like figure, played by Erwin Geschonneck. The director problematised the relationship between victims and victimisers in a critically acclaimed adaptation of the Bruno Apitz novel *Nackt unter Wölfen* (Naked among Wolves, 1963), the first postwar film set in a concentration camp. Finally, Beyer's most famous film, *Spur der Steine* (The Trace of Stones, 1966/1989), which was banned immediately after its release, focused on the organisational problems at a large construction site and, by extension, the difficulties of reconciling political principles with the realities of life and work under socialism. The film's self-reflexive approach to narrative and the question of truth has secured its status as one of the classics of DEFA cinema.

Despite the chilling effect of the Eleventh Plenary, modernist styles continued to offer an analytical framework for challenging established views on the origins of fascism, the legacies of anti-fascism, and the impact of recent political events on the self-understanding of DEFA as both the 'true' and the 'other' German cinema. Thus Joachim Kunert in *Die Abenteuer des Werner Holt* (The Adventures of Werner Holt, 1965) showed the wartime disillusionment of several young middle-class men through a fragmented narrative structure that includes flashbacks and stream-of-consciousness. Other directors introduced highly personal perspectives to explore the affinities between history and narrative. Wolf's autobiographical *Ich war neunzehn* (I Was Nineteen, 1968), about his experiences as a German-born soldier in the Soviet Army, explored the complex meanings of nation and *Heimat* and contemplated their place in the anti-fascist master-narrative. At the same time, Carow in *Die Russen kommen* (The Russians Are Coming, 1968/1987), which was banned, used a young boy's tragic death in the last days of the war to highlight the subjective dimension of world historical events. One of the few promising directors to emerge in the early 1970s, Carow avoided the kind of social typisation found in Maetzig and Dudow but refused the equation of the personal and the political typical of Wolf's contribution to the discourse of anti-fascism. Consequently, his work uncovered more than any other the ideological divide opening up between the founding generation and the first generation born in the GDR.

The Eleventh Plenary may have stifled new artistic initiatives at DEFA but was unable to stop the dissemination of contemporary sensibilities into conventional genres and established forms. This influence was most noticeable in the fashion styles and design choices indebted to an international pop culture and inspired by the counterculture of the 1970s. Yet the new mentality also expressed itself in the looks, moves, and mannerisms of many younger actors. This pervasive modernisation – and, to some degree, commodification – of everyday life extended from entertainment needs and musical tastes to summer vacations and romantic adventures. The resultant shift from public to private life opened up the self-representation of GDR society to lifestyle choices separate from, if not opposed to, the official emphasis on the socialist collective. Defending the need of citizens to take a break from the production quotas, *Das verhexte Fischerdorf* (The Jinxed Fishing Village, 1962) depicted the collective at love and play on the Baltic coast. The return to traditional gender roles and the reaffirmation of bourgeois marriage was made possible through the revival of hybrid forms such as vacation-revues in the style of *Reise ins Ehebett* (Journey into the Conjugal Bed, 1966) and *Hochzeitsnacht im Regen* (Wedding Night in the Rain, 1967). Even the persistence of petty-bourgeois attitudes in the figure of the 'little man' found acknowledgement in the popular Rolf Herricht comedies *Geliebte weisse Maus* (The Small White Mouse, 1964) and *Der Reserveheld* (The Heroic Reservist, 1965). Most famously, the cult film *Heisser Sommer* (Hot Summer, 1968), featuring the popular singers Chris Doerk and Frank Schöbel, showed how young comrades could remain committed to socialist ideals while enjoying American-style pop tunes, sports, and flirtations. Rejecting the conciliatory and compensatory fantasies offered by these contemporary comedies, *Die Glatzkopfbande* (The Skin Head Gang, 1963) remained one of the few films to present a radically different view of GDR youth, one defined by rock 'n' roll, motorcycles, and gratuitous violence and clearly modelled on a Western understanding of counterculture.

All of these examples confirm that DEFA was capable of producing popular films with contemporary relevance. At least in the form of private diversions and lifestyle choices, the modernist sensibilities of the 1960s became an integral part of the filmic imagination. However, even the better contributions limited their portrayals of GDR society to familiar milieux and everyday situations, with the occasional escapes into the extraordinary following established patterns of escapism. To make up for the growing sense of confinement after 1962, DEFA briefly experimented with crime capers such as *Der Dieb von San Marengo* (The Thief of San Marengo, 1963) that, like their French, Italian, and West German equivalents, offered brief escapes to the spectacular settings, cosmopolitan milieux, and luxurious lifestyles found on the Côte d'Azur. The same compensatory function can be attributed to the costume films that, despite their reputation for historical accuracy, failed to offer audiences some much-needed action, adventure, and visual spectacle. Inspired by the robber romances of Kurt Hoffmann and the French cloak-and-dagger films with Gérald Philipe, some directors tried, unsuccessfully, to revive the costume genre by infusing it with anti-feudal attitudes and revolutionary situations. Even the casting of audience favourite Manfred Krug in a folksy adaptation of Kleist's *Der zerbrochene Krug – Jungfer, sie gefällt mir* (Damsel, You Appeal to Me, 1969) – and in a populist episode from the Congress of Vienna in *Hauptmann Florian von der Mühle* (Captain Florian von der Mühle, 1968), the first DEFA film shot in the 70 mm format, failed to overcome the genre's problematic mixture of low-class pleasures and high-class pretensions. Perhaps it was the genre's inherent obsolescence that made the quaint *Die Heiden von Kummerow* (The Heathens of Kummerow, 1967) so well suited as the first German–German co-production.

The conflicting demands of popular entertainment and social relevance found a perfect compromise in the *Indianerfilme* (Indian films) with Yugoslavian actor Goiko Mitic. The films' appearance after the Eleventh Plenary confirms their socio-psychological function as an escape from contemporary problems and a displacement of social and political anxieties on to the threatened culture of the North American Indians. The Indian films appealed to audiences through their fantasies of open space, free movement, and individual and collective heroism – qualities missing from most DEFA films with a contemporary setting. In redefining the typical conflicts of the traditional Western, these productions took advantage of the long-standing German fascination with the Wild West, especially among boys and young men reared on Karl May novels. Influenced by retro-westerns such as *The Magnificent Seven* (1960) and so-called spaghetti westerns in the style of *Per un pugno di dollari* (A Fistful of Dollars, 1964), the DEFA productions offered an alternative to the West German *Winnetou* series by taking the perspective of the Indians and retelling their struggle against colonial interest and imperialist aggression. The story of the proud and defiant Dakota nation in *Die Söhne der grossen Bärin* (The Sons of Great Bear, 1966) established the basic formula for the entire series. That film was followed by *Chingachgook, die grosse Schlange* (Chingachgook, the Great Snake, 1967) and several other Indian films that, every summer season, attracted more than two million spectators. The Indian films contained many explicit and implicit references to the GDR's own attempts to preserve the traditions of working-class culture and resist the temptations of American-style capitalism. Yet whereas the early films romanticised the Indians as icons of struggle and resistance, later contributions paid more attention to their oppression, an indication perhaps also of the growing crisis of socialism in the early 1970s (Hahn 1995, Gemünden 2001).

Whereas the past became the perfect projection screen for retrograde fantasies of Germanness, the relevance of the future to the project of a revolutionary socialism remained the subject of intense debates, as confirmed by the difficulties surrounding Maetzig's *Der schweigende Stern* (Silent Star, 1960), a German–Polish co-production and the most expensive DEFA film ever made (Soldovieri 1998). A product of the Cold War, this adaptation of the popular Stanislaw Lem novel combined deep philosophical reflections on science and technology with a spectacular demonstration of the socialist ethos of international co-operation in the face of nuclear threats. Later contributions to the science-fiction genre offered thinly veiled allegories of the anti-imperialist struggle. As illustrated by *Eolomea* (1972) and, even more importantly, by *Im Staub der Sterne* (In the Dust of the Stars, 1976), the genre provided a spatial imagery through which to envision the socialist state as navigating a dangerous universe and confronting alien civilisations built on workers' exploitation and total mind control. Yet despite the obvious political analogies, these science-fiction films also gave audiences a welcome opportunity to enjoy futuristic fashions and designs and to indulge in some rare psychedelic effects.

Apart from the Indian films that led the studio's annual summer line-up, only three productions attracted more than two million viewers during the 1960s, namely *Die Abenteuer des Werner Holt* in 1965, *Ich war neunzehn* in 1968, and, in 1970, the German–Soviet co-production *Unterwegs zu Lenin* (On the Way to Lenin), which was commissioned for the centennial of Lenin's birth. With most hopes and expectations for an artistically and politically relevant cinema squelched, the studio from then on focused primarily on its younger audience and developed strategies aimed specifically at their needs and desires. For GDR youth, moviegoing offered a much-needed alternative to the obligatory group activities of the FDJ (Freie deutsche Jugend), and the films satisfied desires ignored by official political culture and established high culture. The large percentage of adolescents and young adults in the motion-picture theatres caused some concern among party officials, as these audiences represented a potential source, or measure, of growing dissatisfaction. Obviously, the notion of a national cinema that addressed all viewers as a collective could no longer be upheld either in social or aesthetic terms. Later film-sociological studies would confirm this troubling trend toward audience segmentation and explain the film-makers' growing preference for simple characters, linear narratives, and clear moral oppositions through the cinema's domination by young audiences (Bisky and Wiedemann 1985).

Contributing further to the crisis of cinema, television began to pose a serious threat to the relationship between DEFA and its faithful fans. During the early 1960s, the average citizen still went to the movies 14 times a year; by the early 1980s, that number had fallen to five times a year. Operating since 1952 under the direct control of the Central Committee, the Deutsche Fernsehfunk (DFF) had always been more hierarchical in its organisation but, for that reason, also more flexible in its programming decisions. Thus in the late 1960s, DEFA began to explore more creative arrangements among film, television, broadcasting, and the recording industry. The studio's limited output made such arrangements desirable as well as necessary. Actors and directors participated regularly in co-productions between DEFA and GDR Television, including ambitious multi-part television plays and highly publicised television premieres of big-budget feature films; sometimes television functioned as a refuge for ostracised directors. Further contributing to the blurring of boundaries between film and television, the First Channel and, after 1969, Second Channel (then renamed DDR 1 and DDR 2) regularly showed blockbusters from Italy and France, as well as film classics from other socialist countries. The demand for entertainment even extended to the old Ufa films shown in nostalgia shows like *Willi Schwabes Rumpelkammer* (Junk Room). These programmes helped to create a receptive and more diverse audience for DEFA films as well, an audience that included older citizens, mothers with young children, and viewers in remote rural areas. However, even those changes failed to quell the competition from West German television and, most specifically, the endless stream of Hollywood films broadcast across the border and viewed regularly by many citizens, despite official prohibitions.

The Indian films and their close identification with Goiko Mitic draw attention to the function of actors and actresses in East German cinema (Schenk 1995b). From the beginning, DEFA rejected the profit-driven, market-based star system and its cult of celebrities. The studio found an alternative in topic-based approaches that favoured character actors with a background in the theatre and a talent for ensemble acting. Film-makers occasionally used the identification of audience favourites with particular genres to create recognisable screen personas, as in the case of comedian Rolf Herricht, the East German Heinz Erhardt. But for the most part, directors paid little attention to the usual requirements of female beauty and sex appeal and focused instead on developing a particular physiognomy of class personified since the 1950s by Erwin Geschonneck in his signature roles as a resistance fighter and proletarian hero.

DEFA actors and actresses were often identified with a distinct physiognomy of class that found expression in particular body types, facial features, gestural codes, and individual mannerisms. Many actors looked unmistakably German and, with that elusive quality, resembled either the Ufa stars of the Third Reich or the anti-stars of the New German Cinema. These similarities were particularly pronounced in older male actors such as Geschonneck, with his larger-than-life masculinity reminiscent of Heinrich George. Similarly, the more contemporary ideal of sensitive masculinity found expression in the comparable screen personas of East German Armin Mueller-Stahl and Swiss German Bruno Ganz. The image of female beauty and eroticism projected by East German Angelica Domröse closely resembled that of West German Hanna Schygulla. Even the transition in DEFA productions from the cool modernist aesthetics of the 1960s to the intense personal explorations of the 1970s can be described through a noticeable change in the look of ideal-typical masculinity and femininity. Whereas the monochrome images of the 1960s called for reserved male actors such as the brooding Mueller-Stahl or the quiet Eberhard Esche, the colourful scenes of everyday life in the films of the 1970s cannot be separated from the performances of Jutta Hoffmann and Renate Krößner who combined strength and independence with vulnerability and spontaneity.

Despite its opposition to the star system, DEFA produced one genuine movie star: Manfred Krug. With his large frame, open face, and intensely physical acting style, Krug came to represent the vitality and sensuality of the new society, qualities that made him a perennial favourite with male and female audiences. Repeatedly voted the most popular DEFA actor, Krug also had an impressive career as a jazz singer and political activist. His first appearance in Ralf Kirsten's *Auf der Sonnenseite* (On the Sunny Side, 1962), a love story between a steel-welder-turned-actor and a female project manager, was partly autobiographical. Already his next role in *Beschreibung eines Sommers* (Description of a Summer, 1963), about a similar romantic entanglement between a male civil engineer and a female party secretary, took full advantage of the actor's unique combination of brazenness, tenderness, and warmth. Krug's most famous role in *Spur der Steine* represented yet another contribution to this physiognomy of working-class masculinity, but now in the heightened terms of unrequited love. Krug left the GDR in 1977 and pursued a successful career in West German film and television. Beyer's *Das Versteck* (The Hiding Place, 1978), a delightful comedy about a man taking over his ex-wife's apartment under the pretence of being a fugitive from the law, turned out to be his last DEFA film.

Through their status as public figures, actors and actresses were directly implicated in the back and forth between liberalisation and hard-line dogmatism that in the mid-1970s culminated in the imprisonment and expatriation of dissent thinker Rudolf Bahro and the repressive measures against critical intellectuals. Responding to the expatriation of the popular singer Wolf Biermann in 1976, Eva-Maria Hagen and Armin Mueller-Stahl, as well as Jutta Hoffmann and Angelica Domröse followed Krug and left for the Federal Republic. In *Engel aus Eisen* (Angels of Iron, 1981), author Thomas Brasch referenced these traumatic experiences in the melancholy portrayal of Berlin during the immediate postwar years. Others, like Mueller-Stahl, turned their performative otherness into an internationally recognisable trademark. The West German mass media sometimes exploited these emigration waves from the East for their own political purposes. Meanwhile the more progressive regional television stations, or Third Channels, began to show DEFA films on a regular basis. After 1975, this gradual opening toward the East resulted in the occasional inclusion of a DEFA film in the main competition of the Berlin Film Festival.

Despite the recurring crises of legitimisation, the 1960s and 1970s saw considerable improvements in the institutional support structures that had been established during the 1950s. Founded in 1955, the Staatliche Filmarchiv der DDR (State Film Archives of the GDR) continued to be responsible for the preservation of all German films and film-related materials. Its studio theatre in the centre of Berlin, the Camera, became the main venue for new domestic and foreign releases. The training facilities in Babelsberg, established in 1954, were expanded and renamed in 1969 as the Hochschule für Film und Fernsehen der DDR 'Konrad

Wolf. Since the 1950s, the International Leipzig Festival for Documentary and Animated Film had provided an important showcase for lesser-known Third World cinemas and socialist traditions realised most convincingly in documentary practices. These include the long-term project *Die Kinder von Golzow* (The Children of Golzow, 1980), started by Winfried Junge in the early 1960s to document the coming of age of one generation of GDR citizens. Like the Oberhausen Short Film Festival in the West, the Leipzig Festival during the 1960s functioned as a forum for dissenting voices and sensibilities. For that reason, the organisers frequently experienced interference by the party leadership.

A new tradition of film criticism developed very slowly in the GDR and remained limited to mass dailies such as *Neues Deutschland*, popular magazines such as *Filmspiegel*, and more scholarly publications such as *Deutsche Filmkunst* (1953–63); influential critics included Rolf Richter and Fred Gehler. *Beiträge zur Film- und Fernsehwissenschaft* (formerly *Filmwissenschaftliche Mitteilungen* and *Filmwissenschaftliche Beiträge*) became the most influential publication for film critics and scholars. The *Beiträge* produced an infamous suppressed issue in 1965 that confirmed the close familiarity of DEFA directors with the international New Waves. From the 1970s to the 1980s, the most influential journal was *Film und Fernsehen*, which published sophisticated reviews of foreign as well as domestic films and initiated critical debates on controversial topics, including the persistent problem of audience appeal (Stoff in Allan and Sanford 1999: 43–57). However, the pressure on film critics and scholars to participate in the advancement of GDR society prevented more extensive theoretical and historical investigations (Becker 1999).

The 1970s: the discovery of everyday life

Following the disillusionment of the Eleventh Plenary, the 1970s ushered in a period of relative normalisation in foreign relations, greater attention to social policies that resulted in wage increases and more subsidised housing, and supplementation of the programme of industrial progress through greater concessions to the needs of consumer society. With the ascendancy of Erich Honecker as the new party leader came growing international recognition of the GDR through diplomatic relations with other countries and membership in the United Nations. The Honecker era also brought more relaxed relationships between the two Germanys after the official adaptation of the doctrine of the two German states. These developments had a profound influence on definitions of national identity and the role of Marxist thought in cultural practices. In 1971, the Eighth Party Congress determined that the GDR was already a fully developed socialist society; hence, there would be no more taboos on artistic expression. Film-makers were encouraged to engage with all socially relevant subject matter, including the kind of problems found in non-antagonistic class societies. Finally, the dogma of socialist realism, with its insistence on strong heroes and positive messages, could be replaced by the simultaneously more simple and complicated stories of everyday life. The relative degree of liberalisation reached during the Honecker era allowed artists and intellectuals to explore individual differences, personal perspectives, and alternative forms of consciousness. Yet these creative possibilities could be realised only within the clearly defined demarcations of public versus private, personal versus political, that contributed to the growing marginalisation of cinema culture and that have since been revealed as *Scheinöffentlichkeiten* (illusory public spheres).

DEFA production rate decreased from an annual average of 20 to 25 feature films in the early 1960s to 15 to 20 feature films during the 1970s, an indication both of the growing competition of other mass media and of film's changing role in cultural policy and socialist culture. Two phenomenal successes, *Der Mann, der nach der Oma kam* (The Man Who Came after Grandma, 1972) and *Die Legende von Paul und Paula* (The Legend of Paul and Paula, 1973), announced the new emphasis on the individual. These comedies and dramas about personal problems, especially those related to love, marriage, family, and the workplace, brought a more heterogeneous older audience back to the cinemas. Even more importantly, the films' close attention to everyday life opened up a space for the exploration of individual desires, subjective perceptions, and personal beliefs – perspectives previously ignored in the insistence on typical situations and positive characters and the search for social consensus and collective solutions. Many of these films featured young protagonists who stubbornly pursued their personal dreams within a conformist, intolerant society intent on suppressing difference and denouncing alterity. The provocative ways in which these freethinkers, eccentrics, non-conformists, and individualists exposed the existing contradictions in society, especially in male–female relations, pointed to a growing awareness both of the limits of enlightenment rationality and of the elusiveness of desire and happiness. Seen in the most positive terms, this discovery of the personal brought a long-overdue examination and validation of those aspects of human existence that resisted the determinations of class and, like gender and sexuality, could not be subordinated to the history of class struggle. Yet in a more negative light, the retreat from politics in the traditional sense also meant a continuing marginalisation of cinema within cultural life and a tacit acknowledgement of the failure of both socialist film and socialist society.

The fundamental shift in contemporary narratives from the notion of 'present time' (*Gegenwart*) to that of 'everyday life' (*Alltag*) has been described as a critique of the strict division between the personal and the political in Marxist ideology. Rebelling against that tradition, a new generation of film-makers turned to the quotidian and the ephemeral to explore alternatives to the teleological models of history and narrative that, until that point, had defined the present in relation to the past and the future (Feinstein 2002). For that reason alone, the so-called *Alltagsfilme* (contemporary dramas or films about everyday life) achieved much more than a mere withdrawal to private life; they offered a radically different model of public life and social reality based on individual experiences and personal desires. The new films about an everyday life unmistakably marked by the economic conditions in a socialist society but no longer completely determined by its underlying laws took two very different approaches to the filmic medium. Committed to the ethos of 'documentary realism', one group remained indebted to the tradition established by the Soviet films from the 1920s and the Italian neo-realists of the 1950s. The directors Lothar Warneke and Roland Gräf, the main representatives, often filmed on location, used lay actors, and preferred episodic narratives and a detached camera style. The other group, which included Heiner Carow, favoured a more dramatic, psychological approach and presented their controversial subject matter through conventional narrative structures and identificatory patterns. The difference between an ambitious art cinema with limited appeal and a popular cinema of strong emotions was repeatedly addressed by reviewers who either denounced the second group of directors for their conventional styles or attacked the first one for their lack of storytelling talent.

Documentary realism prevailed in several films about the problems of the new managerial classes and their place in the workers' and peasants' state. Frequently, these dramas aimed at a critique of the cult of productivism associated with socialist realism and a deconstruction of the myth of the indefatigable socialist worker and selfless party cadre (Finke 2002). The renewed interest in documentary styles developed partly in response to the enormously popular *Zeit zu leben* (Time to Live, 1969), whose portrayal of a dying man's selfless efforts to turn a troubled factory into a successful company owed much to idealised representations from the 1950s. Many reviewers rejected the film as socialist kitsch, but several filmmakers were energised to experiment with more differentiated approaches. Accordingly, in *Im Spannungsfeld* (In the Area of Conflict, 1970) the different perspectives of workers and technocrats shed light on the profound impact of technological progress on the workplace. Also set in the nationalised industries, *Netzwerk* (Network, 1970) exposed the inevitable conflict between production goals and technological innovation without offering any easy answers. And in *Bankett für Achilles* (A Banquet for Achilles, 1975), with its haunting images of the barren industrial landscape near Bitterfeld, Gräf used the retirement of a model worker and the resultant change of generations to ask serious questions about the future of traditional working-class culture. Besides diagnosing the limits of organisational and institutional change, all of these contemporary dramas drew attention to the difficulties of balancing work, career, and private life and of reconciling individual desires with collective goals. By returning to the problem of alienation first addressed by the New Waves, the proponents of 'documentary realism' effectively repoliticised cinema through the filmic language of objectivity, whereas more story-based directors such as Carow relied on affect and empathy to create similarly critical effects.

The problems of succeeding in the workplace and of finding personal fulfilment in a career also spilled over into other filmic genres and aesthetic registers. Humorous and farcical treatments proved ill-suited to the critique of institutional power attempted in *Nelken in Aspik* (Carnations in Aspic, 1976). More effective was the dramatic approach taken in *Die Flucht* (The Flight, 1977), about a respected East Berlin paediatrician who decides to leave the GDR for better research conditions in the West but dies tragically during his escape attempt; this film remained one of the few to address the growing problem of *Republikflucht* (literally, flight from the republic). The adventurous life of a resourceful car mechanic allowed Günter Reisch in *Anton der Zauberer* (Anton the Magician, 1978) to explore the possibility, or necessity, of individual survival strategies under socialism. In their choice of farcical, dramatic, and picaresque elements, these three exemplary films attest to the difficult balancing act between critique and compliance required of DEFA directors during the 1970s and acted out by their resourceful, cunning, and ingenious protagonists.

Generic conventions predominated in those comedies about everyday life that presented their social criticism within a basic acceptance of the status quo. Usually, these comedies focus on one specific problem – lack of childcare, the need for a new family car, a weekend house under construction – to test the resourcefulness of GDR citizens in dealing with the inevitable problems and crises. Thus the above-mentioned *Der Mann, der nach der Oma kam* depicts the humorous misunderstandings caused by the arrival of a male nanny into the household of an artistic dual-career couple. In *Einfach Blumen aufs Dach* (Just Flowers on the Roof, 1979), the birth of twins prompts their proud father to buy a used Chaika, the stately limousine issued to East European diplomats and the cause of many slapstick situations. In realising his dream of a summer house, the main character in the hilarious *Der Baulöwe* (The Building Tycoon, 1980) mobilises all of his skills at improvisation and persuasion to overcome the shortages of material and labour that sustain the barter economy in 'real existent socialism'. Similar problems preoccupy a middle-aged single mother who, in *Dach überm Kopf* (A Roof over Your Head, 1980), moves to Berlin to begin a new life in what turns out to be a dilapidated garden shed. As these examples show, criticising the economic structures and social institutions was possible as long as the basic assumptions about socialism as a political reality and historical fact remained unchallenged, an approach realised best in the conciliatory terms and harmonising effects of film comedy and its various registers.

More provocative contributions to the study of everyday life took the perspective of young adolescents, focusing in particular on their first sexual experiences. *Du und ich und Klein-Paris* (You and I and Little Paris, 1971), a declaration of love to the city of Leipzig, still presented the budding romance between a high-school student and a philosophy student in conventional gendered terms. By contrast, *Für die Liebe noch zu mager?* (Too Skinny for Love?, 1974), about the sexual coming of age of a young female textile worker, assumed the female point-of-view in a much more provocative portrayal of the ambiguities of desire. The starkly realist *Sabine Wulff* (1978) by newcomer Erwin Stranka and Gräf's intensely depressing *P. S.* (1979) were two films about young adults growing up in state homes that chose even more confrontational tones. Both films validated the experiences of social outsiders who resist all efforts at integration and repeatedly clash with the philistine attitudes in their social environment. Contributing to the controversial reception of these films, some film-makers intentionally used the

143

disenchantment among the country's youth as a measure of the uncertain future of socialism. Accordingly, not only did the youthful rebellion and defiance depicted in these stories threaten existing assumptions and conventions; it also cast serious doubt on the possibility of social reform and political change.

A significant number of films about everyday life featured strong women characters and focused on 'typical' female problems such as marriage, divorce, pregnancy, single parenthood, and the conflicting demands of love and career. Scholars have interpreted the increase of women's films both as a sign of resignation about the political situation and a more fundamental reorientation in cultural matters (Schütz 1990). The influential *Der Dritte* (The Third, 1972), about a single woman with a career and two children, was one of the first films to acknowledge the fundamental discrepancy between gender equality in the workplace and the persistent inequalities in male–female relationships. Women, subsequently, became the main protagonists in the reassessment of the project of socialism, with the resultant conflation of femininity and sexuality establishing a convenient framework for allegorical meanings and symptomatic readings. Despite the superficial similarities with the so-called New Subjectivity in the New German Cinema, the function of these new gendered discourses remained quite specific to East Germany. For the characters' personal quests reflected less a politicisation of the private sphere than a growing dissatisfaction with the provincialism, conformity, and hypocrisy of public life. In this situation, the validation of the personal was meant to counteract, if not overcome, the shortcomings of the political, and, in so doing, uphold the original dream of fully developed individuals living under socialism. In other words, the critique still functioned as a corrective, and not, as it would later during the 1980s, as a gesture of withdrawal and resignation.

On the most obvious level, the strong female characters confirmed the positive effects of women's rights in the areas of higher education, reproductive rights, family law, and childcare. The problem of femininity allowed film-makers both to affirm the utopian promise of happiness against the power of social conventions and to diagnose the corrosive effect of normative definitions of gender and sexuality on personal relationships. Yet in revealing the continuing problems in love relationships, the women also became a measure of the successes and, more often, the failures of socialism as a whole. Setting the tone for an entire decade, Carow's *Die Legende von Paul und Paula* transformed a young woman's uncompromising pursuit of true love and an authentic life into a compelling parable about the power of desire and the obstacles to its realisation. The phenomenal success of this countercultural fantasy and its celebration of female sexuality as an almost primordial force hinged on the representation of experience as a value in itself. Wolf's surprise hit *Solo Sunny* (1980), with Krößner in the title role of a struggling singer, was both more sobering in its attention to the external constraints on sexual and artistic self-expression and more provocative in its conclusions about the psychological mechanisms behind social conformity and obedience.

In response to these countercultural voices and subversive fantasies, the DEFA studio during the 1970s turned to literary adaptations to find new answers to the old question of national identity and cultural legacy. As in West Germany, though under different conditions, literature was enlisted once more as a stabilising force, institutionally as well as ideologically. The long-established affinity for realism produced two new Fontane adaptations, *Effi Briest* (1970) and *Unterm Birnbaum* (Under the Pear Tree, 1973), which, largely because of the casting of Angelica Domröse, foregrounded the psychological dimensions. Other adaptations (for example, of Eichendorff and E. T. A. Hoffmann) contributed to the ongoing reassessment of romanticism and its subversive effects within German literature, a process that continued well into the early 1990s with several films about, or based on, Hölderlin and Novalis. The main practitioner of literary adaptations, Egon Günther, took full advantage of the critical potential of rereading canonical works. While also interested in modern authors such as Arnold Zweig and Johannes R. Becher, Günther focused specifically on Goethe to affirm the contemporary relevance of the classics but also to question their elevated official status in GDR culture. Thus *Lotte in Weimar* (Lotte in Weimar, 1974), based on the Thomas Mann novel and featuring the internationally known Lilli Palmer, allowed the director to offer a biting critique of the Goethe cult and, more generally, the cult of genius and personality (Mahoney in Rentschler 1986). Yet Günther also gave a conventional class-based interpretation of *Die Leiden des jungen Werther* (The Sorrows of Young Werther, 1976) in place of the cancelled adaptation of Plenzdorf's provocative novel and play, *Die neuen Leiden des jungen Werther* (The New Sorrows of Young Werther), which emphasised the rebellious individualism of this quintessential 'Storm and Stress' hero.

All Goethe films from the mid-1970s were part of a series of public events around the central figure of German classicism that aimed to confirm the state's commitment to high culture. At best, the different approaches, from faithful adaptations to modernised versions, confirmed the relevance of the classics for the present, especially as regards the advancement of enlightenment principles and the notion of the fully developed individual. At worst, these literary adaptations contributed to grandiose self-representations of the political leadership and its manipulation of the humanistic legacy. Some of these problems compromised Siegfried Kühn's attempt to infuse the romantic and intellectual constellations of *Wahlverwandschaften* (Elective Affinities, 1974) with vaguely contemporary references. Similar concerns with historical adaptations haunted the related genre of the artist film that, like *Beethoven – Tage aus einem Leben* (Beethoven – Days in a Life, 1976), tried to update traditional notions of genius, in this case by having the dishevelled composer make an appearance in modern-day East Berlin. Resisting such tendencies, Wolf's contribution to the genre, *Goya* (1971), traces the painter's development from court painter to ally of the people and thereby examines the inherent conflict between art and power. Wolf continued his critical reflections on the public role of the artist in *Der nackte Mann auf dem Sportplatz* (The Naked Man in the Stadium, 1974) and its sobering conclusions about the difficulties of reconciling artistic ambitions with public expectations. His premature death in 1982 had the same effect on DEFA cinema as the death of Fassbinder in the same year. It marked the end of an era of artistic experimentation and social change.

In the same way that the literary adaptations and artist films inspired directors to comment on the conditions of contemporary film-making, the films about the Third Reich and the Second World War allowed them to revisit the place of the anti-fascist tradition in the founding myths of the nation. As a result, a number of film-makers returned to the question of resistance during the Third Reich. Telling the story of the group around Arvid Harnack, *KLK an PTX – Die Rote Kapelle* (KLK Calling PTZ – The Red Orchestra, 1971) acknowledges the existence of bourgeois resistance and argues for the importance of solidarity beyond social and political differences. In the highly acclaimed *Mama, ich lebe* (Mama, I Am Alive, 1977), Wolf explores the difficulties of national identity and political ideology through the individual choices of four Germans soldiers fighting against fascist aggression on the side of the Soviet Union. Focusing on the home front, Kirsten's *Ich zwing dich zu leben* (I'll Force You to Live, 1978) shows the desperate attempts of a disillusioned father to save his son from the mobilisation of the Hitler Youth during the last months of the war. Rücker and Reisch's *Die Verlobte* (The Fiancée, 1980), a co-production with GDR television, similarly gives a complex psychological portrayal of an imprisoned woman communist during the Third Reich. Challenging another aspect of the anti-fascist mythology, in Ulrich Weiß's *Dein unbekannter Bruder* (Your Unknown Brother, 1982), the discovery of a traitor in a communist resistance group raises provocative questions about the ethos of solidarity and its continued relevance for the present. Finally, Beyer's *Der Aufenthalt* (The Turning Point, 1983), based on the well-known Hermann Kant novel, uses the wartime experience of a German soldier in a Warsaw prison for a compelling reflection on collective guilt and national identity.

As part of the renewed interest in the Third Reich, film-makers also began to revisit the complicated relationship between history and narrative from the perspective of the Holocaust. In contrast to the DEFA films from the late 1940s, the contributions from the 1970s and 1980s turned to the history of anti-Semitism to initiate a fundamental reassessment of the categories of class, race, ethnicity, and nation. Thus, in *Jakob der Lügner* (Jacob the Liar, 1974), Beyer's adaptation of the famous Jurek Becker novel and the only DEFA film ever nominated for an Oscar, the possibility of hope and resistance becomes inextricably linked to conflicting definitions of reality and the meaning of truth. The impact of Jacob's lies about advancing Soviet troops on the ghetto inhabitants not only sheds light on the power of hope but also confirms the importance of narrative as a reclaiming, a producing of history. Extending this revisionist process to other historical periods, the adaptation of the Johannes Bobrowski novel *Levins Mühle* (Levin's Mill, 1980), about an anti-Semitic incident in late nineteenth-century West Prussia, draws attention to the changing alliances (for example, between Gypsies and Jews) that give rise to individual acts of political resistance.

The 1980s: the decline of cinema as a public sphere

Politically, the 1980s brought a series of dramatic changes that originated in the Soviet Union under Mikhail Gorbachev but affected all East European countries and eventually resulted in the collapse of the Soviet Union and the end of the Cold War. Whereas Poland, Hungary, and Czechoslovakia led the move toward democratisation, liberalisation, and unionisation, East Germany under Honecker continued to pursue a hard line approach and resist fundamental reforms. Among the few concessions were the loosening of travel restrictions and greater tolerance toward the church groups that later played a key role in the freedom movement. Elsewhere the calls for *glasnost* (transparency) and *perestroika* (restructuring) inspired great hopes for a democratisation of the communist party system and a decentralisation of the state economy and resulted in a wave of heightened cultural activity and intellectual debate; yet political developments in East Germany took a very different turn. With the party confirmed as the central power in all areas of GDR society, the growing separation between ordinary citizens and political cadres only increased the overall sense of disillusionment and dissatisfaction. For artistic production, whether in literature, art, or cinema, the last decade of the GDR meant a period of stagnation, ossification, and accommodation.

Adding to the frustration among writers, artists, and film-makers, the SED leadership refused to be consistent in its cultural policies. Repeated calls for more uplifting stories and heroic characters alternated with frank discussions about more innovative forms and styles. Broad declarations about the responsibility of the feature film in establishing models of social behaviour were followed by repeated complaints about DEFA films' persistent lack of popular appeal. The controversial banning in the GDR of several new films from the Soviet Union confirmed widespread suspicions that the political structure had reached a point of complete fossilisation. Abandoning all dreams of a unified, and unifying, socialist cinema, DEFA had to accept not only the predominance of Western imports in the movie theatres but also the diminished role of cinema in popular culture. Throughout the decade, the studio continued to cater to older audiences with an interest in literary adaptations and contemporary dramas and provide the cultural and political elites with traditional DEFA fare.

Meanwhile, many first-time directors worked in painful awareness of their separation from larger artistic and social movements, which was particularly troubling in light of the promising trends in other East European cinemas and the noticeable liberalisation in literature and the visual arts. Repeatedly, controversial films were released under conditions (for example, limited art house runs and few prints in circulation) guaranteeing that they would never reach their intended audience; as a result, a critical debate no longer took place. Far removed from official film culture, groups of young film artists rediscovered experimental and avant-garde styles and created new outlets for their work through the founding of small film clubs and collectives. This alternative film culture was strongly influenced by contemporary painting and performance art and, with centres in Dresden and

Berlin, played a major role in the emergence of a lively subculture with avant-garde sympathies and dissident energies (Fritzsche and Löser 1996).

In this context, foreign films became increasingly important in satisfying the entertainment needs of the population. Since the 1970s, two-thirds of all new releases had been produced in socialist countries, including the GDR itself. However, the one-third imported from capitalist countries regularly attracted the largest audiences. Rather than fighting these tendencies, the studio leadership aimed at a workable compromise between the conventional genre films imported from the West and the prestige productions by DEFA and other socialist film studios. Major box office successes included Italo-westerns by Sergio Leone and slapstick farces with the French comedian Luis de Funès, as well as a large number of Hollywood blockbusters such as *Flaming Inferno*, *Tootsie*, *Star Trek*, *Beverly Hills Cop*, *E.T.*, and *Dirty Dancing*. Most of these films attracted more than two million viewers. The popularity of West German film-makers extended from old-style professionals such as Hoffmann and oddball comedians such as Otto Waalkes to politically committed directors such as Peter Lilienthal and Margarethe von Trotta. For the most part, the impact of New German Cinema remained negligible, with the filmic sensibilities of a Rainer Werner Fassbinder or Wim Wenders fundamentally foreign to GDR audiences. In the metropolitan areas, the European art cinema of the 1970s and 1980s led by Ingmar Bergman, Damiano Damiani, Louis Malle, and Claude Lelouch found a more receptive audience. The same held true for the directors of the New American Cinema, including Martin Ritt, Arthur Penn, and Sidney Lumet (Jacobi and Janssen 1987).

During these years, DEFA usually produced one-fourth of all new releases. The biannual national film festival in Karl-Marx-Stadt (Chemnitz) functioned as the premiere showcase for these domestic productions. The few that reached more than one million viewers included *Solo Sunny* in 1980 and a re-released *Regalfilm*, *Jahrgang 45*, in 1990; more representative of box office hits from the decade were the light-hearted vacation comedy *Und nächstes Jahr am Balaton* (And Next Year on Lake Balaton, 1980) and a sensationalist drama of corruption set in the West German pharmaceutical industry, *Ärztinnen* (Women Doctors, 1984). The last two examples confirm to what degree popular cinema during the 1980s offered above all a distraction from economic shortages and cultural deficits, including the lack of travel opportunities, consumer goods, and career choices. The films about everyday life continued to celebrate the virtues of individualism, but now within a troubling atmosphere of apathy, resignation, and non-involvement. Under these conditions, the everyday lost much of its provocative force, providing little more than an excuse for the affirmation of entrenched petty-bourgeois tastes and attitudes. Similarly, the preoccupation with mundane things, especially when combined with narrow-mindedness, amounted to little more than an aesthetic and ideological accommodation to the status quo (Hoff and Wiedemann 1992).

On a more positive note, the marginalisation of cinema within GDR culture opened up a space for women directors and taboo subject matter such as homosexuality and religious faith. Until the 1980s, the function of femininity in classical narrative cinema and the role of women as symbols of a more complete life had never been analysed in feminist terms. Nor had the studio produced any female directors during a period that saw the rise of feminist film-making in the West. Until the arrival of Evelyn Schmidt and Iris Gusner, female contributions had remained limited to screenwriting. Their films exhibited considerable differences to those by women film-makers in the West, beginning with the representation of sexual desire and its centrality to female emancipation. Relying on conventional forms, Gusner in *Kaskade rückwärts* (Cascade Backwards, 1984) narrated the adventures of a middle-aged woman as she changes jobs, moves to the city, and sets out to find love and romance. Resisting the standard emancipatory narratives, Schmidt in *Das Fahrrad* (The Bicycle, 1982) portrayed the daily struggles of a young single mother and factory worker unwilling to improve her situation. In contrast to the contemporary dramas from the 1970s, no attempts at mediation or integration take place; even everyday life, it seems, has become meaningless. While largely ignored in the GDR, Schmidt's film became a critical success in the Federal Republic.

In the same way that the 1980s saw more realistic approaches to the woman's question, the new contemporary dramas about love, marriage, and family life avoided simplistic explanations in favour of more complex, open-ended treatments. Carow and Zschoche especially infused more realistic tones into the representation of male–female relationships. Continuing in the documentary tradition of the 1970s, Zschoche in *Bürgschaft für ein Jahr* (Probation for One Year, 1981) told the story of a young single mother fighting to keep custody of her children. By resisting the rhetoric of uplift and reform, the figure of the outsider gave rise to a sobering reflection on the double standards still prevalent in socialist society. Zschoche's critically acclaimed films about adolescents and young adults were distinguished by a similar refreshing lack of didacticism. Already *Sieben Sommersprossen* (Seven Freckles, 1978) stood out through its sensitive treatment of the sexual awakening of two teenagers at a youth summer camp. The boy and the girl returned to the screen in a sequel, *Grüne Hochzeit* (Green Wedding, 1988), as struggling young parents dealing with real-life problems. Earlier, in *Insel der Schwäne* (Island of Swans, 1983), the experiences of a young boy who moves from an idyllic village to the satellite city of Berlin-Marzahn allowed Zschoche to trace a similar process of disillusionment through architectural metaphors indicating that the socialist homeland had become inhospitable and uninhabitable. Relying on melodramatic elements, Carow in *Bis dass der Tod euch scheidet* (Until Death Do Us Part, 1979) presented the problems of a young married couple from the woman's perspective, but without any didactic intentions; the result: a disillusioned commentary on people's inability to change their own lives. Taking a very different approach, Carow, with *Coming out* (1989), made the first DEFA film to address the discrimination against homosexuals. Opening on the night of the fall of the Wall, the film and its important contribution to the history of gays in the GDR were eclipsed by world political events.

Taking a more conciliatory approach, Warneke in his symbolically charged stories about love and friendship upheld the possibilities of a fulfilled life by emphasising its spiritual and religious dimensions. In *Unser kurzes Leben* (Our Short Life, 1981), a free adaptation of Brigitte Reimann's *Franziska Linkerhand*, an ambitious young woman architect on her first assignment confronts the problems in building public housing but eventually learns to be satisfied with small solutions and workable compromises. Similarly, in *Die Beunruhigung* (Apprehension, 1982), a possible diagnosis of cancer persuades a successful divorced woman with a teenage son to re-examine her life and take seriously her need for more meaningful relationships; the hopeful ending rewards her with a supportive new lover. Warneke's last DEFA film, *Einer trage des anderen Last* (Bear Ye One Another's Burdens, 1988), about the friendship between two patients in a tuberculosis sanatorium, a Christian and a Marxist, brings together many of these thematic elements: the power of hope and belief, the need for tolerance and understanding, and the importance of reconciliation and forgiveness.

In contrast to Carow, Zschoche, and Warneke, whose filmic sensibilities found privileged expression in their complex women characters, a growing number of younger directors returned to established generic formulas to reintroduce more traditional attitudes toward marriage and sexuality. Thus *Der Doppelgänger* (The Double, 1985) offered a variation on the marital dramas of the 1970s by having a woman change her mind about divorce after a few months spent with her husband's more charming double. *Rabenvater* (Bad Father, 1985) examined the impact of divorce on children from the perspective of a father who, despite his irresponsible behaviour, is allowed to participate in raising his son. Not surprisingly, the strong women characters from the 1970s, too, produced a backlash in the form of several buddy films that, almost deliberately, reduced their female protagonists to sexual objects. As evidenced by Peter Kahane's *Ete und Ali* (Ete and Ali, 1985), the rituals of male bonding and youthful rebellion allowed for a return of misogynist attitudes, beginning with the equation of femininity with oppressive domesticity. Similarly Erwin Stranka's *Zwei schräge Vögel* (Two Weird Guys, 1989), about two computer programmers in what must be regarded as the GDR's most backward industry, developed its quirky atmosphere at the expense of the women characters.

The only genre that continued to flourish during the 1980s was the children's and youth film, one of the studio's traditionally strong areas (König et al. 1995 and 1996). Approaching the problems of childhood and early adolescence with humour and empathy, the children's films possessed all the qualities – social relevance, formal experimentation, and popular appeal – missing from many contemporary dramas and comedies. The fantastic elements allowed talented directors such as Herrmann Zschoche and Rolf Losansky to explore the miraculous in everyday life but also to address social problems through fantastic or surrealistic perspectives. Thus in Zschoche's *Philipp der Kleine* (Philipp the Small, 1976), the possession of a magic flute allows a timid boy to gain more self-confidence, initially through trickery but eventually on his own accord. *Das Schulgespenst* (The School Ghost, 1987), directed by Losansky, acknowledges the special expectations placed on little girls when the film's unruly heroine exchanges places with a ghost and causes a lot of confusion among her parents, teachers, and friends. Taking a more serious approach to the problems of adolescent girls, *Hasenherz* (Coward, 1987) revolves around a shy tomboy who is cast as the male lead in a fairytale film, an experience that, after a series of difficulties, leaves her more self-assured and accepting of herself.

In the wake of DEFA's fortieth anniversary in 1986, and in anticipation of the fortieth anniversary of the GDR in 1989, the studio experienced one last outpouring of productivity. Just as the myth of anti-fascism and the history of anti-Semitism had posed important challenges to the definition of national identity, the filmic representations of postwar history established the conceptual framework for working through the self-representation of the GDR, including through the filmic images produced by the DEFA studio since its beginnings (Byg 1991). This process had started in the early 1960s with irreverent parodies of early reconstruction films (for example, in *Karbid und Sauerampfer*) and continued during the 1970s in the subversive registers of the picaresque (for example, in *Anton der Zauberer*). With *Das Luftschiff* (The Dirigible, 1983), Rainer Simon enlisted the possibilities of the fantastic in telling the story of an eccentric inventor of dirigibles caught up in the turmoil of twentieth-century German history. In *Märkische Forschungen* (Exploring the Brandenburg Marches, 1982), Gräf used the competing research projects of a respected history professor and an amateur local historian to remind audiences of the continuing provocation of the past for the present. Based on the novel by Günter de Bruyn, the film suggests that the meaning of history can no longer be reduced to simplistic oppositions of true versus false, right versus wrong, but instead involves more complicated forms of rereading. Laying the foundation for the normalisation of German history that would continue in post-unification cinema, a few films reduced the Third Reich to a mere backdrop for personal stories held together by such universal themes as love, friendship, family, and community. Thus the perspective of children in *Kindheit* (Childhood, 1987) allowed its director to relativise the historical events by showing the simple pleasures of country life even under conditions of war, a tendency also found in the West German *Heimat* series. In *Die Schauspielerin* (The Actress, 1988), Corinna Harfouch appeared as a famous theatre actress who, in the 1930s, takes on a Jewish identity to be reconciled with her Jewish lover. By linking Jewishness and, by extension, anti-Semitism to questions of performance and masquerade, the film contributed to the postmodern simulations of history that, after 1989, would become a distinguishing mark of heritage cinema.

In the same way that the building of the Berlin Wall redefined the East German cinema, so its fall on 9 November 1989 brought about that cinema's institutional and ideological demise. Again, a number of *Überläuferfilme*, films begun as DEFA projects but released in another, united Germany, shed light on the wider implications for questions of cinema, nation, and history (Dalichow 1993). Michael Gwisdek's melancholy *Treffen in Travers* (Meeting in Travers, 1988) revisited an episode from the life of the eighteenth-century naturalist Georg Forster in a desperate effort to make sense of the failure of love and revolution. In his adaptation of a well-known Christoph Hein novel, *Der Tangospieler* (The Tango Player, 1991), Gräf returned to the purges of the 1960s to explain the decision of an academic banned from his profession to refuse all offers of professional rehabilitation. Relying on spatial metaphors, Kahane in *Die Architekten* (The Architects, 1990) turned the architectural competition for a community centre in a large public housing estate near Berlin into a compelling allegory of spiritual homelessness and the death of socialism. However, where Kahane still adhered to the DEFA tradition of associating architecture with visions of social change, other film-makers emphatically rejected all forms of utopian thinking. Instead, in *Motivsuche* (Location Research, 1989/1995), Dietmar Hochmuth exposed the manipulations behind documentary practices celebrated during DEFA times as the quintessence of socialist ethics and aesthetics. Starting the difficult process of writing film history, the release of previously banned films such as *Die Russen kommen, Sonnensucher,* and *Berlin um die Ecke* in 1988 and 1989 already gave some indication to audiences of what could have been. Shortly after the fall of the Wall, several other shelved films had their belated premieres and were received with a similar mixture of surprise, sadness, and anxious anticipation. Then, in 1990, the Berlin Film Festival dedicated an entire festival segment to the *Regalfilme.* Yet while the retrospective confirmed DEFA's important contribution to German cinema, it also raised serious questions about the studio's uncertain future.

6

WEST GERMAN CINEMA
1962–90

If the building of the Wall in August 1961 formalised the division between cinema in East and West, the Oberhausen Manifesto announced a radical break with the cinema of the postwar period. On 28 February 1962, a group of young film-makers at the Oberhausen Short Film Festival proclaimed: 'The old film is dead. We believe in the new.' Signed by Edgar Reitz and Alexander Kluge, among others, the manifesto was written to accomplish three things: to formulate a critique of conventional genre cinema, to introduce a new kind of film-making, and to present a list of demands on the government. The 26 film-makers called for public policies and subsidies that would finally acknowledge film as an art form comparable to the other arts. While the signatories shared a basic belief in the importance of film authorship, their manifesto emphasised institutional rather than aesthetic concerns. Unlike the directors of the French Nouvelle Vague, who rebelled against an existing tradition of quality, the representatives of the Young German Cinema first had to establish an art cinema and prove its cultural relevance. Consequently, their contribution to the European New Waves of the 1960s and their relationship to the New German Cinema of the 1970s must be evaluated in light of the structural weaknesses of the West German film industry and the absence of a strong art cinema tradition. Similarly, the Oberhausen approach to the politics of the aesthetic and the later emphasis on cinema as a social practice can be understood only within the turbulent politics of the entire decade (Fischer and Hembus 1981, Koch 1985, Reichmann and Worschech 1991).

The international reception of the New German Cinema has profoundly influenced the historiography of West German cinema after Oberhausen (Rentschler 1984 and 1988). It has contributed to the perception of the 1960s and 1970s as one film-historical period, with the institutional critique and modernist sensibility of the Young German Cinema absorbed into the discourse on authorship, identity, and subjectivity associated with New German Cinema. Despite its embeddedness in new social movements and collaborative practices, New German Cinema has been discussed primarily as an *Autorenkino* (author's cinema) associated with famous names such as Rainer Werner Fassbinder, Wim Wenders, Werner Herzog, and Volker Schlöndorff (Sanford 1980, Franklin 1983, Phillips 1984). While the emphasis on individual creativity has helped experimental film-makers such as

Jean-Marie Straub and Danièle Huillet, writer-activists like Alexander Kluge, and controversial figures such as Hans Jürgen Syberberg, it has also contributed to the neglect of lesser-known directors who did their most innovative work by expanding and revising genre conventions. The women directors Margarethe von Trotta, Helke Sander, and Helma Sanders-Brahms are often marginalised in canonical accounts of New German Cinema but have played a central role in the emergence of feminist film scholarship and a gendered critique of the West German *Autorenfilm* (Möhrmann 1980, Fischetti 1992, Knight 1992, Majer O'Sickey and von Zadow 1998).

Critical analyses of the films themselves have emphasised their function as social commentary and political critique, with narrative strategies, visual styles, and acoustic effects seen as the primary means (and measures) in the new politics of identity, subjectivity, and representation. Reading their stories and images as either a reflection of West German society or an expression of unacknowledged traumas and crises, some scholars have identified recurring topics such as the decline of the family and the conflict between the generations; dramatic changes in the workplace and the disintegration of the public sphere; the impact of the sexual revolution and female emancipation; and individual experiences of isolation, discrimination, and marginalisation (Pflaum and Prinzler 1983, Pflaum 1990). Throughout, special attention has been paid to the pivotal role of Young German Cinema and New German Cinema in uncovering the institutional and ideological legacies of the Third Reich and in making *Vergangenheitsbewältigung* an integral part of public life (Reimer 1992, Wenzel 2000). Moving beyond such thematic approaches, cultural-studies-oriented scholars have used the radical questioning of identity and subjectivity to situate the films within the larger projects of feminism, post-modernism, and, more specifically, the literature of New Subjectivity (McCormick 1991, Kosta 1994). Yet others have used close readings of individual films to trace the continuing German dialogue with America as cultural myth and hegemonic presence (Corrigan 1994). The unifying category of art cinema with its different modes of production and reception has been analysed as an important part both of the struggle against the global dominance of Hollywood and of the search for alternative economic and aesthetic models (Elsaesser 1989). Similarly, the inclusion of non-narrative forms such as the documentary and the essay film has produced a more sophisticated understanding of the politics of film form against the backdrop of the student movement of the 1960s and the wave of terrorism during the 1970s (Alter 2002). More recently, the almost exclusive focus on images and narratives has been challenged by several studies that insist on the importance of film music to the aesthetic vision of New German Cinema and explore the film-makers' heavy reliance on classical music for working through the difficulties of national culture and identity (Flinn 2004, Hillman 2005).

Until 1989, the critical reception of Young German Cinema and New German Cinema remained under the influence of the interpretative paradigms of the Cold War. Apart from a few passing references in feature films made after 1962, the German division became a structuring absence and the GDR an absent other, overshadowed by the omnipresence of American mass culture and Western capitalism. There was no sustained engagement with East German films, despite the surprising parallels in thematic choices and stylistic preferences. By contrast, the ideological orientation of the Federal Republic toward Western Europe and the United States had a profound effect both on the aesthetic revolution associated with the New Waves and the political revolution initiated by the student movement. Under these conditions, the convergence of cinema, aesthetics, and politics was inevitable, given the young generation's desire for new forms of self-expression beyond the traditional high–low culture divide and the artificial national–international distinction. As a result, filmic practices after 1962 developed through a number of oppositions: the fascination with American mass culture versus the critique of US cultural imperialism; the interest in formal experimentation versus the commitment to an alternative public sphere; the privileging of literature versus the search for other non-narrative filmic traditions; and the opposition to political and cultural institutions versus the demand for government funding and support (Bronner and Bronner 1973, Petermann and Thoms 1988).

Just as the Oberhausen Manifesto of 1962 announced a radical transformation of cinema, the resignation of Adenauer in 1963 marked the beginning of a period of great social upheavals and political changes. The Great Coalition of 1966 between the conservative Christian Democrats (CDU) and the more progressive Social Democrats (SPD) institutionalised the historical compromise between stability and reform that guaranteed continuous economic growth but, after 1969, also brought more progressive policies under SPD Chancellors Willy Brandt and Helmut Schmidt. Known as the APO (extra-parliamentary opposition), the radical student movement mobilised in the early 1960s around demands for school and university reform but soon developed a more fundamental critique of postwar society and the capitalist system. In declaring the personal as political, their programmatic calls for radical change gave rise to diverse leftist and alternative groups identified with the label 'the sixties' or 'the 68 generation'. Denouncing mainstream society as reactionary, conformist, and repressive, this heterogeneous counterculture explored alternative lifestyles based on sexual liberation, social experimentation, and individual self-discovery, often with the help of drugs, music, and consciousness-raising. The search for alternatives to bourgeois marriage and the experimentation with different models of family and community (for instance in communes, citizens' initiatives, and women's groups) was an integral part of this process, as was the symbolic role of popular music, fashion, and cinema in providing new identities beyond the oppressive regimes developed during the period of postwar reconstruction and the Economic Miracle.

The Oberhausen Manifesto and the Young German Cinema

The innovative films made after 1962 as a result of better funding opportunities shared a number of formal characteristics and intellectual qualities. Almost all offered an implicit or explicit critique of genre cinema and its stabilising functions within postwar society. Through fragmented narratives, alienation effects, documentary sequences, and self-reflexive commentary, the programme of a politicised modernism facilitated an analysis of the repressive social and political structures of the Federal Republic. Articulated across a range of contemporary themes and motifs, this new alliance between radical aesthetics and radical politics influenced the discourse of art cinema throughout the 1960s and, with considerable modifications, during the 1970s and 1980s as well – until the return to genre cinema in the 1990s. Where other European New Waves engaged with the question of the political in direct and often confrontational ways, West German (and East German) film-makers preferred a more mediated approach, one that used culture and history to address problems of power and identity. In accordance with a much longer tradition of inwardness, contradictions in society were often expressed through the conflict between the generations and its impact on family structures and gender roles. The possibility of resistance and the question of difference often assumed the form of a male subjectivity of crisis, an indication of the profoundly patriarchal structure of postwar society. Similarly, the diagnosis of alienation was predicated, sometimes in problematic ways, on the privileges of class, ethnicity, and citizenship that obliged film-makers to the Eurocentric model, including its presumptions about national culture and identity.

For all of these reasons, Young German Cinema and New German Cinema remained very much a product of the homogeneous, prosperous middle-class society that inspired the Oberhausen Manifesto in the first place. In response to the film-makers' demands, but also in full awareness of the industry's structural problems, the government created an extensive infrastructure of federal offices, funding agencies, and training facilities designed to strengthen and improve the German film. The most important institution for young film-makers was the Kuratorium Junger Deutscher Film (Board for the New German Film), founded in 1965 and initially run under the auspices of the Ministry of the Interior. The Kuratorium provided interest-free loans based on a committee review of submitted screenplays. After 1969, individual states administered this programme, with Bavaria and North-Rhine Westphalia leading the effort to use film funding as a form of regional development. While the Kuratorium gave first-time directors much-needed support, it failed to remedy more endemic problems such as the unwillingness of distributors and exhibitors to show difficult films and the absence of a cinephile culture open to formal experimentation.

The Federal Film Subsidy Law of 1967 promised financial support to the film industry in the name of promoting quality and improving competitiveness; the law has since been revised several times. After intensive lobbying by industry representatives, the Film Subsidy Board, which was overseen by the Ministry of Economics, began to offer loans to companies with a proven record of box office successes. Financed through a tax on box office receipts, this system benefited the so-called 'weepies cartel' and led to a short-lived increase in production – cheaply made sex education films, among others. The chances for more long-term changes improved greatly with the founding of two film schools in 1966 and 1967, respectively, the Deutsche Film- und Fernsehakademie (dffb) in Berlin and the Hochschule für Film und Fernsehen (HFF) in Munich. Whereas the Berlin school developed into a centre of documentary film-making, the Munich school during the 1970s became known for cultivating aesthetic sensibilities. Contributing to this nascent film culture, journals such as *Filmkritik* (under Enno Patalas) and, later, *Film* provided an important platform for ideology critique and aesthetic debates throughout the 1960s and 1970s. Meanwhile Frieda Grafe and Hans C. Blumenberg, both writing for national newspapers, educated readers through their knowledgeable and insightful reviews not only of the most recent European and American films but also of the classics of German cinema.

Already the first wave of films released in 1966 gave a clear indication of the creative and critical energies gathered under the heading of Young German Cinema. In *Abschied von gestern* (Yesterday Girl, 1966), Kluge enlisted episodic narrative structures, analytical montage techniques, and extended documentary sequences in diagnosing the growing sense of amnesia and anomie in public and private life. With clear references to the mass psychology of fascism, Schlöndorff examined the dynamics of brutality and submission in *Der junge Törless* (Young Torless, 1966), his critically acclaimed adaptation of the well-known Musil novella. Set in an upper-class milieu, Peter Schamoni's *Schonzeit für Füchse* (No Shooting Time for Foxes, 1966) captured the symptoms of modern alienation through the explosive combination of disaffected youth and social privilege. Finally, Ulrich Schamoni, in *Alle Jahre wieder* (Next Year, Same Time, 1967), turned the festivities during a typical Christmas season into an almost clinical study on the hypocrisies of bourgeois life.

Several directors used high school and college students as main characters to challenge obsolete social and sexual conventions. Individual gestures of youthful rebellion invaded the liberal upper-class milieu of Johannes Schaaf's *Tätowierung* (Tattoo, 1967), whereas collective forms of resistance prevailed among the graduating seniors of Peter Zadek's hilarious *Ich bin ein Elefant, Madame* (I'm an Elephant, Madame, 1969). May Spils's light-hearted comedies with Werner Enke, *Zur Sache, Schätzchen* (Go for It Baby, 1968) and *Nicht fummeln, Liebling* (No Pawing, Darling, 1970), presented Schwabing's bohemian milieu of daydreamers and good-for-nothings as the epicentre of the counterculture. Yet the problems of the carefree young unmarried couple in *Es* (It, 1965) already revealed some of the limits of free sexuality by ending with the woman's pregnancy and abortion. Questions of gender and sexuality also informed Ula Stöckl's *Neun Leben hat die Katze* (The Cat Has Nine Lives, 1968), a contribution that, with its close attention to the female perspective, remained the exception until the rise of feminist film-making in the mid-1970s. Stöckl's collaboration with Reitz on *Geschichten vom Kübelkind* (Stories of the Trashcan Kid, 1971), a series of brief episodes held together by a highly stylised female figure, was similarly atypical for the times.

The Young German Cinema thrived on a number of productive contradictions. Many film-makers shared an intense frustration with the Federal Republic and its ossified social and political structures. Some used formal means to convey their vision of a different world, while others focused on particular themes to criticise the existing conditions. Some were driven by the desire for self-expression, while others set out to realise film's inherent potential as a form of communication. Some focused on developing a new filmic language, while others devoted themselves to building an alternative public sphere. Some chose innovative forms and techniques to express their dissent, while others reinterpreted established forms in new and creative ways. Ultimately, however, all film-makers channelled their deeply felt separation from the culture of economic liberalism and social conservatism into two equally important thematic concerns: the conflict between the generations and the battle between the sexes.

Unlike in the postwar period, film-makers could no longer articulate and contain these conflicts through traditional forms; instead they examined them through new ways of telling, or not telling, stories. In terms of artistic influences, the historical avant-gardes and the experimental film proved very influential; equally important were the challenges to classical narrative by the European New Waves, and the work of François Truffaut, Jean-Pierre Melville, and Jean-Luc Godard in particular. The enthusiastic German reception of the French and Italian New Waves was directly linked to the rediscovery of social realism and documentary forms, the critique of classical narrative and its ideological underpinnings, and the transformation of film into a political weapon. These diverse influences allowed the Young Germans to approach the relationship between social reality and filmic reality as a more open, dynamic, active, and interventionist one. Accordingly, they used black-and-white cinematography to counter the effects of verisimilitude, experimented with anti-psychological acting styles, and opened up new perspectives through montage, voice-over, and stream-of-consciousness.

It has become common practice to give full credit to the Oberhausen generation for the two-pronged attack on the repressive social and political structures of the Adenauer era and the generic conventions associated with the Hollywood studio system. But in fact, the radicalisation of film form would not have been possible without earlier developments in West German film and literature. The myth of a new beginning served only to distract from the considerable continuities between the 1950s and 1960s. In the cinema, Ottomar Domnick's *Jonas* (1957) already relied on an innovative narrative structure to show the alienation of the individual in the big city. Usually identified with the realist tendencies of the late 1950s, Will Tremper in *Die endlose Nacht* (The Endless Night, 1963) addressed similar existential concerns by documenting one ordinary, and yet also extraordinary, night at Berlin's Tempelhof airport. To add to these patterns of influence, many of the sensibilities associated with the Young German Cinema were prefigured in the looks, gestures, and attitudes promoted by the young actors and actresses of the late 1950s, such as Karin Baal and Horst Buchholz, who combined classic star attributes such as beauty and sex appeal with the cool detachment perfected later by the androgynous anti-stars of the infamous Munich scene, Uschi Obermaier and Marquard Bohm.

The Young German Cinema profited furthermore from the intense interest in modernist experimentation among many postwar writers, including those involved with the literary *Gruppe 47*. These patterns of cultural transfer from literature to film dominated the process of *Vergangenheitsbewältigung* for a long time, and in not always productive ways. The concomitant politicisation of film-makers built on the example of the public intellectual personified by Heinrich Böll and Günter Grass. Not surprisingly, both authors inspired a number of acclaimed film adaptations that functioned as transitional films between 1950s cinema and 1960s cinema. Confirming the status of Böll as the most influential author of the postwar period, Herbert Vesely's *Das Brot der frühen Jahre* (The Bread of Those Early Years, 1962) followed its main character on the difficult journey from social conformity to individual freedom. Based on *Billiard um halb zehn*, Straub and Huillet's *Nicht versöhnt* (Not Reconciled, 1965) mapped the return of the repressed through the political conflicts in a family of architects and, by extension, in modern German history. For *Katz und Maus* (Cat and Mouse, 1967), Hans Jürgen Pohland pursued similar critical intentions by adapting Grass's autobiographical account about a group of high school friends from Danzig during the Second World War. In addition to these contemporary authors, it was Bertolt Brecht who exerted the strongest influence on filmic practices both through his reflections on epic theatre and through his theory of progressive mass media. Especially the writings of Hans Magnus Enzensberger about the consciousness industry confirmed Brecht's relevance to the politicisation of film during the 1960s (Mueller 1989).

In terms of filmic styles, Young German Cinema can be identified with three basic tendencies: the return to social realist forms and documentary influences; the revival of avant-garde and experimental practices; and the direct engagement with popular culture and other modern mass media. The critical impulses received from documentaries prompted some film-makers to deal more directly with problems of social and economic inequality. They adopted narrative strategies first tested by contemporary writers (for example, in protocol literature) in order to give a voice to marginalised social groups. But their films also questioned the conventions of reportage, and its tacit assumptions about objectivity and authenticity, by introducing more subjective and more differentiated point-of-views. Erika Runge's television feature *Warum ist Frau B. glücklich?* (Why Is Mrs B. Happy?, 1968), about an ordinary working-class woman, remains the best-known example of this productive exchange between documentary literature and film.

The Young German Cinema profited equally from the renewed interest in avant-garde traditions. Never part of the mainstream, Birgit and Wilhelm Hein, Werner Nekes and Dore O., and Vlado Kristl experimented with the formal language of film, including the inherent tension between competing notions of the visible and the real. Straub and Huillet emerged as the main representatives of a new avant-garde radical cinema in its aesthetic and political programme (Byg 1995). The austerity of their filmic vision prevented a more extensive reception but guaranteed their influence on other film-makers. *Chronik der Anna Magdalena Bach* (The Chronicle of Anna Magdalena Bach, 1968) showed their systematic refusal to assume a position of narrative authority but also established a conceptual model for formal inquiries into the spatio-temporal relationships unique to the filmic medium. Similar strategies of detachment informed Straub and Huillet's engagement with literary texts, from Brecht in the case of *Geschichtsunterricht* (History Lessons, 1972) to Kafka in the case of *Klassenverhältnisse* (Class Relations, 1984).

Some members of the avant-garde appropriated new filmic techniques for provocative actions and critical interventions. Hellmuth Costard caused a scandal at the 1968 Oberhausen Film Festival with *Besonders wertvoll* (Of Special Merit, 1968) and its close-up of a speaking penis. Throughout the 1970s and 1980s, Costard relied on techniques such as slow motion and time-lapse photography to explore the relationship between the filmic image and the visible world, including more recently in the whimsical *Aufstand der Dinge* (The Revolt of Things, 1994). As one of the main representatives of a radical cinema, Harun Farocki commented extensively on the politics of representation in capitalist societies, from early experimental shorts to ambitious essay films such as *Etwas wird sichtbar* (Something Becomes Visible, 1981), about the role of mass media during the Vietnam War. His compilation of instructional films, titled *Leben: BRD* (1990), has been released under the suggestive English title: *How to Live in the Federal Republic*.

In ways not often acknowledged, the Young German Cinema also developed its unique filmic style through critical re-interpretations of classical Hollywood genres, especially the crime thriller, and through self-conscious references to popular culture, from pop music to Pop Art. Inspired by the New Wave's appropriation of the 1930s gangster film, Klaus Lemke's *Achtundvierzig Stunden bis Acapulco* (Forty-eight Hours to Acapulco, 1967) and Rudolf Thome's *Rote Sonne* (Red Sun, 1970) staged their highly stylised scenarios of sex and murder with scientific precision and ritualistic detachment. The isolated nature of such attempts drew attention to the lack of an established iconography of crime and action adventure in German cinema. Combining elements of the Hollywood melodrama and the American underground film, Robert van Ackeren, Rosa von Praunheim, and, of course, Rainer Werner Fassbinder enlisted dramatic excess, ironic detachment, and formal stylisation in measuring the reverberations of the sexual revolution, and the gay rights movement in particular. Inspired by Andy Warhol, Praunheim in *Die Bettwurst* (Kieler Bettwurst, 1971) and Ackeren in *Harlis* (1972) relied on elements of a camp aesthetic, including its peculiar combination of melancholy and indifference, to capture the spectacle of modern sexuality and its playful scenarios of submission and domination. Through their deconstruction of normative sexual identities and their exploration of new aesthetic sensibilities, both directors extended the formal provocations of the 1960s into the identity-based sexual politics of the 1970s.

Known as a literary author, critical writer, and political activist, Alexander Kluge must be considered the film-maker most closely identified with the original programme of the Young German Cinema (Kluge 1983 and 1999). Reflecting on the social relevance of film, Kluge's *Die Artisten in der Zirkuskuppel: ratlos* (Artists in the Big Top: Perplexed, 1968) offered an allegorical self-representation of Young

160

German Cinema that culminated in an emphatic affirmation of the power of the imagination. By developing further the analytical possibilities of montage and the critical energy of fantasy, Kluge managed to preserve the Oberhausen spirit throughout the 1970s, 1980s, and 1990s, among other ways by applying his energies to other forms and media. In an influential study co-authored with Oskar Negt, *Öffentlichkeit und Erfahrung* (Experience and the Public Sphere, 1972), he discussed the role of experience in a society dominated by modern mass media. The book confirmed Kluge's intellectual debt to Critical Theory, which, from Horkheimer and Adorno's critique of the culture industry to Habermas's writings on the public sphere, influenced an entire generation of critics and scholars committed, like Kluge, to rethinking the relationship between theory and praxis.

Consequently, his approach to film-making brings together two equally important impulses: the transformation of film into a means of critical inquiry and the transformation of cinema into an alternative public sphere. This ongoing process requires the active participation of the audience in creating what Kluge once described as 'the real film in the head of the spectator'. Montage provides him with the most effective strategy of deconstructing and reconstructing meanings. It establishes a discursive model for combining documentary footage, voice-over commentary, legal terminology, and political speeches with extensive references to painting, literature, folklore, mythology, and, time and again, classical music. Together these elements give rise to an anti-illusionist film aesthetic firmly resistant to conventional patterns of identification but fully committed to sense perception as a productive force.

During the 1970s, Kluge continued to critique social institutions and public discourses through his insistence on the productive power of fantasy and its ability to anticipate a society organised around the fulfilment of human desires. The search for more authentic forms of experience linked the episodic documentary style of *Abschied von gestern*, his most famous film, and the conceptual approach of *Gelegenheitsarbeit einer Sklavin* (Part-time Work of a Domestic Slave, 1973) to the dream-like montage sequences in such later works as *Die Patriotin* (The Patriot, 1979) and *Die Macht der Gefühle* (The Power of Emotions, 1983). Frequently, the director relied on women as the representatives of a tradition of human productivity presumably less damaged by the existing power structures. His aesthetic choices confirmed the ability of high culture, including classic opera and canonical literature, to resist the process of commodification; but, in truly dialectical fashion, Kluge made this point most forcefully through a modern mass medium like film and, more recently, television.

Despite the provocation of the Young German Cinema, genre conventions remained a strong influence throughout the decade and allowed the West German film industry to survive intact, though on a greatly reduced level. Film producers frequently used co-productions to reduce their economic risk and expand the framework of cultural and geographical references toward a popular European cinema both inspired by, and distinguished from, Hollywood. With the continuing decline of domestic film production due to the intense competition from television and the diversification of mass culture came a growing fragmentation of the audience into an art house audience, a youth audience, and the small sub-groups served by the porn cinemas near railway stations and the revival cinemas in popular vacation spots. The ageing stars and directors of the 1950s continued to rely on established formulas to connect, though often with little success, to the tastes and styles of the young generation. Offering German alternatives to rock 'n' roll, the *Schlagerfilme* (hit song films) featured popular singers such as Freddy Quinn who, like his predecessor Albers, sought adventures on foreign shores, or Udo Jürgens who appeared as the personification of maturity among the rockers and mods in the German–Italian co-production *Siebzehn Jahr, blondes Haar* (The Battle of the Mods, 1966). The world of teenagers inspired several high school comedies in the style of *Die Lümmel von der ersten Bank* (The Brats from the First Row, 1968) that reduced the spectre of youth insurrection to harmless pranks and adventures. Just as these comedies about free-spirited youth guided younger audiences in their choice of fashion styles, status symbols, and subcultural vernacular, the more exploitative films inspired by the sexual revolution supplied older audiences with more lurid fantasies about adolescent sexuality. The controversial *Helga* series (1967–68) and the various sequels to the *Schulmädchenreport* (School Girl Report, 1970) resorted to the documentary format, and to educational rhetoric, to conceal their lascivious intentions. By contrast, the enormously successful *Oswald Kolle: Das Wunder der Liebe* (Oswald Kolle: The Miracle of Love, 1968) relied on the discourse of public health to enlighten the public about diverse sexual practices. Throughout the 1960s and 1970s, the Munich-based producer Alois Brummer profited greatly from the liberalisation of European screens by specialising in the uniquely German mixture of soft porn, crude humour, and *Heimatfilm*.

Born out of the desperate pursuit of disappearing audiences, the hybridisation of genres during the 1960s and the concomitant increase in European co-productions gave rise to highly arbitrary combinations of crime caper, action adventure, and vacation comedy. Foreign locations, different nationalities, and unusual local customs gave film-makers licence to experiment with the most bizarre plot combinations, involving jewellery heists, fashion shows, adulterous affairs, fake kidnappings, and so forth. This imaginary European topography also allowed them to work with well-known French and Italian stars or shoot their films on (inexpensive) foreign locations. The model for this sort of generic eclecticism was established by the rewriting of German history as a picaresque in the highly successful *Es muss nicht immer Kaviar sein* (Operation Caviar, 1961), based on the best-seller by Johannes Mario Simmel. From then on, French characters and locations initiated audiences into the secrets of *savoir vivre*, whereas English country settings provided an imaginary space for the celebration of old-fashioned eccentricity. Nostalgic tendencies were especially pronounced in the *Pater Brown* series that, beginning with *Das schwarze Schaf* (The Black Sheep, 1960), presented Heinz Rühmann in the role of the inquisitive country priest and amateur detective created by G. K. Chesterton.

The popular Edgar Wallace films combined elements of the murder mystery, Victorian melodrama, and Gothic tale of horror to indulge their fans' lurid fascination with the cruelties and perversions behind the façade of British propriety and reserve. Produced by Constantin, the series started with *Der Frosch mit der Maske* (Face of the Frog, 1959) and continued with countless sequels up through the 1970s that featured the same cast of thieves, murderers, forgers, addicts, perverts, lunatics, and aristocrats. Cult classics from the series include *Die toten Augen von London* (Dead Eyes of London, 1961) and *Das Gasthaus an der Themse* (The Inn on the Thames, 1962), two Alfred Vohrer films that brought together many regulars, including Joachim Fuchsberger as the inspector from Scotland Yard and Eddi Arent as his comic sidekick. The performative excess and formulaic story line of the Edgar Wallace films have contributed to their enduring status as (postmodern) cult movies on late-night television. Reviving one of the great villains of Weimar cinema, CCC's *Mabuse* series failed to achieve similar effects, despite an initial contribution by Lang himself, with *Die tausend Augen des Dr. Mabuse* (The Thousand Eyes of Dr Mabuse, 1960).

Meanwhile, the German love–hate relationship with Hollywood continued in the context of these European co-productions. America remained an integral part of the German imagination through its double identification with the urban jungle and the primordial wilderness. On the one hand, the fascination with crime and violence – and the awareness of their infinite marketability – stood behind the formulaic *Jerry Cotton* series and similar low-budget productions based on the dime novels published by Bastei. Like the Wallace and Mabuse films, these films were often co-productions with British, Italian, French, or Spanish companies, with Constantin one of the studios working in this mode (Bergfelder 2004). On the other hand, the mythical American West inspired romantic dreams of a reconciliation of culture and nature in the figure of the noble savage. Profiting from the great popularity of Karl May, *Der Schatz im Silbersee* (Treasure of Silver Lake, 1962) became the most successful German film from that year and was followed by several other May adaptations, including the *Winnetou* trilogy (1963–65). Produced for Rialto-Film, directed by Harald Reinl, and usually shot in Yugoslavia with lead actors Pierre Brice and Lex Barker, these westerns allowed for a displacement of German history into the mythological spaces of the New World; therein the May adaptations fulfilled a similar socio-psychological function as the DEFA Indian films. The transposition of such regressive patterns into the world of Germanic myth and legend, as attempted by Reinl in the two-part *Die Nibelungen* (The Nibelungs, 1966–67), proved much less successful, an indication perhaps of the continuing need for a clear distinction between American popular culture and German high culture.

The 1970s: the emergence of New German Cinema

The transition from the first to the second generation after Oberhausen was accompanied by significant improvements on the institutional level but also persistent problems in the organisation of the film industry; overshadowing both was an abiding sense of belatedness, or separateness, in comparison to other New Wave cinemas. The inherent contradictions in an art cinema that combined aesthetic innovation and political critique, but did so primarily within the institutional parameters of a national cinema, found expression in the unifying concept of film authorship through which the New German Cinema distinguished itself from the Young German Cinema. From the perspective of the 1960s, the *Autorenfilm* and its emphasis on individual creativity contributed to the depoliticisation of cinema as a public sphere. Yet from the perspective of the 1980s, the 1970s notion of authorship emerged as a logical continuation of earlier debates about the normative function of genre cinema and the search for radically subjective modes of narration and representation. During the decade itself, the identification of New German Cinema with the work of individual directors promised a valid compromise between changing political and economic conditions, on the one hand, and new aesthetic sensibilities and critical agendas, on the other. The film-makers' undiminished desire for political relevance betrayed a continuing belief in film as a reflection of, and intervention into, social reality. At the same time, their authorial styles allowed for more fluid relationships between reality and representation that, according to some directors, made film an integral part of contemporary life, if not a more authentic form of fantasy and experience.

Politically, the 1970s were defined by the ambitious reform initiatives – from the liberalisation of family law and changes in the educational system to improvements in German–German relations – started under the Social Democratic government of Chancellor Brandt. The deterioration of the postwar culture of consensus and status quo coincided with the emergence of radical leftist and autonomous groups and culminated in a wave of terrorist activities in the late 1970s. In response, the government passed several measures, including a much-criticised emergency decree, to restore law and order. These measures only deepened suspicions among many citizens about the return of authoritarian structures, if not a fascist mentality. Widespread disillusionment with traditional politics added to the appeal of alternative movements, including the early ecology movement, women's movement, and gay rights movement. The turn toward the private sphere also gave rise to a heterogeneous counterculture committed both to the defence of traditional civil rights and to new forms of identity politics that, among other things, brought consciousness raising and alternative therapies, autonomous projects and New Age religions, and the various cultural movements – from punk to new wave – that connected the contemporary culture of narcissism and ironic self-referentiality to postmodern sensibilities in literature, theatre, painting, architecture, music, and film.

Sharing basic beliefs with the political elites about the possibility of social change and the importance of critical debate, New German Cinema in some ways functioned as an integral part of SPD cultural policy. Economically and politically, the discourse of art cinema evolving during the 1970s can be described as a form of product differentiation and an aspect of foreign policy that proved particularly successful abroad, both at film festivals and in traditional art house venues and as part of the cultural mission of federal agencies such as the Goethe Institutes and of German studies departments at foreign universities. Under these conditions, the concept of *Autorenfilm* promised not only a new artistic programme but also, and more crucially, a discursive and institutional model for marketing the Federal Republic – a modern democracy, a social welfare state, and a liberal middle-class society – to its citizens and political allies.

The notion of authorship informed a wide range of cultural practices, from the cult of genius surrounding the most famous directors to the founding of new distribution and production companies such as the influential Filmverlag der Autoren. Yet despite the public subsidies and tax breaks and despite the growing awareness of film as an art form, the film industry continued to struggle for economic survival. Faced with the double competition of public television and Hollywood entertainment, producers found most of the available solutions insufficient and ineffective. Feature-film production had increased from fewer than a hundred films in 1960 to 121 films in 1969, a result primarily of the new Film Subsidy Law. During the 1970s, the numbers fell again from a hundred to fifty new releases per year. Some producers, like the Munich-based Franz Seitz, subsidised his more ambitious projects through crassly commercial films. Even the once powerful distribution companies experienced financial problems. By the late 1960s, Constantin was sold to the publishing house Bertelsmann, only to be reconstituted as Neue Constantin in the 1970s by Bernd Eichinger and Leo Kirch, the two men whose ascendancy after 1989 coincided with the demise of the *Autorenfilm*.

The three directors usually associated with New German Cinema – Fassbinder, Herzog, and Wenders – each responded to the social and political upheavals of the 1960s with a filmic style that combined generic conventions, literary influences, avant-garde traditions, and countercultural sensibilities in highly innovative ways. Fassbinder's *Liebe ist kälter als der Tod* (Love is Colder than Death, 1969) resembles the gangster films of other Munich directors such as Thome and Lemke but moves beyond the formal allusions to Hollywood to examine the specifically German constellation of sexuality and violence. Reflecting critically on the preceding decade of political utopias and ideals, Herzog in *Auch Zwerge haben klein angefangen* (Even Dwarfs Started Small, 1970) used documentary techniques to study small-group interactions and diagnose the aggressive nature of human behaviour. And taking advantage of the long tradition of Americanism, Wenders in *Summer in the City* (1970) captured his generation's sense of disillusionment by playing optimistic American pop tunes over pensive images of wintry German cityscapes.

The integrative myth of authorship, including its affinities with auteurism, and the artistic collaborations and patterns of influence that sustained that myth endowed these directors with an aura of authenticity and legitimacy. Their work as writers, critics, and directors secured Fassbinder, Wenders, and Herzog the status of great artists and public figures. Moreover, their professional experiences abroad (for instance, Wenders's work in Hollywood) and their allusions to other filmic oeuvres (the melodramas of Sirk, in the case of Fassbinder) guaranteed their films a strong international reception and made them part of the established traditions of art cinema. In developing their signature styles, all three directors depended to a large degree on a small group of collaborators, beginning with the actors who, like Hanna Schygulla for Fassbinder, Rüdiger Vogler for Wenders, and Klaus Kinski for Herzog, performed the function of a muse or double. The contribution of cinematographers proved equally decisive, with Michael Ballhaus and Xaver Schwarzenberger creating tightly composed frames for Fassbinder; Robby Müller developing elaborate long takes in his work with Wenders; and Thomas Mauch lending his fluid camera style to the on-location shoots preferred by Herzog. Similar patterns of influence, this time in the approach to editing and montage, can be traced in the work of Juliane Lorenz for Fassbinder and of Beate Mainka-Jellinghaus for Herzog and, of course, Kluge.

Rainer Werner Fassbinder was not only the most prolific but also the most talented, influential, and controversial director of the New German Cinema (Katz 1987, Fassbinder 1992, Schmid and Gehr 1992, Watson 1996). His premature death in 1982 marked the end of a career that included 33 feature films, as well as numerous television series, radio plays, and theatre productions. For many, this moment also marked the end of New German Cinema. Such phenomenal creativity over 14 years was possible only through the kind of working relationships with colleagues, friends, and lovers depicted, with shocking openness, in *Warnung vor der heiligen Nutte* (Beware of the Holy Whore, 1970). In his thematic interests and concerns, Fassbinder, who was openly gay, remained preoccupied with the individual's (often futile) struggle against the social structures that preclude the realisation of his or her desires. The director pursued this veritable obsession through the affective registers of a German filmic tradition that included social dramas such as *Warum läuft Herr R. Amok?* (Why Does Herr R. Run Amok?, 1970), critical *Heimatfilme* such as *Wildwechsel* (Jailbait, 1972), chamber play films in the style of *Die bitteren Tränen der Petra von Kant* (The Bitter Tears of Petra von Kant, 1972), as well as acclaimed literary adaptations in the tradition of *Fontane – Effi Briest* (1974). His almost compulsive exploration of power and violence in personal relationships included, to mention three films from one single year, *Angst essen Seele auf* (Ali – Fear Eats the Soul, 1974), a melodramatic study on the destructive effect of racism and ageism; *Martha* (1974), a chilling portrayal of the oppression of women in bourgeois marriage; and *Faustrecht der Freiheit* (Fox and His Friends, 1975), one of the most provocative treatments of gay life and class prejudice.

During the 1970s, Fassbinder resisted the general trend toward self-reflexive interiority and further sharpened his inquiries into the micro-politics of power and desire through a provocatively anti-psychological conception of characters; a marked preference for theatrical conventions and melodramatic effects; and a deliberately anti-realist use of interiors, objects, and settings. Like Warhol, which whom he shared a gay sensibility and pop aesthetic, Fassbinder used melodrama as a distancing device (Shattuc 1995). Formal and emotional excess provided him with a fitting expression of modern alienation and a powerful defence against the false discourse of authenticity; hence the director's highly ritualistic approach to interpersonal relationships. The resistance of his work to interpretative categories such as modernist detachment or postmodern reflexivity originates partly in his compulsive approach to film-making as a more intense form of life. The possibilities and limitations of such extreme stylisation found paradigmatic expression in the director's last film, an adaptation of Jean Genet's controversial *Querelle* (1982).

Fassbinder engaged with the political controversies of the 1970s through melodramatic effects that allowed him to highlight the contradictions between public discourse and the national imagination. His films about left-wing radicalism in *Mutter Küsters Fahrt zum Himmel* (Mother Küsters Goes to Heaven, 1975) and left-wing terrorism in *Die dritte Generation* (The Third Generation, 1979) diagnosed the inevitable corruption of political idealism and revolutionary fervour. From such a position of disillusionment, Fassbinder embarked on his most ambitious project, the so-called FRG trilogy, in which he rewrote the postwar years in the allegorical terms of female melodrama. From *Die Ehe der Maria Braun* (The Marriage of Maria Braun, 1979), about the period of reconstruction, and *Lola* (1981), about the years of the Economic Miracle, to *Die Sehnsucht der Veronika Voss* (Veronika Voss, 1982), about the tragic life of a former Ufa star, he used highly gendered stories to examine the complex emotional investments in the writing of national history. *Lili Marleen* (1981), which recounts the story of the famous song from the Second World War, similarly tries to make sense of Germany in terms of libidinal investments, including the structures of repression that for Fassbinder characterised postwar society from the 1950s to the 1970s (Elsaesser 1996b, Pott 2002).

Among the group of film-makers emerging during the 1970s, Werner Herzog may be described as the most German in his aesthetic sensibilities and romantic pursuits; he also went furthest in exploring uncharted territories and seeking extreme situations (Corrigan 1986, Prager 2007). A firm believer in the transformative power of art, Herzog was greatly influenced by Weimar directors such as Murnau, to whom he paid homage in *Nosferatu: Phantom der Nacht* (Nosferatu, the Vampyre, 1979), and he remained indebted to the legacies of German romanticism, including its explorations of the sublime. These aesthetic traditions found foremost expression in the director's heavy reliance on religious and mythological references and his intense preoccupation with notions such as fate, destiny, and redemption. This romantic tradition defined the main concerns in his work: the motif of the personal journey and the inner quest; the opposition between nature and culture, civilisation and wilderness; the search for liminal states and transgressive experiences; and the fascination with outsiders and foreigners. It is usually a position on the margins, defined in spatial or temporal terms, that in Herzog reveals the power of the imagination and expands the boundaries of reality, and experience, thereby also reconfiguring myth and history, fantasy and reality. From the old folk legend told in *Herz aus Glas* (Heart of Glass, 1976) to the colonial adventures shown in *Aguirre, der Zorn Gottes* (Aguirre: The Wrath of God, 1972) and *Fitzcarraldo* (1982), Herzog insistently evokes images, visions, and dreams in order to overcome the poverty of contemporary existence. During the 1980s, the director continued these inquiries in African and Australian settings with explicitly anthropological and ethnographic themes and what some critics have criticised as a colonialist perspective.

The figure of the outsider functions as a recurring motif in Herzog's films, from the handicapped in his early allegories of the Federal Republic to the tribal groups that inspire his later sojourns to the few remaining areas still untouched by global capitalism and consumerism. Setting the tone, *Jeder für sich und Gott gegen alle* (The Enigma of Kaspar Hauser, 1974) uses the tragic fate of the famous nineteenth-century foundling to show the inherent violence of Western civilisation. The futile search by three outsiders in *Stroszek* (1977) for a better life in Wisconsin and a soldier's descent into madness in *Woyzeck* (Werner Herzog's Woyzeck, 1979), based on the famous Büchner play, follow the same trajectory of disillusionment and betrayal. In most of Herzog's films, heroic gestures of conquest invariably lead to disaster and death, and desperate attempts of liberation only confirm the limits of progress and change. Yet the figure of the outsider not only sheds light on specific German compulsions, including an affinity for nihilism, mysticism, and anti-humanism. The failed stories of civilisation – or the stories of failed civilisation – are also part of a radical critique of enlightenment rationality and classical modernity that continues to motivate the director's daring explorations of the dynamic of creation and destruction, domination and subordination, self-discovery and self-annihilation.

The films of Wim Wenders explore a similar tension between the search for authenticity, immediacy, and belonging and the desire for freedom and movement (Wenders 1989, Bromley 2001, Graf 2002, Behrens 2005). The resultant psychological conflicts culminate in the love–hate relationship with American mass culture and new media technologies. Influenced by New Subjectivity, Wenders addresses the problem of modern masculinity through a number of recurrent themes: the alienation from contemporary society and the dream of an authentic life; the bonds of male friendship and the disillusionment with heterosexual love; the equation of perception with experience and the feared disappearance of the real. Frequently, the episodic, open-ended narratives of his films are structured around a journey or search. Formally, the link between motion and emotion finds expression in the contemplative long takes, elaborate camera movements, and composed still images that distinguish his filmic style. Using the failure of male–female relationships to reflect on the impossibility of story and history, these filmic journeys often function as exercises in the transformative power of images and perceptions. Whereas *Falsche Bewegung* (Wrong Movement, 1975) takes the Goethean motif of the educational journey to examine a society paralysed by post-1960s disillusionment, *Im Lauf der Zeit* (Kings of the Road, 1976) already considers the possibility of visual perception as a redemptive experience. These possibilities are developed further in Wenders's intensely romantic films about America, the melancholy *Alice in den Städten* (Alice in the Cities, 1978) and the more sentimental *Paris, Texas* (1984), which won the Golden Palm at Cannes.

During the 1980s, Wenders continued his inquiries into the power of the filmic image along three axes: the return to storytelling as the prerequisite of romantic love; the rediscovery of place, and *Heimat*, as the foundation of identity; and the reaffirmation of film as a unique visual medium. His homage to the metropolis as the perfect compromise between freedom and belonging inspired several films about Lisbon, Tokyo, and Los Angeles and found full expression in two critically acclaimed films set in Berlin, first as the divided city of *Der Himmel über Berlin* (Wings of Desire, 1987) and then as the unified German capital in *In weiter Ferne, so nah!* (Faraway, So Close!, 1993). Beginning with the noirish *Der Stand der Dinge* (The State of Things, 1982), Wenders repeatedly used self-referential stories about film-making and image production to juxtapose the emotional power of film with the models of simulation provided by the electronic and digital media that dominate the dystopian, post-apocalyptic world of *Bis ans Ende der Welt* (Until the End of the World, 1991). These continuing reflections on the nature of images and perceptions and their contribution to memory, history, and desire reveal the strong influence of postmodern thought on Wenders's ouevre, but they also suggest an essentialist view of the filmic image as the locus of some transcendental truth (Geist 1988, Kolker and Beicken 1993, Cook and Gemünden 1997).

The international reception of New German Cinema in the mid-1970s focused on individual directors and celebrated their special status as representatives of a different Germany. Their films assumed symbolic functions by offering aesthetic alternatives to Hollywood and by announcing a radical break with the legacies of the Third Reich. The degree to which such patterns of reception still relied on national narratives confirmed the role of the national as a category of product differentiation especially on the increasingly international film markets. In West Germany, the critical reception of the *Autorenfilm* was equally marked by contradictions. While often denounced as pretentious and self-indulgent, the films in fact helped to connect the search for more authentic stories and images to new definitions of Germanness as an oppositional, fluid, and contested position unburdened by the ideologies of nationalism. Accordingly, the relevance of cinema as an aesthetic, sensual, and social experience was asserted above all through its affinities with counter-hegemonic social movements and cultural phenomena. Based in the identity politics of civil rights and consciousness-raising, the film-makers' search for more open narrative forms and innovative visual styles was sustained by the widespread desire for a radically different relationship between subjective experience and social reality. This unique quality, which New German Cinema shared with modernist and postmodern aesthetics and which made it a truly transitional phenomenon between the 1960s and the 1980s, was most pronounced in the critical challenges by its leading directors to the enlightenment tradition of rationality and public life, whether through the power–desire nexus examined by Fassbinder, the liminal places and states explored by Herzog or the redemptive moments of vision and specularity pursued by Wenders.

Another unique characteristic of the *Autorenkino* of New German Cinema was its privileging of literary sources and a literary aesthetic. This heavy reliance on literature, including as the foundation of national culture and identity, was considered by many to be the most successful way to elevate film to the level of the other arts and, in ways reminiscent of the 1910s, to re-establish a tradition of quality in German film-making. The resultant convergence of middle-class tastes and institutional rationales with the goals of a politicised art cinema was personified by the director Volker Schlöndorff. Known for skilled adaptations of twentieth-century authors such as Marcel Proust, Max Frisch, and Arthur Miller, Schlöndorff repeatedly enlisted conventional narratives in formal explorations and utilised canonical works for critical rereadings. From *Der junge Törless*, his first feature film, to the later *Der Fangschuss* (Coup de Grace, 1976), Schlöndorff's modernist sensibilities found expression in a marked preference for analytical narrative strategies, minimal dramatic effects, reserved acting styles, and, at least in the early films, a stark black-and-white cinematography. Schlöndorff's greatest commercial and critical successes, his adaptations of the Böll story *Die verlorene Ehre der Katharina Blum* (The Lost Honour of Katharina Blum, 1975) and of the Grass novel *Die Blechtrommel* (The Tin Drum, 1979), both feature protagonists who find themselves confronted with powerful political forces and dramatic historical events. Whereas the earlier film focuses on an innocent victim of the police brutality and public hysteria generated by the terrorist activities of the 1970s, the later one revisits the difficult German past from the perspective of a young boy who, like the nation itself, refuses to grow (up) and see the reality of National Socialism. *Die Blechtrommel* received the Golden Palm and the Oscar for Best Foreign Film. During the 1980s and 1990s, Schlöndorff continued to rely on his deep humanism and sense of artistic responsibility to explore difficult subject matter – the abuses of power, the possibility of resistance, and the importance of individual responsibility – in films made in Europe and the United States (Wydra 1998, Moeller and Lellis 2002).

The difference between the national and international reception of New German Cinema is nowhere more pronounced than in the critical assessment of Hans Jürgen Syberberg. Attacked in Germany for his reactionary views and elitist attitudes, this director frequently won praise in the United States for his willingness to acknowledge the irrational forces in German culture and history. Relying on an array of visual, literary, musical, and philosophical sources, Syberberg transformed cinema into a *Gesamtkunstwerk* in order to perform what he called the necessary labour of mourning – that is, a working through the legacies of German romanticism and nationalism and their pivotal role in the traumas of German history. Revisiting key personages, legends, and myths in the national imagination, Syberberg began with feature films about *Ludwig, Requiem für einen jungfräulichen König* (Ludwig, Requiem for a Virgin King, 1972) and the popular author *Karl May* (1974) and continued in the documentary mode for *Winifred Wagner und die Geschichte des Hauses Wahnfried von 1914 bis 1975* (The Confessions of Winifred Wagner, 1975). The director's preoccupation with the libidinal sources of National Socialism culminated in the monumental, almost seven-hour-long *Hitler – ein Film aus Deutschland* (Our Hitler, 1977). This controversial film explores the collective fantasies associated with Hitler through a mixture of modernist montage and postmodern citation, with a heavy reliance on parody and pastiche and an almost fetishistic use of icons, symbols, and myths. According to Syberberg, these formal elements and rhetorical moves confirm the continuing relevance of the question of nation for the present conjuncture. Cultivating his fascination, if not identification, with Wagner, Syberberg later directed the opera film *Parsifal* (1982) and continues to use the configuration of German literature, music, philosophy, and mysticism to propagate an increasingly conservative agenda (Olsen 2006).

The international reception of New German Cinema was inextricably linked to the difficulty of speaking about Germany in the aftermath of the Third Reich. While foreign audiences praised Syberberg and Herzog for identifying the aesthetic foundations and emotional traumas of German identity, domestic audiences took on a similar project of demystification by confronting the equally problematic notion of *Heimat*. Especially the critical *Heimatfilm* enlisted the generic conventions of its precursor from the 1950s in mapping the continuities in the fantasies of space, place, and belonging and highlighting their connection to historical and contemporary notions of society and community. Through their innovative filmic styles, these films also opened up critical perspectives on the Federal Republic and its spatial antagonisms and regional anachronisms. *Jagdszenen aus Niederbayern* (Hunting Scenes from Lower Bavaria, 1969), *Mathias Kneissl* (1971), and *Jaider, der einsame Jäger* (Jaider, the Lonely Hunter, 1971) offered new interpretations on the familiar figure of the outsider, namely as someone destined to unite and lead the community against a threatening external power. Contributing to larger debates among the New Left, Schlöndorff used the story of *Der plötzliche Reichtum der armen Leute von Kombach* (The Sudden Wealth of the Poor People of Kombach, 1971) to contemplate the possibility of social action and political resistance. The critical *Heimatfilm* provided one of the few contexts in which film-makers after Oberhausen could engage with questions of community, and do so without recourse to the reactionary discourses of folk and nation. The genre's passionate defence of regional against national interests, of rural against urban culture, and of traditional against modern society gave rise to counter-narratives of community that remained relevant throughout the 1980s and 1990s (Schacht 1991).

An equally important institutional context for addressing social questions, this time through the lens of class and labour, developed out of the creative collaboration between film and television. Functioning as exhibition venue and co-producer, public television during the early 1970s emerged as a leading supporter of innovative film-makers and controversial projects, including documentaries and experimental films. In the process, public television asserted its growing influence in a media-based public sphere. The active involvement of WDR (West German Radio) gave rise to the *Arbeiterfilm* (workers' film) that offered realistic portrayals of working class-life in *Liebe Mutter, mir geht es gut* (Dear Mother, I Am All Right, 1972) by Christian Ziewer and Klaus Wiese and in *Die Wollands* (The Wollands, 1973) by Marianne Lüdcke and Ingo Kratisch. By continuing in the Weimar tradition of political film-making, the workers' film provided a rare opportunity for reflecting on the importance of solidarity as an individual and collective virtue (Collins and Porter 1981). Notwithstanding initial concerns, the public's gradual acceptance of the 'amphibian' styles dictated by the television format further strengthened the ties between film and television and led to other arrangements. In 1974, the relationship was formalised in the Television Framework Agreement between public television and the Film Subsidy Board, which subsequently generated more than 30 million marks in funding between 1974 and 1978. On the one hand, cultural programmes such as ZDF's *Das kleine Fernsehspiel* (The Short Television Play) functioned as a showcase for first-time directors and marginalised groups. On the other, the programming structure of television allowed directors to use the mini-series format for literary adaptations of works by Thomas Mann, Hans Fallada, and Jakob Wassermann. These opportunities proved particularly important to monumental undertakings such as Fassbinder's fifteen-and-a-half-hour adaptation of Döblin's *Berlin Alexanderplatz* (1979–80) and Reitz's ongoing *Heimat* project, the 11-part *Heimat: Eine deutsche Chronik* (Heimat, 1984), along with a 13-part sequel, *Die zweite Heimat: Chronik einer Jugend* (The Second Heimat, 1992) and a six-part sequel, *Heimat 3: Chronik einer Zeitenwende* (Heimat 3, 2004).

The building of new film museums and the launching of new book series contributed further to the institutionalisation of art cinema as the dominant mode of national cinema during the 1970s. Modelled after the Cinémathèque Française, the Stiftung Deutsche Kinemathek was founded in Berlin in 1971 as an important film archive and centre for research. The Freunde der Deutschen Kinemathek started the famous Arsenal cinema, Berlin's premier location for film retrospectives, and organised the International Forum of the New Film at the Berlin Film Festival. Even the Bundesarchiv/Filmarchiv, founded in 1953 with the goal of preserving films as historical documents, expanded its holdings in 1978 to become the central national archives for all feature and non-feature films. The Federal Film Archives subsequently moved most of its operations from Koblenz to Berlin; after 1989, it incorporated the holdings of the GDR's State Film Archives. Presenting film as an essential part of the national heritage, film museums opened in the country's major cities, including the Deutsches Filmmuseum in Frankfurt am Main as well as several smaller museums in Munich and Düsseldorf. The proliferation of regional film festivals, all with their own competitions and awards, further underscored film's indispensability to the revitalisation of regional culture and the development of cultural tourism.

Responding to a growing interest in film as a subject of scholarship, several publishing houses began to bring out general film histories and encyclopaedias as well as more specific books devoted to German film. Hanser launched a 'famous directors' series under the editorship of Wolfram Schütte and Peter W. Jansen, Fischer until recently produced the informative Film Almanac yearbooks, and Heyne started a monograph series devoted to popular genres and stars. The ambitious film historical project initiated by the *CineGraph* group under Hans-Michael Bock and several new scholarly journals and monograph series made film a legitimate area of critical inquiry and aesthetic appreciation in the 1970s and 1980s. Contributing to this development, Karena Niehoff for the *Süddeutsche Zeitung* and above all Karsten Witte for the *Frankfurter Rundschau* maintained the high quality of film criticism in national newspapers and played a key role in promoting the *Autorenfilm* as part of an international art cinema. Even the universities began to offer the first film courses in the context of German literature and theatre programmes.

The 1970s have often been identified with the literary movement of New Subjectivity and its validation of psychological reflection over political action. One of its main representatives, the author Peter Handke, collaborated with Wenders on *Die Angst des Tormanns beim Elfmeter* (The Goalie's Fear at the Penalty Kick, 1971) and later directed his own film adaptation of *Die linkshändige Frau* (The Left-handed Woman, 1978). In these paradigmatic works, the retreat to the personal and the cult of inwardness give rise to the prevailing moods of the decade: melancholy, hypersensitivity, reflexivity, and a deep sense of self-alienation. Implicating the problem of modern subjectivity in the traumas of the German past, the films' male leads are compelled to act out the guilt of their fathers by refusing to make decisions or take responsibility; yet this critique of patriarchy remains limited to aesthetic and performative registers. The desperate search for new meaning is acted out in the fragmented narratives, episodic structures, and essayistic forms typical of 1970s cinema, but its underlying ambivalences are most apparent in the physical appearances and performance styles of the decade's leading actors and actresses. Rüdiger Vogler, Hanns Zischler, and Bruno Ganz specialised in playing outsiders, misfits, and loners unwilling or unable to fit into mainstream society but also condemned to inactivity by their hyper-sensitivity, obsessive self-reflection, and narcissistic personalities. The stereotype of the sensitive but self-centred New Man contrasted sharply with the image of the strong, independent woman projected by New German Cinema stars such as Hanna Schygulla, Eva Mattes, and Barbara Sukowa. The fact that this gendered imbalance of power, including in erotic matters, also appeared in many DEFA films from the 1970s, confirms its symptomatic function as a response to more fundamental historical changes, including the demise of the bourgeois patriarchal family as the foundation of authoritarian society.

The new sensibilities conveyed by the actors and directors of New German Cinema transformed cinema into an alternative public sphere and implicated moviegoing more directly in the search for different experiences. After years of cinema closings, especially in smaller towns and rural areas, the numbers during the 1970s finally stabilised around 3,300 cinemas. As a result of urban gentrification, the proliferation of porn cinemas in downtown areas stopped. During the same period, the number of tickets sold was now regularly above 110 million per year. The rising attendance figures reflected a growing interest in film among students, artists, and intellectuals, as well as the educated middle class. The German and European art films never seriously threatened the popular appeal of Hollywood films, which dominated the market with almost 80 per cent of all new releases. The

Autorenfilm, in particular, functioned as a signifier of national identity at international film festivals and in the cultural programming of the Goethe Institutes worldwide. Moreover, European art films gave rise to a small but influential counterculture sustained, among other things, by new exhibition venues and programming practices. In 1971, Hilmar Hoffmann opened the first Kommunale Kino (communal cinema) in Frankfurt am Main; many cities started similar projects under municipal ownership. Functioning like art houses, these theatres organised historical retrospectives and screened films from lesser-known national cinemas and avant-garde traditions. Responding to the changing expectations about moviegoing as a social activity and interactive event, commercial cinema-owners, including the entrepreneurial Hans-Joachim Flebbe (the founder of the CinemaxX chain), built more and more multi-screen cinemas that showed a mixture of difficult and entertaining films and often included cafés, bars, and bookshops on their premises. All of these initiatives responded to the audience's hunger for different perceptions, new sensations, and presumably more authentic identities. In light of such psychological investments, German cinema culture by the end of the 1970s found itself both on the forefront of the postmodern cult of perception and in sharp opposition to its aesthetic of the simulacrum.

While an integral part of this new cinema culture, the large number of literary adaptations during the 1970s was not always an expression of directorial preferences. Instead, it reflected a pragmatic response to diminished funding opportunities and the literary biases of a selection process based on submitted screenplays. Known as the literature adaptation crisis of the mid-1970s, the sudden increase in films inspired by canonical authors such as Goethe, Fontane, Storm, and Ibsen reflected both a reorientation in the public support for contemporary film-makers and a more general change in filmic styles and sensibilities. The modernist aesthetics of formal innovation and political critique gradually gave way to dialogue-driven narratives with clear patterns of identification – a process that cannot be separated from the larger cultural and political developments known as the *Tendenzwende*, the turn toward conservatism. Only German romanticism still allowed for a more creative engagement with the tradition of irrationalism and its relevance for definitions of national identity. Especially the figure of the romantic genius inspired several projects about the life and work of Heinrich von Kleist, including Eric Rohmer's critically acclaimed *Die Marquise von O.* (The Marquise of O, 1976), that promised both a retreat from overtly political subject matter and a rediscovery of the aesthetic as a subversive quality.

Notwithstanding the favourable reception of its leading directors and literary adaptations, New German Cinema remained to a large degree defined through the topics and agendas that dominated West German society during the 1970s and 1980s, a fact often forgotten by auteurist readings. Usually made by lesser-known directors, these topical films combined social relevance and popular appeal in order to address a wide range of pressing problems such as the brutality of public life, the alienation of urban youth, the disappearance of regional culture, the power of large corporations, and the threat of ecological disasters. Repeatedly the narratives examined the tension between the safety of the social welfare state and the coldness of a totally administered world, and they juxtaposed the benefits of an open and mobile society with the dangers of dislocation and disconnection. Young protagonists proved ideally suited to articulate this tension in their desperate or violent opposition to family, society, and the state. Thus Hark Bohm, the main representative of the critical youth film, showed the alienation of adolescent boys in *Nordsee ist Mordsee* (North Sea Is Dead Sea, 1976) and *Moritz, lieber Moritz* (Moritz, Dear Moritz, 1978), two top-grossing films from the decade. In one of the earliest films about Turkish immigrant families, *Yasemin* (1988), Bohm approached the problem of integration and assimilation through the inspirational story of a female high school student. Uwe Frießner in *Das Ende des Regenbogens* (The End of the Rainbow, 1979) promised no such redeeming qualities in his sobering portrayal of a West Berlin youth involved in street prostitution and petty theft. Set in the same milieu, the cautionary tale of a young girl's descent into the world of hard drugs and sexual tricks in Ulrich Edel's *Christiane F. – Wir Kinder vom Bahnhof Zoo* (We Children from Bahnhof Zoo, 1981) catered primarily to sensationalist impulses and, because of these qualities, became a commercial success at home and abroad.

The films about social outsiders shared an intense sense of fear, anger, and paranoia and often used violence as a metaphor of contemporary life. Action, suspense, and high drama emerged as the preferred modalities for examining social problems such as the dehumanising conditions in the prison system depicted in Reinhold Hauff's *Die Verrohung des Franz Blum* (The Brutalisation of Franz Blum, 1974), the criminalisation of homosexuals in Wolfgang Petersen's *Die Konsequenz* (The Consequence, 1977), and the threat of pandemics raised by Peter Fleischmann's *Die Hamburger Krankheit* (The Hamburg Disease, 1979). Political thrillers such as *Messer im Kopf* (Knife in the Head, 1978) and *Kamikaze 1989* (Kamikaze 89, 1982) offered cautionary tales about the uncontrollable power of state institutions and large corporations. Despite the anti-imperialist rhetoric of the 1960s, only a few film-makers addressed the problem of political persecution, such as Sohrab Shahid Saless in the German–Canadian co-production *Dar Ghorbat / In der Fremde* (Far from Home, 1975), a moving portrayal of Iranians exiled by the Shah regime, and Ziewer in *Aus der Ferne sehe ich dieses Land* (I See this Land from Afar, 1978), about Chilean refugees escaping from the Pinochet regime. Yet the voice of international solidarity sounded loud and clear in Peter Lilienthal's films about Latin America, from *Es herrscht Ruhe im Land* (Calm Prevails over the Country, 1976), which showed the reality of everyday life under a totalitarian regime, to *Der Aufstand* (The Uprising, 1980), which explored the possibility of resistance under conditions of political oppression.

Sometimes, the figure of the outsider motivated more humorous treatments, especially in narratives about disenfranchised social groups or declining industrial regions. With considerable commercial success, Adolf Winkelmann in *Die Abfahrer* (On the Move, 1978) and *Jede Menge Kohle* (Lots of Dough, 1981) told quirky stories of individual rebellion against the backdrop of the dying steel industry in the Ruhr region. A similar combination of nostalgia, humour, and eccentricity characterised the surprise hit *Lina Braake* (1975), about a feisty old woman's fight against a bank, and *Das Brot des Bäckers* (The Baker's Bread, 1976), about a small-town bakery resisting mechanisation and mass production. Yet such light-hearted approaches remained the exception in a decade of film-making dominated by serious dramas and haunted by a pervasive sense of malaise.

It was under such conditions that the so-called *Frauenfilm* (woman's film) of the late 1970s emerged as a logical continuation of, and a powerful challenge to, the New German Cinema. The not unproblematic term *Frauenfilm* usually refers to films by women directors, films about 'women's issues' (for example, marriage, pregnancy, motherhood), and films with a pronounced feminist orientation. The critical reception of the woman's film in the mainstream press was dismissive, with 'one-sided', 'self-indulgent', 'boring', and 'depressing' frequent complaints that, in a way, only confirmed the underlying provocation. Many of the early women directors developed their filmic styles through a critical engagement with the student movement of the 1960s and the women's movement of the 1970s. Rejecting the narrow understanding of politics prevalent even on the radical left, Helke Sander, Helma Sanders-Brahms, Jutta Brückner, and Margarethe von Trotta focused their attention on personal relationships as the starting point for all social and political changes. Making films for these women represented a form of self-expression, consciousness-raising, and political activism. Some enlisted their stories of discrimination and oppression in feminist critiques of a male-dominated society, whereas others addressed public issues such as unequal pay, job discrimination, sexual violence, and reproductive rights, and yet others explored intimate relationships among women, including lesbianism as a personal and political choice. The diagnosis of institutional sexism and the critique of patriarchy sometimes gave way to a not unproblematic essentialist celebration of women's otherness. The growing divisions within the women's movement (socialist versus feminist, heterosexual versus lesbian, reformist versus autonomous) during the 1980s contributed to the gradual disappearance of the women's film, with individual women directors continuing their work in different contexts. The anti-feminist backlash in the early 1990s further diminished the core audience for these films, except within the feminist and lesbian subcultures found in all the major cities.

Most women's films shared a number of key characteristics, beginning with the preference for autobiographical forms, for stories of everyday life, and for what some critics have called a female aesthetic. The feminist movement remained an important reference point by providing the implied audience for these films, by establishing the model of a different public sphere, and by serving as an important source of inspiration for their stories and characters. The basic feminist tenet that 'the private is political' guided the film-makers' search for alternative filmic forms and styles. Their radical programme extended to various autonomous film and media activities, organisations for women film professionals, and feminist film festivals such as the Cologne Feminale. Founded in 1974, the feminist film journal *Frauen und Film* contributed actively to the emergence of an autonomous women's film culture and, later, to the advancement of feminist film theory (Riecke 1998).

The international orientation of the feminist and lesbian movements was largely responsible for the positive reception of German women directors in other countries. The productive exchanges between feminist and avant-garde practices extended to the work of video artists such as the Austrian Valie Export and, as in the work of Rebecca Horn, strengthened film's affinities with painting, video, and performance art.

The early women's films pursued two equally important goals: to tell different stories and to tell stories differently. The preference for melodramatic forms helped film-makers to reaffirm emotionality as a female strength, but this time from a female point-of-view. Autobiographical and biographical approaches allowed them to validate personal perspectives and individual experiences, to formulate a new aesthetics and erotics of female subjectivity, and to explore the gendered body as the site of oppression as well as liberation. In the early years, women directors emphasised the power of female solidarity, as did Sanders-Brahms through the stories of the young people depicted in *Unter dem Pflaster liegt der Strand* (Below the Pavement Lies the Strand, 1975) and Sander through the problems of the single working mother from *REDUPERS: die allseitig reduzierte Persönlichkeit* (The All-around Reduced Personality, 1978). Instead of offering political explanations, both films used the unique setting of West Berlin to examine the difficult situation of women through the prohibitions on female sexuality and creative expression. Working within a feminist framework, Sander continued to document the intricate connections between the personal and the political in *Der subjektive Faktor* (The Subjective Factor, 1981) and *Der Beginn aller Schrecken ist Liebe* (Love Is the Beginning of All Terror, 1984). By contrast, Sanders-Brahms moved from the sense of social responsibility that informed the tragic portrait of an unmarried Turkish woman in Germany, *Shirins Hochzeit* (Shirin's Wedding, 1976), to the highly allegorical interweaving of family story and national history in what became her most famous and most controversial film, *Deutschland bleiche Mutter* (Germany Pale Mother, 1980).

In the early 1980s, feminist film-makers also began to examine the relationship between autobiography and historiography and to pay closer attention to the suppression of female voices in the master-narratives of German history and cultural identity (Weinberger 1992, Linville 1998). The discovery of forgotten historical figures such as the feminist and socialist Flora Tristan, who inspired Claudia Alemann's imaginative filmic journey in *Die Reise nach Lyon* (1980, Blind Spot), or von Trotta's moving portrait of *Rosa Luxemburg* (1986) as both a female revolutionary and a woman in love represented only one side in this ongoing process; the other side involved a fundamental reinterpretation of established modes of historical narration and explanation. In their contribution to the process of coming to terms with the Nazi past, women film-makers paid special attention to the role of traditional gender roles and family structures in the rise of National Socialism and subsequent theories about its mass appeal. Challenging implicit assumptions about traditional masculinity as the guarantor of political stability, and of normative heterosexuality as the foundation of public life, feminists emphatically insisted on a sharp distinction between the historical experiences of women and their allegorical status in historical narratives, including those offered by the male directors of New German Cinema.

Mother–daughter relationships played a key role in these explorations, as did the ambiguous figure of the stranger and the experience of otherness. Uncovering the past in the present, Jeanine Meerapfel in *Malou* (1981) showed a woman's increasingly desperate attempts to reconstruct the tragic life story of her mother and, in so doing, to come to terms with her own conflicted identity of being Catholic, Jewish, and Argentine in West German society. By focusing on the contested nature of femininity, women film-makers also opened up new perspectives on the conservative Adenauer era. Jutta Brückner in *Hungerjahre* (Hunger Years, 1980) used a young girl's experience of growing up during the 1950s to uncover the connection between sexual repression and economic prosperity during the Economic Miracle. Taking a more playful approach in her use of dream sequences and fantastic elements, Marianne Rosenbaum in *Peppermint Frieden* (Peppermint Peace, 1983) recreated the sense of hope, confidence, and infinite possibility during the postwar years by assuming the perspective of an imaginative young girl.

As the most famous female director of the 1980s, von Trotta remained closely identified both with the specific concerns of the woman's film and with more general developments within New German Cinema. From the beginning, her films exhibited a remarkable consistency in the preference for middle-class settings and the emphasis on symbiotic relationships between sisters or close friends. *Schwestern oder die Balance des Glücks* (Sisters or The Balance of Happiness, 1979) and *Heller Wahn* (Sheer Madness, 1982) offer psychological insights into the complicated dynamics of closeness and distance and the underlying processes of identification and projection in all personal relationships. Her most famous film, *Die bleierne Zeit* (The German Sisters / Marianne and Juliane, 1981), tells the story of Christiane and Gudrun Ensslin both to measure the effect of terrorism on everyday life and to illuminate the connection between revolutionary politics and individual biography. By combining psychological and political perspectives, von Trotta was very effective in communicating feminist concerns to a wider public; but she also contributed to the compromises that made the films of the 1980s more conventional in form and content (Wydra 2000).

The 1980s: crises and transformations

The preoccupation with personal relationships as the primary site of power struggles and social changes reached a critical impasse when film-makers had to confront the momentous political events of the late 1970s known as the 'German Autumn'. The wave of terrorism initiated by the Red Army Faction (RAF) shook the political foundations of the Federal Republic and forced artists, intellectuals, and public figures to confront the resultant legitimisation crisis. Following a wave of bombings, kidnappings, and assassinations intended to force the release of the prisoners of Stammheim, several directors made an omnibus film, *Deutschland im Herbst*

(Germany in Autumn, 1978), which addressed the far-reaching effects of terrorism on West German society, including in new forms of censorship and self-censorship. Similar critical intentions informed a later project, *Der Kandidat* (The Candidate, 1980), about the election campaign of conservative Franz Josef Strauß. During the 1980s, film-makers continued to deal with the psychological causes and social consequences of left-wing terrorism, whether through the dramatic re-enactment of the RAF trials in *Stammheim* (1986) or the screen adaptation of Bernhard Vesper's autobiography, *Die Reise* (The Journey, 1986). All of these films participated in the labour of mourning that connected the 'German Autumn' to the repressed legacies of the Third Reich and the betrayed utopias of the student movement. The pervasive sense of failure and loss in filmic treatments of terrorism and the West German left continued to haunt subsequent attempts to preserve, transform, or overcome the politicised discourses of cinema developed during the 1960s and 1970s (Kraus et al. 1997).

Many film historical surveys characterise the 1980s as a period of decline, with the death of Fassbinder in 1982 marking the end of cinema as a formally innovative and politically provocative force. The election in 1982 of the CDU-dominated government under Chancellor Helmut Kohl coincided with a conservative turn in social and economic policies as well as cultural tastes. The public scandal surrounding Herbert Achternbusch's *Das Gespenst* (The Ghost, 1983), which started with accusations of blasphemy by the Catholic Church, prompted the new Minister of the Interior to speak out against the critical art films of the 1970s and demand the production of more entertainment films. The threat to the future of art cinema loomed in the further reduction of public subsidies on the national level and the denial of already approved loans to controversial projects. For the film industry, this steady erosion of support coincided with an intensified competition for audiences after the introduction of home video and, later, cable television. Some companies like the Kirch group diversified their holdings by buying the rights to old Hollywood films and television programmes.

Meanwhile the pursuit of commercial success and the appeal of big budgets contributed to the exodus of yet another generation of German film-makers to Hollywood. After the phenomenal international success of *Das Boot* (The Boat, 1981), which depicts the heroic fight of a German submarine crew during the Second World War, Petersen made *Die unendliche Geschichte* (The Never-ending Story, 1984), based on Michael Ende's popular children's book, with an eye already toward international markets. In Hollywood, he subsequently developed a reputation for suspenseful political thrillers. As a master of special effects, Roland Emmerich in the 1990s had great commercial success with horror films and political thrillers. Both Petersen and Ende bring a uniquely German perspective to their apocalyptic views of the American empire and the future of a planet threatened by extragalactic attacks and ecological disasters. Other Germans now working in Hollywood include cinematographer Michael Ballhaus, known for his work with Martin Scorsese and Francis Ford Coppola, and composer Hans Zimmer, famous for his lush Wagnerian scores (Haase 2007).

While some producers and directors turned to big-budget films to become more competitive, others took advantage of the close connections within film, television, and the recording industry. The affinities between music and film proved particularly profitable, as evident in the commercial success of *Panische Zeiten* (Panic Times, 1980), with rock star Udo Lindenberg, or *Theo gegen den Rest der Welt* (Theo Against the Rest of the World, 1980), with singer Marius Müller-Westernhagen. The exploitation of regressive tendencies and parochial sensibilities in these mainstream successes was most noticeable in the registers of a regionally defined humour. With their adolescent pranks and inane jokes, comedians Otto Waalkes in *Otto – der Film* (Otto – the Film, 1985) and Dieter Hallervorden with *Didi auf vollen Touren* (Didi in Full Form, 1986) acquired large cult followings. Among the few television personalities who made the successful transition to the screen was the eccentric Loriot (alias Vicco von Bülow), who appeared in two box office hits, *Ödipussi* (1988) and *Pappa ante Portas* (1991).

Meanwhile, the return to generic conventions once again opened up the history of the Third Reich to more probing investigations into the possibility of individual resistance and the involvement of ordinary Germans in anti-Semitic atrocities. The central role of mass media in this process of remembering became overwhelmingly clear after two surprise successes: the retelling of the Holocaust as family melodrama in the American television series *Holocaust*, which sparked intense public debates in 1979; and, two years later, the spectacle of German wartime heroism presented by *Das Boot* through a careful avoidance of all political references. These revisionist tendencies continued in two German co-productions with Switzerland that thematised the Swiss involvement with the Third Reich, *Das Boot ist voll* (The Boat Is Full, 1981) and *Glut* (Embers, 1984). The renewed interest in the Nazi past during the 1980s cannot be separated from the so-called Historians' Debate about the origins of National Socialism and the singularity of the Holocaust. First signs of a normalisation of German history appeared in the changing forms of public commemoration, including the fortieth anniversary in 1985 of the end of the Second World War. Yet the very existence of these tendencies also brought additional urgency to the question of historical representation and its meaning to the self-understanding of the Federal Republic.

The West German films about the Third Reich followed two basic models: studies of significant historical figures and events and more generic investigations into the fascism of everyday life. For a fictional account of the life of Rudolf Höss, the commandant of the Auschwitz concentration camp, in *Aus einem deutschen Leben* (Death Is My Trade, 1977), director Theodor Kotulla chose a detached documentary style in tracing the banality of evil. Chilling factuality also prevailed in *Die Wannseekonferenz* (The Wannsee Conference, 1984), which records the eponymous secret meeting in January 1942 concerning the Final Solution. The more dramatic reflections on art and politics, and the dangers of blind ambition, informed the intense performances by Klaus Maria Brandauer in two Istvan Szabo films, *Mephisto* (1981), about the phenomenal career of the actor Gustav Gründgens during the Third Reich, and *Hanussen* (1988), about a famous

180

clairvoyant from the Berlin of the 1920s who fatally predicted the rise of the Nazis. Both of these films belonged to the 1980s European art film, big-budget co-productions with a European cast and crew that promoted the European heritage in their choice of locations, literary sources, and historical subject matter; the less distinguished products are referred to dismissively as Euro-pudding.

The second type of film about the Third Reich concentrated on average characters, typical situations, and ordinary lives. As illustrated by *David* (1979) and *Die Kinder aus Nr. 67* (The Children of Number 67, 1980), some film-makers chose the perspectives of children to challenge familiar patterns of historical explanation. Others, such as Alf Brustellin and Bernhard Sinkel in *Berlinger* (1975), explored the consequences of individual choice through the different careers of two friends, a calculating opportunist and a stubborn individualist – an approach reminiscent of Hoffmann's *Wir Wunderkinder* of 1958 and oddly similar to the DEFA production *Anton, der Zauberer* of 1978. All of these films introduced alternative points-of-view from which to confront the complexities of history beyond the dichotomies of guilt and innocence and with greater attention to questions of individual agency and personal responsibility. Along similar lines, Wicki's television adaptation of Alfred Andersch's *Sansibar oder der letzte Grund* (Sansibar or the Last Reason, 1987) told a moving parable of reconciliation, with a communist man and a Jewish woman joining forces to save a Christian artefact from imminent destruction by the Nazis.

Many of these new attitudes came together in the work of Michael Verhoeven, whose Third Reich trilogy recounts remarkable stories of individual resistance based on real historical figures and events. Whereas *Die weisse Rose* (The White Rose, 1982), about the Munich student resistance group around Sophie and Hans Scholl, still followed a conventional narrative pattern, *Das schreckliche Mädchen* (The Nasty Girl, 1990) presented a young woman's research about her hometown during the Third Reich through an imaginative combination of pseudo-documentary scenes, grotesque dream sequences, and other critical strategies reminiscent of Brechtian distanciation. The last film in the Verhoeven trilogy, *Mutters Courage* (My Mother's Courage, 1995), relied on a provocative mixture of grotesque, comedy, and burlesque to link George Tabori's account of his mother's survival during the Holocaust to larger questions about the decisive moments of life and death.

The renewed interest in the Third Reich brought a long overdue confrontation with the historical roots of anti-Semitism and the Holocaust, on the one hand, and a growing awareness of their importance to then-current debates about German history and national identity, on the other. As an integral part of this difficult process, the rediscovery of *Heimat* introduced an appealing alternative to the tainted political history of nation and *Volk*. More problematically, the nostalgia for *Heimat* also promised an escape from the discourse of collective guilt by relocating German identity in idyllic villages and beautiful landscapes. The ordinary story of one such village, the imaginary Schabbach in the Hunsrück, was thus elevated to grand epic scale in one of the most ambitious German television projects, Reitz's production of *Heimat* and its sequels, *Die zweite Heimat* and *Heimat 3*. The original *Heimat* tells the history from 1918 to the present of a small village in the Hunsrück mountains through the everyday problems and personal relationships of its inhabitants. The first sequel follows one young man to Munich where he joins the bohemian milieu of artists and intellectuals during the 1960s and 1970s; the second sequel extends his story to the momentous events surrounding German unification. Criticised for its apolitical celebration of community and heritage but also hailed for its close attention to the micro-levels of story and history, the original *Heimat* series inspired heated debates about history, memory, narrative, and national identity (Kaes 1989, Santner 1990).

Several directors during the 1970s and 1980s became closely identified with the alternately uncanny, absurd, and humorous scenarios inspired by this critical re-evaluation of *Heimat*. Bringing an outsider's sensibility to familiar landscapes such as the Lüneburg Heath and the Rhine valley, the Swiss-born director Niklaus Schilling turned the cold idylls and beautiful still-lives of *Nachtschatten* (Night Shades, 1972), *Rheingold* (Rhinegold, 1978), and *Der Willi Busch Report* (The Willi Busch Report, 1979) into morbid allegories of the Federal Republic. The eccentric Herbert Achternbusch made a name for himself by celebrating the whimsical, scurrilous, and zany nature of everyday life in Bavaria with a mixture of anthropological detachment, confrontational techniques, and deeply felt personal ambivalence. From Munich films like *Servus Bayern* (Bye-bye Bavaria, 1977) to the reincarnation story of *Ab nach Tibet* (Gone to Tibet, 1994), Achternbusch carried on in the tradition of anarchic humour started by Valentin during the 1920s. With almost compulsive regularity, the director combined elements of vaudeville, burlesque, passion play, and absurd theatre in order to work through his love–hate relationship with a city and a region ruled by institutions of the Catholic Church, haunted by the legacies of the Third Reich, and defined by the beer-drinking rituals of the Hofbräuhaus. One of the few other directors to preserve the authorial ethos of New German Cinema during the politically and aesthetically conservative 1980s was Munich-born Percy Adlon. From the quirky *Zuckerbaby* (Sugar Baby, 1985) and the enormously successful *Out of Rosenheim* (Bagdad Cafe, 1987) to his recent German–American productions, Adlon regularly worked with Marianne Sägebrecht as a buxom Bavarian woman who finds personal happiness despite prevailing beauty standards and sexual stereotypes.

In less obvious ways, these regional sensibilities and ethnic identities also made possible the acceptance, no matter how tentative, of the Federal Republic as a contemporary version of *Heimat*. The resultant reflections on identity, place, and belonging found their favourite protagonists among the urban counterculture of artists and intellectuals as well as the successful members of the educated middle class. The growing dissatisfaction with the narcissistic cult of subjectivity opened up a space for reclaiming romance, love, and sexuality as an essential human experience. Two directors from the 1960s played a key role in initiating this change in erotic and romantic matters. Specialising in romantic comedies, Rudolf Thome during the 1980s presented his stories of ordinary men and women against the backdrop of urban life in West Berlin and, later, a reunited Berlin. The symptomatic shift from the public debates about gentrification that still complicated romantic love in *Berlin Chamissoplatz* (1980) to the sentimental images of couples and families in *Das Mikroskop* (The Microscope, 1988) and *Liebe auf den ersten Blick* (Love at First Sight, 1991) became possible through the reaffirmation both of traditional notions of gender and of the private sphere as the locus of individual happiness. Fascinated with the rituals of heterosexual desire, Robert van Ackeren introduced a more cynical tone and became an observant chronicler of the manifold erotic constellations between strong women and weak men. From *Die Reinheit des Herzens* (Purity of the Heart, 1980) and *Die flambierte Frau* (A Woman in Flames, 1983) to *Die wahre Geschichte von Männern und Frauen* (The True Story of Men and Women, 1992), the spectacle of female sexuality allowed van Ackeren simultaneously to demonstrate the liberalisation in public attitudes toward sexuality and to measure the reverberations of the sexual revolution in individual passions and perversions.

Significantly, the disappearance of art cinema as the predominant model of national cinema opened up a space for the cultivation of diverse audiences and marginal tastes. Resisting the trend toward verisimilitude, two prolific film artists from the 1960s continued to probe the affinities between sexuality and aesthetics from an openly gay perspective. Beginning with *Der Tod der Maria Malibran* (The Death of Maria Malibran, 1972), with cult star Magdalena Montezuma, Werner Schroeter relied on an eclectic mixture of opera, melodrama, religion, ritual, and performance art to explore the connection between beauty and desire in the sexually ambiguous terms of a camp aesthetic. His social melodramas about Italian guest workers, *Neapolitanische Geschwister* (Kingdom of Naples, 1978) and *Palermo oder Wolfsburg* (Palermo or Wolfsburg, 1980), used realist and theatrical elements to open up a space for compassionate identification and transgressive desire. Continuing his fascination with otherness, Schroeter's most compelling contribution to gay aesthetics, *Der Rosenkönig* (The Rose King, 1986), explored the eroticism of the filmic image through the lens of Italy as the incarnation of beauty and sensuality.

Representative of a more activist stance on gay rights issues but also known for combining kitsch and underground elements in the most irreverent ways, the work of Rosa von Praunheim can be divided into three groups: polemics about the discrimination against homosexuals such as *Nicht der Homosexuelle ist pervers, sondern die Situation, in der er lebt* (Not the Homosexual Is Perverted but the Society in Which He Finds Himself, 1971) and *AIDS-Trilogie: Schweigen = Death* (Silence = Death, 1990); low-budget melodramas in the style of *Anita – Tänze des Lasters* (Anita – Dances of Vice, 1987) and other homages to Weimar expressionism; and documentaries about the ordinary lives of extraordinary people such as the elderly male cross-dresser Charlotte von Mahlsdorf of *Ich bin meine eigene Frau* (I Am My Own Woman, 1992). In contrast to Schroeter and Praunheim, who remained committed to the political project of sexual liberation, the Berlin underground film-maker Lothar Lambert made a career for himself by promoting gay sensibilities through the kind of misogynist overtones found in *Die Alptraumfrau* (Nightmare Woman, 1981) and *Was Sie nie über Frauen wissen wollten* (What You Never Wanted to Know about Women, 1992). Earlier the surprise hit *Taxi zum Klo* (Taxi to the Toilet, 1981) by Frank Ripploh, a controversial depiction of the promiscuous gay scene in Berlin before the times of AIDS, had confirmed to what degree the taboos on homosexual representations had been eroded in the course of the 1980s.

In what ways films with gay and lesbian themes conveyed a distinct queer sensibility – in other words, a challenge to established notions of gender, sexuality, and desire – became evident in the few films committed equally to sexual liberation and formal experimentation. Since the late 1970s, Ulrike Ottinger produced the visually most imaginative body of work by appropriating the means of postmodern citation, modernist defamiliarisation, and postcolonial ethnography for beautiful mise-en-scènes of female love and adventure. Whether caught on a junk in the Chinese Seas or drunk in the streets of Berlin, the women of *Madame X, eine absolute Herrscherin* (Madame X, an Absolute Ruler, 1978) and *Bildnis einer Trinkerin* (Ticket of No Return, 1979) asserted their otherness through the means of parody, theatricality, and artifice. Ottinger's ambition to reclaim visual pleasure for the cinema continued in the excursions of *Johanna d'Arc of Mongolia* (Joan of Arc of Mongolia, 1989) and found privileged expression across three discursive registers: erotic allegory, exoticism, and ethnography. Rejecting the essentialism of feminist identity politics, Monika Treut likewise appropriated the aesthetics of sadomasochism in *Verführung: Die grausame Frau* (Seduction: The Cruel Woman, 1985), a highly stylised film shot in black-and-white by the well-known cinematographer Elfi Mikesch. The later *Die Jungfrauenmaschine* (The Virgin Machine, 1988), the coming-out story of a young German woman during a stay in San Francisco, allowed Treut to explore the performative nature of gender and sexuality in more playful tones, an indication also of the changing function of sexual politics in the postmodern politics of representation (Kuzniar 2000).

The only new director to emerge during the 1980s, Doris Dörrie, was also the one who most successfully enlisted the conventions of romantic comedy in diagnosing the complications of male–female relationships from a post-feminist perspective. Inspired by Hollywood genre cinema but with a distinct German sensibility, committed to the goals of feminism but also surprisingly open about the messiness of ordinary life, Dörrie quickly established her reputation after the phenomenal success of *Männer* (Men, 1985). This humorous take on the myth of the New Man and the endurance of traditional gender roles showed her talent of combining precise social observation with a deep understanding of human foibles. By presenting individualistic characters and unusual lifestyles through familiar generic elements, Dörrie became an important transitional figure between the ethos of self-discovery cultivated by New German Cinema and the greater emphasis on entertainment in post-unification cinema. To a large degree, this transition was predicated on the rearticulation of gender troubles through the lens of multiculturalism and transnationalism. Thus Dörrie in *Happy Birthday, Türke!* (Happy Birthday!, 1992) appropriated elements of *film noir*, including its myth of the urban jungle, to present the complications of German-Turkish identity – in fact of all identities – in conscious opposition to the liberal rhetoric of integration. Likewise, references to black comedy in *Keiner liebt mich* (Nobody Loves Me, 1994) and to the road movie in *Bin ich schön?* (Am I Beautiful?, 1998) allowed Dörrie to explore the productive alliances among various 'others' – women, gays, foreigners – while avoiding all too simplistic solutions to the central question of identity in a world of postmodern simulation (Birgel and Phillips 2004).

The one significant political issue linking the West German cinema of the 1980s to the post-unification cinema of the 1990s was the growing awareness among film-makers of the many immigrants, exiles, and foreigners living in the Federal Republic. Their profound impact on definitions of German culture and society reverberated throughout filmic practices, from the familiar ethnic and national stereotyping and the dynamics of self and other to various efforts at promoting tolerance and understanding. This process had begun as early as the 1950s with the first cameo appearances by Italian and Spanish guest workers in the revue films, youth films, and *Heimatfilme*. It had continued during the 1970s with dramatic stories about Turkish men and women arriving in the Federal Republic and beginning the difficult process of social integration and cultural assimilation, a process extended to the present through the problems in first- and second-generation immigrant families. This development culminated during the 1980s in the growing number of contemporary dramas that, through their stories and characters, confirmed the existence of an ethnically, culturally, and socially diverse society. The underlying shifts in the representation of West Germany's various 'others' – the Turkish immigrants, the African refugees, the Iranian exiles, and all the other foreigners and visitors – did more than just reflect a gradual and not uncontested recognition of Germany as an immigrant society. These filmic representations also participated in the redefinition of national culture and identity in an increasingly multiethnic, multicultural world. Yet, as the immigrants became an integral part of the self-representation of the Federal Republic, the Germans from the East remained absent from the filmic imagination, except as embodiments of fundamental otherness. From television productions such as *Berlin Mitte* (Central Berlin, 1979) to feature films such as *Der Mann auf der Mauer* (The Man on the Wall, 1982), the few German–German encounters in films of the 1980s invariably ended in disorientation, dissatisfaction, and disillusionment. Little did film-makers know that these fictional moments would in a few years be surpassed by the world historic events that brought about the end of the Cold War division of Germany and marked the beginning of the very different world of globalisation, mass migration, multiculturalism, and cultural hybridity.

15   Sabine Sinjen and Bruno Dietrich in *Es*. Courtesy BFI Stills, Posters and Designs.

16   Renate Blume and Eberhard
Esche in *Der geteilte Himmel*.
Courtesy BFI Stills, Posters and
Designs.

17 Rainer Werner Fassbinder and Peter Chatel in *Faustrecht der Freiheit*. Courtesy BFI Stills, Posters and Designs.

18 Eva Mattes and Bruno S. in *Stroszek*. Courtesy BFI Stills, Posters and Designs.

19 Lutze and Tabea Blumenschein in *Bildnis einer Trinkerin*. Courtesy BFI Stills, Posters and Designs.

20 Uwe Ochsenknecht, Ulrike Kriener, and Heiner Lauterbach in *Männer*. Courtesy BFI Stills, Posters and Designs.

21 Bruno Ganz and Solweig Dommartin in *Der Himmel über Berlin*. Courtesy BFI Stills, Posters and Designs.

7

POST-UNIFICATION CINEMA
1990–2007

The collapse of the Wall on 9 November 1989 and the signing of the Unification Treaty on 3 October 1990 marked the end of the postwar period and the Cold War. The difficult process of unification, a process also known as the *Wende* (change, transition), fundamentally altered the social and political landscape in the old Federal Republic and the so-called new states. Whether thought of as reunification, unification, or the coming together of two unequal partners, the making of the Berlin Republic has taken place in the context of European unification, globalisation, and mass migration, on the one hand, and increased ethnic and religious resentments and new provincialisms, on the other. German unification has once again resulted in confrontation with the legacies of the past (i.e., the Third Reich and the GDR) and given rise to a complex and contradictory culture of remembrance, retrospection, and nostalgia. It has provoked heated debates on the meaning of Germanness, whether defined in legal, ethnic, linguistic or cultural terms, and put into question the role of the nation state in a post-communist Europe defined less by ideological differences than by social and economic inequalities. At the same time, the 1990s and early 2000s have seen a greater tolerance toward ethnic, religious, and sexual minorities and a growing acceptance of pluralism, multiculturalism, and hybridity in social attitudes and cultural practices. The equally dramatic changes in the world economy, from the ascendancy of multinational corporations to the creation of new information technologies, have only intensified the sense of unprecedented mobility and dislocation and resulted in repeated confrontations over issues of immigration, citizenship, and asylum laws and over the costs and benefits of the neo-liberal world order.

In 1998, after 16 years of CDU rule, the new SPD/Greens coalition government led by Chancellor Gerhard Schröder initiated ambitious social and economic reforms intended to make the country more competitive on global markets and less inflexible on labour and employment issues. Many initiatives provided new opportunities but also raised a number of serious concerns: about the dismantling of the social welfare state and the growth of federal, state, and city deficits; about a decline in the standard of living and a deterioration of the fabric of public life; about the collapse of the old consensus model binding together big corporations, labour unions, political parties, and special interest groups; and about continuing problems in the new states such as mass unemployment, population loss, and right-wing violence. Since 2005, the coalition government under CDU Chancellor Angela Merkel has had to deal with these complex social and political questions. Yet in the same way that the re-emergence of Germany as a global player on export markets has alleviated some of these problems, the difficult foreign policy issues in the wake of the continuing problems in the Middle East and the challenges posed by Islamic radicalism have exposed the Berlin Republic more than ever to international conflicts and made it much more dependent on transnational alliances. The continued imbalance of power between the old and the new states and the consequences of several decades of immigration in what de facto is a country of immigration has focused renewed attention to the real and imaginary topographies of space, place, and belonging, especially among a younger generation of film-makers.

From the beginning, the difficulty of merging two ideological systems has been accompanied by intense anxieties, resentments, and projections, including the complementary stereotypes of *Wessies* (West Germans) and *Ossies* (East Germans). After the government's move to Berlin, a number of architectural projects, from the new Reichstag and Potsdamer Platz to the Holocaust Memorial, have generated intense public discussions about the importance of commemoration and the meaning of nation and history. The newly found sense of national pride in conjunction with Germany's hosting of the 2006 World Soccer Cup, the subject of Sönke Wortmann's surprise hit *Deutschland. Ein Sommermärchen* (Germany. A Summer's Fairytale, 2006), has fuelled hopes about a normalisation of German identity. At the same time, growing resistance to economic and cultural globalisation and the rise of new religious and political fundamentalisms have heightened concerns about the future of a multicultural, multiethnic, and transnational Europe, as evidenced by the exclusionary strategies associated with 'fortress Europe' and the more enlightened transnationalism favoured by progressive politicians and intellectuals. The beginning of the Iraq War in 2003 and the resultant strain in transatlantic relations has caused a new wave of anti-Americanism and inspired visions of Europe as both a counterweight and an alternative to US global hegemony. Yet the problems of Muslim Europe have also given rise to heated debates about a European or German *Leitkultur* (core culture or shared values) that defines itself as modern, secular, pluralist, and committed to Enlightenment notions of civil society or, in its more conservative version, as western, Christian, and founded on compulsory social integration and cultural assimilation. With earlier dreams of multiculturalism giving way to more sober assessments of the problems of immigration, the binary logic behind such positions has been questioned by many who now insist on some basic acceptance of the core values of freedom, democracy, solidarity, diversity, and tolerance, and human rights represented by the European Union (EU).

The historical events of 1989/90 coincided with an unexpected revival of popular cinema in the 1990s, a development judged critically as a 'cinema of consensus' by the advocates of a formally advanced art cinema (Rentschler 2000). Accordingly, the recent signs of an emerging cinema of dissent have been welcomed by scholars used to associating German cinema with critical perspectives. In Germany, the return of commercially successful film-making has been described as a repudiation of the social and cultural legacies of the '68 generation and an affirmation of post-ideological society and its promotion of consumerism, materialism, and fun mentality (Amend and Bütow 1997, Blum and Blum 1997, Töteberg 1999). In the English-speaking world, film scholars have taken a more nuanced approach by focusing on the challenges of presenting serious issues in a light-hearted, conciliatory fashion (Brady and Hughes 1995, Clarke 2006). In considering the wider implications of such developments for the writing of German film history, some scholars have begun to reassess older critical models, beginning with the emphasis on famous directors and canonical films, and to pay more attention to the continuities of genre cinema and the function of multimediality in competing definitions of the national, international, and transnational (*Arachne* vol. 3, no. 2 (1996), *Seminar* vol. 33, no. 4 (1997), *Camera Obscura* no. 44 (2000), *New German Critique* no. 87 (2002), *Germanic Review* vol. 79, no. 3 (2007)).

Film-making in the new Germany and a unified Europe

Subject to the process of privatisation that affected all state-owned industries of the former GDR, the DEFA studio was taken over by the Treuhand, the government agency in change of privatisation, and sold in 1992 to a French Conglomerate, Compagnie Général Des Eaux, now known as Vivendi Universal. In 2004, Vivendi sold Studio Babelsberg to Filmbetriebe Berlin Brandenburg GmbH (FBB), an investment company. Since Volker Schlöndorff's early tenure as artistic director from 1992 to 1997, Studio Babelsberg has been promoted as a centre of European film and television production; increasingly, the city of Berlin is also used as an attractive location by international productions. Reflecting fundamental changes in film production, distribution, and exhibition, the old oppositions of film versus television, and of public versus private funding have given way to more fluid arrangements and pragmatic approaches. Independent production companies, international distribution companies, public and private television stations, and regional and local film boards now all work together in developing mixed forms of film financing and moving toward transnational modes of production.

To a large degree, film funding remains committed to the mixed financing model and the underlying rationales developed in the old Federal Republic (Berg and Hickethier 1994, Storm 2000). What has changed is the balance between the demands of economic profitability and regional development and the preservation of film art and local cinema culture, with the former taking precedence over the latter and with public–private ventures clearly becoming the norm. To the degree that film art has been replaced by film entertainment as the dominant model of national cinema, the state is more and more withdrawing from film-funding and making room for private interests and commercial uses (Halle 2008). Since the revision of the Federal Film Subsidy Law in 1992, the Film Subsidy Board has reduced its overall support for film-making; it has also changed its criteria from those based on artistic quality to those of economic expediency. Confirming the shift to the individual states, the main players now include regional agencies such as Filmboard Berlin-Brandenburg, Filmstiftung NRW, and FilmFernsehFonds Bayern. The choice of areas in Brandenburg or Schleswig-Hollstein for location shooting confirms the continued use of film funding as an instrument of regional development and job creation. Even major cities such as Munich and Hamburg rely on film productions to boost the local economy and promote their cities as tourist attractions. In addition to public television channels such as WDR, MDR, and NDR, the Franco-German cultural channel Arte, founded in 1992, plays an ever more important role in the financing of European co-productions; the same holds true for French Canal Plus and British Channel Four.

The growing significance of film and media culture to the self-representation of the Berlin Republic can be measured by the re-emergence of the star system and the promotion of a new generation of celebrities on television, fan websites, and in the yellow press. From the increasingly glamorous Berlinale in February, which awards the Golden and Silver Bear in the international competition, to the award ceremony every May of the Deutsche Filmpreis, the LOLA, which honours the best of a year's production based on the recommendations of the newly founded Deutsche Filmakademie (German Film Academy), the film industry has become more active in promoting German films at home and abroad. The long overdue recognition of film as an essential part of the cultural heritage culminated in the opening in 2000 of the Filmmuseum Berlin on Potsdamer Platz. This spectacular complex unites the city's premier retrospective film theatre, the Arsenal, the archival collections of the Deutsche Kinemathek, and a permanent exhibition on German film history in one location. On a more troubling note, the creation of a more commercially oriented, consumer-friendly film culture has gone hand in hand with the disappearance of those institutions that defined film culture in the Federal Republic, including the municipally owned communal cinemas.

At the same time, film production in Germany and Europe is becoming a transnational affair, with the definition of what constitutes a German film more and more difficult; particularly noteworthy in this context is the opening toward Eastern Europe. The European Union continues to treat film as a cultural good, as evidenced by the 1993 GATT talks during which the Europeans reaffirmed their view of film as a cultural good worthy of protection through subsidies and quotas. Such positions reflect prevailing attitudes toward American cultural hegemony and globalisation in general. At the same time, the European Union during the 1990s has started initiatives such as the European Commission's MEDIA Plus and the Council of Europe's Eurimages that support the European audio-visual industries by co-ordinating film and television productions, helping the distribution and exhibition sectors, subsidising film festivals, and training media professionals (Jäckel 2003, Elsaesser 2005). The preservation of cultural diversity within Europe and the goal of greater competitiveness on global markets have created their own set of contradictions. On the one hand, the many similarities among European approaches to minority cinema, heritage film, and socially conscious film-making suggest the emergence of a self-consciously European cinema modelled on Hollywood but with distinct artistic traditions and regional sensibilities. These new transnational ethics and aesthetics emphasise shared concerns across national boundaries and find privileged expression in the celebration of marginal voices, hybrid identities, and diasporic perspectives. On the other hand, the new conditions of production, distribution, and exhibition have contributed to the reaffirmation and commodification of national identities that, in the German context, is most apparent in the international marketing of films about modern German history.

The revival of the German film industry, the expansion of the European Union, and the intricacies of European film financing have brought many foreign-born film professionals to Berlin and Munich, a trend that accounts for the many stories about border crossings, multiple identities, and cross-cultural encounters and the many experiments with hybridisation, appropriation, and transculturation. The impact on subject matter has been most noticeable in the case of Turkish directors working in Germany who, together with second- and third-generation Turkish immigrants, have radically expanded and transformed the filmic imagination. Aside from attracting the usual number of Austrians and Swiss such as Stefan Ruzowitzky and Dani Levy, the German film industry now employs a large number of actors and directors from Eastern Europe, including Czech-born Dana Vavrova, Romanian-born Alexandra Maria Lara, and German-Hungarian Fred Kelemen, creating a situation reminiscent of 1920s Film Europe.

Meanwhile German-born Michael Haneke, to mention the most famous director operating in a European framework, started his career in Austria, works primarily in France, and finances most of his films as European co-productions. The European sensibility of his oeuvre, from the German–Austrian co-production *71 Fragmente einer Chronologie des Zufalls* (71 Fragments of a Chronology of Chance, 1994) to the European co-production *Die Klavierspielerin* (The Piano Teacher, 2001), based on the novel by Elfriede Jelinek, is evident in the intense preoccupation with the educated, affluent bourgeoisie and the systematic deconstruction of Hollywood conventions of storytelling. Confirming the new division between the transnational and the regional as the two models of European film-making, the rise of a transnational production mode and art cinema tradition has coincided with the rediscovery of local and regional sensibilities in the conventional formats cultivated by Helmut Dietl in his explorations of the Munich yuppie scene and by Detlev Buck through his North German affinity for rural milieux and quirky outsiders.

Just like the new models of film funding, film production remains divided between global ambitions and artisanal solutions. Bernd Eichinger who, as the producer and director of Constantin-Film, has consolidated his position as Germany's most powerful and versatile film professional, personifies the first model (Rauch 2000). Alternating between international blockbusters such as the science-fiction film *Resident Evil* (2002) and prestige productions about German history from the Nazis to the RAF, Eichinger works in the producer-based tradition established by Pommer for Ufa in the 1920s. Similarly, the actor-writer-director-producer Til Schweiger divides his attention between European and American projects since the successful marketing of his directorial debut *Der Eisbär* (The Ice Bear, 1998) as a German *Pulp Fiction* (1994).

X Filme Creative Pool, the production company founded in 1994 by Tom Tykwer, Dani Levy, Wolfgang Becker, and Stefan Arndt embodies the second model, which may be compared to the low-budget and less commercially driven independent film. Like the Filmverlag der Autoren in the 1970s and 1980s, X Filme has produced the most innovative films of the 1990s and early 2000s and continues to specialise in dramas and comedies with a distinctly contemporary sensibility. Especially the younger generation associated with the independent film seems eager and willing to work in transnational contexts, a development illustrated by the careers of Tom Tykwer and Franka Potente after the phenomenal success of *Lola rennt* (Run Lola Run, 1998), with Tykwer directing English-language co-productions such as *Heaven* (2002) and *Das Parfüm: Die Geschichte eines Mörders* (Perfume: The Story of a Murderer, 2006), and with Potente appearing as the female lead in several major Hollywood films. Established older directors and innovative film artists, too, continue to be attracted to the greater creative possibilities available elsewhere, with Wenders since *Million Dollar Hotel* (2000) shuttling between Babelsberg and Hollywood and with Treut pursuing her gender-bending explorations wherever she can find funding for her provocative documentaries and essay films.

The changes in film financing and modes of production must be seen as an integral part of the transformation of the German media landscape and the proliferation of new digital technologies. Since the privatisation of public broadcasting in the early 1980s, cable stations and media concerns like the Kirch group (now sold) have played a key role in financing domestic productions, sponsoring international projects, developing further the synergies among film, television, and video, and strengthening the existing ties with the music and publishing industries. All of these initiatives have contributed to what some welcome as a long-overdue maximisation of resources and others denounce as excessive commercialism. Joining established German distributors such as Filmverlag der Autoren (now part of Kinowelt), Warner, Columbia, United International Pictures, and Buena Vista International have increased their presence on German markets and begun to promote new films through elaborate marketing campaigns. During the same period, German investors seeking tax shelters have become actively involved in the financing of Hollywood movies, with German Film Funds co-financing between 15 and 20 per cent of all major Hollywood productions in 2001. The considerable flows of venture capital into film projects, made possible by German tax laws, international tax policies, and the stock market bubble, have made film a viable investment and global commodity and a powerful symbol of the post-unification culture of shareholder value and capitalist growth.

The promotion after 1989 of a consciously popular and commercially viable German film was not just a response to the intense competition with electronic and digital media and the new arrangements between public and private funding; the return to genre cinema also seemed to offer the best solution to the steady decline of film culture since the early 1980s. In the former East, unification had a devastating effect on local film exhibition. With higher admission prices and lower discretionary incomes, ticket sales plummeted – in some areas by almost 40 per cent – and many motion-picture theatres stopped operations. This wave of closings in the East coincided with a diminished public interest in the offerings of revival houses in the West and a general trend toward large and spectacular multiplexes. These multiplexes brought older and more diverse audiences back to the movies – namely as part of the new event culture generated by Hollywood blockbusters – but they also provided a perfect showcase for the romantic comedies that started the revival of German cinema during the early 1990s. As a consequence, the number of new releases increased from approximately 60 films per year in the early 1990s to 80 per year in the early 2000s. In 2006, 122 German feature films were released, with more than one-third as co-productions; there has also been a marked increase in documentaries. The total number of tickets sold in 2001 reached almost 118 million, a considerable improvement compared to West German numbers from the 1960s to the 1980s but still very low measured against the 'golden age of German film' from the 1930s to the 1950s. During the 1990s, the German market share of films in distribution was usually between 6 and 15 per cent; the US share decreased slightly but remained between 70 and 88 per cent. In the last few years, the German market share has fluctuated between 10 and 20 per cent, with Hollywood productions providing between 70 and 80 per cent, and other European cinemas contributing about 5 per cent of all new releases.

During the early 1990s, two kinds of films dominated movie programming: big-budget Hollywood productions and low-budget domestic productions. Hollywood continued to satisfy the need for blockbusters with famous stars, spectacular settings, and special effects. *Pretty Woman* headed the list of box-office hits in 1990, followed by *Home Alone* in 1991, *Basic Instinct* in 1992, *Jurassic Park* in 1993, *While You Were Sleeping* in 1994, *The Lion King* in 1995, *Independence Day* in 1996, *Men in Black* in 1997, and *Titanic* in 1998; the early 2000s saw the ascendancy of Disney animated films and the *Harry Potter* series. Hollywood blockbusters continue to generate most profits at the box office, but some German films performed surprisingly well, with *Der Schuh des Manitu* (Manitou's Shoe, 2001) the top-grossing film of 2001, *(T)Raumschiff Surprise – Periode I* (Dreamship Surprise, 2004) and *Sieben Zwerge* (Seven Dwarfs, 2004) among the top three films of that year, *Die weisse Massai* (The White Massai) among the top ten in 2005, and *Das Parfüm* reaching more than five million viewers in 2006. These successes confirm to what degree cinema after 1989 has become mainstream entertainment aimed primarily at a mass audience and, more specifically, at young film fans in their teens and twenties.

The division of labour between the global trends and styles propagated by the Hollywood film industry and the local traditions and alternative sensibilities captured by the surprisingly successful but largely non-exportable examples of German humour has left little room for the kind of formal innovation and critical reflection usually identified with art cinema. East and West German film-makers from the 1970s and 1980s continue to make films but with little commercial success and virtually no international resonance, with the exception of Wenders, Herzog, and Schlöndorff. Several directors, including von Trotta and Beyer, found a temporary refuge in television. In a cultural climate that no longer associates filmic practices with cultural critique, reassigning this function once again to literature and theatre, even Schroeter's ambitious adaptation of Ingeborg Bachmann's *Malina* (1991) attracted fewer than fifty thousand viewers. Outside the metropolitan centres, the lack of interest in French, British, or Italian films has further undermined established traditions that, since the 1920s, have provided alternatives to Hollywood through the foreign art film. This new provincialism in audience tastes, combined with an overwhelming preference for trivial entertainment, is all the more surprising in light of the new synergies in European film production and film financing and the remarkable similarities among leading European directors in their experiments with generic conventions, social realist traditions, and postmodern styles.

Since the introduction of home VCRs in the 1970s and the introduction of DVD players in the 1990s, the German film industry has profited greatly from the expansion of the home entertainment sector and the growing market for VHS and DVD rentals and sales, with the percentages now evenly divided among VHS and DVD rentals, VHS sales, and DVD sales. Often containing special features such as director's commentary, actors' interviews, and deleted scenes, DVDs have created a new culture of movie viewing that, despite its commercial orientation, functions as an occasional corrective to the forces of cultural levelling, especially in the case of niche markets such as minority cinema or experimental film. The official film sites and discussion groups on the World Wide Web play an increasingly important role in identifying cult films, promoting new stars, and facilitating the occasional crossover successes. With most new German films easily available on DVDs, and with many older films re-released in the digital format, film reception may have become more privatised in the process; but it has also allowed for new forms of spectator identification and consumer choice. Together with the many film festivals organised by cities large and small as an integral part of cultural tourism and urban renewal, these new delivery systems for audio-visual media have helped German film classics and independent productions to reach their target audiences, which has been especially important in the marketing of gay and lesbian films, the preservation of the DEFA heritage, and the international reception of Turkish-German films.

Last but not least, the changing media landscape with its hybrid formats and diverse exhibition venues has given rise to new documentary and experimental forms and sparked a renewed interest both in film as a form of social and political commentary and in formal reflections on the primacy of the image in contemporary media society. The documentaries made after 1989 proved very effective in addressing such social problems as unemployment, youth violence, and xenophobia. Several films dealt specifically with the impact of unification on everyday life in the provinces and small towns of the former GDR. At the same time, the filmic experiments of Farocki, Ottinger, Herzog, and others suggest that non-narrative genres remain ideally suited to push the boundaries of representation and interrogate film's contribution to constructions of identity, nation, and history (Alter 2002). Whereas the essay film has allowed some film-makers to reintroduce the notion of authorship and subjectivity, the documentary aesthetic has been used by others to respond to changing definitions of realism and reality. For similar reasons, the possibilities of experimental film have been greatly enriched by installation art, video art, and digital technologies. The productive alliance between filmic and digital technologies has resulted in closer collaborations among motion-picture theatres, art museums, and alternative exhibition spaces and profoundly transformed the function of film art in what some scholars now call the age of post-cinema (Halle and Steingroever 2008).

The different systems of distribution identified with cinema, television, video, and the World Wide Web, and the changing alliances between public and private, and national and international, modes of financing have profoundly affected existing definitions of film as a medium with distinct technical and aesthetic qualities and unique conditions of reception. The departure from earlier concepts of media specificity and film art is nowhere more apparent than in the creative synergies between German film and television, especially after the deregulation of television and the introduction of new commercial channels. In light of the seemingly unstoppable trend toward 'amphibian' forms and practices, a clear distinction between film and television can no longer be maintained. The strong trend toward serials and sequels in both media confirms the concomitant erosion of the filmic text (i.e., a distinct, self-contained entity) as the central category of film analysis. Conventional films intended for theatrical release end up being shown only on television, whereas innovative television plays receive prestigious media prizes. For the most part, the feature films made during the 1990s were aesthetic hybrids without a distinctive visual or narrative style. Their close adherence to the format of the television play is evident in the limited number of locations and characters, the heavy emphasis on dialogue, and the overarching concern with average situations, typical characters, relevant problems, and meaningful solutions. However, RTL2, a private channel known for its crass commercialism, also produced the critically acclaimed media thriller *Der Sandmann* (The Sandman, 1995), and SAT 1 launched *German Classics*, a successful series of remakes from the 1950s that included *Das Mädchen Rosemarie*. Public television during the same decade reaffirmed its original function as an advocate for high culture and an alternative to the commercialisation of private television. Literary adaptations, in particular, benefited immensely from the synergies between film and television – in terms of financing models and creative personnel – that made possible expensive multi-part adaptations of novels by Thomas Mann, Joseph Roth, and Lion Feuchtwanger. *Jahrestage* (Anniversaries, 2000), based on the acclaimed novel by Uwe Johnson, and Breloer's *Die Manns* (The Mann Family, 2001), about the first family of twentieth-century German literature, proved particularly successful; but middle-brow authors such as Erich Kästner and Vicki Baum profited equally from the rediscovery of literature on German television. In this context, the adaptations of

East German authors Erwin Strittmatter and Erich Loest attested to a concerted effort by former DEFA directors to keep alive other literary traditions, especially in the context of historical fiction.

In the tradition of Reitz's *Heimat* series, public television stations have also devoted considerable resources to historicising the history of the Federal Republic, the Third Reich and, most recently, the Second World War. Whereas mainstream films tend to present the recent past through personal stories, television productions take on more controversial political subject matter, a tradition that began with *Todesspiel* (Deadly Games, 1997), Heinrich Breloer's acclaimed docudrama about the RAF and the 'German Autumn' of 1977. A mixture of sentimental recollection and authentic reconstruction emerged as the dominant audio-visual style across a range of narrative formats, with television specialising in more fact-based genres but also competing with the cinema in the production of epic formats and visual spectacles. The rediscovery of the 1950s – and, later, of the 1960s and 1970s – extended the process of historical retrospection and nostalgic appropriation to the postwar period and, with that, to the project of national reconstruction. What Sönke Wortmann's *Das Wunder von Bern* (The Miracle of Berne, 2003) achieved on the big screen, the rebirth of Germany's national pride after its team's victory at the 1954 World Soccer Cup, numerous television mini-series and docudramas have since performed on the small screen, the transformation of German history into an object of affective investments and affirmative identifications. During the last decade, the history of the Federal Republic has been retold in a series of productions about influential figures such as the publisher Axel Springer, espionage scandals such as the Guillaume Affair, and newsworthy stories such as the mass escape through a tunnel under the Berlin Wall in the early 1960s or the catastrophic North Sea flood of 1962. More recently, the Third Reich and the Second World War have once again assumed centre stage in the televised imagination, with several mini-series devoted to key figures among the Nazi leadership such as Albert Speer and with more and more projects focused on Germans as the victims of history, whether in the bombing of Dresden or the expulsion of ethnic Germans from the East.

Elements of popular cinema: the return to genre

Made possible by new models of film financing and sustained by the changing division of labour between film and television, the 1990s gave way to a hedonistic culture of fun, pleasure, and entertainment that marked a radical break with the legacies of the 1960s and 1970s. Promoting an unabashedly materialist and consumerist individualism, the new star-driven cinema shared this new preoccupation with glamour, fame, beauty, and celebrity with other popular diversions such as spectator sports, gossip magazines, pop music, high-end fashion, and television talk shows. In some cases, the underlying anti-intellectualism produced expressions of crudeness and vulgarity uniquely German in the animosity toward bourgeois culture. In other cases, the search for personal happiness established a framework for combining retrograde fantasies of family and community with more tolerant attitudes toward alternative sexualities and hybrid identities. By validating individual ambition and self-interest, the new genre films, and the romantic comedies in particular, provided not only convenient models of identification for the managerial, technical, and cultural elites brought forth by globalisation and neo-liberalism. These contemporary narratives also assigned different functions to socially and economically marginalised groups, either by turning them into symbols of the post-unification culture of openness and tolerance (for instance, in the depiction of homosexuals and immigrant groups) or by enlisting them in a nostalgic celebration of provincialism and parochialism (for instance, through the stories of simple country folk). With such contradictory investments, the popular comedies and dramas provided a convenient vehicle for the attitudes, dispositions, and mentalities that, translated into political terms, sustained the Berlin Republic through the various crises of the 1990s.

Commercial success in the 1990s required the adaptation of directorial visions, performance styles, and generic conventions to contemporary tastes and sensibilities, including an acute awareness of the performativity of identity. The unexpected rediscovery of genre cinema, German style, began with a number of undistinguished but very influential romantic comedies made by women directors for a largely female audience. Not surprisingly given the centrality of sexual difference in classical narrative cinema, the crisis of heterosexuality functioned as a main topic and structural device, with the post-feminist approaches to gender and sexuality facilitating a precarious balancing act between affirmation and subversion. The director Sherry Hormann codified the main elements of the genre in several yuppie comedies about troubled marriages, romantic relationships, and love triangles, including *Frauen sind was Wunderbares* (Women Are Simply Wonderful, 1994) and *Irren ist männlich* (Father's Day, 1996). A number of films were based on novels by best-selling author Hera Lind, including Peter Timm's *Ein Mann für jede Tonart* (A Man for Every Situation, 1993) and Sönke Wortmann's *Das Superweib* (The Superwife, 1996) with Veronica Ferres. The ideal of contemporary femininity found a perfect embodiment in blonde Katja Riemann who, whether as a newspaper cartoonist in *Abgeschminkt!* (Making Up!, 1993) or as a radio talk show host in *Stadtgespräch* (Talk of the Town, 1995), combined professional competence with romantic incompetence, and pseudo-feminist arguments with traditionally female wiles.

Showing attractive young professionals in stylish middle-class and upper-middle-class settings, these so-called *Beziehungskomödien* (relationship comedies) derived much of their humorous appeal from the alleged discrepancy between the 'eternal' problems in male–female relationships and the contemporary culture of gender trouble and post-feminist malaise. Katja von Garnier's *Abgeschminkt!* set the tone by simultaneously evoking the lifestyle markers of the emancipated woman and demonstrating the inevitable failure of feminist demands in the face of true love. Most of these comedies reduce the problems of femininity to that of sexuality, and, to add to the essentialist tone, to motherhood (even if outside marriage). Sustained by this timely compromise between progressive and conservative attitudes, even unconventional living arrangements and sexual entanglements end up affirming the importance of love, friendship, and family as a refuge from the pressures of the workplace. At times, the anti-feminist backlash resulted in satirical attacks on the culture of political correctness, as evident by the screen adaptation of *Der Campus* (Campus, 1998), the best-seller by Dieter Schwanitz. Even Sandra Nettelbeck's surprise hit *Bella Martha* (Mostly Martha, 2001) with Martina Gedeck in the title role, participated in the subtle denunciation of female careerism that can be healed only through the sudden arrival of a child – solutions that the women directors of the 1970s would have rejected as sexist. No wonder that the film was remade by Hollywood with Catherine Zeta-Jones as *No Reservations* (2007).

Typically, the romantic comedies from the 1990s feature young women who want it all: lovers, friends, children, and a successful career. Yet invariably, their professional ambition upsets the balance of power between the sexes; this point is usually made through the stereotypical figure of the unreconstructed male. The ensuing dramatic complications – arguments, fights, affairs, and break-ups – aim at the restoration of traditional femininity and masculinity, but in more enlightened, tolerant terms. The underlying message: men must control their selfish and aggressive impulses without becoming overly feminised, and women must embrace their feminine qualities without falling back into complete dependency. Most romantic comedies achieve this conciliatory effect by first diagnosing the excesses of male chauvinism and then documenting the miraculous transformation of unreconstructed males into mature, supportive partners. As a rule, this process takes place through the arrival of the main protagonist in an environment perceived as hostile or different. In Wortmann's audience hit *Der bewegte Mann* (Maybe, Maybe Not, 1994), the re-education of the arrogant macho comes about through a gay friend; a feminist commune performs the same task in *Allein unter Frauen* (Alone among Women, 1991). Buck's *Männerpension* (Jailbirds, 1996) offers yet another variation on this theme by delivering male prisoners during a weekend on furlough to the female volunteers intent on rehabilitating them.

Within such generic conventions, the new stars from the relationship comedies usually play well-adjusted, upwardly mobile, reasonably happy, but also incredibly self-centred men and women in their twenties and thirties. In countless stories about love and marriage, family and friendship, career and money, the leading protagonists must make the difficult transition to an adulthood symbolised no longer by changed family status (marriage, parenthood) but by an acute awareness of the limits of individual self-realisation. The inevitable conflicts are articulated through personal relationships and, more specifically, the main character's competing needs for personal independence and a sense of belonging. At times, these problems erupt in the context of corporate intrigues, professional rivalries, and publicity scandals. At other times, stressful summer vacations, endless traffic jams or ambitious house renovations provide some much-needed comic relief. Yet in the obligatory happy endings, all the machos, feminists, careerists, homemakers, single mothers, and divorced fathers invariably find common ground in their unshaken belief in the pursuit of personal happiness.

For one thing, the romantic comedies of the 1990s promoted the versions of modern love considered the most compatible with middle-class attitudes toward marriage and family life. For another, the films advertised the affluent lifestyles and consumerist tastes personified by the new class of yuppies. Featuring attractive young urban professionals working in consulting, advertising, mass media, and investment banking, the comedies evoke a contemporary society unburdened by ideology, politics, and history and held together by the unbridled pursuit of money and status. Yet below the glossy surface, the characters' compulsive optimism and unmitigated narcissism also suggest an unwillingness or inability to confront the frightening prospect of an adult world marked by responsibilities, compromises, failures, and regrets. Not surprisingly, from Dietl's much-discussed *Rossini, oder die mörderische Frage, wer mit wem schlief* (Rossini, 1997), about a fashionable Munich restaurant favoured by local celebrities from stage and screen, to *Workaholic* (1996), about the marital difficulties of a dual-career couple, these cautionary tales about the new affluent classes rarely followed their own half-hearted calls for moderation and humility and instead remained intoxicated by the trappings of status and wealth.

A few film-makers mocked the affirmative character of the relationship comedies by cultivating the subversive energies of the grotesque and the absurd. Working in this mode, Oskar Roehler combined highly stylised images, fantastic devices, and cheap shock effects in the castration comedy *Suck My Dick* (2001), a satirical comment on the erotic predilections of the new *nouveaux riches*. His adaptation of *Elementarteilchen* (Elementary Particles, 2006), based on the controversial novel by Michel Houellebecq, confirmed Roehler's reputation as the most cynical observer of human sexuality to emerge in the age of gender performance and post-identity. Meanwhile, most post-unification films dealing with questions of gender and sexuality now regularly feature gay characters, challenge hetero-normative assumptions, and accept the possibility of same-sex desire. Since the decriminalisation of homosexuality in 1994, gay characters have been used repeatedly to evoke an atmosphere of sexual tolerance and worldly sophistication. More problematically, the function of gay characters in the relationship comedies has often been limited to resolving the crisis of heterosexuality and affirming the monogamous couple, whether homosexual or heterosexual, as the foundation of society (Halle 2000). Using love, or the pursuit of love, in promoting social and racial harmony and cross-cultural understanding, such films mark a radical break with the politics of gay rights advocated by Rosa von Praunheim or the queer sensibilities explored by Monika Treut; yet they also complicate the filmic manifestations of gender and sexuality in interesting ways. Similar tendencies toward more ordinary stories and characters can be observed in the relationship comedies made from a gay or lesbian perspective, including the charming lesbian love story between a German and an Afro-German woman in *Alles wird gut* (Everything Will Be Fine, 1998) by Angelina Maccarone. Her portrayal in *Fremde Haut* (Unveiled, 2005) of a lesbian from Iran seeking asylum in male disguise acknowledges both the power of love and the pervasiveness of homophobia, but without the didactic intensions that marred the first lesbian films from the early 1980s.

Whereas Praunheim has maintained his activist stance even in mainstream productions such as *Der Einstein des Sex* (The Einstein of Sex, 1999) about Weimar sexologist Magnus Hirschfeld, conventional genre films in the style of *Wem nutzt die Liebe in Gedanken* (Love in Thoughts, 2004) have taken to mining other historical periods for sentimental treatments of homosexual youth. Conceptually, the resultant depoliticisation of gay cinema is reflected in the move from 'homosexual' and 'gay' to 'queer' as the preferred category of self-identification and artistic exploration (Kuzniar 2000). With the gradual disappearance of a radical gay cinema that still treated sexual preference as a political choice, alternative visions have survived primarily in experimental films in the style of Michael Stock's *Prinz in Hölleland* (Prince in Hell, 1993) and the video work and shorts by Michael Brynntrup where queer identity becomes aligned with an aesthetic of marginality. Combining an underground aesthetic with hardcore gay pornography, Bruce LaBruce's controversial *The Raspberry Reich* (2004) mocks the 1970s' politicisation of sexuality in its exploitative portrayal of RAF terrorism, an indication of the difficulties of gay and lesbian cinema to find new directions.

The unwillingness of many protagonists to enter adulthood and become productive members of society is nowhere more striking than in the popular road movies and buddy films of the 1990s. Modelled on established Hollywood formulas but also inspired by the spatial and social topography of a unified Germany, these films responded to a growing frustration with the available social models and lifestyle options. Alternatives are subsequently found in the renunciation of heterosexual love in favour of all-male or, less frequently, all-female groups; the flight from metropolitan centres to provincial towns and deserted landscapes; and the rejection of basic comforts and securities for the adventures of coincidence and circumstance. Informed by such personal choices, the road movies conjured up dream images of a new homeland in which all differences and difficulties can be overcome through a shared opposition to middle-class values. In Buck's unification comedy *Wir können auch anders* (No More Mr Nice Guy, 1993), two dim-witted brothers and a Red Army soldier venture on their own educational journey through the former East. Already with *Bunte Hunde* (Wild Guys, 1995), which was inspired by an actual hostage drama, the promises of the road deteriorate into romantic and sentimental clichés. The last trip taken by two terminally ill young men in *Knockin' on Heaven's Door* (1997) similarly remains fraught with symbolic references to travelling as a form of self-discovery. An exception at least in terms of gender dynamics, *Burning Life* (1994) features two young women who find new meaning in life by robbing banks and distributing their loot among the poor. Less convincing in her take on girl power, von Garnier in *Bandits* (1997) follows four escaped female convicts from their dramatic prison break to their media-driven fame as punk stars and folk heroines.

Perennial favourites with younger audiences, the petty-bourgeois comedies of the 1990s performed similar socio-psychological functions as the relationship comedies, though with a very different audience in mind. Their quirky, silly, or hilarious stories aimed to reconcile individual desires with social realities, but this time from the perspective of the lower classes. Frequently, the male protagonists in these films compensate for their diminished social or economic status by preserving a sense of self in the pursuit of hobbies, sports, and other recreational activities. Some stories offer insightful vignettes of everyday life in the provinces, the kind depicted in the northern flatlands of Buck's *Karniggels* (Rabbits, 1991). Other characters acquire surrogate identities through their association with certain car brands, as shown in the weekend activities of young Opel Manta aficionados in Peter Timm's *Manta, Manta* (1991) and the travel adventures of the East German family from *Go Trabi Go* (1991), two films that, through celebrating the regional cultures of provincial Saxony and the declining Ruhr region, contributed to the nostalgic patterns of *Ostalgie* and *Westalgie*. Yet other protagonists, like the fanatical soccer fans in Winkelmann's *Nordkurve* (North Curve, 1993), enlist the rituals of male bonding to preserve some of the traditions of working-class culture, a tendency also observed in several films that romanticise the decrepit industrial landscapes and depopulated villages of the former GDR, thereby turning them into the imaginary sites of a new Wild East.

While the road movies and petty-bourgeois comedies offered important alternatives to the materialistic yuppie culture depicted in the romantic comedies, other comic genres expressed their class resentments through a deliberate crudeness and simple vulgarity. Combining elements of farce, parody, and grotesque and alluding to older traditions of slapstick comedy, these cheap productions derived much of their emotional appeal from their aggressive, if inarticulate protest against bourgeois conventions and standards of taste. Comedian Gerhard Polt created the formula for these so-called *Proll-Lustspiele* (proletarian comedies) with *Man spricht deutsh* (German Spoken Here, 1988), about one of the countless 'typical' German families populating the beaches on the Adriatic coast, and he continued with a similar vacation farce about the drinking rituals of Mallorca tourists in *Ballermann 6* (1997). The mockery of middle-class notions of normalcy stood behind the infantile pranks that made Tom Gerhardt from *Voll normaaal* (Totally Normal, 1994) the German equivalent of Jim Carey. Film adaptations of popular novels and cartoons proved particularly effective in establishing a domestic tradition in film animation. Michael Schaack started the trend with *Werner Beinhart* (1990) and its numerous sequels about the adventures of a simple-minded, beer-drinking biker dude. A popular television show hosted by two Bavarian comedians with pseudo-Turkish rap personas spawned the situation comedy *Erkan & Stefan* (2000). Its director, Michael 'Bully' Herbig, also made the cult comedy *Der Schuh des Manitu*, with its 11 million tickets the most successful German film ever made. This puerile spoof of the 1960s *Winnteou* films even spawned *Manitu*-related products such as T-shirts and car stickers with nonsense quotes from the film. The similar success of the Star Trek spoof *(T)Raumschiff Surprise – Periode 1* confirmed the actor, screenwriter, director, producer (and television personality) Herbig as one of the commercially most successful people working in contemporary German cinema.

Not surprisingly given the youthfulness of movie audiences, a large number of films made since 1989 dealt with the joys of childhood and the problems of adolescence. The steady stream of films aimed specifically at children included the delightful *Rennschwein Rudi Rüsssel* (Rudi, the Racing Pig, 1995), whose anthropomorphising depiction of a lovable pig anticipated the *Babe* films, and the fairytale-like *Bibi Blocksberg* (2002), an adaptation of the popular children's book about a resourceful little witch and the German answer to Harry Potter. The long overdue acknowledgement of children as consumers also started yet another wave of Kästner adaptations with the multicultural version of *Emil und die Detektive* (Emil and the Detectives, 2001). Since unification, film-makers have turned youth into a heuristic device through which to diagnose the deterioration of family ties and social networks and to analyse the effects of alienation and dislocation on society's most vulnerable members. Growing up in these films frequently means poverty, violence, homelessness, addiction, depression, and sexual abuse. At times the young protagonists have little interaction with their parents or friends. They not only seem utterly lost and confused but also determined to sever all ties to mainstream society; at other times, they become resourceful and confident in confronting the challenges of personal independence.

Inspired by Hollywood, the more conventional treatments usually focused on budding sexuality, first love, and family conflict; a large number of teen comedies and slacker comedies also displayed a puerile scatological humour. Perhaps it was the audience's desire for more substantial problems that contributed to the surprise success of Caroline Link's *Jenseits der Stille* (Beyond Silence, 1996), about a young woman who fulfils her dream of becoming a musician despite the opposition of her deaf-mute parents. And perhaps it was exasperation with middle-class narratives that contributed to the critical acclaim of *Oi! Warning* (1999) about young people in the skinhead milieu. Hans-Christian Schmid made a name for himself with several coming-of-age stories, beginning with *Nach fünf im Urwald* (It's a Jungle Out There, 1995), one of the few films that featured an intact and surprisingly tolerant family with teenagers. The early hacker subculture of the 1980s depicted in *23* (1998) provided him with a conduit to the more existential problems of young adulthood and the chilling new world of information technologies. In *Crazy* (2000), based on the much-discussed novel by 16-year-old Benjamin Lebert, Schmid applied the same filmic sensibility to the boarding school experiences of a handicapped young man. While the genre of the critical youth film continues to combine didactic intentions with social messages, more recent productions have emphasised the subversive power of love, fun, and irreverence, with *Fickende Fische* (Do Fish Do It?, 2002) a touching portrayal of adolescent love in the age of AIDS.

In measuring the impact of unification on social structures, psychological dispositions, and cultural tastes, film-makers during the 1990s re-enlisted the stabilising function of classical narrative in their effort to make sense of everyday life in the Berlin Republic. Younger directors in particular found their subjects and styles through both an emphatic rejection of the legacies of the parent generation (that is, of New German Cinema) and an enthusiastic return to the cinema of their grandparents: that is, the genre cinema of the postwar period. Their version of Zero Hour subsequently found expression in their declared opposition to films with artistic ambitions or critical intentions. Many directors rejected the old vision of film authorship for a more workable, and profitable, compromise between art and commerce. Regrets about such blatant commercialism and fears about the demise of cinema inspired sentimental reminiscences of the silent era in the style of *Der Kinoerzähler* (The Film Narrator, 1993). Meanwhile, the new world of mass entertainment found telling expression in Helmut Dietl's *Late Show* (1999) and similar self-congratulatory films about media professionals. Firmly committed to entertainment as the primary function of cinema, some directors enthusiastically and unabashedly emulated concurrent Hollywood trends. Others cultivated the more intimate, smaller German formats as alternatives to the formulaic blockbusters and star vehicles dominating US imports during the 1990s. And yet others enlisted the harmonising effects of genre in the rewriting of the German past and the remapping of the German present within the changing ethnic, national, and geopolitical topographies of post-Wall Europe. All of these films accommodated the audience's desire both for less complicated narratives of German identity and for more optimistic visions of a multiethnic, multicultural society.

These developments were spearheaded by a new generation of film-makers raised on Hollywood films, cable television, and music videos (Schäffler 2002). A surprising number started out by directing television series, commercials, and music videos and continue to move effortlessly between television plays and feature films. Many young film professionals were trained at the country's leading film schools: the dffb Berlin, the HFF Munich, and as the most recent addition, the Hochschule für Film und Fernsehen 'Konrad Wolf' Potsdam-Babelsberg; several newcomers attended US film schools. Sönke Wortmann, Detlev Buck, and Hans-Christian Schmid are products of the HFF Munich, which is known for training its graduates in the kind of generic formulas employed by Wortmann in his playful experiments with gender roles or refined by Buck in his hilarious portrayals of contemporary masculinity. The Hochschule für bildende Künste Hamburg (HFBK) has produced such diverse talents as Fatih Akin, Lars Becker, and Oliver Hirschbiegel. Andreas Dresen, one of the few young directors born and trained in the East, studied at the HFF Potsdam-Babelsberg, a school known for its commitment to documentary formats and registers. Seeking alternatives to the lure of digital media and its aesthetics of simulation, other directors continue to work in the tradition of filmic realism and auteurist film-making. Here the so-called New Berlin School, a group of dffb graduates, most notably Christian Petzold and Thomas Arslan, has attracted special attention because of their belief in film as a medium with a unique ability to create reality effects and illuminate social reality. The formal characteristics of the New Berlin School are particularly pronounced in the films of Angela Schanelec and her preference for long takes, few dialogues, lay actors, and episodic narratives.

The most famous young director to emerge during the 1990s but, like Fassbinder, without any film school training is Tom Tykwer (Schuppach 2004). His highly stylised use of visual symbols and filmic ciphers was already noticeable in *Die tödliche Maria* (Deadly Maria, 1993) and *Winterschläfer* (Winter Sleepers, 1997) and their philosophical reflections on temporality and causality and the power of fate and coincidence. But it was *Lola rennt* that showed off his considerable talents as a director, screenwriter, and composer, beginning with its formal explorations of coincidence and contingency and its visual reflections on the highly mediated nature of subjectivity and experience. Praised for its multi-layered narrative structure and profoundly filmic sense of movement and space, this MTV-inspired city symphony with Potente in the title role received several film prizes and became the most successful German film internationally since *Das Boot*. With its heavy reliance on popular music, modern fashion, and contemporary lifestyles, *Lola rennt* captured perfectly the spirit of the generation that reached adulthood during the Berlin Republic. At the same time, with its sparse use of dialogue, self-reflexive approach to sounds and images, and fragmented urban topography, the film came to represent the quintessential postmodern film. With *Der Krieger und die Kaiserin* (The Princess and the Warrior, 2000), Tykwer continued some of his formal inquiries into fate and coincidence but also opened up the narrative toward the redemptive qualities of romantic love.

The mass appeal of a hybridised genre cinema owes much to directors such as Wortmann and Buck, and the emergence of an innovative but popular art cinema remains inseparable from Tykwer. Yet post-unification cinema would not have been able to contribute to the new fun mentality without its young and attractive stars, many of whom started their careers without prior training in the theatre. Again the similarities to the postwar years are pronounced, with heartthrob Til Schweiger a contemporary version of Horst Buchholz and perky Katja Riemann a combination of Liselotte Pulver and Ruth Leuwerik. At the same time, these leading German stars of the 1990s modelled themselves on then-popular Hollywood versions of youthful masculinity and femininity, with Schweiger a German Tom Cruise and Riemann a German Meg Ryan. Less famous actors and actresses have become closely identified with particular dramatic registers and gender stereotypes. Whereas Heino Ferch revived the tradition of charming rogues, Kai Wiesinger convinced in the role of the eternal boy. Joachim Król built an impressive career by playing sensitive, thoughtful, and often slightly quirky characters. Moritz Bleibtreu has been repeatedly cast as the charming hero of slick action films, and Daniel Brühl has recently gained much attention as the young sensitive guy and brooding idealist. After *Lola rennt*, Franka Potente emerged as an international star by turning her version of the girl next door into an icon of contemporary femininity and art cinema chic. Other actresses relied on more conventional and 'typically German' registers. Thus the screen persona of Veronica Ferres alternates between the stereotypical blonde beast and the equally clichéd blonde with a heart. Whereas Maria Schrader performs the role of the dramatic heroine with a touch of *femme fatale*, Meret Becker infuses the classical *ingénue* with a rebellious punk sensibility. Meanwhile, character actors Corinna Harfouch and Sebastian Koch have lent their dramatic talents to more serious treatments of German history. The return to provocative subject matter has also come with trained actors who use their experience in the intimate format of television to add psychological depth and complexity. The impressive results, from Martina Gedeck's performance of middle-age lust in

Sommer '04 (Summer '04, 2006) and Jürgen Vogel's provocative portrayal of a rapist in *Der freie Wille* (The Free Will, 2006), suggest that some recent films are taking a more mature view of human nature and the inscrutability of desire.

Last but not least, the diversity of a popular genre cinema defined as much through its actors and actresses as through its leading directors opened the door for marginal forms and genres, including those either neglected during the heydays of art cinema or absent from the German film tradition. Some film-makers worked entirely outside the mainstream, with horror providing a particularly useful venue for a return of the repressed (Hantke 2006). Taking the need for shock effects to an extreme, Jörg Buttgereit combined horror, gore, perversion, and bad taste in low-budget horror films such as *Nekromantik* (1987) and *Schramm* (1993) and acquired a small but international underground following mainly through video releases. More mainstream genres included action adventures, crime capers, horror films, and science fiction films. The prolific Dominik Graf, who directed the well-made police thriller *Die Sieger* (The Invincibles, 1994), still had to confront long-established prejudices against the sensationalist mixture of family tragedies and corporate power struggles that eventually became his speciality. Yet a series of box office hits in the early 2000s validated those film-makers who ventured into the familiar Hollywood terrain of action, horror, and suspense. Austrian-born Stefan Ruzowitzky in *Anatomie* (Anatomy, 2000) combined elements of the medical drama and the slasher film, whereas Oliver Hirschbiegel in *Das Experiment* (The Experiment, 2001) based his prison drama on a scientific experiment about human behaviour in a master–slave situation. Surprisingly successful at the box office, both films spawned sequels, another phenomenon reminiscent of the 1950s and 1960s. Last but not least, in the multimedia work of theatre producer, film director, and media artist Christoph Schlingensief, the subversive energies of violence, anarchy, and the grotesque were repeatedly mobilised for explicitly political interventions, first in the irreverent unification farce *Das deutsche Kettensägenmassaker* (The German Chain Saw Massacre, 1990) and then in the equally bizarre *Terror 2000* (1992) about right-wing terrorism in the former East. Schlingensief's shock aesthetic has remained the exception in the decade's prevailing modes of coming to terms with the past(s).

Once again: coming to terms with the past(s)

Simultaneously with the culture of narcissism and hedonism, the 1990s saw the emergence of a pervasive sense of nostalgia and retrospection. Working through the past after 1989 meant dealing with the legacies of the Third Reich and the Cold War but also using the changing relationship to the past to measure the slow and painful process of unification. The experiences of West and East Germans were treated in alternately dramatic, sentimental, comical, and ironic tones, and they continue to serve as a reference point even in films without explicit references to the German division (Naughton 2002). The first filmic responses to the events leading up to the collapse of the GDR relied heavily on realist styles and the formal conventions of the docudrama. They used classical narrative structures in presenting the historical events and in measuring their impact on public and private lives. In recounting the process, most film-makers preferred socio-psychological models of explanation. In the two-part television series *Nikolaikirche* (Nikolai Church, 1995), based on the Loest novel, Frank Beyer concentrated on a middle-class family from Leipzig to show the possibility of individual choice even under an oppressive regime. Based on a true story, *Der Blaue* (The Blue One, 1994) reconstructed the informal power structures that allowed an informer for the East German secret police to become a state secretary in the unified Germany. Indicative of the underlying conflation of historical periods, several films use the geographical and ideological terrain identified with the former GDR to gain access to the legacies of the Third Reich. Thus *Die Spur des Bernsteinzimmers* (The Mystery of the Amber Room, 1992) brings together three very different characters in a detective-like search for the legendary treasure lost during the Second World War. Similarly, the protagonists in Schilling's *Die blinde Kuh* (Project Blind Cow, 1994) find important historical documents about early Nazi television research in the crumbling military installations left behind by the Red Army, a narrative construction that speaks to a growing tendency in public discourse and scholarly debate to describe the Third Reich and the GDR both as totalitarian regimes.

In many of the early films about unification, a profound sense of loss, failure, and regret coexists with the kind of fearless pragmatism displayed by the old woman from *Der Brocken* (Rising to the Bait, 1992), who defends her idyllic life on the island of Rügen against old and new enemies, and the less confident young heroine of Helke Misselwitz's *Herzsprung* (1992), who tries to build a new existence in a small town located near the nation's new geographical centre. However, such nuanced reflections on the victims of history were soon forgotten in favour of either more forward-looking or more backward-looking narratives; hence the painful belatedness of a film like Gwisdek's gloomy *Abschied von Agnes* (Farewell to Agnes, 1994). In later treatments, life in the new states either inspires the sense of melancholy that keeps together the group of small-town friends paralysed by boredom and hopelessness in *Vergiss Amerika* (Forget America, 2000), or it requires the painful confrontation with the past initiated by five former East German border guards in *Hundsköpfe* (Dog Heads, 2002).

The young generation of writers and directors born and raised in the GDR contributed to the process by sharing their memories of everyday life under socialism. The rediscovery of the GDR as *Heimat*, and of its consumer products as objects of nostalgic appropriation, started with the re-releases of DEFA classics, the regular programming of DEFA films on MDR regional television, and the popular success of post-communist compilation films in the style of *East Side Story* (1997). However, *Ostalgie* meant not only sugar-coating the past in light of a bleak present; it also involved a painful working through memories, identifications, and lost political beliefs. With its cheerful tunes and colourful characters, Leander Haußmann's *Sonnenallee* (Sun Alley, 1999), based on the novel by Thomas Brussig, struck a perfect balance between sentimental recollection and ironic reconstruction. Another Brussig adaptation, the picaresque *Helden wie wir* (Heroes Like Us, 1999), added a hilarious new element – an enormous, wall-shattering erection – to the official narratives about the fall of the Wall. The audience hit *Good-Bye Lenin!* (2003) by Wolfgang Becker continued in this tradition of humour and satire by recognising the need of all generations to deal with their experiences of loss: the mother by never really awaking from her coma, the son by simulating historical continuity, and all the other characters by either denying or forgetting their participation in the collective fantasy called GDR. Whereas Haußmann's *NVA* (2005) offers a rather clichéd view of military service in the National People's Army, the narrative of Stasi surveillance and dissident culture told by first-time director Florian Henckel von Donnersmarck in *Das Leben der Anderen* (The Lives of Others, 2006) stands out through its profound insights into the insidious mechanisms of compliance and self-censorship in a surveillance state; the film received the 2007 Oscar for Best Foreign Film.

In the same way that the first films about unification repeated narrative formulas from the postwar period (for example, compare *Der Blaue* with *Mein Schulfreund*), so the first big-budget films about the history of the German division drew upon established models of explanation involving an all-powerful regime and its hierarchical power structures; the excesses of party leaders and the insidious effects of state surveillance; and, to introduce the most critical point, the continuities of authoritarianism across the ideological divides of the Cold War. In a significant departure from earlier films about the German division, including *Himmel ohne Sterne* and *Der geteilte Himmel*, these unification narratives typically involve a West German woman and an East German man. Two directors from New German cinema were among the first to address these difficult legacies openly. Von Trotta in *Das Versprechen* (The Promise, 1995) presented the postwar division as the tragic story of two young lovers separated by politics and ideology. Significantly, the happy ending not for the couple but for the unified nation arrives under the conditions of post-ideology. As noted by critics of the film, the retrospective construction of the German division as a love story makes unification appear natural and inevitable; moreover, the validation of the female perspective draws upon a not unproblematic tradition of female allegories of nation. Using unification as a conduit to the equally problematic history of the Federal Republic during the 1970s, Schlöndorff in *Die Stille nach dem Schuss* (The Legends of Rita, 2000) followed a female member of the RAF from life in the underground in the West to several failed new beginnings in the East. His nuanced portrayal of everyday life in the GDR made it possible to contemplate the losses and losers on both sides of the German–German border.

Meanwhile, the films about the old Federal Republic gave rise to a very different kind of *Westalgie*, namely nostalgia for the prosperous, comfortable, and self-contained West during the Cold War era. It found expression in the yearning for more authentic forms of youth and counterculture and for more meaningful political convictions and commitments. Part of broader retro trends in fashion, design, and pop music, the subsequent rediscovery of the 1960s, 1970s, and 1980s spawned such peripheral phenomena as homages to the German New Wave in the style of *Verschwende deine Jugend* (Play It Loud!, 2003). Focusing more specifically on the legacy of the RAF, the autonomous political groups of the 1970s, and the alternative lifestyles of the 1980s, several films approached the failure of the student movement and the death of communism from the perspective of post-ideology and post-memory: that is, of a disillusioned generation without utopian projects or revolutionary gestures. In contrast to the austere treatments of the subject by directors of the New German Cinema, the younger film-makers used linear narratives and strong character identification, the seductive lure of set and costume design, and the self-reflective play with the respective decade's musical sounds to work through the myths and mystifications of the New Left.

Exploring terrorism's devastating impact on family life, Christian Petzold in *Die innere Sicherheit* (The State I Am In, 2000) told the sobering story of a girl's coming-of-age while living in the underground with her ex-terrorist parents. Yet already *Was tun, wenn's brennt?* (What to Do in Case of Fire, 2001) promised a sentimental trip down memory lane into the anarchist scene in West Berlin during the 1970s. Whereas essay films such as *Black Box BRD* (Black Box Germany, 2001) reflected critically on the causes and effects of West German terrorism, the portrayal of one of its leading figures in *Baader* (2002) offered little more than an exercise in radical chic, complete with fancy cars, cool clothes, big guns, and macho posturing. In an ambiguous comment on the self-isolation of the intelligentsia and the counterculture, two critically acclaimed films captured the end of the Federal Republic through protagonists who decide to ignore or fail to notice its demise. Thus Roehler used a starkly beautiful black-and-white cinematography in *Die Unberührbare* (No Place to Go, 2000) to capture the lost world of the Federal Republic through the melodramatic figure of the writer Gisela Elsner, his mother, whereas Haußmann in the quirky *Herr Lehmann* (Berlin Blues, 2003) described the habitués of West Berlin's pub scene as utterly unprepared for the fall of the Wall.

The filmic contributions to *Ostalgie* and *Westalgie* thrived on widespread frustration with the consequences of unification and residual attachments to the social and cultural networks and the comfortable living conditions threatened by neo-liberalism, globalisation, and multiculturalism. Moreover, the renewed interest in the question of nation and national identity confirmed both the presentness of the past and the disappearance of that past into media-produced images and narratives. With the gradual passing of the generation of the Third Reich and the Second World War, the terms of historical narrative had to be redefined from the perspective of post-memory; that is, of those who did not live through these events but are part of them through collective processes of forgetting and remembering. As a result, the constitutive elements of history are once again reassessed and reconfigured in the difficult act of working through the past, but this time as part of an alternately feared or desired normalisation of history. Its broader implications continue to be pondered in scholarly debates about history, memory, and identity, especially in relationship to contemporary practices of commemoration and continuing public controversies about the involvement of ordinary Germans in the mass killings in the East, the repressed history of German wartime suffering, and the difficulty, if not impossibility, of speaking about Germans as the victims of their own history. As if to confirm the diagnosis of a gradual disappearance of history into media simulations and filmic spectacles, the filmic contributions to this ongoing process tend to be more conventional in their reliance on visual pleasure and their validation of the personal in opposition to the political – with the exception of a new wave of documentaries.

Just as the end of the Cold War changed the meaning of the Nazi past, so the opening of the Wall brought back the threat of neo-Nazis activities. A number of documentaries examined the milieu of neo-Nazis in the new states, including Thomas Heise's feature *Stau – jetzt gehts los* (Jammed – Let's Get Moving, 1992) and Winfried Bonengel's *Beruf Neonazi* (Profession: Neo-Nazi, 1993). Both films caused public controversies, the first because of its sensationalist style, and the second because of its refusal to judge the central characters. Responding to the continuing fascination with fascist imagery, other documentary film-makers approached the legacies of the Third Reich through the complicated relationship between ideology and aesthetics and the central role of film in rewriting history and memory. Ray Müller's two-part documentary *Die Macht der Bilder* (The Wonderful, Horrible Life of Leni Riefenstahl, 1993) made possible a direct confrontation with the life and work of the most infamous film-maker of the Third Reich. The affinities between cinema and warfare inspired essayistic reflections on the limits of visual representation in *Mein Krieg* (My Private War, 1990), a compilation film made up of home movies by German soldiers on the Eastern front. Taking a decidedly feminist perspective with *BeFreier und Befreite* (Liberators Take Liberties, 1992), Helke Sander presented a much-discussed two-part documentary about the mass rapes of German women by Soviet soldiers during the last months of the war. She relied on historical documents, personal interviews, and critical commentary to challenge prevailing views on gender, power, and history – but not without exposing herself to accusations of essentialism (*October* no. 72). André Heller used a more conventional film portrait of Hitler's secretary Traudl Junge in *Der tote Winkel* (Blind Spot, 2002) to confront questions of historical knowledge and personal accountability.

In the films about the Third Reich made since 1989, several tendencies can be discerned: a recognition of the survival of the past in the present and of the changing terms and modes of engagement; a growing focus on the Holocaust and its impact on German–Jewish relations today; and a renewed interest in the role of ordinary Germans in choosing between resistance and accommodation. A number of films thematised the continuing obsession with the past and made the return of the repressed a constitutive part of their narratives. The process began with Dietl's *Schtonk!* (1992), a political satire featuring Götz George about the forged Hitler diaries and the widespread fascination with Nazi memorabilia. Blurring the boundaries between past and present, Mueller-Stahl's Hitler film *Gespräch mit dem Biest* (Conversation with the Beast, 1996) confronts the audience with a 100-year-old man claiming to be Hitler, whereas George's *Nichts als die Wahrheit* (After the Truth, 1999) introduces a senile Josef Mengele seeking public validation. Both films develop their revisionist projects through showing the historical figures as old, ailing, but unmistakably and frighteningly alive in the present.

Contemporaneous with the documentary approaches and self-reflexive historical narratives, more and more feature films focused on the lives and choices of ordinary Germans during the Third Reich. This kind of inquiry found rich material in the real-life story of *Die Denunziantin* (The Denunciation, 1993), a simple woman who denounced Carl Goerdeler, an opponent of the Nazi regime, and was subsequently denounced and tried for crimes against humanity. The love story between a young man and an older woman during the 1936 Olympic Games depicted in Gordian Maugg's *Der olympische Sommer* (The Olympic Summer, 1993) highlights the precarious relationship between public and private life through the interlacing of documentary materials with fictional black-and-white scenes. Taking the opposite approach, Schlöndorff used highly stylised settings and melodramatic effects to conjure up a dream-like hallucination of the Third Reich in the German–French co-production of *Der Unhold* (The Ogre, 1996), based on the controversial Michel Tournier novel.

The Nazi past since the 1990s has become an object of historicist retrospection and nostalgic longing. At the same, history has emerged as a privileged site for the imaginary reconstruction of German identity. In what is sometimes referred to as heritage films, history is increasingly being used for spectacular treatments and spectatorial desires, with revisionist tendencies and consumerist attitudes inspiring uniquely postmodern history effects (Koepnick 2002b). The films produced under these conditions have been accused of depoliticising the Nazi period through their preference for melodramatic or sentimental treatments, their affinity for popular traditions and conventional styles, and their heavy reliance on personalisation and psychologisation. All take advantage of the commercialisation, banalisation, and kitschification of the Third Reich through the culture industry, on the one hand, and the highly circumscribed discourse of guilt, mourning, and taboos prevalent in political life and scholarly debate, on the other. With history reduced to a consumable good, the Nazi past can finally be explored, experienced, and enjoyed without guilt, qualities that have played a key role in the domestic reception of recent German films about the Nazi past.

Significantly, the desire for the symbolic reconciliation of self and other frequently finds expression in the heightened terms of romantic love. In the process, anti-Semitism is sometimes reduced to a mere background effect, a diminishment already found in Joseph Vilsmaier's *Die Comedian Harmonists* (The Harmonists, 1997), the story of the famous *a capella* singing group torn apart by anti-Semitic laws and bad German-Jewish marriages. Continuing this trend, Max Färberböck in *Aimée und Jaguar* (Aimée & Jaguar, 1999) used the memoirs of Erica Fischer to rewrite the history of everyday life during the Third Reich from the perspective of a German-Jewish lesbian love story. A similarly exceptional story inspired *Rosenstrasse* (2003), Trotta's homage, based on true events, to a group of German wives protesting against the deportation of their Jewish husbands. Profiting from a renewed interest in exiles and émigrés, *Nirgendwo in Afrika* (Nowhere in Africa, 2002) shows the difficulties of a German-Jewish family adjusting to their farming life in Kenya. Directed by Caroline Link, this filmic adaptation of an auto-biographical story won the Oscar in 2003 for Best Foreign Film.

The workings of the heritage film can be exemplarily studied in the work of Joseph Vilsmaier, the commercially most successful director-producer-cinematographer of the 1990s. Vilsmaier started out with *Herbstmilch* (Autumn Milk, 1989), which recounts the life story of a peasant woman from Lower Bavaria. Evoking the tradition of German romanticism, *Schlafes Bruder* (Brother of Sleep, 1995) allowed the director to adapt the popular Robert Schneider novel about a nineteenth-century musical prodigy to his own grand visions of a national cinema reborn through the convergence of history, mythology, and nostalgia. Vilsmaier continued his revisionist project with three films about the Third Reich: *Stalingrad* (1993), a graphic war spectacle about the senseless sacrifice of the Sixth Army in the Second World War; the above-mentioned *Die Comedian Harmonists*; and the ambitious biopic *Marlene* (2000), with Katja Flint in the role of the most famous German movie star. Significantly, Vilsmaier's films about the Third Reich give no social or political explanations for the origins of National Socialism. Instead his heavy reliance on production design contributes to the normalisation of German history by reducing the past to a visual spectacle. Moreover, his nostalgic re-enactments of the past remain firmly within a historicist aesthetic and thus serve the stabilisation of national identity in the present.

More recently, film-makers have begun to probe the libidinal investments that sustained Nazi rule and continue to inform contemporary audiences' relationship to cinema's favourite villains. *Napola – Elite für den Führer* (Before the Fall, 2004) infuses its story of two adolescents in a boarding school with homoerotic overtones that suggest a close connection between fascism and homosexuality. Introducing a rarely seen female perspective, Jutta Brückner's *Die Hitlerkantate* (Hitler Cantata, 2005) makes a related point through a young woman composer deeply in love with Hitler. Rejecting simplistic views of political indoctrination and authoritarian rule, both films focus on the micro-politics of power and desire and subsequently locate the continuing fascination with fascism in the ways it promises to transcend average lives and do away with the separation between public and private sphere. The degree to which such attractions are also exploited for their emotional investments and spectacular effects remains a question of debate.

The vacillation between historical detachment and contemporary relevance in filmic revisions of Nazi history has been most pronounced in a group of mainstream features about anti-Semitism and the Holocaust. Many were inspired by the overwhelmingly positive German reception of *Schindler's List* (1993) that, like the *Holocaust* series 14 years earlier, used an American perspective both to reflect on the causes of the Holocaust and to confront the enormity of Jewish suffering. Sparked by the publication of Daniel Goldhagen's *Hitler's Willing Executioners*, the Goldhagen debate in 1996 served similar purposes in drawing attention to the involvement of ordinary Germans in the mass killings. On the one hand, the process of historicisation resulted in a renewed interest in historical figures and events and in a preference for realist or naturalist styles. Here, the insistence on accuracy and authenticity did not always succeed in increasing historical understanding. These problems are particularly apparent in films that, like *Babij Jar – Das vergessene Verbrechen* (Babiy Yar – The Forgotten Crime, 2003) or *Der letzte Zug* (The Last Train, 2006), attempt to capture the reality of genocide without acknowledging the limits of representation. A similar problem compromises Eichinger and Hirschbiegel's ambitious *Der Untergang* (The Downfall, 2004), with Bruno Ganz in the Hitler role. Their meticulous recreation of the last days in the bunker inspired heated debates about what some critics denounced as a normalisation of the Nazi past; but it also revealed the central role of filmic illusionism in achieving psychological detachment. Intent on avoiding such effects, *Sophie Scholl: Die letzten Tage* (Sophie Scholl: The Final Days, 2005) relies instead on a police interrogation protocol to pay tribute to the quiet dignity and religious faith of the most famous member of the White Rose resistance group.

On the other hand, the highly formalised rituals of commemoration in public life opened up a space for the exploration of other affective registers in genre cinema, including humour and satire (Frölich et al. 2003). This process started with the (real-life) picaresque story of a German-Jewish boy, as told by Agnieszka Holland in *Hitlerjunge Salomon* (Europa Europa, 1990), who miraculously survives the Third Reich by assuming different racial, national, and political identities. Holland's use of humour in depicting Jewish suffering and survival was one of the reasons why this Polish–German–French co-production was not chosen as Germany's submission to that year's Best Foreign Language Film Oscar. However, her playful exploration of the performativity of identity resonated with some of the projections and displacements that continue to haunt German-Jewish culture and complicate the situation of Jews living in post-unification Germany. International trends in Holocaust representation also seem to have given some film-makers licence to apply humorous perspectives to the Nazi leadership, until recently considered a taboo in Germany. Thus *Goebbels und Geduldig* (Goebbels and Geduldig, 2001) reintroduces the double motif from Chaplin's *Great Dictator* through the figure of a Jewish prisoner forced to appear as Goebbels's stand-in. A similar German–Jewish encounter between a depressed Hitler and a Jewish thespian takes place in Levy's *Mein Führer: Die wirklich wahreste Wahrheit über Adolf Hitler* (Mein Führer: The Truly Truest Truth about Adolf Hitler, 2007), a crass mixture of drama, comedy, and farce with comedian Helke Schneider in the title role.

The recent German films about the Third Reich and the Holocaust attest as much to a growing German interest in Jewish culture and religion as to a hidden yearning for essentialist categories of identity that, in a strange reversal of terms, sometimes finds expression in nostalgic celebrations of Jewishness. The over-determined nature of such reconciliation narratives is most apparent in *Meschugge* (The Giraffe, 1998), a collaboration of Dani Levy and Maria Schrader that relies on sexual desire to move beyond the effects of trauma and guilt and achieve closure for the children of Holocaust survivors and Nazi perpetrators. The hilarious treatment of contemporary German–Jewish relations in Levi's *Alles Zucker!* (Go for Sugar, 2004) similarly remains under the influence of the taboos that have defined

Jewish representations after the Holocaust. At the same time, these contemporary settings open up the German–Jewish narrative to the issues that have dominated political and cultural debates since unification: the transformation of Germany into a multiethnic, multicultural society and the emergence of a transnational aesthetics founded equally on German and European traditions.

The future of national cinema

The self-celebratory images of the New Berlin Republic that initially prompted film scholars to describe early post-unification cinema as a 'cinema of consensus' in the early 2000s has given way to more critical narratives and complex images in what many now call a new 'cinema of dissent'. The move from the initial reclamation of nation as an integral part of German identity to the challenges of a distinctly European identity has played a pivotal role in this complicated process; so have the experiments with the creative possibilities of a transnational cinema founded on cross-cultural exchanges and creative border crossings. Several developments and events contributed to the making of such a transnational cinema: the fall of the Wall and the subsequent influx of Eastern Europeans to Germany; the establishment of the European Union in 1992 and the ensuing integration of Germany into a European labour market; the centralisation of global capital and the disintegration of the nation state; the rise of cosmopolitan and international youth cultures and professional elites located in the continent's metropolitan centres; the increasing visibility and empowerment of first- and second-generation immigrants as active members of German society and public life; and the challenges to earlier dreams of happy multiculturalism by Islamic radicalism and global terrorism after the events of 11 September 2001 depicted in Färberböck's *September* (2003) as a first disappointing attempt to map the new configurations of the local and the global.

In the cinema, the impact of these fundamental changes has been most pronounced in the emergence of what scholars call either minority cinema, accented cinema or hyphenated cinema and what, in the German context, has become known as Turkish-German or German-Turkish cinema (Göktürk 2000). All of these contributions thematise the consequences of migration, displacement, diaspora, and exile from the perspective of private lives and personal relationships and through the key categories of identity: gender, sexuality, class, ethnicity, and race. On the one hand, these new kinds of films are part of a cinema of border crossings that celebrates identities as hybrid, provisional, and contingent and that presents the process of transculturation and hybridisation as transgressive and potentially subversive. On the other, they contribute to a discourse of identity that, even in its anti-essentialist rhetoric, often uses identity as a fixed category through which to distinguish self and other, create a sense of community, and make sense of shared experiences of exclusion and discrimination. Formally and thematically heterogeneous and multi-voiced in their artistic visions and critical goals, these films bring into relief the complex and often contradictory meanings of the culture of identity in a post-national Germany and transnational Europe; they also draw attention to

216

the increasing difficulties of writing about 'German' films and film-makers in the age of transnational film production, distribution, and reception.

The making of a distinct Turkish-German cinema has been the most productive and most written-about outcome of these larger developments. Turkish-German film-makers started out by drawing attention to the realities of immigration, from the experiences of economic hardship in Anatolia to the difficulties of social integration in the Berlin Republic. Yet, unlike the Turkish men and women in New German Cinema, characters were no longer presented as exotic foreigners or threatening others. Instead their alterity became a function of the ongoing redefinition of Germanness, a process recognised both in the changes to the citizenship and naturalisation laws in 2000 and in the self-definition of a nation of immigrants now home to more than seven million foreigners, among them two and a half million people of Turkish descent. Since the early 1990s, two tendencies have prevailed: the affirmation of an essential difference located in ethnicity and the exploration of new forms of cultural hybridity. The encoding of otherness in melodramatic form, including through gendering, was particularly evident in early films that articulated their dramatic conflicts through the spatial terms of evictions, deportations, and illegal border crossings. Tevfik Baser, one of the first Turkish-German directors, chose such spatial tropes for the claustrophobic scenario of female confinement in *40 m2 Deutschland* (Forty Square Metres of Germany, 1986) and the elegiac reflection on the trauma of exile in *Lebe wohl, Fremde* (Farewell, Stranger, 1991). Ethnic cleansing and civil war in the former Yugoslavia caused the young Serbian woman in *Das serbische Mädchen* (The Serbian Girl, 1991) to leave her home for an uncertain life with an elusive German boyfriend. Similarly concerned with experiences of displacement, Kadir Sözen in *Winterblume* (Winter Flowers, 1997) used a starkly documentary style to show the failed attempts of a group of Turkish deportees to re-enter the Federal Republic. And in *Yara* (1999), Yilmaz Arslan recounted the sad story of a young woman equally homeless in Turkey and Germany.

In some of the first contributions, the identification of Turkishness with essential qualities sometimes allowed for the displacement of German guilt into stories of ethnic discrimination and oppression that revolved around the Turkish woman as a quintessential figure of victimhood. In the meantime, the rhetoric of social integration has given way to more nuanced treatments that recognise Germany as an immigrant society and seek to find a balance between the calls for complete assimilation and the dangers of retreating to a 'parallel society'. Similarly, the early discourse of pity and compassion, with its implicit social and ethnic hierarchies, has been replaced by more self-critical approaches to the representation of ethnic identities and the play with national stereotypes. Subsequently, the Turkish-German cinema has opened up a space for the possibility of living between cultures and of assuming multiple identities, with the difficulty of translating linguistic and cultural differences a recurring motif. This process has resulted in more complex, and sometimes also more controversial, treatments of the living conditions of second- and third-generation immigrants.

In that tradition, Hussi Kutlucan's *Ich Chef, Du Turnschuh* (Me Boss, You Sneakers!, 1998) portrays a group of illegal workers on a construction site in the new centre of Berlin but eschews the rhetoric of social tolerance and cultural diversity found in more mainstream films about Turkish, Italian, Spanish, and Greek 'guest workers'. Yüksel Yavuz's *Aprilkinder* (April Children, 1998) follows several second-generation immigrants dealing with their Turkish-German identities without succumbing to romantic visions of multicultural diversity and harmony. Since the haunting *Schattenboxer* (Shadow Boxer, 1992) and the violent *Kanak Attack* (2000), both by Lars Becker, film-makers have repeatedly turned to Hollywood genres such as the gangster film and *film noir* to identify the new lines of demarcation separating these new outsiders from mainstream society. In a sharp departure from earlier treatments, compassion has been replaced by male aggression, and the promise of integration undercut by disillusioned views on the emergence of a growing social underclass. The connection between marginalisation, criminalisation, and alternative lifestyles has confirmed the centrality of normative notions of masculinity to Turkish-German narratives of empowerment, from its identification with the brutal world of drug dealing depicted in *Dealer* (1999) to the homosexual and transgender milieu celebrated in *Lola und Bilidikid* (Lola and Bilidikid, 1998). Challenging the domination of Turkish-German cinema by male directors and actors, Ayse Polat has recently introduced a rarely seen female perspective, first from the perspective of a young girl in the television production *Auslandstournee* (Tour Abroad, 2000) and then through the friendship between two girls in *En garde* (2004); that film won several prizes at international film festivals.

The tension in Turkish-German cinema between the affirmation of identity as a foundation of community and society and the celebration of hybrid identities as transgressive and subversive has found paradigmatic expression in the films of Fatih Akin. His first feature-length film *Kurz und schmerzlos* (Short Sharp Shock, 1998) established his reputation as a promising new director and a powerful critical voice, at once optimistic, romantic, provocative, uncompromising, and humorous. Rejecting the clichéd image of Turkish guest workers as passive victims, *Kurz und schmerzlos* takes elements from the gangster film, the noir aesthetics, and a hip-hop inspired ghetto sensibility to show how three good friends, a Turk, a Serb, and a Greek, succumb to a glamorous life of crime, violence, murder, and death. At the same time, the director uses these generic conventions and ethnic stereotypes to deconstruct the patterns of projection that contribute to the construction of the other as other. Akin's ongoing reflections on the meaning of place, home, identity, and belonging in a fundamentally transformed Europe also found expression in the road movie narrative of the charming *Im Juli* (In July, 2000) and the diasporic family romance of the more sentimental *Solino* (2002). Featuring newcomer Sibel Kekilli in a brilliant performance, his most uncompromising contribution to Turkish-German cinema, *Gegen die Wand* (Head On, 2004), received the Golden Bear at the Berlin Film Festival for its taboo-breaking depiction of a young Turkish's woman's quest for sexual freedom. Taking a more conciliatory approach, his screenplay for the kung-fu comedy *Kebab Connection* (2005) is both an homage to his native Hamburg and a celebration of love in the age of multiculturalism and global consumer culture. Confirming Akin's rising status as a European director, the second film in his trilogy on 'love, death, and the devil', *Auf der anderen Seite* (The Edge of Heaven), premiered in 2007 at the Cannes Film Festival.

The Turkish-German films have contributed to the repoliticisation of cinema around issues of identity and their relationship to practices of exclusion and discrimination. Unification fundamentally changed the real and imaginary landscapes of Europe, bringing not only new patterns of mass migration but also increasing the level of mobility, both in the physical sense and in the form of attitudes and beliefs. Yet the mobilisation of film characters across this imaginary European landscape has not remained limited to immigrants and foreigners. Already an early film by Jan Schütte, *Winckelmanns Reisen* (Winckelmann's Travels, 1990), used the figure of a travelling salesman to suggest that even 'natives' sometimes move through familiar cities and landscapes as if in a foreign country. Especially the critics of neoliberalism have introduced troubled characters displaced in their own hometowns, the victims of the global movements of capital and labour and the politics of regional development and social welfare. Especially the cities and small towns in the former East have inspired depressing stories of unemployment, poverty, homelessness, and domestic violence. At the same time, film-makers have used social realist conventions and documentary styles to endow their characters with a sense of dignity and self-sufficiency and validate these struggle against economic hardship and downward mobility. In Dresen's *Halbe Treppe* (Grill Point, 2002) and Schmid's *Lichter* (Distant Lights, 2003) the location of Frankfurt an der Oder at the German–Polish border functions as an allegory of the thin line between becoming destitute and getting by and between having opportunities and being crushed by circumstances.

The changing landscape of post-unification cinema has found privileged expression in countless films set in contemporary Berlin, the capital of the Federal Republic, the centre of a united Europe, the city with the largest Turkish population outside Turkey, and, in ways not yet fully acknowledged, the entry point of countless immigrants from Eastern Europe. These new urban topographies first came into view through the diasporic narratives that motivated the journey from Poland to New York via Berlin in Michael Klier's *Überall ist es besser, wo wir nicht sind* (Things Are Always Better Elsewhere, 1989) and that continued with the return of Polish-Americans to Warsaw via Berlin in Schütte's *Auf Wiedersehen, Amerika* (Bye Bye America, 1993). Berlin's proximity to Eastern Europe, and with it to Slavic culture as yet another exotic other, also inspired a number of films that, in the style of Fred Kelemen's uncompromisingly dark *Abendland* (Nightfall, 1999), used the underworld of Polish and Russian thieves and prostitutes to challenge earlier dreams of enlightened urbanism and postmodern flânerie. Within these transnational constellations, the city's spatial images have opened up a space for formal experiments with fragmented or multiple narratives and documentary, realist, fantastic, and surrealist styles. As such an overdetermined mise-en-scène, the metropolis has become a privileged site for contemplating the difficulties of unification and globalisation and for measuring the consequences of mass migration and mobilisation through the quintessential urban figures of the migrant, exile, immigrant, and foreigner. At the same time, the familiar cityscape of famous monuments and typical neighbourhoods has allowed film-makers to explore the survival of German history in the layered history of the capital and to map new directions for post-unification cinema that situate the continuities of German identity within more open and less stable constellations.

Since 1989, several socially conscious directors – some of them trained or born in the GDR – have enlisted the social and cultural topographies of post-unification Berlin in diagnosing the failures of unification. A distinct DEFA sensibility has been preserved in the use of lay actors, real locations, documentary camera styles, episodic narratives, and an affinity for ordinary people and everyday life. Czech-born Klier offers an unrelentingly bleak view in *Ostkreuz* (1991), a television play about a mother–daughter relationship destroyed by poverty and homelessness, and the more nuanced *Heidi M.* (2001), about a single, middle-aged East Berlin woman played by former DEFA actress Katrin Saß. Kleinert's noirish *Wege in die Nacht* (Paths in the Night, 1999), with Hilmar Thate, another former DEFA actor, follows an ex-factory-manager as he acts out his own vision of law and order in post-Wall Berlin. Focusing on the younger generation growing up in the unified city, several directors have drawn attention to the disintegration of social structures and the consequences of economic inequality. The affinities between established subcultures and the new urban underclass were already glaringly apparent in Becker's critically acclaimed *Das Leben ist eine Baustelle* (Life Is All You Get, 1997), its title a telling reference to Berlin as a construction site of new national and post-national identities. Similarly, Dresen's *Nachtgestalten* (Night Shapes, 1999) drew attention to the growing number of young derelicts in the capital and their difficult lives on the other side of middle-class comfort and prosperity. More positive portrayals of the unemployed and under-employed can be found in the urban idylls of *Sommer vorm Balkon* (Summer in Berlin, 2004), also directed by Dresen. The first signs of a new culture of youthful rebellion made *Die fetten Jahre sind vorbei* (The Edukators, 2004) a popular success at home and aboard, with its message of 'The fat years are past!' a witty comment on the limits of the neoliberal world order and the return of anti-capitalist activism.

Last but not least, the Berlin films have functioned as an incubator for filmic styles and sensibilities that respond to the crisis of cinema with a renewed commitment to the intermediality and multimediality that have distinguished this quintessential mixed medium from the very beginning. Beginning with Ottinger's sparse chronicle of the days leading up to the introduction of a single currency on 1 July 1990 in *Countdown* (1990), Berlin has subsequently inspired a virtual murder mystery in the interactive *Killer.berlin.doc* (1999), a contemporary remake of the Ruttmann city symphony in Thomas Schadt's *Berlin, Sinfonie einer Grossstadt* (Berlin Symphony, 2002), and an adaptation of the Renee Pollesch play in *Stadt als Beute* (Berlin Stories, 2005), a process of appropriation and recontextualisation that is bound to continue. These films take full advantage of the recycled, remixed, remastered, and reloaded sounds and images that constitute the real and imaginary spaces of the contemporary metropolis. Thus in the same way that the East Berlin of *Sonnenallee* and the West Berlin of *Herr Lehmann* may be described as filmic elegies to a once divided city, the films set in unified Berlin build their stories around the layers of history and memory preserved in the spatial organisation of social relations. And in the same way that *Goodbye Lenin* and *Lola rennt* draw attention to the reliance of urban experience on media-produced images and narratives, many recent Berlin films are acutely aware of the close affinities between urbanism and cinema and their shared dependency on the hybrid aesthetics of simulation, appropriation, and performativity developed in the interspaces between fiction and documentary, film and theatre, and film and video.

As the last decade of the twentieth century has shown, the future of German cinema will require more than the perfection of well-tested generic formulas and the creative contribution of a few talented directors. And as the first decade of the twenty-first century suggests, the survival of this influential filmic tradition will involve the productive interplay among the constitutive elements that have characterised German cinema from the very beginning. Now as then, this process requires a workable compromise between art film and popular cinema, generic tradition and formal innovation, political ideology and mass diversion, public interest and corporate profit, cultural heritage and culture industry, and, last but not least, between the national, international, and transnational as overlapping categories of identity in the global media landscape. Above all, the continuing vibrancy of national cinema in a transnational age will depend on the ways in which film-makers respond to the challenges posed by new information and communication technologies and engage with changing conceptions of image and spectatorship in the age of digital media.

Of course, the absorption of film into other audio-visual media once again raises serious questions about the very meaning of the terms 'national' and 'cinema'. Does film – as film – still have a future in the twenty-first century? Or will the digital revolution in film production and exhibition make superfluous the formal language of narrative film and radically alter its relationship to reality and realism, on the one hand, and fantasy and illusionism, on the other? Are the dramatic changes in media culture a new chance both for films in history and for the history of film? Or will these developments end up undermining traditional notions of the work and the role of the *auteur*, not to speak of the established hierarchies among the existing technologies of looking, including surveillance? Will the category of national cinema still have a place between the discourses of the local and the global? Will film-making be transformed by the changing dynamics of identity, spatiality, and spectacle or will the national become a repository for the equally marginalised positions of the documentary and the experimental? Will feature film-makers enter into new alliances with video art, performance art, and installation art? Or will they fully embrace the commercialism of music videos and television commercials? Finally, will narrative remain the central organising principle in German films? Or will storytelling be absorbed into the spectacular effects developed by Hollywood and be replaced by the scopic regimes associated with other visual media? It will be up to the next generation of German film directors, film producers, and film audiences to formulate answers to these questions.

221

22 Til Schweiger and Joachim Król in *Der bewegte Mann*. Courtesy of Neue
Constantin / Olga Film / The Kobal Collection.

23 Franka Potente and Moritz Bleibtreu in *Lola rennt*. Courtesy of Sony Pictures
Classics / The Kobal Collection.

24 Sibel Kekilli and Birol Ünel in *Gegen die Wand*. Courtesy of NDR / PanFilm / The Kobal Collection.

25 Martina Gedeck and Sebastian Koch in *Das Leben der Anderen*. Courtesy of Creado Film / BR / Arte / The Kobal Collection.

BIBLIOGRAPHY

The following Reference Works and List of Works Cited represent a comprehensive list of books and articles on German cinema. Preference has been given to monographs and anthologies; articles have been included only where few other sources are available. More extensive bibliographies on individual periods can be found in the following English-language monographs and anthologies: in Elsaesser 1996a for Wilhelmine cinema; in Elsaesser 2000b for Weimar cinema; in Rentschler 1996 and Reimer 2000 for Third Reich cinema; in Fehrenbach 1995 for postwar cinema; in Allan and Sanford 1999 for East German cinema; in Elsaesser 1989 and Corrigan 1994 for West German cinema; and in Clarke 2006 for post-unification cinema.

Reference works

Bock, H.-M. (ed.) (1984 ff.) *CineGraph: Lexikon zum deutschsprachigen Film*: Munich: edition text + kritik.

Bock, H.-M. and Jacobsen, W. (eds) (1997) *Recherche: Film. Quellen und Methoden der Filmforschung*, Munich: edition text + kritik.

Borra, A. and Mader-Koltay, R. (2007) *German Through Film*, New Haven: Yale University Press.

Cramer, T. (ed.) (1995) *Reclams Lexikon des deutschen Films*, Stuttgart: Philipp Reclam jun.

Elsaesser, T. and Wedel, M. (eds). (1999) *The BFI Companion to German Cinema*, London: bfi Publishing.

Heinzlmeier, A. and Schulz, B. (2000) *Lexikon der deutschen Film- und TV-Stars*, Berlin: Lexicon.

Helt, R. C. and Helt, M. E. (1987) *West German Cinema since 1945: A Reference Handbook*, Metuchen: Scarecrow Press.

Helt, R. C. and Helt, M. E. (1992) *West German Cinema 1985–1990: A Reference Handbook*, Metuchen: Scarecrow Press.

Holba, H. et al. (eds) (1984) *Reclams deutsches Filmlexikon: Filmkünstler aus Deutschland, Österreich und der Schweiz*, Stuttgart: Reclam.

Jacobsen, W., Kaes. A. and Prinzler, H. H. (eds) (2004) *Geschichte des deutschen Films*, rev. and enlarged ed., Stuttgart: Metzler.

Klaus, U. J. (1988–92) *Deutsche Tonfilme: Filmlexikon der abendfüllenden und deutsch- sprachigen Tonfilme nach ihren deutschen Uraufführungen*, 3 vols (for 1929/30, 1931, and 1932), Berlin and Berchtesgarden: Klaus.

Prinzler, H. H. (1995) *Chronik des deutschen Films 1895–1994*, Stuttgart: Metzler.

Reimer, R. C., Zachau, R. and Sinka, M. (2005) *German Culture Through Film: An Intro- duction to German Cinema*, Newburyport: Focus Publishing.

Schmidt, K. M. and Schmidt, I. (2001) *Lexikon Literaturverfilmungen: Verzeichnis deutschsprachiger Filme 1945–2000*, Stuttgart: Metzler.

Smith, D. C. (2000) *The German Filmography 1895–1949*, Jefferson: McFarland.

Vogt, G. (2001) *Die Stadt im Kino: Deutsche Spielfilme 1900–2000*, Marburg: Schüren.

List of works cited

Agde, G. (1987) *Kurt Maetzig – Filmarbeit: Gespräche, Reden, Schriften*, Berlin: Henschel.

Agde, G. (ed.) (1991) *Kahlschlag: Das 11. Plenum des ZK der SED 1965*, Berlin: Aufbau.

Agde, G. (1998) *Flimmernde Versprechen: Geschichte des deutschen Werbefilms im Kino seit 1897*, Berlin: Das neue Berlin.

Agde, G. (2001) *Kämpfer: Biographie eines Films und seiner Macher*, Berlin: Das neue Berlin.

Albrecht, G. (1969) *Nationalsozialistische Filmpolitik: Eine soziologische Untersuchung über die Spielfilme des Dritten Reiches*, Stuttgart: Enke.

Albrecht, G. (ed.) (1979) *Der Film im 3. Reich*, Karlsruhe: DOKU.

Allan, S. and Sanford, J. (eds) (1999) *DEFA: East German Cinema, 1946–1992*, New York and Oxford: Berghahn Books.

Alter, N. (2002) *Projecting History: Non-Fiction German Cinema 1967–2000*, Ann Arbor: University of Michigan Press.

Alter, N. and Koepnick, L. (eds) (2004) *Sound Matters: Essays on the Acoustics of German Cinema*, New York and Oxford: Berghahn.

Amend, H. and Bütow, M. (eds) (1997) *Der bewegte Film: Aufbruch zu neuen deutschen Erfolgen*, Berlin: VISTAS.

Andriopoulos, S. (2007) *Possessed: Hypnotic Crimes, Corporate Fiction, Hypnotism, and the Invention of Cinema*, Chicago: University of Chicago Press.

Arnheim, R. (1974) *Film as Art*, Berkeley: University of California Press.

Arnheim, R. (1977) *Kritiken und Aufsätze zum Film*, ed. H. H. Diederichs, Munich: Hanser.

Ascheid, A. (2003) *Hitler's Heroines: Stardom and Womanhood in Nazi Cinema*, Phila- delphia: Temple University Press.

Asper, H. (2002) *'Etwas Besseres als der Tod' . . . Filmexil in Hollywood*, Marburg: Schüren.

Aurich, R., and Jacobsen, W. (eds) (1998) *Werkstatt Film: Selbstverständnis und Visionen von Filmleuten der zwanziger Jahre*, Munich: edition text + kritik.

Aurich, R., Jacobsen, W., and Jatho, G. (eds) (2001) *Bilder / Stories / Filme: Der Pro- duzent Joachim von Vietinghoff*, Berlin: Filmmuseum.

Baird, J. W. (1974) *The Mythical World of Nazi War Propaganda 1933–1945*, Minneapolis: University of Minnesota Press.

Balázs, B. (1982–84) *Schriften zum Film*, 2 vols, eds H. H. Diederichs, W. Gersch, and M. Nagy, Berlin: Hanser.

Barkhausen, H. (1982) *Filmpropaganda für Deutschland im Ersten und Zweiten Weltkrieg*, Hildesheim: Olms.

Barlow, J. D. (1982) *German Expressionist Film*, Boston: Twayne.

Barsam, R. M. (1975) *Filmguide to 'Triumph of the Will'*, Bloomington: Indiana University Press.

Bartetzko, D. (1985) *Illusionen in Stein: Stimmungsarchitektur im deutschen Faschismus. Ihre Vorgeschichte in Theater- und Film-Bauten*, Reinbek: Rowohlt.

Barthel, M. (1986) *So war es wirklich: Der deutsche Nachkriegsfilm*, Munich: F. A. Herbig.

Bechdolf, U. (1992) *Wunsch-Bilder? Frauen im nationalsozialistischen Unterhaltungsfilm*, Tübingen: Vereinigung für Volkskunde.

Becker, D. (1999) *Zwischen Ideologie und Autonomie: Die DDR-Forschung und die deutsche Filmgeschichte*, Münster: LIT.

Becker, W. (1973) *Film und Herrschaft: Organisationsprinzipien und Organisationsstrukturen der nationalsozialistischen Filmpropaganda*, Berlin: Spiess.

Becker, W. and Schöll, N. (1995) *In jenen Tagen . . . Wie der deutsche Nachkriegsfilm die Vergangenheit bewältigte*, Opladen: Leske + Buderich.

Behn, M. (ed.) (1994) *Schwarzer Traum und weiße Sklavin: Deutsch-dänische Filmbeziehungen 1910–1930*, Munich: edition text + kritik.

Behrens, V. (2005) *Man of Plenty: Wim Wenders*, Marburg: Schüren.

Belach, H. (ed.) (1979) *Wir tanzen um die Welt: Deutsche Revuefilme 1933–1945*, Munich: Hanser.

Belach, H. (1986) *Henny Porten: Der erste deutsche Filmstar 1890–1960*, Berlin: Haude & Spener.

Belach, H. and Jacobsen, W. (eds) (1990) *Richard Oswald: Regisseur und Produzent*, Munich: edition text + kritik.

Belach, H. and Prinzler, H. H. (eds) (1983) *Exil: Sechs Schauspieler aus Deutschland*, Berlin: Stiftung Deutsche Kinemathek.

Benzenhöfer, U. and Eckart, W. U. (eds) (1990) *Medizin im Spielfilm des Nationalsozialismus*, Tecklenburg: Burgverlag.

Berg, J. (1993) *Am Ende der Rolle: Diskussion über den Autorenfilm*, Marburg: Schüren.

Berg, J. and Hickethier, K. (eds) (1994) *Filmproduktion, Filmförderung, Filmfinanzierung*, Berlin: edition sigma.

Berger, J. (ed.) (1977) *Erobert den Film: Proletariat und Film in der Weimarer Republik*, ed. Neue Gesellschaft für Bildende Kunst und Freunde der deutschen Kinemathek, Berlin: NGBK.

Berger, J., Reichmann, H.-P. and Worschech, R. (eds) (1989) *Zwischen gestern und morgen: Westdeutscher Nachkriegsfilm 1946–1962*, Frankfurt am Main: Deutsches Filmmuseum.

Bergfelder, T. (2004) *International Adventures: Popular German Cinema and European Co-productions in the 1960s*, New York and Oxford: Berghahn Books.

Bergfelder, T. and Cargnelli, C. (2007) *German-Speaking Émigrés in British Cinema, 1925–1950*, Oxford and New York: Berghahn.

Bergfelder, T., Carter, E. and Göktürk, D. (eds) (2002) *The German Cinema Book*, London: bfi Publishing.

Berg-Ganschow, U. and Jacobsen, W. (eds) (1987) *. . . Film . . . Stadt . . . Kino . . . Berlin . . .*, Berlin: Argon.

Berghahn, D. (2005) *Hollywood Behind the Wall: The Cinema of East Germany*, Manchester and New York: Manchester University Press.

Berghahn, D. and Bance, A. (eds) (2002) *Millennial Essays on Film and Other German Studies*, Oxford: Peter Lang.

Bertram, T. (ed.) (1998) *Der rote Korsar: Traumwelt Kino der fünfziger und sechziger Jahre*, Essen: Klartext.

Bessen, U. (1989) *Trümmer und Träume: Nachkriegszeit und fünfziger Jahre auf Zelluloid. Deutsche Spielfilme als Zeugnisse ihrer Zeit. Eine Dokumentation*, Bochum: Studienverlag Dr. N. Brockmeyer.

Beyer, F. (1991) *Die Ufa-Stars im Dritten Reich*, Munich: Heyne.

Birett, H. (1980) *Verzeichnis in Deutschland gelaufener Filme: Entscheidungen der Filmzensur 1911–1920*, Munich: Saur.

Birett, H. (1991) *Das Filmangebot in Deutschland 1895–1911*, Munich: Winterberg.

Birett, H. (1994) *Lichtspiele: Der Kino in Deutschland bis 1914*, Munich: Q-Verlag.

Birgel, F. A. and Phillips, K. (eds) (2004) *Straight through the Heart: Doris Dörrie, German Filmmaker, and Author*, Landham: Scarecrow Press.

Bisky, L. and Wiedemann, D. (1985) *Der Spielfilm – Rezeption und Wirkung. Kultursoziologische Analysen*, Berlin: Henschel.

Bliersbach, G. (1989) *So grün war die Heide: Die gar nicht so heile Welt im Nachkriegsfilm*, Weinheim: Beltz.

Blum, H. R. and Blum, K. (1997) *Gesichter des neuen deutschen Films*, Berlin: Parthas.

Blunk, H. (1984) *Die DDR in ihren Spielfilmen: Reproduktion und Konzeption der DDR-Gesellschaft im neueren DEFA-Gegenwartsspielfilm*, Munich: Profil.

Blunk, H. and Jungnickel, D. (eds) (1990) *Filmland DDR: Ein Reader zu Geschichte, Funktion und Wirkung der DEFA*, Cologne: Verlag Wissenschaft und Politik.

Bock, H.-M. and Behn, M. (eds) (1988) *Film und Gesellschaft in der DDR*, Material-Sammlung, Hamburg: CineGraph.

Bock, H.-M. and Lenssen, C. (eds) (1992) *Joe May: Regisseur und Produzent*, Munich: edition text + kritik.

Bock, H.-M. and Töteberg, M. (eds) (1992) *Das Ufa-Buch: Kunst und Krisen, Stars und Regisseure, Wirtschaft und Politik*, Frankfurt am Main: Zweitausendundeins.

Bongartz, B. (1992) *Von Caligari zu Hitler – von Hitler zu Dr. Mabuse? Eine 'psychologische' Geschichte des deutschen Flms von 1946 bis 1960*, Münster: MAkS.

Borgelt, H. (1993) *Die UFA – ein Traum: Hundert Jahre deutscher Film. Ereignisse und Erlebnisse*, Berlin: edition q.

Brady, M. and Hughes, H. (1995) 'German Film after the *Wende*', in Lewis, D. and McKenzie, J. R. P. (eds) *The New Germany: Social, Political and Cultural Challenges of Unification*, Exeter: Exeter University Press.

Brandt, H.-J. (1987) *NS-Filmtheorie und dokumentarische Praxis: Hippler, Noldan, Junghans*, Tübingen: Niemeyer.

Bredow, W. von and Zurek, R. (eds) (1975) *Film und Gesellschaft in Deutschland: Dokumente und Materialien*, Hamburg: Hoffmann & Campe.

Brennicke, I. and Hembus, J. (1983) *Klassiker des deutschen Stummfilms 1910–1930*, Munich: Goldmann.

Bretschneider, J. (ed.) (1992) *Ewald André Dupont: Autor und Regisseur*, Munich: edition text + kritik.

Bromley, R. (2001) *From Alice to Buena Vista: The Films of Wim Wenders*, Westport: Praeger.

Bronner, B. and Brocher, C. (1973) *Die Filmemacher: Zur neuen deutschen Produktion nach Oberhausen*, Munich: Bertelsmann.

Bruns, K. (1995) *Kinomythen 1920–1945: Die Filmentwürfe der Thea von Harbou*, Stuttgart: Metzler.

Budd, M. (ed.) (1990) *The Cabinet of Dr. Caligari: Texts, Contexts, Histories*, New Brunswick: Rutgers University Press.

Bulgakowa, O. (ed.) (1995) *Die ungewöhnlichen Abenteuer des Dr. Mabuse im Land der Bolschewiki*, Berlin: Freunde der Deutschen Kinemathek.

Byg, B. (1980) 'The anti-fascist tradition and GDR film', in *Proceedings, Purdue University Fifth Annual Conference on Film*, West Lafayette: Purdue University.

Byg, B. (1990) 'What might have been: DEFA films of the past and the future of German cinema', *Cineaste* vol. 17, no. 4.

Byg, B. (1991) 'Two approaches to GDR history in DEFA films', *Studies in GDR Culture and Society* vol. 10.

Byg, B. (1995) *Landscapes of Resistance: The German Films of Danièle Huillet and Jean-Marie Straub*, Berkeley: University of California Press.

Byg, B. und Moore, B. (eds) (2002) *Moving Images of East Germany: Past and Future of DEFA Film*, Washington, DC: Johns Hopkins University Press.

Calhoon, K. (2001) *Peripheral Visions: The Hidden Stages of Weimar Cinema*, Detroit: Wayne State University Press.

Carter, E. (2004) *Dietrich's Ghosts: The Sublime and the Beautiful in Third Reich Film*, London: bfi Publishing.

Clarke, D. (ed.) (2006) *German Cinema since Unification*, London: Continuum.

Coates, P. (1991) *The Gorgon's Gaze: German Cinema, Expressionism, and the Image of Horror*, Cambridge: Cambridge University Press.

Collins, R. and Porter, V. (1981) *WDR and the Arbeiterfilm: Fassbinder, Ziewer and Others*, London: British Film Institute.

Cook, R. and Gemünden, G. (eds) (1997) *The Cinema of Wim Wenders: Image, Narrative, and the Postmodern Condition*, Detroit: Wayne State University Press.

Corrigan, T. (1994) *New German Film: The Displaced Image*, rev. and exp. ed., Bloomington: Indiana University Press.

Corrigan, T. (ed.) (1986) *The Films of Werner Herzog: Between Mirage and History*, London: Methuen.

Courtade, F. and Cadars, P. (1975) *Geschichte des Films im Dritten Reich*, Munich: Hanser.

Crofts, S. (1993) 'Reconceptualizing national cinema/s', *Quarterly Review of Film & Video* vol. 14, no. 3.

Currid, B. (2005) A *National Acoustics: Music and Publicity in Weimar and Nazi Germany*, Minneapolis: University of Minnesota Press.

Dahlke, G. and Karl, G. (eds) (1988) *Deutsche Spielfilme von den Anfängen bis 1933: Ein Filmführer*, Berlin: Henschelverlag.

Dalichow, B. (1993) 'Die jüngste Regiegeneration der DEFA – Aufbruch oder Abgesang'?, *Augenblick* vol. 14.

Dassanowsky, R. von (2005) *Austrian Cinema: A History*, Jefferson, NC: McFarland.

Davidson, J. E. (1999) *Deterritorializing the New German Cinema*, Minneapolis: University of Minnesota Press.

Davidson, J. E. and Hake. S. (2007) *Framing the Fifties*, New York and Oxford: Berghahn Books.

Degenhardt, A. (2001) '*Bedenken, die zu überwinden sind . . .' Das neue Medium Film im Spannungsfeld reformpädagogischer Erziehungsziele. Von der Kinoreformbewegung bis zur handlungsorientierten Filmarbeit Adolf Reichweins*, Munich: Kopäd-Verlag.

Deutsches Filminstitut (ed.) (2001) *Die Vergangenheit in der Gegenwart: Konfrontationen mit den Folgen des Holocaust im deutschen Nachkriegsfilm,* Frankfurt am Main: Deutsches Filminstitut.

Diederichs, H. H. (1986) *Anfänge deutscher Filmkritik,* Stuttgart: Robert Fischer & Uwe Wiedlerroither.

Diestelmeyer, J. (ed.) (2003) *Tonfilmfrieden/Tonfilmkrieg: Die Tobis 1928–1945,* 2 vols, Munich: edition text + kritik.

Diestelmeyer, J. (ed.) (2006) *Spaß beiseite, Film ab: Jüdischer Humor und verdrängendes Lachen in der Filmkomödie bis 1945,* Munich: edition text + kritik.

Dillmann-Kühn, C. (1990) *Artur Brauer und die CCC: Filmgeschäft, Produktionsalltag, Studiogeschichte 1946–1990.* Frankfurt am Main: Deutsches Filmmuseum.

Donner, W. (1995) *Propaganda und Film im 'Dritten Reich',* afterword Andreas Kilb, Berlin: TIP-Verlag.

Dost, M., Hopf, F. and Kluge, A. (1973) *Filmwirtschaft in der Bundesrepublik Deutschland und in Europa: Götterdämmerung in Raten,* Munich: Hanser.

Downing, T. (1992) *Olympia,* London: British Film Institute.

Drawer, C. (ed.) (1996) *So viele Träume: DEFA-Film-Kritiken aus drei Jahrzehnten von Heinz Kersten,* Berlin: VISTAS.

Drewniak, B. (1987) *Der deutsche Film 1938–1945,* Düsseldorf: Droste.

Eisner, L. (1973) *Murnau,* Berkeley: University of California Press.

Eisner, L. (1977) *The Haunted Screen,* trans. R. Greaves, Berkeley: University of California Press.

Elsaesser, T. (1982) 'Social mobility and the fantastic: German silent film', *Wide Angle* vol. 5, no. 2.

Elsaesser, T. (1984) 'Film history and visual pleasure: Weimar history', in Mellencamp, P. and Rosen, P. (eds) *Cinema Histories, Cinema Practices,* Los Angeles: American Film Institute.

Elsaesser, T. (1989) *New German Cinema: A History,* New Brunswick: Rutgers University Press.

Elsaesser, T. (ed.) (1996a) *Early German Cinema: The First Two Decades,* Amsterdam: University of Amsterdam Press.

Elsaesser, T. (1996b) *Fassbinder's Germany: History Identity Subject,* Amsterdam: Amsterdam University Press.

Elsaesser, T. (2000a) *Metropolis,* London: bfi Publishing.

Elsaesser, T. (2000b) *Weimar Cinema and After: Germany's Historical Imaginary,* London: Routledge.

Elsaesser, T. (2002) *Filmgeschichte und frühes Kino: Archäologie eines Medienwandels,* Munich: edition text + kritik.

Elsaesser, T. (2005) *European Cinema: Face to Face with Hollywood,* Chicago: University of Chicago Press.

Elsaesser, T. and Wedel, M. (eds) (2002) *Kino der Kaiserzeit: Zwischen Tradition und Moderne,* Munich: edition text + kritik.

Esser, M. (ed.) (1994) *Gleißende Schatten: Kamerapioniere der zwanziger Jahre,* Berlin: Henschel.

Fassbinder, R. W. (1992) *The Anarchy of the Imagination: Interviews, Essays, Notes,* ed. M. Töteberg and L. A. Lensing, Baltimore: Johns Hopkins University Press.

Fehrenbach, H. (1995) *Cinema in Democratizing Germany. Reconstructing National Identity after Hitler,* Chapel Hill: University of North Carolina Press.

Feinstein, J. (2002) *The Triumph of the Ordinary: Depictions of Daily Life in the East German Cinema, 1949–89,* Chapel Hill: University of North Carolina Press.

Feldmann, S. et. al. (eds) (1980) *Werner Schroeter*, Munich: Hanser.

Filmmuseum Potsdam (ed.) (1999) *Leni Riefenstahl*, Berlin: Henschel.

Finke, K. (ed.) (2001) *DEFA-Film als nationales Kulturerbe?*, Berlin: Vistas.

Finke, K. (ed.) (2002) *Politik und Mythos. Kader, Arbeiter und Aktivisten im DEFA-Film*, Oldenburg: BIS Verlag.

Fischer, R. and Hembus, J. (1981) *Der neue deutsche Film 1960–1980*, Munich: Goldmann.

Fischetti, R. (1992) *Das neue Kino – Filme von Frauen. Acht Porträts von deutschen Regisseurinnen*, Dülmen-Hiddengsel: tende.

Fisher, J. (2007) *Disciplining Germany: Youth, Reeducation, and Reconstruction after the Second World War*, Detroit: Wayne State University Press.

Fisher, J. and Prager, B. (eds) (2008) *Politics in Post-1989 Cinema*, Amsterdam: Rodopi.

Flinn, C. (2004) *The New German Cinema: Music, History, and the Matter of Style*, Berkeley: University of California Press.

Fox, J. (2000) *Filming Women in the Third Reich*, Oxford: Berg.

Franklin, J. (1983) *New German Cinema: From Oberhausen to Hamburg*, Boston: Twayne.

Frieden, S., McCormick, R. W., Petersen, V. P. and Vogelsang, L. M. (eds) (1993) *Gender Perspectives in German Cinema*, 2 vols, Providence, RI: Berg Publishers.

Fritz, W. (1984) *Kino in Österreich 1945–83: Film zwischen Kommerz und Avantgarde*, Vienna: Österreichischer Bundesverlag.

Fritz, W. (1988) *Der Wiener Film im Dritten Reich*, Vienna: Österreichische Gesellschaft für Kommunikations- und Medienforschung.

Fritz, W. (1991) *Kino in Österreich: Der Tonfilm*, Vienna: Österreichischer Bundesverlag.

Fritzsche, K. and Löser, C. (eds) (1996) *Gegenbilder: Filmische Subversion in der DDR 1976–1989*, Berlin: Janus press.

Frölich, M., Schneider, C. and Visarius, K. (eds) (2003) *Lachen über Hitler – Auschwitz-Gelächter?*, Munich: edition text + kritik.

Gandert, G. (1993) *Der Film der Weimarer Republik: Ein Handbuch der zeitgenössischen Kritik 1929*, Berlin: de Gruyter.

Garncarz, J. (2007) *Die Entstehung des Kinos in Deutschland, 1896–1914*, Frankfurt am Main: Stroemfeld/Roter Stern.

Garncarz, J. (2008) *Importing Entertainment: The Globalization of German Film Culture*, Oxford and New York: Berghahn.

Gehler, F. and Kasten, U. (1990a) *Friedrich Wilhelm Murnau*, Berlin: Henschel.

Gehler, F. and Kasten, U. (1990b) *Fritz Lang: Die Stimme von Metropolis*, Berlin: Henschel.

Geiss, A. (ed.) (1994) *Filmstadt Babelsberg: Zur Geschichte des Studios und seiner Filme*, Berlin: Nicolai.

Geist, K. (1988) *The Cinema of Wim Wenders: From Paris, France to Paris, Texas*, Ann Arbor: UMI Research Press.

Gemünden, G. (2001) 'Between Karl May and Karl Marx: The DEFA "Indianerfilme" (1965–83)', *New German Critique* vol. 82.

Georgi, R. and Hoff, P. (eds) (1990) *Konrad Wolf: Neue Sichten auf seine Filme*, Berlin: VISTAS.

Gersch, W. (1975) *Film bei Brecht: Bertolt Brechts praktische und theoretische Auseinandersetzung mit dem Film*, Munich: Hanser.

Gersch, W. (2006) *Szenen eines Landes: Die DDR und ihre Filme*, Berlin: Aufbau.

Ginsberg, T. and Thompson, K. M. (eds) (1996) *Perspectives on German Cinema*, New York: G. K. Hall.

Glaß, P. (1999) *Kino ist mehr als Film: Die Jahre 1976–1990*, Berlin: AG-Verlag.

Goergen, J. (ed.) (1989) *Walter Ruttmann: Eine Dokumentation*, Berlin: Freunde der Deutschen Kinemathek.

Göktürk, D. (2000) 'Migration und Kino – Subnationale Mitleidskultur oder transnationale Rollenspiele?', in Chiellino, C. (ed.) *Interkulturelle Literatur in Deutschland: Ein Handbuch*, Stuttgart: Metzger.

Graf, A. (2002) *The Cinema of Wim Wenders: Celluloid Highway*, London: Wallflower.

Grafe, F. (2003) *Licht aus Berlin: Lang Lubitsch Murnau und Weiteres zum Kino der Weimarer Republik*, Berlin: Brickmann & Bose.

Greffrath, B. (1995) *Gesellschaftsbilder der Nachkriegszeit 1945–1949*, Pfaffenweiler: Centaurus.

Guerin, F. (2005) *A Culture of Light: Cinema and Technology in 1920s Germany*, Minneapolis: University of Minnesota Press.

Gunning, T. (2000) *The Films of Fritz Lang: Modernity, Crime and Desire*, London: bfi Publishing.

Güttinger, F. (1984a) *Kein Tag ohne Kino: Schriftsteller über den Stummfilm*, Frankfurt am Main: Deutsches Filmmuseum.

Güttinger, F. (1984b) *Der Stummfilm im Zitat der Zeit*, Frankfurt am Main: Deutsches Filmmuseum.

Haase, C. (2007) *When "Heimat" Meets Hollywood: German Filmmakers in America, 1985–2005*, Rochester: Camden House.

Habel, F.-B. (2001) *Das große Lexikon der DEFA-Spielfilme*, Berlin: Schwarzkopf & Schwarzkopf.

Hagener, M. (ed.) (2000) *Geschlecht in Fesseln: Sexualität zwischen Aufklärung und Ausbeutung im Weimarer Kino 1918–1933*, Munich: edition text + kritik.

Hagener, M. and Hans, J. (eds) (1999) *Als die Filme laufen lernten: Innovation und Tradition im Musikfilm 1928–1938*, Munich: edition text + kritik.

Hahn, F.-B. (1995) *Goiko Mitic, Mustangs, Marterpfähle: Die DEFA-Indianerfilme*, Berlin: Schwarzkopf & Schwarzkopf.

Hake, S. (1990) 'Chaplin reception in Weimar Germany', *New German Critique* no. 51.

Hake, S. (1992a) *Passions and Deceptions: The Early Films of Ernst Lubitsch*, Princeton: Princeton University Press.

Hake, S. (1992b) 'Self-referentiality in Early German Cinema', *Cinema Journal* vol. 31, no. 3.

Hake, S. (1993) *The Cinema's Third Machine: Writing on Film in Germany 1907–1933*, Lincoln: University of Nebraska Press.

Hake, S. (2002) *Popular Cinema in the Third Reich*, Austin: University of Texas Press.

Halle, R. (2000) ''Happy ends to crisis of heterosexual desire: toward a social psychology of recent German comedies', *Camera Obscura* vol. 2, no. 2.

Halle, R. (2008) *German Film after Germany: Toward a Transnational Aesthetic*, Urbana and Chicago: University of Illinois Press.

Halle, R. and McCarthy, M. (eds) (2003) *Light Motives: German Popular Film in Perspective*, Detroit: Wayne State University Press.

Halle, R. and Steingroever, R. (eds) (2008) *After the Avant-garde: German and Austrian Experimental Film*, Rochester: Camden House Press.

Hanisch, M. (1991) *Auf den Spuren der Filmgeschichte: Berliner Schauplätze*, Berlin: Henschel.

Hansen, M. (1983) 'Early silent cinema, whose public sphere?', *New German Critique* no. 29.

Hantke, S. (ed.) (2006) *Caligari's Heirs: The German Cinema of Fear after 1945*, Lanham: Scarecrow.

Happel, H. G. (1984) *Der historische Spielfilm im Nationalsozialismus*, Frankfurt am Main: R. G. Fischer.

Hardt, U. (1996) *From Caligari to California: Eric Pommer's Life in the International Film Wars*, Providence: Berghahn Books.

Hasenberg, P. and Thull, M. (eds) (1991) *Filme in der DDR 1987–90*, Cologne: Verlag Katholisches Institut für Medieninformation.

Hauser, J. (1989) *Neuaufbau der westdeutschen Filmwirtschaft 1945–1955 und der Einfluß der US-amerikanischen Filmpolitik*, Pfaffenweiler: Centaurus.

Heath, S. (1978) 'Questions of property: film and nationhood', *Cinetracts* vol. 1, no. 4.

Heimann, T. (1994) *DEFA, Künstler und SED-Kulturpolitik: Verständnis von Kulturpolitik und Filmproduktion in der SBZ/DDR 1945 bis 1959*, Berlin: VISTAS.

Heimann, T. (2000) 'Erinnerung als Wandel: Kriegsbilder im frühen DDR-Film', in Sabrow, M. (ed.) *Geschichte als Herrschaftsdiskurs. Der Umgang mit der Vergangenheit in der DDR*, Cologne: Böhlau.

Heller, H.-B. (1984) *Literarische Intelligenz und Film: Zu Veränderungen der ästhetischen Theorie und Praxis unter dem Eindruck des Films 1910–1930 in Deutschland*, Tübingen: Max Niemeyer.

Hembus, J. (1981) *Der deutsche Film kann gar nicht besser sein: Ein Pamphlet von gestern. Eine Abrechnung von heute*, Munich: Rogner & Bernhard.

Hesse, S. (2003) *Kamera-Auge und Spürnase: Der Detektiv im frühen deutschen Kino*, Frankfurt am Main: Stroemfeld/Roter Stern.

Hickethier, K. (1986) *Grenzgänger zwischen Theater und Kino: Schauspielerporträts aus dem Berlin der Zwanziger Jahre*, Berlin: Edition Mythos Berlin.

Hickethier, K. (1998) *Geschichte des deutschen Fernsehens*, Stuttgart: Metzger.

Hilchenbach, M. (1982) *Kino im Exil: Die Emigration deutscher Filmkünstler 1933–1945*, Munich: Saur.

Hillman, R. (2005) *Unsettling Scores: German Film, Music, and Ideology*, Bloomington: Indiana University Press.

Hinton, D. B. (1991) *The Films of Leni Riefenstahl*, 2nd ed., Metuchen: Scarecrow Press.

Hjort, M. and MacKenzie, S. (2000) (eds) *Cinema and Nation*, London: Routledge.

Hobsch, M. (1999) *Liebe, Tanz und 1000 Schlagerfilme*, Berlin: Schwarzkopf & Schwarzkopf.

Hochmuth, D. (ed.) (1993) *DEFA NOVA – nach wie vor? Versuch einer Spurensicherung*, Berlin: VISTAS.

Hoff, P. and Wiedemann, D. (eds) (1992) *Der DEFA Spielfilm in den 80er Jahren – Chancen für die 90er?* Berlin: VISTAS.

Hoffmann, H. (1996) *The Triumph of Propaganda: Film and National Socialism, 1933–1945*, trans. J. A. Broadwin and V. R. Berghahn, Providence: Berghahn Books.

Höfig, W. (1973) *Der deutsche Heimatfilm 1947–1960*, Stuttgart: Ferdinand Enke.

Hollstein, D. (1983) *'Jud Süß' und die Deutschen: Antisemitische Vorurteile im nationalsozialistischen Spielfilm*, Frankfurt am Main: Ullstein.

Horak, J.-C. (1984) *Fluchtpunkt Hollywood: Eine Dokumentation zur Filmemigration nach 1933*, Münster: MAkS.

Horak, J.-C. (1993) 'Rin-Tin-Tin in Berlin or American cinema in Weimar', *Film History* vol. 5, pp. 49–62.

Horak, J.-C. (1996) 'German exile cinema, 1933–1950', *Film History* vol. 8, pp. 373–89.

Hull, D. S. (1973) *Film in the Third Reich: A Study of the German Cinema 1933–1945*, New York: Simon & Schuster.

Hurst, H. and Gassen, H. (eds) (1991) *Kameradschaft – Querelle: Kino zwischen Deutschland und Frankreich*, Munich: Institut Français.

Jäckel, A. (2003) *European Film Industries*. London: British Film Institute.

Jacobi, R. and Janssen, H. (eds) (1987) *Filme in der DDR 1945–1986: Kritische Notizen aus 42 Kinojahren*, Cologne: Verlag Katholisches Institut für Medieninformation.

Jacobsen, W. (1989) *Erich Pommer: Ein Filmproduzent macht Filmgeschichte*, Berlin: Argon.

Jacobsen, W. (ed.) (1992) *Babelsberg: Ein Filmstudio 1912–1992*, Berlin: Argon.

Jacobsen, W. and Aurich, R. (2005) *Der Sonnensucher Konrad Wolf*, Berlin: Aufbau.

Jacobsen, W. and Prinzler, H. H. (eds) (1992) *Käutner*, Berlin: Volker Spiess.

Jansen, P. W. and Schütte, W. (eds) (1977) *Film in der DDR*, Munich: Hanser.

Jary, M. (1993) *Traumfabriken made in Germany: Die Geschichte des deutschen Nachkriegsfilms 1945–1960*, Berlin: edition q.

Jochum, N. (ed.) (1979) *Das wandelnde Bild: Der Filmpionier Guido Seeber 1879–1940*, Berlin: Elefanten Press.

Jordan, G. and Schenk, R. (eds) (1996) *Schwarzweiß und Farbe: DEFA-Dokumentarfilm 1946–92*, Berlin: Henschel.

Jörg, H. (1994) *Die sagen- und märchenhafte Leinwand: Erzählstoffe, Motive und narrative Strukturen der Volksprosa in 'klassischen' deutschen Stummfilm (1910–1930)*, Sinzheim: Pro Universitate.

Jung, U. (ed.) (1993) *Der deutsche Film: Aspekte seiner Geschichte von den Anfängen bis zur Gegenwart*, Trier: WVT Wissenschaftlicher Verlag.

Jung, U. and Schatzberg, W. (1999) *Beyond Caligari: The Films of Robert Wiene*. New York and Oxford: Berghahn Books.

Jung, U. and Schatzberg, W. (eds) (1992) *Filmkultur zur Zeit der Weimarer Republik*, Munich: K. G. Saur.

Kabatek, W. (2003) *Imagerie des Anderen im Weimarer Kino*, Bielefeld: Transcript.

Kaes, A. (1989) *From 'Hitler' to 'Heimat': The Return of History as Film*, Cambridge: Harvard University Press.

Kaes, A. (1995) 'German cultural history and the study of film: ten theses and a postscript', *New German Critique* no. 65.

Kaes, A. (2000) *M*, London: bfi Publishing.

Kaes, A. (2008) *Shell Shock: Film and Trauma in the Weimar Republic*, Princeton: Princeton University Press.

Kaes, A. (ed. and intro.) (1978) *Kino-Debatte: Texte zum Verhältnis von Literatur und Film 1909–1929*, Tübingen: Max Niemeyer.

Kannapin, D. (1997) *Antifaschismus im Film der DDR: DEFA-Spielfilme 1945–1955/56*, Cologne: PapyRossa.

Kannapin, D. (2005) *Dialektik der Bilder: Der Nationalsozialismus in deutschen Film: Ein Ost-West Vergleich*, Berlin: Karl Dietz.

Kanzog, K. (1994) *'Staatspolitisch besonders wertvoll'. Ein Handbuch zu 30 deutschen Spielfilmen der Jahre 1934 bis 1945*, Munich: diskurs film.

Kapczynski, J. (2008) *The German Patient: Crisis and Recovery in Postwar Culture*, Ann Arbor: University of Michigan Press.

Kasten, J. (1990) *Der expressionistische Film: Abgefilmtes Theater oder avantgardistisches Erzählkino? Eine stil-, produktions- und rezeptionsgeschichtliche Untersuchung*, Münster: MAkS.

Katz, R. (1987) *Love Is Colder than Death: The Life and Times of Rainer Werner Fassbinder*, New York: Random House.

Keiner, R. (1987) *Hanns Heinz Ewers und der phantastische Film*, Hildesheim: Olms.

Keiner, R. (1991) *Thea von Harbou und der deutsche Film bis 1933*, Hildesheim: Olms.

Keitz, U. and Hoffmann, K. (2001) *Die Einübung des dokumentaren Blicks: Fiction Film and Non Fiction Film zwischen Wahrheitsanspruch und expressiver Sachlichkeit 1985–1945*, Marburg: Schüren.

Kelson, J. F. (1996) *Catalogue of Forbidden German Feature and Short Film Productions held in Zonal Film Archives of Film Section, Information Services Division, Control Commission for Germany (BE)*, Westport: Greenwood Press.

Kessler, F., Lenk, S. and Loiperdinger, M. (eds) (1992) *Früher Film in Deutschland*, Frankfurt am Main: Stroemfeld/Roter Stern (*KINtop* 1).

Kessler, F., Lenk, S. and Loiperdinger, M. (eds) (1994a) *Oskar Messter – Filmpionier der Kaiserzeit*, Frankfurt am Main: Stroemfeld/Roter Stern (*KINtop* 2).

Kessler, F., Lenk, S. and Loiperdinger, M. (eds) (1994b) *Oskar Messter – Erfinder und Geschäftsmann*, Frankfurt am Main: Stroemfeld/Roter Stern (*KINtop* 3).

Kester, B. (2003) *Film Front Weimar: Representations of the First World War in German Films of the Weimar Period (1919–1933)*, Amsterdam: Amsterdam University Press.

Kilchenstein, G. (1997) *Frühe Filmzensur in Deutschland: Eine vergleichende Studie zur Prüfungsarbeit in Berlin und München (1906–1914)*, Munich: diskurs film.

Kinkel, L. (2002) *Die Scheinwerferin: Leni Riefenstahl und das Dritte Reich*, Munich: Europa.

Kinter, J. (1985) *Arbeiterbewegung und Film (1895–1933): Zur Geschichte der Arbeiter- und Alltagskultur und der gewerkschaftlichen und sozialdemokratischen Kultur- und Medienarbeit*, Hamburg: Medienpädagogik-Zentrum.

Kleinhans, B. (2003). *Ein Volk, ein Reich, ein Kino: Lichtspiel in der braunen Provinz*, Cologne: PapyRossa.

Kluge, A. (1983) *Bestandaufnahme Utopie Film: Zwanzig Jahre neuer deutscher Film*, Frankfurt am Main: Zweitausendeins.

Kluge, A. (1999) *In Gefahr und größter Not bringt der Mittelweg den Tod: Texte zu Kino, Film, Politik*, ed. C. Schulte, Berlin: Vorwerk.

Knight, J. (1992) *Women and the New German Cinema*, London: Verso.

Knight, J. (2003) *New German Cinema: Images of a Generation*, London and New York: Wallflower Press.

Koch, K. (1985) *Die Bedeutung des 'Oberhausener Manifestes' für die Filmentwicklung in der BRD*, Frankfurt am Main: Peter Lang.

Koebner, T. (ed.) (1997) *Idole des deutschen Film: Eine Galerie von Schlüsselfiguren*, Munich: edition text + kritik.

Koebner, T. (ed.) (2003) *Diesseits der 'Dämonischen Leinwand': Neue Perspektiven auf das späte Weimarer Kino*, Munich: edition text + kritik.

Koepnick, L. (2002a) *The Dark Mirror: German Cinema Between Hitler and Hollywood*, University of California Press: Berkeley.

Koepnick, L. (2002b). 'Reframing the past: heritage cinema and Holocaust in the 1990s', *New German Critique* no. 87.

Koepnick, L. and Schindler, S. (2007) *The Cosmopolitan Screen: German Cinema and the Global Imaginary, 1945 to the Present*, Ann Arbor: University of Michigan Press.

Kolker, R. and Beicken, P. (1993) *The Films of Wim Wenders: Cinema as Vision and Desire*, Cambridge: Cambridge University Press.

König, I., Wiedemann, D. and Wolf, L. (eds) (1995) *Zwischen Bluejeans und Blauhemden: Jugendfilm in Ost und West*, Berlin: Henschel.

König, I., Wiedemann, D. and Wolf, L. (eds) (1996) *Zwischen Marx und Muck: DEFA-Filme für Kinder*, Berlin: Henschel.

Korte, H. (ed.) (1980) *Film und Realität in der Weimarer Republik*, Frankfurt am Main: Fischer.

Korte, H. (1998) *Der Spielfilm und das Ende der Weimarer Republik: Ein rezeptionshistorischer Versuch*, Göttingen: Vanderhoeck und Ruprecht.

Kosta, B. (1994) *Recasting Autobiography: Women's Counterfictions in Contemporary German Literature and Film*, Ithaca: Cornell University Press.

Kotulla, T. (2005) *Theodor Kotulla: Regisseur und Kritiker* (Film & Schrift, vol. 1), Munich: edition text + kritik.

Kracauer, S. (1990) *Schriften 5*, 3 vols, ed. I. Mülder-Bach, Frankfurt am Main: Suhrkamp.

Kracauer, S. (1995) *The Mass Ornament*, ed. and trans. T. Y. Levin, Cambridge, MA: Harvard University Press.

Kracauer, S. (2004) *From Caligari to Hitler: A Psychological History of the German Film*, rev. and exp. ed., ed. Leonardo Quaresima, Princeton: Princeton University Press.

Krah, H. (ed.) (1999) *Geschichte(n) NS-Film – NS-Spuren heute*, Kiel: Ludwig.

Kraus, P. et al. (ed.) (1997) *Deutschland im Herbst: Terrorismus im Film*, Munich: Filmzentrum.

Kreimeier, K. (1973) *Kino und Filmindustrie in der BRD: Ideologieproduktion und Klassenwirklichkeit nach 1945*, Kronsberg: Scriptor.

Kreimeier, K. (1996) *The Ufa Story: A History of Germany's Greatest Film Company, 1918–1945*, trans. R. and R. Kimber, New York: Hill and Wang.

Kühn, G., Tümmler, K. and Wimmer, W. (eds) (1975) *Film und revolutionäre Arbeiterbewegung in Deutschland 1918–1932: Dokumente und Materialien*, 2 vols, Berlin: Henschel.

Kuzniar, A. (2000) *The Queer German Cinema*, Stanford: Stanford University Press.

Ledig, E. (1990) *Paul Wegeners Golem-Filme im Kontext fantastischer Literatur*, Munich: diskurs film.

Ledig, E. (ed.) (1988) *Der Stummfilm: Konstruktion und Rekonstruktion*, Munich: diskurs film 2.

Leiser, E. (1974) *Nazi Cinema*, trans. G. Mander and D. Wilson, New York: Macmillan.

Leonhardt, S. (1989) 'Testing the borders: East German film between individualism and social commitment', in Goulding, D. G. (ed.), *Post New Wave Cinema in the Soviet Union and Eastern Europe*, Bloomington: Indiana University Press.

Linville, S. (1998) *Feminism, Film, Fascism: Women's Autobiographical Film in Postwar Germany*, Austin: University of Texas Press.

Loacker, A. and Prucha, M. (eds) (2000) *Unerwünschtes Kino: Der deutschsprachige Emigrantenfilm 1934–1937*, Vienna: Filmarchiv Austria.

Loiperdinger, M. (ed.) (1991) *Märtyrerlegenden im NS-Film*, Opladen: Leske + Budrich.

Loiperdinger, M. (1999) *Film & Schokolade: Stollwercks Geschäfte mit lebenden Bildern*, Frankfurt am Main: Stroemfeld/Roter Stern.

Lowry, S. (1991) *Pathos und Politik: Ideologie in Spielfilmen des Nationalsozialismus*, Tübingen: Niemeyer.

Lüdeke, W. (1973) *Der Film in Agitation und Propaganda der revolutionären deutschen Arbeiterbewegung (1919–1933)*, Berlin/West: Oberbaumverlag.

Lutze, P. C. (1998) *Alexander Kluge: The Last Modernist*, Detroit: Wayne State University Press.

McCarthy, M. and Halle, R. (eds) (2003) *Light Motives: German Popular Film in Perspective*, Detroit: Wayne State University Press.

McCormick, R. (1991) *Politics of the Self: Feminism and the Postmodern in West German Literature and Film*, Princeton: Princeton University Press.

McCormick, R. (2002) *Gender, Sexuality in Weimar Modernity: Film, Literature and New Objectivity*, New York: Palgrave.

Maiwald, K.-J. (1983) *Filmzensur im NS-Staat*, Dortmund: Nowotny.

Majer O'Sickey, I. and von Zadow, I. (eds) (1998) *Triangulated Visions: Women in Recent German Cinema*, Albany: State University of New York Press.

Manvell, R. and Fraenkel, H. (1971) *The German Cinema*, New York: Praeger.

Marquardt, A. and Rathsack, H. (eds) (1981) *Preußen im Film*, Reinbek: Rowohlt.

Marsiske, H.-A. (ed.) (1992) *Zeitmaschine Kino: Darstellungen von Geschichte im Film*, Marburg: Hitzeroth.

May, R. and Jackson, H. (eds) (2001) *Filme für die Volksfront: Erwin Piscator, Gustav von Wangenheim, Friedrich Wolf – antifaschistische Filmemacher im sowjetischen Exil*, Berlin: Stattkino Berlin e.V.

Meurer, H. J. (2000) *Cinema and National Identity in a Divided Germany, 1979–1989*, Lewiston: Edwin Mellen Press.

Minden, M. and Bachmann, H. (eds) (2000) *Fritz Lang's 'Metropolis': Cinematic Visions of Technology and Fear*, Rochester: Camden House.

Möbius, H. and Vogt, G. (1990) *Drehort Stadt: Das Thema 'Großstadt' im deutschen Film*, Harburg: Hitzeroth.

Moeller, F. (1998) *Der Filmminister: Goebbels und der Film im Dritten Reich*, Berlin: Henschel.

Moeller, H.-B. und Lellis, G. (2002) *Volker Schlöndoff's Cinema: Adaptation, Politics, and the 'Movie-Appropriate'*, Carbondale: University of Illinois Press.

Möhrmann, R. (1980) *Die Frau mit der Kamera: Filmemacherinnen in der Bundesrepublik Deutschland. Situationen, Perspektiven. Zehn exemplarische Lebensläufe*, Munich: Hanser.

Moldenhauer, G. and Zimmermann, P. (eds) (2000) *Der geteilte Himmel: Arbeit, Alltag und Geschichte im ost- und westdeutschen Film*, Constance: UVK Medien.

Moltke, J. von (2005) *No Place Like Home: Locations of Heimat in German Cinema*, Berkeley: University of California Press.

Monaco, P. (1976) *Cinema and Society: France and Germany during the Twenties*, New York: Elsevier.

Mückenberger, C. (ed.) (1990) *Prädikat: Besondes schädlich: 'Das Kaninchen bin ich' 'Denk bloß nicht daß ich heule'*, Berlin: Henschel.

Mückenberger, C. and Jordan, G. (1994) *'Sie sehen selbst, Sie hören selbst' . . . Die DEFA von ihren Anfängen bis 1949*, Marburg: Hitzeroth.

Mueller, R. (1989) *Bertolt Brecht and the Theory of Media*, Lincoln: Nebraska University Press.

Mühl-Benninghaus, W. (1997) 'German film censorship during World War I', *Film History* vol. 9, pp. 71–94.

Mühl-Benninghaus, W. (1999) *Das Ringen um den Tonfilm: Strategien der Elektro- und der Filmindustrie in den 20er und 30er Jahren*, Düsseldorf: Droste.

Mühl-Benninghaus, W. (2004) *Vom Augusterlebnis zur UFA-Gründung: Der deutsche Film im 1. Weltkrieg*, Berlin: AVINUS.

Müller, C. (1994) *Frühe deutsche Kinematographie: Formale, wirtschaftliche, und kulturelle Entwicklungen 1907–1912*, Stuttgart: Metzler.

Müller, C. (2003) *Vom Stummfilm zum Tonfilm*, Munich: Fink.

Murray, B. (1990) *Film and the German Left in the Weimar Republic*, Austin: University of Texas Press.

Murray, B. and Wickham, C. (eds) (1992) *Framing the Past: The Historiography of German Cinema and Television*, Carbondale: University of Southern Illinois Press.

Naughton, L. (2002) *That Was the Wild East: Film Culture, Unification, and the 'New' Germany*, Ann Arbor: University of Michigan Press.

Neale, S. (1977) 'Propaganda', *Screen* vol. 18, no. 3.

Negt, O. and Kluge, A. (1993) *The Public Sphere and Experience: Toward an Analysis of the Bourgeois and Proletarian Public Sphere*, trans. P. Labanyi, Minneapolis: University of Minnesota Press.

Noack, F. (2000) *Veit Harlan: 'Des Teufels Regisseur'*, Munich: belleville.

O'Brien, M.-E. (2003) *The Politics of Entertainment in the Third Reich*. Rochester: Camden House.

Oksiloff, A. (2001) *Picturing the Primitive: Visual Culture, Ethnography, and Early German Cinema*, New York: Palgrave.

Olsen, S. (2006) *Hans Jürgen Syberberg*, Lanham: University Press of America.

Omasta, M., Mayr, B. and Cargnelli, C. (eds) (2003) *Carl Mayer: Scenarist*. Vienna, Synema.

Orbanz, E. (ed.) (1977) *Wolfgang Staudte*, Berlin: Volker Spiess.

Osten, U. von der (1998) *NS-Filme im Kontext sehen! 'Staatspolitisch besonders wertvolle' Filme der Jahre 1934–1938*. Munich: diskurs film.

Ott, F. W. (1986) *The Great German Films: From Before World War I to the Present*, Secaucus: Citadel.

Paech, A. and Paech, J. (2000) *Menschen im Kino: Film und Literatur erzählen*, Stuttgart: Metzler.

Paech, J. (1988) *Literatur und Film*, Stuttgart: Metzler.

Pages, N. C., Majer-O'Sickey, O. and Rhiel, M. (eds) (2007) *Screening Riefenstahl: An Anthology of New Riefenstahl Criticism*, New York: Continuum.

Petermann, W. and Thoms, R. (eds) (1988) *Kino Fronten: 20 Jahre '68 und das Kino*, Munich: Trickster.

Petley, J. (1979) *Capital and Culture: German Cinema 1933–45*, London: British Film Institute.

Petro, P. (1989) *Joyless Streets: Women and Melodramatic Representation in Weimar Germany*, Princeton: Princeton University Press.

Pflaum, H. G. (1990) *Germany on Film: Theme and Content in Cinema of the Federal Republic of Germany*, trans. R. Helt and R. Richter, Detroit: Wayne State University Press.

Pflaum, H. G. and Prinzler, H. H. (1983) *Cinema in the Federal Republic of Germany*, Bonn: Inter Nationes.

Pflügl, H. (ed.) (2001) *Der geteilte Himmel: Höhepunkte des DEFA-Kinos 1946–1992*, 3 vols, Vienna: Filmarchiv Austria.

Phillips, K. (ed.) (1984) *New West German Filmmakers: Fom Oberhausen through the 1970s*, New York: Frederick Ungar.

Pinthus, K. (ed.) (1983) *Das Kinobuch*, afterword W. Schobert, Frankfurt am Main: Fischer.

Plummer, T. G. et al. (eds) (1982) *Film and Politics in the Weimar Republic*, New York: Holmes & Meier.

Poss, I. (ed.) (1997) *DEFA 50: Gespräche aus acht Filmnächten*, Brandenburgische Zentrale für Politische Bildung.

Poss, I. and Warnecke, P. (eds) (2006) *Spur der Filme: Zeitzeugen über die DEFA*, Berlin: Ch. Links.

Pott, S. (2002) *Film als Geschichtsschreibung bei Rainer Werner Fassbinder: Fassbinders Darstellung der Bundesrepublik Deutschland anhand ausgewählter Frauenfiguren in seiner 'BRD Trilogie': Die Ehe der Maria Braun (1978), Lola (1981), und Die Sehnsucht der Veronika Voss (1982)*, Frankfurt am Main: Peter Lang.

Prager, B. (2007) *The Cinema of Werner Herzog: Aesthetic Ecstasy and Truth*, London: Wallflower.

Prawer, S. S. (1980) *Caligari's Children: The Film as Tale of Terror*, London: Oxford University Press.

Prawer, S. S. (2002) *The Blue Angel (Der blaue Engel)*, London: bfi Publishing.

Prawer, S. S. (2005) *Between Two Worlds: The Jewish Presence in German and Austrian Film, 1910–1933*, New York and Oxford: Berghahn Books.

Prinzler, H. H. (ed.) (2003) *Friedrich Wilhelm Murnau: Ein Melancholiker des Film*, Berlin: Bertz.

Prinzler, H. H. and Patalas, E. (eds) (1984) *Lubitsch*, Munich: C. J. Bucher.

Prommer, E. (1999) *Kinobesuch im Lebenslauf: Eine historische und medienbiographische Studie*, Constance: UVK Medien.

Prümm, K. and Wenz, B. (eds) (1991) *Willy Haas: Der Kritiker als Mitproduzent, Texte zum Film 1920–1933*, Berlin: Edition Hentrich.

Putz, P. (1996) *Waterloo in Geiselgasteig: Die Geschichte des Münchener Filmkonzerns Emelka (1919–1933) im Antagonismus zwischen Bayern und dem Reich*, Trier: Wissenschaftlicher Verlag.

Rapp, C. (1997) *Höhenrausch: Der deutsche Bergfilm*, Vienna: Sonderzahl.

Rauch, A. M. (2000) *Bernd Eichinger und seine Filme*, Frankfurt am Main: Haag + Herchen.

Rayns, T. (ed.) (1979) *Fassbinder*, London: British Film Institute.

Reeves, N. (1999) *The Power of Film Propaganda: Myth or Reality?*, London and New York: Cassell.

Reichmann, H.-P. and Worschech, R. (eds) (1991) *Abschied von gestern: Bundesdeutscher Film der sechziger und siebziger Jahre*, Frankfurt am Main: Deutsches Filmmuseum.

Reimer, R. and Reimer, C. (1992) *Nazi-Retro Films: How German Narrative Cinema Remembers the Past*, New York: Twayne.

Reimer, R. C. (ed.) (2000) *Cultural History through a National Socialist Lens: Essays on the Cinema of Nazi Germany*, Rochester: Camden House.

Reiss, E. (1979) *'Wir senden Frohsinn': Fernsehen unterm Faschismus*, Berlin: Elefanten Press.

Rentschler, E. (1984) *West German Film in the Course of Time*, Bedford Hills: Redgrave.

Rentschler, E. (1996) *The Ministry of Illusion: Nazi Cinema and its Afterlife*, Cambridge, MA: Harvard University Press.

Rentschler, E. (2000) 'From New German Cinema to the postwall cinema of consensus', in Hjort, M. and MacKenzie, S. (eds) *Cinema and Nation*, London: Routledge.

Rentschler, E. (ed.) (1986) *German Film and Literature: Adaptations and Transformations*, London and New York: Methuen.

Rentschler, E. (ed.) (1988) *West German Filmmakers on Film*, New York: Holmes & Meier.

Rentschler, E. (ed.) (1990) *The Films of G. W. Pabst: An Extraterritorial Cinema*, New Brunswick: Rutgers University Press.

Reuter, M. (1997) *Ärzte im bundesdeutschen Spielfilm der Fünfziger Jahre*, Alfeld: Aufsätze zu Film und Fernsehen.

Richter, H. (1968) *Filmgegner von heute – Filmfreunde von morgen*, intro. W. Schobert, Frankfurt am Main: Fischer.

Richter, H. (1986) *The Struggle for the Film: Towards a Socially Responsible Film*, ed. J. Römhild, trans. B. Brewster, foreword A. L. Rees, New York: St Martin's Press.

Richter, R. (ed.) (1983) *DEFA-Spielfilm-Regisseure und ihre Kritiker*, 2 vols, Berlin: Henschel.

Riecke, C. (1998) *Feministische Filmtheorie in der Bundesrepublik Deutschland*, New York: Peter Lang.

Riefenstahl, L. (1993) *Leni Riefenstahl: A Memoir*, New York: St Martin's Press.

Riess, C. (1985) *Das gab's nur einmal: Die große Zeit des deutschen Films*, 3 vols, Frankfurt am Main: Ullstein.

Robinson, D. (1997) *Das Cabinet des Dr. Caligari*, London: bfi Publishing.

Romani, C. (1992) *Tainted Goddesses: Female Film Stars of the Third Reich*, trans. R. Connolly, New York: Sarpedon.

Rosen, P. (1984) 'History, textuality, nation: Kracauer, Burch, and some problems in the study of national cinemas', *Iris* vol. 2, no. 2.

Rossell, D. (1998) 'Beyond Messter: aspects of early cinema in Berlin', *Film History* vol. 10, pp. 52–69.

Rossell, D. (2001) *Faszination der Bewegung: Ottomar Anschütz zwischen Photographie und Kino*, Frankfurt am Main: Stroemfeld/Roter Stern.

Rother, R. (2000) *Leni Riefenstahl: Die Verführung des Talents*, Berlin: Henschel.

Rügner, U. (1988) *Filmmusik in Deutschland zwischen 1924 und 1934*, Hildesheim: Olms.

Rutz, G.-P. (2000) *Darstellungen von Film in literarischen Fiktionen der zwanziger und dreißiger Jahre*, Münster: LIT.

Salt, B. (1979) 'From *Caligari* to who?', *Sight and Sound* vol. 48, no. 2.

Sanford, J. (1980) *The New German Cinema*, Totowa: Barnes and Noble.

Santner, E. (1990) *Stranded Objects: Mourning, Memory, and Film in Post-War Germany*, Ithaca: Cornell University Press.

Saunders, T. J. (1994) *From Berlin to Hollywood: American Cinema and Weimar Germany*, Berkeley: University of California Press.

Saunders, T. J. (1997) 'The German-Russian film (mis)alliance (DERUSSA): commerce & politics in German-Soviet cinema ties', *Film History* vol. 9, pp. 168–88.

Schacht, D. A. (1991) *Fluchtpunkt Provinz: Der neue Heimatfilm zwischen 1968 und 1972*, Münster: MAkS.

Schäffler, S. (2002) *Neun Interviews (Becker, Buttgereit, Glasner, Gröning, Huettner, Karmakar, Roehler, Schmid, Tykwer)*, Munich: belleville.

Schaudig, M. (ed.) (1996) *Positionen deutscher Filmgeschichte: 100 Jahre Kinematographie: Strukturen, Diskurse, Kontexte*, Munich: diskurs film.

Schebera, J. (1990) *Damals in Neubabelsberg: Studios, Stars und Kinopaläste im Berlin der zwanziger Jahre*, Leipzig: Edition Leipzig.

Schenk, I. (ed.) *Dschungel Großstadt: Kino und Modernisierung*, Marburg: Schüren.

Schenk, R. (ed.) (1994) *Das zweite Leben der Filmstadt Babelsberg, DEFA 1946–92*, Berlin: Henschel.

Schenk, R. (ed.) (1995a) *Regie: Frank Beyer*, Berlin: Edition Hentrich.

Schenk, R. (ed.) (1995b) *Vor der Kamera: Fünfzig Schauspieler in Babelsberg*, Berlin: Henschel.

Scheunemann, D. (ed.) (2003) *Expressionist Film: New Perspectives*, Rochester: Camden House.

Schittly, D. (2002) *Zwischen Regie und Regime: die Filmpolitik der SED im Spiegel der DEFA-Produktionen*, Berlin: Links.

Schlüpmann, H. (1990) *Unheimlichkeit des Blicks: Das Drama des frühen deutschen Kinos*, Frankfurt am Main: Stroemfeld/Roter Stern.

Schmid, M. and Gehr, H. (eds) (1992) *Rainer Werner Fassbinder: Dichter, Schauspieler, Filmemacher*, Berlin: Argon.

Schmieding, W. (1961) *Kunst oder Kasse: Der Ärger mit dem deutschen Film*, Hamburg: Rütting & Loening.

Schmitt-Sasse, J. (ed.) (1993) *Widergänger: Faschismus und Antifaschismus im Film*, Münster: MAkS.

Schnurre, W. (1950) *Rettung des deutschen Films: Eine Streitschrift*, Stuttgart: Deutsche Verlags-Anstalt.

Schönemann, H. (1992) *Fritz Lang: Filmbilder Vorbilder*, Berlin: Hentrich.

Schöning, J. (ed.) (1989) *Reinhold Schünzel: Schauspieler und Regisseur*, Munich: edition text + kritik.

Schöning, J. (ed.) (1995) *Fantaisies russes: Russische Filmmacher in Berlin und Paris 1920–1930*, Munich: edition text + kritik.

Schöning, J. (ed.) (2005) *FilmEuropa-Babylon: Mehrsprachenversionen der 1930er Jahre in Europa*, Munich: text + kritik.

Schulte-Sasse, L. (1996) *Entertaining the Third Reich: Illusions of Wholeness in Nazi Cinema*, Durham: Duke University Press.

Schulz, G. (ed.) (1989) *DEFA-Spielfilme 1946–1964: Filmografie*, Berlin: Staatliches Filmarchiv.

Schuppach, S. (2004) *Tom Tykwer*, Mainz: Bender.

Schuster, A. (1999) *Zerfall oder Wandel der Kultur? Eine kultursoziologische Interpretation des deutschen Films*, Wiesbaden: DUV.

Schütz, R. (1990) 'Zur Erkundung individueller Glücksansprüche in DEFA-Spielfilmen der achtziger Jahre' in *Junge Filmemacher zwischen Innovation und Tradition*, Berlin: VISTAS.

Schweinitz, J. (ed.) (1992) *Prolog vor dem Film: Nachdenken über ein neues Medium 1909–1914*, Leipzig: Reclam.

Segeberg, H. (ed.) (1996) *Die Mobilisierung des Sehens*, Munich: Wilhelm Fink.

Segeberg, H. (ed.) (1998) *Die Modellierung des Kinofilms*, Munich: Wilhelm Fink.

Segeberg, H. (ed.) (2000) *Die Perfektionierung des Schein*, Munich: Wilhelm Fink.

Segeberg, H. (ed.) (2004) *Mediale Mobilmaching I: Das Dritten Reich und der Film*, Munich: Wilhelm Fink.

Segeberg, H. (ed.) (2006) *Mediale Mobilmaching II: Hollywood, Exil und Nachkrieg*, Munich: Wilhelm Fink.

Seidl, C. (1987) *Der deutsche Film der fünfziger Jahre*, Munich: Heyne.

Shandley, R. (2001) *Rubble Films: German Cinema in the Shadows of the Third Reich*, Philadelphia: Temple University Press.

Shattuc, J. (1995) *Television, Tabloids, and Tears: Fassbinder und Popular Culture*, Minneapolis: University of Minnesota Press.

Sigl, K., Schneider, W. and Tornow, I. (eds) (1990). *Jede Menge Kohle? Kunst und Kommerz auf dem deutschen Filmmarkt der Nachkriegszeit*, Munich: Filmland Presse.

Silberman, M. (1990) 'Remembering history: the filmmaker Konrad Wolf', *New German Critique* no. 49.

Silberman, M. (1994) 'Post-wall documentaries: new images from a new Germany', *Cinema Journal* vol. 33, no. 2.

Silberman, M. (1995) *German Cinema: Texts and Contexts*, Detroit: Wayne State University Press.

Silberman, M. (1996) 'What is German in the German cinema?', *Film History* vol. 8, pp. 297–315.

Silberman, M. (ed. and trans.) (2000) *Bertolt Brecht on Film & Radio*, London: Methuen.

Soldovieri, S. (1998) 'Socialists in outer space', *Film History* vol. 10, pp. 382–98.

Soldovieri, S. (2008) *Managing the Movies. Censorship, Modernisation and the East German Film Crisis of 1965/66*, Toronto: University of Toronto Press.

Spieker, M. (1999) *Hollywood unterm Hakenkreuz: Der amerikanische Spielfilm im Dritten Reich*, Trier: WVT Wissenschaftlicher Verlag.

Spielhagen, E. (ed.) (1993) *So durften wir glauben zu kämpfen . . . Erfahrungen mit DDR-Medien*, Berlin: VISTAS.

Spiker, J. (1975) *Film und Kapital: Der Weg der deutschen Filmwirtschaft zum national-sozialistischen Einheitskonzern*, Berlin: Volker Spiess.

Stationen der Moderne im Film II: Texte Manifeste Pamphlete (1989) Berlin: Freunde der Deutschen Kinemathek.

Steinle, M. (2003) *Vom Feindbild zum Fremdbild. Die gegenseitige Darstellung von BRD und DDR im Dokumentarfilm*, Constance: UVK.

Stettner, P. (1992) *Vom Trümmerfilm zur Traumfabrik: Die 'Junge Film-Union' 1947–1952*, Hildesheim: Olms.

Storm, S. (2000) *Strukturen der Filmfinanzierung in Deutschland*, Potsdam: Verlag Berlin-Brandenburg.

Stratenwerth, I. and Simon, H. (eds) (2004) *Pioniere in Celluloid: Juden in der frühen Filmwelt*, Berlin: Henschel.

Strauß, A. (1996) *Frauen im deutschen Film*, Frankfurt am Main: Peter Lang.

Sturm, S. and Wohlgemuth, A. (eds) (1996) *Hallo? Berlin? Ici Paris! Deutsch-Französische Filmbeziehungen 1918–1939*, Munich: edition text + kritik.

Syberberg, H.-J. (1982) *Hitler: A Film from Germany*, trans. J. Neugroschel, New York: Farrar, Straus and Giroux.

Thomas, H. A. (1962) *Die deutsche Tonfilmmusik: Von den Anfängen bis 1956*, Gütersloh: Bertelsmann.

Thompson, K. (1996) 'National or international films? The European debates during the 1920s', *Film History* vol. 8, pp. 281–96.

Tornow, I. (1990) *Piroschka und Wunderkinder oder: Von der Unvereinbarkeit von Idylle und Satire. Der Regisseur Kurt Hoffmann*, Munich: Filmland Presse.

Töteberg, M. (ed.) (1999) *Szenenwechsel: Momentaufnahmen des jungen deutschen Films*, Reinbek: Rowohlt.

Traudisch, D. (1993) *Mutterschaft mit Zuckerguss? Frauenfeindliche Propaganda im NS-Spielfilm*, Pfaffenweiler: Centaurus.

Trumpener, K. (forthcoming) *The Divided Screen: Cinemas of Postwar Germany*, Princeton: Princeton University Press.

Turner, G. (1986) *National Fictions*, Sydney: Allan Unwin.

Uhlenbrok, K. (ed.) (1998) *MusikSpektakelFilm: Musiktheater und Tanzkultur im deutschen Film*, Munich: edition text + kritik.

Uricchio, W. (ed.) (1990) 'Introduction to the history of German television 1935–1944', *Historical Journal of Film, Radio and Television* vol. 10, no. 2, pp. 115–240 [special issue].

Usai, P. C. and Codelli, L. (eds) (1990) *Before Caligari: German Cinema 1895–1920*, Pordenone: Le Giornate del Cinema Muto.

Vogelsang, K. (1990) *Filmmusik im Dritten Reich: Eine Dokumentation*, Hamburg: Facta Oblita.

Vonderau, P. (2007) *Bilder vom Norden: Schwedisch-deutsche Filmbeziehungen 1914–1939*, Marburg: Schüren.

Wager, J. B. (1999) *Dangerous Dames: Women and Representation in the Weimar Street Film and Film Noir*, Athens: Ohio State University Press.

Walsh, M. (1996) 'National cinema, national imaginary', *Film History* vol. 8, no. 3.

Warstat, D. H. (1982) *Frühes Kino der Kleinstadt*, Berlin: Volker Spiess.

Watson, S. W. (1996) *Understanding Rainer Werner Fassbinder: Film as Private and Public Art*, Columbia: University of South Carolina Press.

Wedel, M. (1996) *Max Mack: Showmann im Glashaus*, Berlin: Freunde der Deutschen Kinemathek.

Weinberger, G. (1992) *Nazi German and Its Aftermath in Women Directors' Auto-biographical Films of the late 1970s: In the Murderer's House*, San Francisco: Mellen Research University Press.

Welch, D. (1985) *Propaganda and the German Cinema 1933–1945*, Oxford: Oxford University Press.

Welch, D. (1993). *The Third Reich: Politics and Propaganda*, London: Routledge.

Wenders, W. (1989) *Emotion Pictures: Reflections on the Cinema*, trans. S. Whiteside, London: Faber and Faber.

Wenzel, E. (2000) *Gedächnisraum Film: Die Arbeit an der deutschen Geschichte in Filmen seit den sechziger Jahren*, Stuttgart: Metzler.

Werner, P. (1990) *Die Skandalchronik des deutschen Films*, Frankfurt am Main: Fischer.

Westermann, B. (1990) *Nationale Identität im Spielfilm der fünfziger Jahre*, Frankfurt am Main: Peter Lang.

Wetzel, K. and Hagemann, P. A. (1982) *Zensur – verbotene deutsche Filme 1933–1945*, Berlin: Volker Spiess.

Willemen, P. (1994) 'The national', in *Looks and Frictions: Essays in Cultural Studies and Film Theory*, London: bfi Publishing.

Wilmesmeier, H. (1994) *Deutsche Avantgarde und Film: Die Filmmatinee 'Der absolute Film' 3. und 10. Mai 1925*, Münster: LIT.

Winkler, C. and Rauch, J. von (2001) *Tanzende Sterne und nasser Asphalt: Die Filmarchitekten Herbert Kirchhoff und Albert Becker und das Gesicht des deutschen Films in den fünfziger Jahren*, Munich: Dölling und Galitz.

Witte, K. (1995) *Lachende Erben, toller Tag: Filmkomödie im Dritten Reich*, Berlin: Vorwerk.

Worschech, R., Schurig, M. and Worschech, M. (eds) (1995) *Lebende Bilder einer Stadt: Kino und Film in Frankfurt am Main*, Frankfurt am Main: Deutsches Filmmuseum.

Wottrich, E. (ed.) (2001) *Deutsche Universal: Transatlantische Verleih- und Produktionsstrategien eines Hollywood-Studios in den 20er und 30er Jahren*, Munich: text + kritik.

Wottrich, E. (ed.) (2002) *M wie Nebenzahl: Nero-Filmproduktion zwischen Europa und Hollywood*, Munich: text + kritik.

Wulf, J. (1989) *Theater und Film im Dritten Reich: Eine Dokumentation*, Frankfurt am Main: Ullstein.

Wuss, P. (1990) *Kunstwert des Films und Massencharakter des Mediums*, Berlin: Henschel.

Wydra, T. (1998) *Volker Schlöndorff und seine Filme*, Munich: Heyne.

Wydra, T. (2000) *Margarethe von Trotta: Filmen, um zu überleben*, Berlin: Henschel.

Zeutschner, H. (1995) *Die braune Mattscheibe: Fernsehen im Nationalsozialismus*, Hamburg: Rotbuch.

Zglinicki, F. von (1986) *Die Wege der Traumfabrik: Von Guckkästen, Zauberscheiben und bewegten Bildern*, Berlin: Transit.

Zilinski, L. et al. (ed.) (1970) *Spielfilme der DEFA im Spiegel der Kritik*, Berlin: Henschel.

Zimmermann, P. (ed.) (2005). *Geschichte des dokumentarischen Films in Deutschland*, 3 vols, Stuttgart: Reclam.

The following German-language journals and newsletters regularly publish articles and special issues on all aspects and periods of German cinema:

Apropos: Film (2000–5). Das Jahrbuch der DEFA-Stiftung, Berlin: Bertz + Fischer.

Augenblick: Beiträge zu Film, Fernsehen Medien, Marburg; Schüren.

diskurs film: Münchener Beiträge zur Filmphilologie, Munich: Schaudig-Ledig.

KINtop: Jahrbuch zur Erforschung des frühen Films (1–14/15) Frankfurt am Main: Stroemfeld/Roter Stern.

Filmexil: Zeitschrift über die Film-Emigration während des Nationalsozialismus, ed. Filmmuseum Berlin / Deutsche Kinemathek, Munich: edition text + kritik.

Filmblatt: Zeitschrift für Filmgeschichte, ed. CineGraph Babelsberg, Berlin-Brandenburgisches Centrum für Filmforschung.

FilmGeschichte, Filmmuseum Berlin / Deutsche Kinemathek

Film und Kritik, Frankfurt am Main: Stroemfeld/Roter Stern.

Frauen und Film, Frankfurt am Main: Stroemfeld/Roter Stern.

montage/av, Zeitschrift für Theorie & Geschichte audiovisueller Kommunikation, Marburg: Schüren.

The following English-language journals regularly publish articles on German film and have published special issues on German cinema:

Arachne, vol. 3, no. 2 (1996), ed. U. Lischke Mc-Nab and C. Flinn, special issue on German film and culture.

Camera Obsura, no. 44 (2000), special issue on post-Wall German cinema.

Discourse, no. 6 (1983), ed. R. Mueller, special issue on German avant-garde cinema.

Film Criticism, vol. 23 (1999), nos 2–3, ed. G. Gemünden, special issue on Detlef Sierck / Douglas Sirk.

Film History, vol. 18 (2006), no. 1, ed. M. Silberman, special issue on 'Cold-War German Cinema'.

German Quarterly, vol. 64, no. 1 (1991), special issue on literature and film.

Germanic Review, vol. 79 (2007), ed. J. Kapczynski, special issue on 'Newer German Cinema: Between Nostalgia and Nowhere'.

Monatshefte, vol. 82, no. 3 (1990), special issue on German film studies.

New German Critique, nos 24–25 (1981–82), ed. D. Bathrick and M. Hansen, special double issue on New German Cinema.

New German Critique, no. 49 (1990), ed. M. Hansen, special issue on Alexander Kluge.

New German Critique, no. 60 (1993), ed. D. Bathrick and E. Rentschler, special issue on German film history.

New German Critique, no. 63 (1994), ed. D. Bathrick and G. Gemünden, special issue on Rainer Werner Fassbinder.

New German Critique, no. 74 (1998), ed. D. Bathrick and E. Rentschler, special issue on Nazi cinema.

New German Critique, no. 87 (2002), ed. E. Rentschler, special issue on post-Wall cinema.

New German Critique, no. 80 (2004), ed. G. Gemünden and A. Kaes, special issue on film and exile.

October, no. 21 (1982), ed. D. Crimp, special issue on Rainer Werner Fassbinder.

October, no. 46 (1988), ed. S. Liebman, special issue on Alexander Kluge.

October, no. 72 (1995), ed. S. Liebman, special issue on 'Berlin 1945: war and rape in *Liberators take liberties*'.

Quarterly Review of Film Studies, vol. 5, no. 2 (1980), ed. E. Rentschler, special issue on West German film in the 1970s.

Seminar: A Journal of Germanic Studies, vol. 33, no. 4 (1997), ed. U. Lischke-McNab and K. Hanson, special issue on recent German film.

Wide Angle, vol. 12, no. 1 (1990), ed. J. Shattuc, special issue on 'the other Fassbinder'.

The following websites offer information on various aspects of German film and provide links to other German film sites:

http://www.CineGraph.de

http://www.defa-stiftung.de

http://www.filminstitut.de

http://www.filmmuseum-berlin.de

http://www.filmmuseum-potsdam.de

http://www.Filmportal.de

http://www.german-films.de

http://www.goethe.de/kue/flm/enindex.htm (Goethe Institute)

http://www.imdb.com (Internet Movie Database)

http://www.spio.de (Spitzenorganisation der deutschen Filmwirtschaft)

http://www.germanhollywood.com (German Hollywood Connection)

http://www.umass.edu/defa (DEFA Film Library UMass Amherst)

INDEX OF FILMS

NOTE: Film titles beginning with a German definite article have the article transposed to the end of the heading, e.g., *Bergkatze, Die*, but film titles beginning with an indefinite article do not, e.g., *Ein Walzertraum*. The years refer to the year of first German release, not the year of production; censored films usually have two dates. The English translations of titles are taken from the Internet Movie Database (IMDb); U.S. release titles are given preference over British, Australian or Canadian ones.

NAME INDEX

SUBJECT INDEX

abstract films 40–1
action adventures 19, 160, 208
actors: character actors 18, 21–2, 47,
  81–2, 138; female stars 18, 47, 82–3,
  115, 138, 173, 207–8; male stars 47–8,
  83, 115, 139, 207–8; reception of
  Hollywood stars 39, 48, 49, 69, 82,
  207; star system 17, 18, 81, 138, 193
animation 12, 25, 40–1, 51, 75, 196
anti-Semitism: 22, 53, 56, 80, 102, 103,
  146, 181, 213, 214; Holocaust:
  representation of 93, 94, 97, 102–3,
  146, 180, 181, 212, 214, 215; Jewish
  film-makers 16, 66
audiences: middle class 51; women
  audiences 9, 12, 29, 43; working class
  13; young audiences 70, 110, 111–12,
  120, 136, 137, 143–4, 150–1,196
authorship: in film 17, 40, 85, 92, 129,
  153, 164, 165, 198; and auteurism
  165; *Autorenfilm* 23, 39, 154, 164–5,
  169, 173, 174
avant-garde 41, 49, 130, 158, 159–60,
  177

Berlin: as centre of film production 9, 12,
  13, 24, 49, 50, 56, 95, 97, 109–10;
  images of Berlin during the Third
  Reich 76; the Weimar Republic 40, 41,
  46, 55; Wilhelmine Empire 11;
  representations of East Berlin 109,
  101, 133–4, 139, 143, 145, 149, 152;
  of unified city 219–21; of West Berlin
  158, 169, 175, 177, 182, 183, 184,
  185
biographical films: artist films 79, 145,
  198; genius films 79, 102, 103;

political leaders 44–5, 78, 79, 84, 102,
  114, 170, 212, 214, 215
broadcasting 57, 66, 76, 95, 122, 166

chamber play film 21, 38, 42, 43, 104,
  117, 166
children's films 111, 150, 179, 204–5
cinemas *see* motion-picture theaters
cinematography 11, 15, 17, 31–2, 33–4,
  45, 75, 113, 161, 171, 179
class: representation of the middle class 37,
  42, 142, 156, 170; petty bourgeoisie
  21, 43, 83–4, 87, 101, 106, 120, 135,
  148, 203, 204; white-collar workers
  52, 58, 87; working-class 13, 102, 106,
  107, 109, 171, 204; yuppies 200
colonialism 14, 26, 78, 84, 90, 167–8
comedies: ethnic comedies 21; romantic
  comedies 35, 36, 50, 82, 89, 111,
  182–3, 184, 196, 200–1; slapstick
  comedies 19, 204; white-collar
  comedies 58
co-productions 5, 34, 50, 56, 71, 97, 119,
  122, 138, 161, 180, 193, 194, 195,
  196, 213
cosmopolitanism 53, 65, 70, 80, 108,
  112, 216
costume films *see* period films
crime dramas 19, 37, 38, 86, 103, 110,
  131, 132, 175, 179, 208
criticism and scholarship: film journals
  51–2, 54, 70, 121, 140, 157, 172,
  176; film criticism 40, 51, 52, 70, 121,
  130, 140, 173; film scholarship 2, 8–9,
  28–9, 65, 93, 121, 128, 153–4, 192
cultural films 24, 26, 40, 41, 45, 51, 69,
  75, 121

268

Related titles from Routledge

South African National Cinema
Jacqueline Maingard

South African National Cinema examines how South African cinema represents national identities, especially with regard to race.

Jacqueline Maingard establishes interrelationships between South African cinema and key points in South Africa's history. She discusses how cinema figures in the making, entrenching and undoing of apartheid through detailed analyses of selected films, including *De Voortrekkers* (1916) at one end of the twentieth century and *Mapantsula* (1988) at the other, as well as films that have been produced post apartheid, including *Drum* (2004), *Tsotsi* (2005) and *Zulu Love Letter* (2004).

South African National Cinema focuses on how early cinema screened 'the colonial' and appropriated 'the national' in ways that both reproduced and helped construct a white national identity. It takes readers through cinema's role in building white Afrikaner nationalism in the 1930s and 1940s, and examines film culture and modernity in the development of black audiences from the 1920s to the 1950s, especially in a group of films including *Jim Comes to Joburg* (1949) and *Come Back, Africa* (1959). Jacqueline Maingard considers the effects of the state film subsidy system in the 1960s and 1970s, and discusses cinema against apartheid in the 1980s. She shows how shifting national cinema policies after the first democratic election in 1994 made it possible for the first time to imagine and begin to develop an inclusive national film culture.

ISBN 13: 978-0-415-21679-1 (hbk)
ISBN 13: 978-0-415-21680-7 (pbk)

Available at all good bookshops
For ordering and further information please visit:
www.routledge.com

Related titles from Routledge

Spanish National Cinema
Núria Triana-Toribio

A nation is nothing without the stories it tells about itself. In *Spanish National Cinema*, Núria Triana-Toribio studies some of the stories told through film, as well as the demands made on Spanish cinema to provide new stories to contribute to the formation of the nation. She also examines the changing national qualities of Spanish cinema, such as the 'Spanishness' of its filmmakers, while taking issue with studies of national cinemas that focus on 'important moments'.

Núria Triana-Toribio's insightful study examines the discourses of nationalism as they intersected or clashed with Spanish film production from its inception to the present. While the book addresses the discourses around filmmakers such as Almodóvar and Medem, whose work has achieved international recognition, Spanish National Cinema is particularly novel in its treatment of a whole range of popular cinema rarely touched on in studies of Spanish cinema. Using accounts of films, popular film magazines and documents not readily available to an English-speaking audience, as well as case studies focusing on the key issues of each epoch, this volume illuminates the complex and changing relationship between cinema and Spanish national identity.

ISBN 13: 978-0-415-22059-0 (hbk)
ISBN 13: 978-0-415-22060-6 (pbk)

Available at all good bookshops
For ordering and further information please visit:
www.routledge.com

Related titles from Routledge

Brazilian National Cinema
Lisa Shaw and Stephanie Dennison

Brazilian cinema is one of the most influential national cinemas in Latin America and this wide-ranging study traces the evolution of Brazilian film from the silent era to the present day, including detailed studies of more recent international box-office hits, such as *Central Station* (1998) and *City of God* (2002).

Brazilian National Cinema gives due importance to traditionally overlooked aspects of Brazilian cinema, such as popular genres, ranging from musical comedies (the *chanchada*) to soft-core porn films (the *pornochanchada*) and horror films, and also provides a fresh approach to the internationally acclaimed avant-garde *cinema novo* of the 1960s.

Lisa Shaw and Stephanie Dennison apply recent theories on stardom, particularly relating to issues of ethnicity, race and gender, to both well-known Brazilian performers, such as Carmen Miranda and Sonia Braga, and lesser known domestic icons, such as the Afro-Brazilian comic actor, Grande Otelo (Big Othello) and the *uber*blonde children's TV and film star, and media mogul, Xuxa.

This timely addition to the National Cinemas series provides a comprehensive overview of the relationship between Brazilian cinema and issues of national and cultural identity.

ISBN 13: 978-0-415-33815-8 (hbk)
ISBN 13: 978-0-415-33816-5 (pbk)

Available at all good bookshops
For ordering and further information please visit:
www.routledge.com

Related titles from Routledge

Chinese National Cinema
Yingjin Zhang

What does it mean to be 'Chinese'? This controversial question has sparked off a never-ending process of image-making in Chinese-speaking communities throughout the twentieth century. This introduction to Chinese national cinema covers three 'Chinas': mainland China, Hong Kong and Taiwan. Historical and comparative perspectives bring out the parallel developments in these three Chinas, while critical analysis explores thematic and stylistic changes over time.

As well as exploring artistic achievements and ideological debates, Yingjin Zhang examines how - despite the pressures placed on the industry from state control and rigid censorship - Chinese national cinema remains incapable of projecting a single unified picture, but rather portrays many different Chinas.

ISBN 13: 9-78-0-415-17289-9 (hbk)
ISBN 13: 9-78-0-415-17290-5 (hbk)

Available at all good bookshops
For ordering and further information please visit:
www.routledge.com

Related titles from Routledge

Mexican National Cinema
Andrea Noble

Mexican National Cinema offers an account of the development of Mexican cinema from the intense cultural nationalism of the Mexican Revolution, through the 'Golden Age' of the 1940s and the 'nuevo cine' of the 1960s, to the renaissance in Mexican cinema in the 1990s.

The book moves from broad historical and theoretical context, particularly theories of nation, emergent discourses of 'mexicanidad' and the establishment and development of the Mexican industry, towards readings of key film texts and genres. Films considered include:

- Y tu mama también
- ¡Que viva México!
- La mujer del Puerto
- El Castillo de la pureza

In each case, Andrea Noble considers the representation of nation inherent in these films and genres, placing an emphasis on the ways in which they intersect with debates in cultural history, particularly Mexico's quest for modernity.

Mexican National Cinema provides a thorough and detailed account of the vital and complex relationship between cinema and national identity in Mexico

ISBN 13: 9-78-0-415-23009-4 (hbk)
ISBN 13: 9-78-0-415-23010-0 (pbk)

Available at all good bookshops
For ordering and further information please visit:
www.routledge.com